# The C.O.R.P.O.R.A.T.I.O.N.
## (Crooked Officials Robbing People of Rights Against Truth in Our Nation)
## VS. WE THE PEOPLE
## AUTONOMOUS WARRIOR'S MENTALITY
## YOUR PARAMOUNT MANUAL FOR
## GREATNESS AND SUCCESS

By Roosevelt Tankard & agent Tazadaq Shah

ISBN: 9798704663324

Dedicate to Marty Bradley Raymond Smith Denis Pitman (Israel) And Malachi Dean for showing a strong sense of support doing this economic war. Stay on your grind, hustle harder and always make creditor move. Romans 13: 8 Owe no man anything, but to love one another DEBTORS love to hate, therefore use their energy to soar to greater heights. I love you for who you are.

# CONTENTS

1   Put on the Full Armor of Yahawah (GOD) Warrior's Mentality

2   A WARRIOR'S MENTALITY Soldier in the Army of the Highest

3   Develop the Mindset of the Blessed and Unstoppable

4   Get your Mind Right King/Queen!

5   Prosperity and Success is on the opposite side of difficulty and struggle., go get it!

6   You must Suffer and Endure Struggle to be Great and Success.

7   Only Three letters Required for Absolute Success, W. H. Y.

8   The Issues of law Contract is Now the Law of the Land

9   Born: The Ill Mind of a Creditor

10   Acknowledge knowledge Cipher.

11   Acknowledge the Power Within

12   Eliminate Debtor, haters, and Critics.

13   Day 11 Diminish the Satan of Self and All Negative Thoughts

14   Be Quick to Listen and Slow to Speak

15   Day 13Its Grind Season, allow your Grind to Speak for You

16   Day 14 The Wisdom of this World is Foolishness.

17   Live in the Now Not Yesterday or Tomorrow

18   Employ Your Sovereignty Stand Up Like a

19   Never quit or give up to being average.

20   Day Take the Limits of Yahawah (YHWH, God) Awaken the roach hakes within you!

21   Take the Limits of Yahawah (YHWH, God) Awaken the Ruach ha kodesh within you!

22   Wisdom Moon all being born to Culture Freedom.

23   How to Live Utterly Free as An American National

24   A Creditor in Commercial Warfare

25   Control the Corporation Keep Grinding Hustle Harder.

The C.O.R.P.O.R.A.T.I.O.N.

(Crooked Officials Robbing People of Rights Against Truth in Our Nation) BOOK TITLE

Subscribe to all four of my channels on YouTube now! They are as follows...

Deprogramed Enlightener/ Undaunted National/ Aspokesman4men/U-N-I-versal Indigenoustv7 on YouTube.

Book mark our websites: www.truedisciplesofchrist.org/shop and Deprogrammed Enlightener on YouTube

Email: tazadaqshah@yahoo.com or tazadaqshah@yahoo.com@yahoo.com

Phone coaching: 347-618-1783

Contact Us now!

"The CORPORATION is your AUTONOMOUS WARRIOR'S MENTALITY your paramount manual for greatness. And success. This book this the revised edited ultimate manual for greatness, motivation, and success that will compel you to observe and change your inner self. This book is instilled with the fundamentals that will teach you to crush your alter ego and begin living the marvelous life that Yahawah (God) has created you to live. Placing this effective program into actions, will move you to enjoy the unequivocal liberty and fulfillment of God's true blessings. It is not coincidental that you purchased this book. It was part of Yahawah (God's) plan for your life to intersect with Tazadaq, God's man, to arm you with the warrior's mentality, Right Knowledge, and over-standing and enlightenment required for you to inherit a blessed and amazing future. Once you embrace the warrior's mentality which trains you to be a solider in the army of the lord you will be blessed and utterly unstoppable. This is much more than just another self-help or motivational manual, this book that you are holding in your hands or reading on your computer screen, is the answer to your prayers and a blueprint that you should follow to accomplish your goals and dreams. Qam Yahsharahal!

Tazadaq the Mindset of an Alpha Male "Return of Real men" tazadaqshah@yahoo.com
www.truedisciplesofchrist.org Phone coaching available

# ACKNOWLEDGMENTS

Shalom, Family,

This is Yahawah's work. You are about to embark on a journey that will change your life for the better. Use this blueprint of my daily life to improver yours. I acknowledge I can do all thing s through Yahawashi.

You are about to embark on a journey that will be challenging, difficult, yet mind altering if you adhere to the messages herein. This manual will alter your world and change the world in which you live. "The World Is Mind!" If you change the thoughts that you think within your mind you can change your world around, you. The world is mind! There is a 9th dimension that is unknown to the average man, it consists of sight, sounds, and is only limited by your mind, "The world is mind". You have not just picked up another book that you will throw aside, you do not know it yet, but you just embarked on a journey into the 9th dimension. This book will take you into another realm within time; it is an exodus. You purchased this book because you are not satisfied with somethings in your life, they are insufficient, and you are not content with your current circumstance. Circumstance reveal the man/ wombman. The mere fact that you purchased this book suggest that you intend to do something to improve your life. Do not allow anyone, not even yourself to stop you from this goal.

This didactic, life altering book comes complete with everything that you need to change your life. This book was composed with Lessons, motivational positive affirmations, empowering prayers, inspirational message to awaken god's warrior within you. This is Yahawah's (God's) work. Use these steps to take actions which are your works, and finally a deluge of Self-Assessment Question to assist you and provoke you to get your mind right or perish in your ignorance. I suggest that you write down your goals and finally a self-assessment workbook. Essentially this book is designed to change your life in 31 days. One might ask, if this book is written to change my life in 34 days, why are there so many lessons? The crux is to teach you to be seven (7). Then you men bless women with Right Knowledge and wisdom which eventually brings forth a true understanding (3) to teach the children. When you observe the mathematical equation involved when we add 3 + 4 we arrive at the sum of seven. Seven represent god.

The first 3 days designed to instill proper overstanding of whom you really are and what you must do by the 3rd day to prepare for the 34 days. The second day is where you will begin to learn wisdom (2) which is the wise words that will be spoken into existence by man womb-man and child. Wisdom represents the womb-man (2) where you will begin to birth new thoughts and eliminate all negative thinking. Finally, it takes us back to the 1st chapter which represents putting on the true amour of Yahawah (God). Knowing how to protect yourself against the deceit and trick knowledge of the devil is paramount. This is the first chapter because contrary to what you have been taught the man (knowledge) is first. Man is represented by 1 because the Highest God created man first and then created womb-man 2nd. Thus, when knowledge goes into wisdom, they bring forth a proper understanding (3) which are their children. Genesis chapter 2 verse 18 reads, "Then the Lord, God said it is not good that man should be alone I will create a help meet for him." If the woman was created for man, she cannot be equal to man as this society falsely teaches.

I therefore encourage both brothers and sisters to take heed to the divine warning that the creator has instilled within Tazadaq that is being dispatched to you from this manual. Henceforth before you do anything, I encourage you to be quick to listen slow to speak and slow to anger that's James Chapter 1 verse 19. Everything that I say is rooted in the word because I am Yahawah's (God's) man. This divine message is inspired by God and you have been blessed to receive this Right Knowledge within this manual that will change your life and make you successful.

The C.O.R.P.O.R.A.T.I.O.N.

(Crooked Officials Robbing People of Rights Against Truth in Our Nation) BOOK TITLE

Humbled thyself and be in accordance with Proverbs 18 verse 13, which says he who answers before listing that it is folly and shame. The Bible was written in a masculine form therefore when God uses words like man, he is often referring to the women as well. Through the spirit of the Highest in Christ this book has been strategically designed to align your thinking with paramount laws of success. As you follow the step-by-step life altering guides you will begin to discover amazing breakthroughs and new doors of opportunity will open within your life. Greatness, success, and an indomitable spirit will not chase you down. One does not become successful by following the trend. One becomes successful by pushing beyond what you have been told was

# 1 PUT ON THE FULL AMOR OF YAH (GOD) HAVE A WARRIOR'S MENTALITY

Bible verses Ephesians 6: 13 Wherefore take unto you the whole armour of God, that ye may be able to withstand in the evil day, and having done all, to stand.[14] Stand therefore, having your loins girt about with truth, and having on the breastplate of righteousness;[15] And your feet shod with the preparation of the gospel of peace.

This book has 25 chapters all being born to myself (2+5 = 7). Seven represent God, I am god according to psalms 82:6. The first section of this book is designed to help you to establish the proper mind state. If you skip it, you will regret it later. I do not teach you what to think like a schoolteacher or professor that want you to clone what they say and not grow. I teach you how to think freely for yourself. Edward Joseph Snowden is an American computer professional, former Contractor for Central Intelligence Agency employee, and former contractor for other the United States government who copied and leaked classified information from the National Security Agency in 2013.

He merely told people what we already knew that there was a crooked government, but he never gave the people remedy. Snowden ran like a coward as Esau usually does unless he has the foe out numbered. Tazadaq stand has a man, and I do not only tell you the problem I expose the solution that they have hidden from the masses. I am a Martyr for the truth. This book is a remedy for a chronic disease that is rapidly spreading throughout every corner of the world. This disease is more common than Cancer; it is more contagious than the common cold. This sickness will destroy your dreams and demolish your goals. This is a sickness known as "average". The disease of average has spread throughout the world and 99% of the population are affected by the sickness known as average. Average is an Achilles heel to success. Average is not a diminutive barrier. To overcome average, you must don a warrior's mentality. Your mind must become tranquil. You must endure vitriolic people that will adulterate your thinking. A warrior's mentally is essentially aberrant; a warrior's mentally is not average. A warrior's mentality is not amenable. You must be driven and focused. One that possession a warrior's mentality develops the mind of god. Psalms 82 verse 6 reads "I have said you are God's and all of you are children of the highest".

If the Bible informs us that we are Gods, why are so many of you placing limitations on God? Stop placing limitations on God; stop leasing success. You cannot lease success and proclaim yourself to be God. You must own success. Now take the limitations off God because you are made in his image and likeness. Greatness and success are only ascertained through difficulties, struggle, and perseverance. The difficulty factor is always attached to greatness. Anything that has value has the difficulty factor attached.

Case in point: The gift of life is an exceedingly difficult process for both the mother and the baby; it is difficult for the mother because she undergoes excruciating pain because the baby stretches her birth canal. It is difficult for the baby because the baby must go through the tight birth canal and experience a deluge of pain. However thereafter is the most beautiful gift which is the gift of life. From this we can all bare witness or discover that even from the inception of us coming into this world that the difficulty factor is attached from birth. Knowing thus, why would you think that you could have anything of true value without struggle? Struggle and the difficulty factor are attached to the lonely road to greatness. If you decide to travel down this road you will witness a deluge of dead corpses along the road of those that tried and failed. Most people do not have the perseverance to push beyond normality or their limitations. This should inspire you to keep striving, and to do so you must take on the Warrior's Mentality. We have borne witness from our being born into the world that the process of evolution and growth is a difficult journey. But thereafter is the most beautiful gift that one could have, the gift of life. I ask you, what are you going to do with this exhaustive manual that can change life?

What is your passion that God has created you to do? Are you working on a job that you do just for money or survival? If so, you are not happy as you should be if you are happy at all. Is your marriage the marriage that you prayed for? Or are you with a borderline spouse that you are afraid to leave because you fear being alone? This is the average person in the world today.

The enemy does not want you to succeed. The word states in 1st peter 5:8 "Be sober, be vigilant; because your adversary the devil, as a roaring lion, walketh about, and seeking whom he may devour." Are you doing what the creator Yahawah has created you to do? Are you just suffering from the disease of average? Or you just following the trend and are emulating everyone else? Are you acting like everyone else, talking like others, thinking like others, suffering from the sickness of average like others? I refuse to be a clone! If you want to be successful, if you want to be great you must take the limitations off God and be limit less because the disease of average will destroy your dreams of greatness and success. Right now, you are what the world sees as normal. Normality to me is failure because you are akin to what everyone else is.

You cannot expect to leave a legacy if you are just average. Normality is what degenerate people consider as living. I refuse to be average. I have chosen to take the higher road, the more difficult road, the more challenging road; and anyone that is intended to be on that journey with me will take the higher road with me, yes, a much more challenging and difficult road but a much more rewarding one.

From today forth you must promise yourself that anyone in your life or anything in your life that is not helping you achieve your goals and your dreams you will kick them out of your life because they are a hindrance to you being the great man or woman that the creator created you to be. Stop being in average! Everything that I say is rooted in the word. So, the Scriptures for today's lesson are Ephesians 6 and 13 to 17.

How can we make it in a world that is so diluted with sin and wickedness? A world in which our own mothers, fathers, sisters, brothers, cousins turned their back against us because of us desiring to live in accordance with the laws, statutes, and commandments of God? Well, allow me to explain why. Christ says in the book of John chapter 14 verse 30 "hereafter I will not talk much with you for the prince of this world cometh and have nothing in me".

The prince of this world is Satan. You and I were created to live in accordance with the word of God and to be Christ like, but our very own children war against us. The global elite has transformed the earth into a world so corrupt in which our own wives or husbands plot against us or commit lustful acts as adultery, wickedness such as murder for insurance policies to be with another. This is a world where every wicked abominable act is glorified. Satan grants you a reward for selling your soul and you shy away from righteousness. A world where homosexuality, lesbianism, pedophilia, incest, and all forms of sexual wickedness is practiced. Yet, there is a way to survive in the Basic Instructions Before Leaving Earth (B.I.B.L.E.) which the Most High gave us, his beloved and today brother or sister you will learn the ways to protect yourself from the wickedness of this corrupt degenerate world?

In the book of Ephesians chapter 6 verse 11 it reads "put on the whole armor of God that you may be able to stand against the wiles of the devil". What is the Scripture speaking about? What does the word armor mean? Armor is all the tools used to wage war or to protect one's self in battle. However, this is allegorical. The battle spoken of in these next verses is a type of spiritual battle which has been weighed against the people of Zion by the children of perdition, the children of hell the children of Satan. Too many of you are attempting to fight physical in spiritual fight. Get your mind right King! Get your mind right queen! In Ephesians Chapter 6 verse 12 it reads "for we wrestle not against flesh and blood but against principalities against powers, against the rulers of the darkness of this world, against spiritual wickedness in high places". The Illuminati is real and there are those that take oaths in secrecy to control and deceive the masses.

So, we must take on this armor of God that he has given us to guard ourselves. Our fleshly bodies we must protect with the word of Yahawah (God) as does soldiers. Again "for we wrestle not against flesh and blood but against principalities against powers against the rulers of the darkness of this world against spiritual wickedness in high places". Here we are not wrestling with the physical powers but against spiritual evil that is trying to take away the Holy Spirit that gives us righteousness, because these spirits out there want us to fall victims to the lust of the flush and the lust of the world. That is to be carnally minded which is death. A spirit does not have flesh and bones. The book of Luke 24 and 39 reads, "behold my hands and my feet that it is I myself and to me and see for a spirit have not flesh and bones as you see me have."

Satan's angels and Satan's agents war against us spiritually the book of Matthew chapter 25 verse 41 states, "then shall he say unto them on the left-hand depart from me, depart into everlasting fire prepared for the devil and his angels". Satan and his angels are not after anything of the world because the world belongs to Satan already. Satan's agents and his angels are after those of us that has been taken out of the world if you are in Christ and the spirit of Christ within you, than you are a new creature so the Scriptures read in the book of John chapter 15 verse 19 "if you was of the world the world will love his own but because ye are not of the world but I have chosen you out of the world therefore the world hated a you". If you are in Christ, you are a new creature and you were not of this world.

Satan's has been in control of this world since the time that Christ walked the earth in the flesh. Satan has controlled the world, and still does. Let us prove that in the book of Job chapter 9 verse 24. "The earth is given into the hands of the wicked he covered the faces of the judges thereof. Who painted Christ as a so-called white man, who painted all the Angels as so-called white people, who painted all the prophets as so-called white people? The rulers of this world? Who rules the world right now? So-called rich white men. I speak the truth. That is what the Scripture means he cover the faces of the judges thereof. So, we see this Scripture coincides with the book of John 14 verse 30 "hereafter I will not talk much with you for the prince of this world cometh and have nothing in me". This Scriptures is saying that at this current time the earth is under Satan's authority. U.S.A (UNDER SATAN'S AU¬THORITY).

First and foremost, I did not say that the earth was given into the hands of the wicked the Bible stated that. Next who rules the earth? This is rhetorical, you do not have to answer it because both you and I know the answer. The people that rule the world how has it been? Is it just? Is it justice? Not is just us frozen as just-ice at negative 32 degrees mentally.

Just as he was after Job in the book of Job chapter 1 verse 6 to, Satan went to God when the sons of men went to God and challenged Job's faith in God. Just as he did this with Job, he does this with us day in and day out. Therefore, it is extremely important to guard ourselves with the armor of God.

We must be ready spiritually and do all that we can to withstand the evils of this world, resist the devil and he will flee from you. Ephesians chapter 6 verse 13 says wherefore take into you the whole armor of God that ye may be able to stand (meaning he will be fighting to get you) in these days of evil if you have not done all that you can, you must stand and show thyself to be a man. Verse 14 says stand therefore having your loins girt (to girt is to encircle or bring something close to you) about with truth and having on the breastplate of righteousness. What are our loins and how do we keep them in truth? Our l loins are our private areas, but we also must girt our minds which are to be scarce and holy which means set apart in truth. God says in first Peters chapter 1 verse 16 "For it is written be holy for I am holy". Brothers and sisters, we are not to be committing acts of sex and intimacy or intimate conversations with anyone besides our spouse if we are married. If you have a so-called girlfriend or boyfriend, you are married because in the Bible there is no such thing as a boyfriend or a girlfriend; the act of sex constitutes marriage according to the book of Exodus chapter 22 verse 16. "And if a man entices a maid that is not be throbbed which means engage and lie with her meaning to have sex with her, he shall surely endow her made him promise her to be his wife".

Therefore, we are not supposed to be out in the world talking or committing any acts of affection with anyone other than the person we are espoused to. The other intimate relationships or wicked but marriage is honorable. The book of Hebrews chapter 13 verse 4 reads "marriage is honorable in all in the bed undefiled both warmongers and adulterers God will judge". Fornication is sexual wickedness or setting up partners with god. This includes porn movies, dirty music, walking with your private parts exposed on beaches, or any type of wickedness that most deem as being okay because you are just looking or listening to this world. To look on someone or even think anything that has to do with sex or sexuality is sin if they are not your spouse. It is lust for man to look upon a woman in her nakedness that is not his wife and it is sin. There are many women out there that choose to go to male doctors and have the male doctors looking up into their Vagina. There are many men out there that choose to go to female doctors and have female doctors looking at them in the nude. You cannot say that you are in a godly mind state if you are doing this intentionally. If you are going to a doctor of the opposite sex you may be enticing that man or woman to sin. A doctor is still a man or a woman and sin like everyone else. Stop placing them on a pedestal. This is not of God this is of the world this is sin. But many of you do not comprehend the Bible, because you are not spiritual, you would think that I am deranged. But what does the Lord say? The book of James chapter 1 verse 15 says "then when lust have conceived it is bringing forth sin and sin when it is finished it bringing forth death". So, when a man looks upon a woman in lust that sin it does not matter if the man's a doctor. When a woman looks upon a man unless it is her husband that is sin, it does not matter if the woman is a doctor. You are inviting sin into the world and you will be judge. Let us see what the Lord says regarding this. The book of Matthew chapter 5 verse 28 "but I say unto you that whosoever look at on a woman to lust after her hath committed adultery with her already in his heart". I have heard of many cases where male doctors have been charged with molesting women in the doctor's office. There has been many cases where the male doctors have performed certain procedures on females that was totally.

unnecessary. This is when lust have conceived. Therefore, any woman or man that puts themselves in this position intentionally and think little of it get ready for the judgments of God. The most high tells us that we are not to associate with those that do not obey the will of God. Second Thessalonians chapter 3 verse 6. "now we command you brethren in the name of our Lord Yahawashi that ye abstain yourselves from every brother that walk disorderly and not after the traditions which he receives of us".

That is crystal clear that people that are not following this Bible we are not supposed to be around them, we are not supposed to befriend them we are not supposed to be with them. We are being told to withdraw from such people in the name of our Lord. Second Thessalonians chapter 3 verse 14 says and "if any man obeys not our words by this epistle note that man and have no

company with him that he may be ashamed".

These worldly people and their positions are Satan's devices of getting to our spirits because everything we see hear, touch, smell, and feel go into our mental. Everything we do and interact with becomes who we are. If we are constantly reading, watching listening and associating with evil corrupt worldly things and people, then that is who we will become. God says we are a temple in

which he dwells first Corinthians chapter 3 verse 16          "that ye are the temple of God and the spirit of God dwells in you if any

man defiles the temple of God himself God destroy for the temple of God is holy which temple ye are". If we do not put on the armor of God, we are susceptible to the wiles of the devil and will be defiled and God will not dwell in us but will destroy us mentally and eventually physically because we will be unholy. Ephesians chapter 6 verse 14 talks about a breastplate of righteousness. Beloved a breastplate was a form of protection used to protect soldiers in battle. It protected their middle section. The heart is in the part that the breastplate protected but this scripture is speaking in a spiritual sense meaning to be righteous as a breastplate of honor in truth. Preparing wherever we go with the breast plate of righteousness that will be in front protecting you.

Ephesians chapter 6 verse 15 "your feet shod with the preparation of the gospel of peace". Shod means to put on foot gear. To prepare your feet means to put on protection of foot gear before heading out to battle. Christ ever walked in peace using only the word of God to teach, he cashed out evil spirits. Therefore, we must study and be born in the gospel of the word of the Highest in Christ. Our feet become just as Christ traveling throughout day in and day out with our feet to where God directs them to takes us physically, and to not go in the direction which is of the devil and against God. We must have the word of God firmly planted within us teaching the Scriptures in our everyday steps. When we go against God's laws, statutes, and commandments we are sinning. When we sin, we go against God himself.

King David said in the book of Psalms chapter 51 verse 4, "against thee, there only have I sin and done this evil in thy sight". Here we hear King David saying that sin is evil, and it is only against the Lord that he sins because he is our ultimate Redeemer. James in the book of James chapter 4 verse 17 "Therefore to him that knoweth to do good, and doeth it not, to him it is sin". Here we read that if we know to be good if we do not do it is sin. 1st John chapter 5 verse 17 says "all unrighteousness is sin". God goes on to say through John in 1st John chapter 3 verse 4 "whosoever committed sin transgressive also the law for sin is transgression of the law". We must not go against the Lord we will be put to death not only physically but mentally and will not receive the gift of God's eternal life. Romans 6 verse 23 says "for the wages of sin is death but the gift of God is eternal life through Yahawashi Lord". Eternal life is something given from God we will never receive it if we go against his law's statutes and commandments. God is very merciful he forgives but only if our sins is confessing and not hidden. The book of Proverbs chapter 28 verse 13 "he that covers his sins shall not prosper but whoso confess it and forsake it then shall have mercy".

If we sin, we must admit unto God what we have done and that we must do our absolute best to never go back to committing those sins again. God has given us the tools necessary to use to lead by his will but if we cover our wickedness and do not confess, God will not have mercy on us, and we will not inherit the gift of eternal life. We must do the work of God to stay clean from the wicked devices of Satan and his angels and agents.

The book of Psalms chapter 119 verse 9 "Wherewithal shall a young man cleanse his way? by taking heed thereto according to thy word.". The word is the laws, statutes, and commandments of the highest God. We must do our absolute best to obey them no matter what! There are no excuses. God does not play games. Satan and his angels are going all over the earth in every direction trying to take our spirit away from God. We need to be sober and ready because Satan deals deceitfully. Once the spirit of Satan is on you, you will deal deceitfully when one deals deceitfully, he conceals the truth knowingly. This is the same as a lie and is of the devil and is also breaking God's commandments. One of the major tools Satan uses is the lust of the world, such as sex, drugs, cars, jobs, money, a new house, clothes, fame, power etc. We must withhold ourselves from fleshly lusts because they are in opposition to God. First Peter's chapter 2 verse 11 "dearly beloved beseech you as strangers and pilgrims abstain from fleshly lusts which war against the soul". When we complete the act of lust whether it is mental or physical it is sin and will bring us not only a spiritual death but eventually a physical death. A spiritual death is separation from God then you eventually die physically. It is okay to lust for your spouse but lust for others lead to sin and wicked practices. So, the book of James chapter 1 verse 15 says "then when lust hath conceived It bring forth sin and sin when it is finished bring forth death". Satan knows this and is going every which way to get this to happen, so he can turn you against God.

First Peter's chapter 5 verse eight through 9 "be sober and diligent (this means keeping careful watch for possible dangers or difficulties) because your adversary the devil is a roaring lion walking about seeking whom he may devour". Satan is not under the earth with horns and a long tail, or on a hot sauce bottle. With a pitchfork this is just a fable. Satan is real, and his spirit is here throughout the earth. The loin is the king of the jungle and his roar is fearless so likewise Satan is the king of this world and he is persistent and fearless and doing all he can to get us to commit sin against not only ourselves, and the ones we love, but against God. Therefore, God gave us this armor and his laws, statutes, and commandments. These were given to us to uphold us in this day and time because this day and time is evil. Most importantly we need to believe in God himself with his promise that he has sent his Redeemer to deliver us from this wicked devil and all his attempts to take our souls.

The book of Ephesians chapter 6 verse 16 says "above all taking the shield of faith were withal you shall be able to quench all the fiery darts of the wicked". Darts are used in battle to kill the physical body but here the wicked have darts that they used to kill our spirits. An animal who is shot with a dart in the wilderness not from which it came only suffers from the blow and the affliction that follows. This armor God has given us will allow us to see the dart before it hits the flesh and be able to show it away and overcome it. For example, how water quenches a flame of fire or cold rain on a hot burning mountain top. With faith, we overcome. Now let us ask ourselves what is faith? The Scriptures are noticeably clear on this. Hebrews chapter 11 verse 1 "now faith is the substance of things hoped for the evidence of things not seen". This clearly states that faith is something that you long for and wish for, something you think about having, it is a substance you cannot readily obtain because it has not come yet. In this thing you hope for as evidence meaning it exists even though it is not yet or has not been seen. Just as we have not seen the father, we have faith in him and what he says. Though we may not have seen the father or have not seen the son in this life we have faith that he is, he was, and still lives with the father. It is our very faith that will carry us through hard times and temptations. God says in first Corinthians chapter 10 verse 13 "therefore have no temptations taking you but such as common to man but God is faithful who will not suffer you to be tempted above that ye are able but will with the temptation also make a way to escape that ye be able to bear it". The Scriptures is saying that there is not any temptation that we cannot handle that these type of temptations are not unknown, we know what he does and are fully aware of his tricks as the Scripture say in first Corinthians chapter 2 verse 1 We shouldn't allow Satan to get an advantage of us for we are not ignorant of his devices and that God believes and will not allow us to be tempted with something we cannot rebuke but will with all the temptation give us a way out and a choice which we will choose to stay on the right hand side of God.

We must stand in Christ and stand with the armor he provided for us or we will fall to the left side with Satan and his angels and agents. Every time we are combating with Satan and use our armor, we will overcome Satan and be closer and closer to the Highest. Ephesians 6 and 17 "and take the helmet of salvation and the sword of the Spirit which is the word of God". This verse says that helmet of salvation because of all the armor a soldier's wear in battle to protect the body the head is most vital. The head is.

made up of the eyes to see and, the ears to hear, the nose to smell, the mouth to speak and most of all the brain which direct all these features to call the body into order. The head is most important because it is the point at which we have faith to arrive and abstain through these daily struggles. We must fight earnestly to protect our salvation. Just as the head is at the top of the body and where the head goes the body must follow. Salvation is above all and is the point at which we hope to attain in the sword of the Spirit which is the word of God because the sword was used in battle to cause defeat. But this sword is spiritual and is God's very words written here in the Scripture of his holy book, the Bible. The sword was used in battle to kill. But this sword is spiritual and is God's very words written here in the Scriptures of his holy book.
The sword of the Spirit is our weapon to maneuver in this day and time to arrive before Yahawah sends Christ to return and seal our salvation in the great book of life.
In this chapter we have discussed the entire armor of God our private parts not only physically but mentally girt with truth, a breastplate of righteousness and our feet shod in righteousness, a shield of faith, helmet of salvation, and the sword of the Spirit which is the word of God. This is the armor that is described in the beginning of Ephesians chapter 6 verse 13. This very armor is our wisdom that God blessed us with to endure in this wicked corrupt world of sin. We are soldiers for God when we do his will. Second Timothy chapter 2 verse 3 reads "therefore endure hardness as a good soldier of Christ". Matthew 10 :22 "and ye shall be hated of all men for my namesake but he that endure to the end shall be saved". We are hated because we do not live for this world but with this armor fight against the evil and wickedness of this world. If we continue as the Lord stated in the commandments of God until the very end, we will receive the gift of eternal life. The end is when Christ returns or if we die before the end in this life will be resurrected with eternal life. First Corinthians 15 and 26 the "last enemy that shall be destroyed is death".
If some of us feel like taking on the armor is a hard thing or a difficult task, God says in Philippians 4 verse 13 "I could do all things through Christ which strengthens me". If what we are doing is in accordance with the highest our power is limitless, and we could do anything. Second Timothy's 1 verse 7 says "for God have not given us the spirit of fear but of power and love". This fear is not the same as the fear of God because that fear will keep us from sinning and from disobeying God. The fear God did not give us is to be tricked by Satan and his angels to get us to disbelieve because we have all the attributes to believe and with these, we could do all things as God has promised. We have the power to overcome and accomplish, to love, and to forget to be patient, and persevere with a sound mind to discern right from wrong, good from evil, and how to conduct ourselves as ambassadors of Christ.
Daily Affirmation: Dear Father Yahawah (God) I forgive all the people that have caused me harm, done me wrong, hurt

me and betrayed me. I forgive myself as well for any ill that I have caused others. I accept your forgiveness and I am placing your freedom of peace and I will walk in your law's statutes and commandments henceforth. The more I let go of the internal hate, discontentment, and self-loathing, the more I am free thank you Lord.

**Tazadaq Motivational Quotes for Success.**

If you affiliate with losers and naysayers, you will render yourself to be a loser and a naysayer. You will emulate their ways, pick up their habits, and clone their attitudes about life. If you are around cynical negative people, most of the time you will end up cynical and negative. It is imperative to align yourself with positive people.

The fiercest foe and enemy that you will have to deal with is the Satan of self. If you extract the enemy within the enemy outside can do you no harm.

How you define yourself right now, how you view yourself right now is who you truly are. You are what you think about all day, as a man think within his heart so is, he. Who are you right now and what must you change to create who you want to be? What must you leave behind to get where you want to go, whom I shall leave behind to accomplish my goals my dreams? If you want to keep on getting what you are getting simply keep on doing what you are doing, and you are guaranteed to be average, to be a failure and to suffer from the disease of normality.

80% of your self-talk is negative, you must start concentrating on the positive and live now, life is not about tomorrow it is about right now, it is about today. Tomorrow is a great dream, but is not real, yesterday may be a great memory but it is not real. Your only reality is right now. When you can envision the invisible you can accomplish the impossible. So, my question is what you are dreaming that you intend to make possible?

You must eliminate self-negativity; you must eliminate all negative thinking and thoughts. If you think something negative you must not speak it, because the very moment that you speak it you are speaking it into existence and you will live it out. Some people are so negative that even when I attempt to give you a positive statement, or positive energy you take everything that I articulate and transform it into something negative. You are so undetermined to be positive and so determine to be negative that it is astonishing. You have thought your way into extreme depression and being negative, yet you are expecting to produce positive results. The outcome of your life is based upon your thinking and the choices that you make. If you choose negative thoughts, you will yield negative results.

Self-Assessment Questions:

1. Why did Yahawashi die on the cross?
2. Is there any resentment within my heart that needs to be addressed?
3. Am I in denial or have I rendered true forgiveness?
4. Have I totally utterly forgiven those people that have hurt, me cause me pain, done me wrong, or am I just in denial?
5. Am I searching deep inside releasing and letting go?
6. What is the mindset of a person who has truly forgiven?
7. Have I honestly forgiven myself of the wrong things that I have done in the past?

Today's prayer:

I pray to the father Yahawah, to reveal to me any unforgiveness within my heart. Help me to address it and completely turn it over to you. Give me the strength to let go of the past and any destructive irrational emotions, I cannot carry this burden any longer, it gets in the way of our relationships in Yahawashi name amen.

**Daily Prayer:** I pray dear God Yahawah for you to show me any resentment and unforgiveness that is within my heart. Most high please help me discover it completely and allow you to diminish it. Father God provide me with the strength to let go of my dreadful past and destructive emotions. Help me let go of any burden that I have been carrying around that has been a barrier between the relationship of you and others in Yahawashi (Christ) name I pray amen.

Acting: Now please take out a sheet of paper and write down or type the names of any and every one that has ever hurt you. Also, why. Then anyone that is ever betrayed you. Once you have accomplished this pray over that list of names, it will not be easy but pray over that list of names. Ask God to bless these people that have hurt you and betrayed you in every aspect of their lives. Do this daily until you flush all the negative energy away from your mind about these people, completely out of your system.

This is the point, where everything in your circumference, within your entire life is about to change for the better. The highest is about to instill you with the knowledge, wisdom, and the understanding and faith to alter your life.

# 2 A WARRIOR'S MENTALITY SOLIDER IN THE ARMY OF THE YAH

Bible Verse: 1st Chronicles 11: 9 So David waxed greater and greater: for the LORD of hosts was with him. 10 These also are the chief of the mighty men whom David had, who strengthened themselves with him in his kingdom, and with all Israel, to make him king, according to the word of the LORD concerning Israel.

Please reflect deeply on these words of wisdom that you are about to read this is not another book to be read and laid aside. This book is to be read no less than five times as repetition is the father of learning and will enable you to supplant this profound divine spiritual message into your subconscious mind.

Let us reflect on being a soldier of Christ or emulate King David's mighty men. Christ is not an average man, he is extraordinary. He realized that the disease of average was not his calling. Upon his second term he is said to be seen in the clouds with a bloody garment and a sword bathe in blood. This is a metaphor which is symbolic to Christ returning for war not peace. This is not taught in your churches today because 501 C3 grants or C4 grants prevent them from telling the whole truth.

If we are to be soldiers in the Lord's army, we must develop a warrior's mentality. We must develop the mind of Christ. We must essentially become Christlike. A warrior's mentality does not know average. A warrior's mentality does not embrace defeat. A warrior's mentality becomes Christ like. Hamashiyach, Christ is the God of this world. When I say a warrior's mentality it is not just alluding to the battle, its suggesting that you be a champion in your marriage, on your job, in your studies etc. The book of John says in the beginning was the word, the word was with God, and the word was God. Going deeper we see that the word became flesh and dwelt among us. Christ was God on earth. if you want to be Christ like it is essential that you develop a warrior's mentality. A warrior's mentality does not know defeat, its is do not know failure, it does not know quitting or giving up. A warrior's mentality only knows, perseverance, success, being blessed and unstoppable and great. It is parallel to a champion mindset; this is the mind of Christ and God's mind. When you develop the mind of God, you begin to think like a God, you begin to act like a God, you began to walk like a God. When you think like God, you act like God, walk like God; then what have you become? You have become an agent of God, and a direct reflection of God. The book of Psalms 82 verse 6 says have I not said you are God's.

So, we realize to developing a warrior's mentality is a prerequisite of being a soldier in the Army of the Lord. This is not for the weak heart, the feebleminded, or the fearful. This is for those with an indomitable spirit, with the ability to push beyond the pain, the ability to endure hardships, to push beyond struggle, the ability to fall 10 times and get back up 11. You must comprehend that just because you have fallen it does not render you a failure. What separates champions and warriors from average is that those with a warrior's mentality, those with the mind of God, push beyond what is impossible because Philippians 4 verse 13 says I can do all things through Christ which strengthens me. It is having a warrior's mentality, developing the mind of God being Christlike is to know your true calling. You must ask yourself what did God create me to be? And am I doing it? If I am not, then I could never be the great man or woman that my creator intended me to be, because my path is not aligned with what God has destined me to be. Therefore, I would never feel content.

Just about anyone could be a soldier that is one thing but, being a soldier in the Army of the Lord is unlike your typical average soldier. Being a solider of God is a special kind of different. Soldiers in the army of the Lord sweats victory, we drink the preparation of the difficulties, and transform it into victory. These are just a few of the essential elements that you must possess to become great. Difficulties and struggle will define the moral character within you. It is falling, yet never quitting that produce winners. I have never learned from anything that I already did well. It has always been the failure that made champions great. Champions conquer the agony of defeat, crush competition with training, and going beyond what is expected then is reward with success and winning. This is the 300 mentality, this reflects King David's mighty men, and if we follow the path that Yahawah has designed for us we will be successful and prosperous. in 2 Kings 2: 2-3. It reads, 2 "go the way of all the earth: he thous strong therefore and shew thyself a man;3 And keep the charge of the LORD thy God, to walk in his ways, to keep his statutes, and his commandments, and his judgments, and his testimonies, as it is written in the law of Moses, that thou mayest prosper in all that thou do, and whithersoever thou turpeth thyself".

The C.O.R.P.O.R.A.T.I.O.N.

(Crooked Officials Robbing People of Rights Against Truth in Our Nation) BOOK TITLE

The Mighty Men in the Lord's army has a warrior's mentality. King David's Mighty Men were a group of 37 men known as the

Gibb rim (Mighty Men) who fought with king David who are also identified in 2nd Samuel 23:8-38. These Mighty men had a warrior's mentality. Abishai raised his spear and killed 300 men. The Scriptures clearly reveal that there is a season and time for everything. The highest is not all about peace yet he is also about war as well. We bear witness that there is a season and time for everything. Ecclesiastes chapter 3 verse 8 says "there is a time to love, a time to hate a time of war and a time of peace". Warriors do not attempt to make peace in the heat of battle. A warrior's mentality is having the capacity to discern the time for peace. Warriors have a champion mentality, and champion do not chase peace in competition, they strive for victory. This is your time; this is your moment. Every second that you allow to past is a second wasted on becoming a soldier in the Army of the Lord.

The highest cannot use week feebleminded men and women. True warriors and those that want success must change their minds to push beyond the perceived limitations placed upon them by society. Mediocracy is eliminated from the minds of champions in the warrior mentality. Greatness and success are allergic to the disease of average and normality. True champion and warriors are never average. Normality is what the feebleminded, the weak, and the average person considers adjustment, I consider it death. From this moment forth, you must embed into your subconscious mind that you will not accept failure, average is not an option. Greatness can only be achieved through hard work, overcoming difficulties, and burning the midnight oil. The warrior mindset and your success are achieved through your failure. You must learn to view your fall as an opportunity to learn. Get up! Now go and be great!

Daily Affirmation: Each day I spend time in prayer with the Highest that grants me strength and power to strive for my goals and maintain a peace of mind.

**Self -Assessment Question:**

Is God the first thing on my mind when I awake?
What motivates me to have positive day?
How much time do I spend alone with Yahawah?
What type of foods do I put into my holy temple?
What time do I sit aside each day to spend time with Yahawah?
Do I give Yahawah my full attention when I am alone with him?
How often do I read the Bible?
Do I stay connected to the spirit throughout the day?

**Daily Prayer:** Lord help me establish a better relationship with you. Show me how to be a better listener and receive your divine message. Give me strength to bring my concerns to you in prayer. Help me establish set times in the morning and at night for prayer. In the name of Christ, I pray amen.

Successful Quotes:

I contend that prayer is a monologue and not a dialogue. God's voice is the most vital part listening to the voice of God is your secret of the assurance that he will listen to your voice.

Silence is the room we create when searching for God, where we hear his voice and follow his command.

We can be both tired, and weary, and emotionally drained, but spending time alone with God, we find that he interjects our thinking and instills into our bodies a powerful spirit and strength.

When our quiet times have become less how can we expect to give God the time that he is due? How can we receive the guidance that God desires to give us? How can our hearts fill the energy of his divine power? How can we have deep fellowship with those purposes that are really mirrors to the heart of God?

But thou when thou are entering the closet, and when thou hast shut thy door, pray to the father which is in secret; and thou father which seeth in secret. Shall reward the openly. Matthew 6;6.

Your Action Step: put aside at least 20 minutes every day to be alone with the highest. You should spend the first five minutes plan for others, the next five minutes being grateful and thinking God for you and all your needs, and that last five minutes just listening to God talking back to you. The more that you do this, the more divine revelation the highest will give you about his plans for your life.

**Inspiration for Victory:** The highest God has very amazing things that he intends to share with you. Each time that you get alone with God, the more he will use you fulfill his purposes.

# 3 DEVELOP THE MINDSET OF THE BLESSED AND UNSTOPPABLECHAPTER NAME

Bible Verse: Jeremiah 17: 7 Blessed is the man that trusteth in the LORD, and whose hope the LORD is.

The crux of being blessed and unstoppable, is utilizing an exhaustive supply of all the talents and gifts that God has instilled within you. However, this is just the beginning of your journey to being great. You must conflate your talents with perseverance and a never dying spirit to be tremendously successful, to be blessed and unstoppable. Struggle must become common; difficulties must become desirable if you are to achieve greatness. You must have a capacity to excel as a champion, to develop a warrior mentality, and you must be desperate over any negative thoughts and energy that you formally possessed.

You must trust in the highest God with all your heart and soul and relinquish all doubt. There must be no desultory within your thinking because this will destroy you from your objective which is being blessed and unstoppable. An aporia within your mind will not only hinder success but it will demolish your dreams. You must be impervious about anyone distracting you, positive thinking must become embedded into your subconscious mind. You must promise yourself that you will kicking anyone out of your life that attempts to belittle you, or misdirect you, and any negative people or any negative energy that would misguide you from your goals.

There are many people that claim to trust in the Lord but, when they are faced with challenges, when they are faced with difficult ties, they fall victim of their self-doubt rendering them to the epitome of their own internal failure. Because you fall does not make you a failure, if you fall 21 times, must get up 22 times. What differentiates the great, the champions, the warriors, from the com-mon people, from the losers, from those that say I should have, and I could have, is determination, perseverance and getting back up. For once in your life, you must make a rational decision, you must have the willpower to prevent yourself from doing the things that you have always done and push yourself to do the things that you were previously afraid to do. You just did not try hard enough. This is how greatness is accomplished, this is how a warrior mentality is developed, this is having faith in the Lord thy God.

Once again, the Scripture say in the book of Jeremiah 17 verse seven Blessed is the man that trusted in the Lord, whose hope the Lord is. There are only two forces in this world brothers and sisters are good and evil, his lightness and there is darkness is God and is the devil.

There is no mediocrity, so you are either on the side of the devil are you on the side of God in Christ, but you will be compelled to choose. Choose life brother, choose life sister. The problem is most of you instead of placing your trust in God, you place your trust in man, so we read in the Scriptures because everything that I say is rooted in the word of God; Jeremiah 17 verse 5 "cursed be the man that trusted in man and make it flesh his arm". Essentially what this Scriptures is saying sister, is that if you trust in man you will not be blessed. Because if that man falls so shall you. Stop trusting in man who is mortal, trust in God who is immortal if you want immortality and you must put your trust in the Lord.

Many of you have trusted in a marriage, yet the marriage fell, your spouse may have committed adultery; you trusted in a job, and got laid off or fired, you trusted in Barack Obama, but you did not get the change that you anticipated, and that he promised; many whites trusted in Donald Trump only to be let down again. We must stop trusting man and trust in the Lord Philippians 4 verse 13 says I could do old things through Christ that strengthens. No one finds what they are seeking trusting in man. Are you not sick and tired of being sick and tired of getting the same old thing? That is the definition of insanity. I challenge you brother, I challenge you sister, from this moment forward to trust in the Lord and he will push yourself beyond what others told you was impossible. If we were to dissect that word impossible, within the word itself lies the word possible, so we must start to look at the word impossible as I'm-possible. Greatness is on the other side of your negative thinking, greatness is on the other side of doubt, greatness is on the other side of failure. What is separating you from being great is your lack of faith, and you being content with being average. Average has no place within the realm of the blessed and unstoppable. I dare you to challenge yourself to be his great as you can be. I dare you to challenge yourself to get back up each time that you fall. I dare you to push yourself beyond your limitations. I dare you, because if you do at the end of that struggle will be success.

**Daily Affirmation:** What you think of most is what you will bring them to fruition. It is been said over and again as a man think in his heart so is, he. The heart here is not the heart within the chest the heart here is the mind which is the core of your thinking. You

become what you think about. You cannot think negative thoughts and get positive results there is a war going on within you, you must extinguish the fire the battle between success and failure that you have been allowing to bind within you all these years. Greatness is on the other side of your doubt, of your self-loathing go get.

**Self-Assessment Question:**

What can I do to make me have a closer relationship with God?

Have I eliminated all negative people out of my life that would prevent me from having a better relationship with God?

Am I holding onto dead relationships that is preventing me from accomplishing my dreams and goals? Do I have any relationships with negative cynical people it is operating in the lower level of vibration?

Am I holding onto any type of relationship that render me to be unhappy, yet I continue to hold onto it because I am accustomed to it?

Are the relationships in my life bringing me joy or depression; if it did not bring me joy and the relationships are unrepairable because the other person does not want to change am, I willing to walk away from that relationship?

**Daily Prayer:** Dear father God I come to you as your servant in the name of Christ I ask that you strengthen me to have the capacity to walk away from any relationship that is not bringing something positive to my life. Please bless me with the wisdom, knowledge, and understanding to have the capacity to be able to discern when it is time to walk away from any given away situation. Do not allow me to fall to the wayside into the trick knowledge of the devil. Understand that Satan's angels are ever before me and they may come in the form of a loved one, or of a child, and of a friend. Dear God please protect me against the evil demonic forces and give me the ability to walk away from every relationship that you do not intend to be in my life amen.

**Positive Quotes:**

stop looking for external sources or external people to blame for your internal problems. You can change your clothes, you change your home, you go out and purchase a new car and thereby you change your car. You are content with changing all these external things yet because it is dark within, it is cold within, and it is scary within you refuse to look within and change your thinking. And since you do not change your mind yet change relationships, change the person, get a different car, you change the car, but you have not changed your thinking. And until you change your mind, you will put that same old problematic person and thinking into the new relationship, into the new home, into new car, and end up with the same old problems. If you want to change, you must first change yourself and your life will change. By Tazadaq. Shah.

To be a champion must be willing to burn the midnight oil, to be blessed and unstoppable you must resist sleep and you feel like sleeping must burn the midnight oil and training your mind and push your body beyond your limitations beyond your perceived limitation to greatness. I seldom sleep as much as I would like to because sleep is a cousin of death. I do the work now and I surmise I will sleep more when I die. Tazadaq.

Action Step: From today forth you will put your trust in the Lord. I dare you to trust the Lord in prayer to fulfill your dreams. I dare you. You want to write down on a cue card, or index card what you want to accomplish for this year, and you going to read that card three times a day. By doing so you will begin to materialize this into your subconscious mind, and you will subconsciously begin to act out towards accomplishing those things which you have written down.

Inspiration for Victory: Greatness and success are a lonely road, traveling this road he would discover a lot of dead corpse of those that attempted to accomplish greatness that wanted to be successful, yet they fell. They felt that because they fell but because they gave up. Because I could have, and I should have has never made it into the arena with the hands held. I tried is 100 times greater than I should have, what I could have done. At least you tried but if you never even gave it a chance you fell before you even tried. Greatness and success are challenging roads march them with dedication and consistency, walked out one step at a time. Onward God's soldiers! # Tazadaq Shah.

# 4 GET YOUR MIND RIGHT KING/QUEEN! MAKE CREDITOR MOVES

Bible Verse: Jeremiah 17: 9 The heart is deceitful above all things, and desperately wicked: who can know it?
Most of the people that would give you advice, will tell you always follow your heart. I contend that this is the most inaccurate ad¬vice one could ever give. Following your heart can result in a quitting during challenge. If you want to be successful, if you want to be blessed and unstoppable, it is imperative that you put your trust in the Lord. Once again, everything that I say is rooted in the word of God. The book of Proverbs chapter 3 verse five says trust in the Lord with all thine heart and lean not unto thine own un¬derstanding. This overlays what the Scripture Jeremiah 17 verse 9, the heart is deceitful above all things. The heart spoken of here is not the muscle that is within one's chest the heart spoken of here is the core of one is thinking and is the brain.
Your brain is a central processing unit like a computer. Without that central processing unit of the computer, the computer cannot think, nor can it carry out the actions. It requires a brain to call will of the other units of your body into order. If there is a deficiency in your brain it can be a hindrance or a hold to performance. One cannot anticipate being great by doing what is easy. And not capable of sound thought, a sound mind and an insatiable will to succeed. One must be driven, and to do so it is essential that you exercise the muscles of the brain daily. Just as one goes to the gym and you push the bicep, the triceps, and the chest muscles be¬yond the limitations; you must push your brain beyond what you anticipate being average to be exceptional. Remember whatever you think in your mind, this is what you will begin to live out. Because it is our thoughts that is deep within our subconscious, that we consciously respond to. You must repeat to yourself daily I can, I will, I must be blessed successful and unstoppable.

Many of you may have been baffled by that last paragraph, because at the inception of this chapter we started it by stating that the heart is deceitful of things. We further explained that the heart spoken of here is the brain. So, we first must place our trust in the highest, to direct our thinking in a positive direction to bring forth, a positive outcome result. What I am suggesting to you is you do not follow your understanding, until you have first taken to the Lord in prayer. Do not follow your heart, do not listen to the average person, that suggest that you follow your heart. Again, Jeremiah chapter 17 verse 9 says the heart is deceitful above all things, and desperately wicked, who can know it? So, you may think that you have an answer, but we should always take our de¬sires first to the Lord in prayer and pray that he gives us the correct answer. Wait for, listen for, he will respond if you are asking.

**Daily Affirmation**: I even like to see any challenge or any possibility of defeat as a temporary barrier I am trying to get across and overcome as a test. Each minute, each second, I shall with supreme divine revelation move forward. Second by second minute by minute I will push my mind into the portion that the creator has destine me to be.

**Self – Assessment Question**:
in which areas of my life do I most need improvement?
What are my weaknesses that I need more training to strengthen these weaknesses?
What is your mind concerned with that is hindering you from accomplishing success?
Do I currently have the paradigm that it requires to be blessed and unstoppable, and successful?
How do those people that are successful responding to failure or a loss?
Do I focus on overcoming with determination or shut down when I am challenge or things do not go my way?
In what ways can I enhance my talents, in what ways can I expand my goals?
What can I do today within this moment that will improve my life?

**Today's prayer: I** pray to you today God, for improvement in my mindset. Dear father please help me overcome the obstacles, overcome setbacks, and overcome the losses and see them as a learning process. Lord I submit all my beliefs to you, please assist me in mentally framing each of my experiences in a proper and constructive way for mountain improvements in Christ name I pray amen.

**Success Quotes**:
I hated every minute of training, but I said do not quit. Suffer now and live the rest of your life as a champion. Mohammad Ali

The last three or four reps is what makes the muscle growth. This area pain drives to champion from someone else who is not a champion. That is what most people live, having the guts to go on and just saying they will go through the pain no matter what happens. Arnold Schwarzenegger

Life is not about how hard of a hit we can give it is about how many you can take and keep moving forward Sylvester Stallone.

Most of the important things in the world have been accomplished by people who have Been trying when there seem to hold Dale Carnegie.

Too many people are falsely proclaiming to possess a warrior mindset but when faced and confronted with a challenge that they consider to be unbearable they tap out to the challenge; an obstacle is merely just challenge however it becomes a barrier once you bow to it. You tap out because of doubt and fear. I see every challenge and barrier as an opportunity to test my determination, I will overcome any challenge or barrier that face me with the warrior mentality within. By Tazadaq Shah

**Action Steps:**

To truly carry out the most high's plan for your life you must be Deprogrammed and reprogram your mind. Most people in the world today, about 99% of the population suffers from cognitive dissonance. To break this program that has been imposed upon you by the global elite, you must be Deprogramed. Henceforth listen to positive motivational videos, listen to self-help audio, and read the Bible daily. The objective here is to pour so much positivity into your mind that there is no room for anything else.

**Inspiration for Victory:** Yahawah, who is mightiest of all, challenges you to trust him with all your dreams and goals. Trust in the Lord his commandments, and his judgments, and his testimonies, as it is written in the law of Moses, that thou mayest prosper in all that thou doest, and whithersoever thou turnest thyself:

Faith is the four winds that blows the oxygen of a life into your lungs for you to be the artist. But what the paint brush of your mind, you could decide to paint success, or you could paint failure. If you go the way alone, you will see your footprints in the sand, and when you fall, no one will be there to pick you back up, or to assist you in getting back on. But if you traveled this course of God, when you see one set of footprints in the sand, it is not that you are walking alone, it is to when God is carrying you through these difficult times.
But we must first show him that we believe in him, and that we obey him. We do this by keeping his laws, statutes, and commandments and walking how he has ordered us to. Thus, if you want to be successful, if you want to be blessed and unstoppable keep his laws statutes and commandments as written the words of Moses, that you may have prosperity and all the things that you do.

 This is God's promise to us. The one limitation that God has it he cannot break his promise. It must be natural to be obedient to the highest, to keep his laws, statutes, and commandments. The father chastised those whom he loves and if you have not chastisement you are bastards and not sons, Hebrews 12:6. Do not ever assume that you are going walk with God and you do not undergo struggle, difficulties, and pain. You will not be able to properly walk with God if you attempt to follow him emotionally. You must have a modicum of rules that will prevent you from aborting the path that leads you to success. Yahawah, is despot he has no equal there is no power besides him. He is omnipotent. The wisdom of this world is in aporia compared to the knowledge of God. The naysayers, your envious of family members, may construct a diatribe of attacks to deter you. Do not yield to these negative people. Their lives are desultory, whereas the creator has a perfect plan for you to be successful. However, the greatest enemy that you will face is your Satan of self, that will attempt to talk you out of pushing yourself beyond what you have been taught to believe is a limitation. You were created in the image and likeness of God, stop placing the limitation on God. God is limit less, and you being created in his image and likeness should be limit less as well. Took the limitations were for God the book of Psalms chapter 82 verse 6, I have said you are God's and all of you for the children of the highest. If the highest God is my father, and I am his son, then I am a son of God and God. Stop placing limitations on God.

You must believe, to call it into existence. Doubt is the enemy to success; self-loathing is a chronic illness that cripple you from greatness. Excuses are crutches that prevent you from obtaining your goals and dreams. You must run to the challenge and, leap over the hurdle of hinderance into success. To effectively do so you must have the mind of a champion. A true champion is driven by a warrior's mentality. Success is not going to reach for you, you must strive for success. It is a lonely road, a more challenging journey, yet a much more rewarding one. Anyone that is truly in favor of you being successful and great will support you on your mission to greatness. Those that attempt to talk you out of greatness, envy you, and secretly yearn to see you fall as they have fallen. Do not allow the naysayers or the negative people to define you.

 You must extirpate all negative people and thoughts out of your life! Do it now. Dethatch your emotions and make a rational decision to eliminate all people and things that has a negative impact on your life. Such people will drain you mentally and spiritually and thereby destroy what Yahawah has planned for you to be. They are not a part of what Yah has planned for you. They are just a small section in your life, but that chapter is over, and you must move forward unto new heights. They are not on your level of vibration. Will you sacrifice your goals and dreams for someone that does not genuinely care for you even though they claim to? Or will you align yourself with God's divine will and eliminate these unclean spirits that dwell in those people around you? Your times is now, you will not have a second opportunity. All things are relevant to time. This is your time. Do it now.
Daily Affirmation: You need to place yourself within a mental state where you can visualize where you want to be five years from now, when year from now, one month from now, one minute from now, do it now. You must

rapidly develop a sense of urgency.

for success, you must sweat the perspiration of victory. Success will not come to those sitting around on a sofa about, success comes to those that has the willpower to push beyond their perceived limitations.

**Self-Awareness Questions:**
Am I allowing outside forces resources to distract me from accomplishing my mission?
Am I still talking about what I am going to accomplish, or am I speaking my thoughts into existence and making it my reality right now?
Have I done the things that are necessary to align me with the path that the highest has created me to follow?
Are you working on a job that you hate going into, but you do it because you need the money for survival, and you fear without that job you will not be able to make it?
Are you still in a relationship that is causing you stress, worrying, and making you mentally and physically sick?
Why am I still holding on to things and people that are not beneficial towards me accomplishing my goals and what my creator has planned for me?
What is more imperative, is it for me to remain in a relationship with someone that is keeping me on a lower level of vibration; or to detach that negative person and those negative emotions and work on accomplishing my dreams and goals?

**Today's Prayer:**
Dear father God please keep me focuses on the things that I need to be focused upon that will keep me on the straight and narrow path. Please do not let me fall to temptation, and lust. Please instill the spirit in me to have a positive mental attitude, to persevere during times of difficulty and struggle when I feel as if I am about to give up, give me the strength to push forward and keep a positive mental attitude, give me that faith that with God its possible in Yahawashi name, I pray amen.

**Successful Quotes:**
I contend that it is the week that is cruel kindness and gentleness can only be anticipated from the strong.
We all need a target, if there is no target then you have no goal to aim at. If you have not taken aim at any goal, then you have no focus. Where there is no focus there is no goals, there is no dreams, there is no reason for why. What is your why, or reason for being born? Unless you know this, you will always be just average and should never expect to be great.

There is a land of the living and there is a land of the dead the bridge to cross this great divide is love, love me fully or leave me alone fully, I am still becoming me, therefore accept me as I embark on this journey or leave me alone, because both God and Satan is not done with me yet.
We must awake and peer into the mirror of our mind's reflection is to cast off the war that is going on between the person who that were striving to become to be the person that society attempts to program us to be. Some of us give into the pressures of society and consider that is what is known as adjustment, but there is a selected few, there is 1%, that says I will not be another clone, I will not surrender to the pressures of society I am becoming, and I will continue to develop into me.

**Action Step:** from today forth you are going to commit to be a better you than you were yesterday, if you have done 10 repetitions in the gym manager 12 today, if you devoted 30 minutes to reading yesterday, develop to be devoted to 35 today. Your goal from this point forward is to be a better you.

**Inspiration for Victory:**
If you want to be successful you must find the passion and change your passion do not chase money, money will not bring true happiness. When you are doing your passion, it is no longer a job it is enjoyment. follow your passion and not a lust for money. Turn off the television, pick up a book, practice or put in the work towards accomplishing your goals.

The C.O.R.P.O.R.A.T.I.O.N.

(Crooked Officials Robbing People of Rights Against Truth in Our Nation) BOOK TITLE

# 6 YOU MUST SUFFER AND ENDURE STRUGGLE TO BE GREAT AND SUCCESS.

Bible Verse: Hebrews 12: 6 For whom the Lord loves He chastens and scourges every son whom he receives. 7. If you endure chastening, Yahawah deals with you as a son, for what son is there whom a father does not chasten? 8 But if you are without chastening, of which all have become partakers, then you are bastards and not sons.

Shalom, I would like to begin this chapter by stating that one should never anticipate him being successful, great, or extraordinary if they do not endure suffering and struggle. If you detest correction, if you detest corrective criticism, then you will about his plan for you and miss your blessing. The process of evolution, growth, and success always is inclusive of pain and suffering. I was compelled to peer into the mirror of truth in face my undesired reality which is to suffer to be successful and great. I had to endure long suffering. The only way that I discovered my true calling was to indulge myself to the most difficult, the most excruciating, painful situation that one would deem intolerable. And to do so I realized that I had to undergo suffering, so I walked away from two professional jobs working in corporate America as a computer network administrator, and as a computer architectural instructor.

I just walked in one day and prayed to my God and I handed in my resignation. I did not know how I was going to eat; I did not know how I was going to live, but what I did know is that these jobs were not allowing me to wear the spiritual clothing that my creator had designed specifically for. I realize that I had been living a life that others told me would be successful, I was working a job that others said was a good job even though I did not like it. So, I am talking to you right now, if you are not doing what the creator has planned for you, if you are not following that, then you are not really living. You will never actually be successful despite the amount of money that you make because that's not your true calling. And when I quitted that job people said this guy's crazy, this guys to stupid, because they did not comprehend my passion to be alone with the path that Yahawah had planned for me.

When I converse with people, I will often be asked what is your passion? Some people do not know, and if you do not know your passion that moves you, and do not know your primary target then you are lost. This is suggesting that you truly do not have something essential to take aim at. If you are not aiming at anything, if you are not shooting at anything, then there is no focus because you have no target.

I can sense if you are doing something that is not your true calling, because you are not genuinely happy, so you become complacent if you adapted something that you really don't enjoy doing. Many people, they do this in relationships, they remain in relationships that causes them a deluge of pain and mental challenges, and then it physically destroys them. Why are you trying to force someone to love you if it is not in them? Love is not just saying I love you but is an expressed act. And if you have anyone in your life that is not supporting your goals, your dreams, to be aligned with the path that God has designed for you, then you need to extirpate them out of your life. This is inclusive of your mother, of your father, of your spouse, and of your children. Perhaps this sounds harsh, but this is what it requires to truly be what the creator has called you to be. This is what it takes to walk in his light with out of darkness. Look it up the word, look it up second Corinthians 6 chapter start reading at the 14 verse.

I also ask people that I converse with what is your passion? Some of them can somewhat answer the question but the vast majority really do not know, and 99% of the people or not living in their passion. Therefore, five years from now they would still be talking about what they should have done, or what they could have done, or that they are almost ready to do it, but I know that they would never truly accomplish their dreams or truly be successful. To truly be successful they must stop succumbing to that fear they must be willing to suffer, and they must be willing to take risk. See beloved I cannot tell you what you what to hear, I tell you the polar opposite of what you want to hear, or what the world instills into you, and I tell you what's really required to be that 1%, that is truly living their passion. This is truly the warrior mentality. Now when I quit those jobs, I was at an all-time low, and I was transpiring into what everyone told me I would be if I quit those jobs, "nothing". See I had developed the mindset of a loser, of a failure. And then the spirit of truth touched me, and I realize that just because I had fallen did not mean that I was an utter failure. I had already taken the first step of taking the risk of leaving jobs that was not in my calling.

Essentially, if you are reading my book right now, and you are because you are reading this, and you are still fearful of looking into the mirror of adversity, this is what I suggested you do. First of all, you're not going to like or enjoy what I say to you because I give you righteous rebuke. What I am about to tell you right now is something that you have actually never heard in your life, is the exact opposite of what you want to hear, or what the world has told you. What you have been doing is you been cloning others, you have cloned your college professor, you have cloned your peers, you clone celebrities. You have been taught to follow program to to follow someone else or what others are doing, and you have aborted individuality. I challenge you to do what you have never done before, which is to develop some to truth inside instead of looking at external sources, look inwardly. restart, where it is cool, where is difficult to admit your shortcomings and your issues that you need to check and be sure to become who you are supposed to be. I challenge you to peer deep within yourself and see what it is that you want. Start doing it right now.

What are you passionate about? You listen to a lot of self-help gurus different, slogans, but they will all just words unless you speak it into existence. Most people be just talking, they never will do what they say, many of you right now will say Tazadaq he is just talking, because you do not truly know I speak from experience. What I am telling you right now young king, young queen, older King, older queen, is that the only way to get to the other side of this journey is it is imperative that you suffer to truly grow. When I hit rock bottom, I realized that no one was there to assist or to help me. Three was only my creator. When I would actually look into the mirror, I felt degenerate, I felt subordinate, I felt awful, and I did not want to feel that way anymore, so I decided that I was suffering now, to change my mind, my body, now to be great and successful later.

This is what I tell you, watch this watch this.... most people would have run to someone for help, most people would have tried to abort the path for a path of lesser resistance, but I did not ask for help, no one was there to help, so I suffered. No one, absolutely no one had sympathy for me. No one felt sorry for me, no one said help Tazadaq out his cars broken, he is in a strange city where he did not grow up in, having no family here no one helped me. Even my wife at the time abandoned me.

She knew I did not have a job, I had moved to her hometown, she abandoned me several times and so not only did I had to deal with not having a job, but I also had to endure the emotional distress that one undergoes when they are leaving a marriage. No one was there for me, but I pushed through the pain, and maybe that was intense. having been abandoned by someone that had claimed to love me. And therein I became stronger. And want to say this to you family, we are all great and unique within our own way.

No one could be me like, only I can be me, and no one could be you as you could. Then be you. So, stop trying to be what others want you to be, and be who you are because no one can be you as good as you can. But sister, you have greatness within. Discover that greatness, because on the other side of difficulty and the struggle is greatness is success. You must search that inner core, and blackout the naysayers, to blackout all the negative thoughts and supplant into your mind "I am going to be great, successful, blessed and unstoppable: and then do it. But this is not an easy journey, it will take hard work, it will take enduring difficulties, it would take struggle, all those noncognitive skills are required to be successful and great. You might be looked upon as being intelligent, so many may say you are very smart, oh yeah that is cool, great but it is those noncognitive skills that will make you bless and unstoppable to be a winner is the other side of struggle, go and get it. Too many people put on an act as if this is stage play, to be accepted into the world of others. Because you are not writing a story you are reading from someone else's story and that has become the story of your life. You must read the life God has destined for you. And if you want to remain a loser you, you can complain about where your life is, not where it should be.

The C.O.R.P.O.R.A.T.I.O.N.

(Crooked Officials Robbing People of Rights Against Truth in Our Nation) BOOK TITLE

You could blame other, and then you will remain on a degenerate substandard abase level, and you will remain miserable. Until you learn to look within, you are never going to change.

For you to change your life, for you to truly be successful, you must look within and say what is it that is wrong with me? You must build calluses in your thinking just as a labor worker may build calluses on his hands., you have to suffer and endure struggle. We may fall but, you must get back up, you must have faith. Again, everything that I say is rooted in the word the book of Hebrews chapter 11 verse 1 says now faith is the substance of things hoped for the evidence of things not seen." Real faith is the process of believing in a future with everything your prayed without any evidence or assurance to prove it. One cannot see or experience a dream prior to it taking place, but you must still align your thought, your words, and actions with the full anticipation and expectation of that dream materializing into reality.

To truly walk in the fullness of being blessed and unstoppable one must, when you walk with absolute confidence, when you operate with full anticipation, you create a powerful presence of undeniable influence. When you function with this type of trust and conviction it makes all things possible fulfilling the Scriptures again.

Your destiny has an obligation by the Lord of the universe to concede, to the demands of unwavering faith. The level of strength that you receive will all wait to be equivalent to the level of your belief. Your vision for the future needs corresponding expectations in order to bring it into fruition. Your dreams, not back by faith is just an impotent hard thought and wish, so you are destining to failure. Now you can keep ejaculating to the madness of the world or have mental intercourse with your thinking in both a new mentality. The only person that could turn this person around is you. Others may not be able to see or understand your vision be¬because destiny hides itself in the mind of the one who will inherit it. If you want to receive this inheritance protect your faith at all times. Especially in the initial stages of this development. The world will attempt to fuck you and impregnate you with a deadly disease called average, or doubt, or mediocrity. This contagious disease is more detrimental than cancer, or HIV. It is a dream killer, and it is fixed on murdering your future. You must diminish, you must destroy, you must eliminate, and annihilate any traces of this sickness from your life. True faith never attains or accepts any other outcome then the one best for. You must slam the door, close of your internal circle to anyone that does not support you in your dreams or that is not aligned with your path for you to be successful and great. If you cannot extirpate the naysayers, then you must quarantine the doubters and naysayers around you and you must limit their ability to access your thinking and refused to let them infect your mind with doubt and discontentment. You must surround yourself with people that believe in what you believe and by people that are clear warriors, by people that has a warrior's mentality, and people that or akin to your thinking.

Faith unwavering can move mountains. And when properly understood and applied it becomes a torchlight for change. Every miracle that Christ performed he used faith to do it. True Israelites have access to the same power for he said in the book of John 14 verse 12 "greater works than these will you do because I'm going to the father. I am paraphrasing that go look it up yourself. So, you as a believer in Christ you have access to this same power, so with him interceding on your behalf you could do even greater works and wonders. I will tell you family faith is essentially the sole language spoken in the kingdom of God, which means it is utterly the only language that the universe yields to. You are thinking your, belief is the chosen method that releases the blessings, so the quality of your future depends on how fluent you become in your faith. When your anticipation your goals, your dreams, and your expectations collide, they expose with blessings a manifestation of greatness. Your faith can pull your goals, your, dreams your desires from an imaginary wall into the core of your reality. Whatever it is that you want to be, whatever it is that you wanted to have, you must have faith that it will happen, anticipate it happening and it will come into fruition. Hold fast to your dreams, hold fast to your visions, and it will happen.

**Positive Affirmation**: I walked circumspectly fully in faith knowing that what I had envisioned for my life the highest will bring it to pass. I am devoted, I am sold out, and I am committed to achieving and fulfilling all my gods given assignments that he has aligned me with. I will not be denied my dreams, or my goal.

**Self-Assessment Question:**

what does it mean to be truly faithful?

What is differentiating between having true faith or just is having hope? Am I currently showing expectations and my life?

Who are the biggest naysayers, dream killers and doubters that I know?

How can I limit the naysayers and doubters from access in my mind?

Who encouraged me to accomplish my dreams?

What is the body language of a man or woman that believes they are going to succeed?

When in my past did, I exemplify unwavering faith?

Do I know the difference between trust and faith?

**Daily Prayer**: I pray that you will escalate my faith to its highest level and work miracles through me. Father I thank you for strengthening my belief in you. Father God help me to achieve a spirit of exceptional faith so that I can fulfill the purpose that you.

Created me for. May your mind and will be glorified in everything that I accomplish in the name of Christ I pray amen.

**Success Quotes:**

second Corinthians chapter 5 verse 7 for we walk by faith not by sight.

Feed your faith and your fears will starve to death.

Faith activates God fear activates the enemy.

In faith there is enough light for those who want to believe and enough saddles to bind those that do not.

Faith is to believe what you do not see the reward of this faith is to see what you believe.

Therefore, I tell you whatever you ask in prayer believe that you have received it and it will be yours Mark chapter 11 verse 24.

Action Step: pray for God to help you with your unbelief. Emotions self in the word of God. Study to show thyself approved. From this moment forward begin to distance yourself from anyone that cast doubt on you achieving your goals and dreams. Surround yourself with people who inspire you and encourage you to pursue your calling.

**Inspiration for Victory**: You are a child of the most high-power, the modern-day illuminati, Goliaths, our deceivers                are                no                match                for                you.

# 7 ONLY THEIR LETTERS REQUIRED FOR ABSOLUTE SUCCESS, W. H.Y.

Bible Verse: Proverbs 19:21 many are the plans in the mind of man, but it is the purpose of the Lord that will stand.

If you are to be tremendously successful, you must have a purpose. Your true purpose is your "why". Why do you want to be great, why do you want to be successful? Whatever you truly desire and aspire to accomplish it is imperative to dissect it and deeply comprehended. It is your why that is essential, however more important what is imperative is that your goal that you are striving for is to be driven. Motivation is just not enough; you need to be driven. Because if you are driven behind your why you will move to accomplish what you desire. This essential reason, this purpose, or belief that drives you and motivate you will move you to consistently work towards your desires. There will be a Days of trials and tribulations during this journey, and you will see a lot of dead carcasses of those that attempted to do what you are doing, and they fell. Do not be deterred by this, allow this to be your motivation that you are pushing past the deceased with the motivational purpose in life. This why will be your transportation that will carry you through the difficult times. The more that you desire to accomplish the stronger your why should be. Alas, when you develop an insatiable desire, and undeniable motivation to be driven to achieve something then will you achieve it. I contend that you can accomplish anything if there is a good enough reason, if there is a strong enough why. Whatever it takes to put yourself into this warrior's mentality of never quitting, of not being denied, do it. There is absolutely nothing that can stop a man or a woman who has no other choice but to be successful and succeed.

That is your why.
Before I wrote this book, before I begin writing this book, I said this book will be a bestseller, and this book is a bestseller. The principles, your motives, the check that will thrust you into your goals and orbit into your dreams. You surely do not want to run out of gas during your travels to ascertaining your goals. Warriors do not give up, champions know inside why they want what they want, and it may be years, know that it takes determination to get them through the battlefield of the marriage, through the battlefield of a gym sculpting your body into that of a God; through the battlefield of a dead-end you are that you must fight your inner demons and be able to walk away from them. Warriors, and champions move into a course that drives them and to a belief that inspires them to go beyond normality, to go beyond mediocrity. This is what pushes a true warrior, into a champion behind normality it is consistency, it is out working the competitive, it is sticking it out doing the most turbulent times. Why is the father to all legends that had been born and made themselves great in the fill? It does not matter if it is a family issue, if it is a corporation issue, if it is a marriage issue, or if it is an individual you can defeat each one of them, you need a strong why to accomplish what you want to accomplish. You must ensure that what you learn that your desires are constructed around righteousness. You must filter all your motives and intentions through the fruits of the spirit which are faithfulness, goodness, kindness, patient's, peace, joy, and most importantly love. Motives planted in revenge, contention, polemics, or self-destructive and will ultimately prevent your success. You must never make your why depended on some external force or external person. If you make your why depended upon some external force, you will make yourself vulnerable to outside circumstances and situations.

Success is a remote journey; it is an extremely lonely road. This journey must be traveled day after day, day in and day out, so if what you are doing does not wake you up early and keep you up late burning the midnight oil then you need to do something else. If you fill stagnated and seemed to be not driven and lack motivation, examine your why, examine your reasons for doing it in the first place. There must be burning desire, a deep-felt connection to what you are doing, because all your energy flows out this con¬nection. The deeper you are connected to that which you are doing the more likely you will accomplish it. You must be driven, find the motive that ignites you on the inside and make that the core of your thinking and your life. Awaken to your own why and you will be destined for success, destined for greatness and you will be unstoppable.
Daily Affirmation: I am extremely driven, and I commit myself to living a life that is totally successful. I have good incentive and pure motives that drives me daily. I know what I want and why I wanted. I will not be denied success.

**Self-Assessment Question:**
**what is the reason that I want to** be successful in my life?
Is my wife strong enough?
Do I need to be more honest with myself?
How did successful people become successful?
What is the why?
What happens if I forget?
What belief inspire me to do what I do? What are the reasons behind me wanting what I want?
Am I deeply connected to my purpose?
Is my why truly and aligned with the path God has planned for me?
Daily Prayer:
Dear father God, I pray that you will help me examine me why behind the things that I desire for me and my loved ones in life. Help me father to sort out any internal motives that are out of line with you. Watch me dearly, purifying my intentions and my thinking so that I can walk the straight and narrow path that will please you in Christ name I pray a man.
**Successful Quotes**:
When something is not enough. You must hunger for it. Your motivation must be compelling in order to overcome the obstacles that will invariably come in your way. Les Brown
power is not alarming to pure minds. Thomas Jefferson
when you want to be successful as bad as you want to breath you will be successful. Eric Thomas
he who has a reason to live for can bear almost any how. Frederick Nietzsche
The moment there is suspicion about a person's motives, everything he does becomes tainted Gandhi.
great thoughts and a pure heart, that is what we should ask from God.
Talent is a wonderful thing, but it will carry quitter. Stephen King

**Action Steps**: write down 12 powerful reasons why you want to be successful the top three from this list that motivates and inspires you the most.
Write those down on a separate business card, or cue card or index card. Now you have your why. Carry it with you wherever you go. Read it three times a day. Whenever things get hard in life pull out your why and let it remind you of the reasons you must keep pushing forward.

**Inspiration for Victory**: today you need to tell your problems, struggles, difficulties, and your pain how small they look standing adjacent to God.

Insert chapter seven text here. Insert chapter seven text here. Insert chapter seven text here. Insert chapter seven text here. Insert chapter seven text here. Insert chapter seven text here. Insert chapter seven text here. Insert chapter seven text here. Insert chapter seven text here. Insert chapter seven text here. Insert chapter seven text here. Insert chapter seven text here. Insert chapter seven text here. Insert chapter seven text here. Insert chapter seven text here. Insert chapter seven text here. Insert chapter seven text here. Insert chapter seven text here. Insert chapter seven text here. Insert chapter seven text here. Insert chapter seven text here. Insert chapter seven text here. Insert chapter seven text here. Insert chapter seven text here. Insert chapter.

# 8 THE ISSUES OF LAW CONTRACT IS NOW THE LAW OF THE LAND

Bible Verse Habakkuk 1: 4 Therefore the law is slacked, and judgment doth never go forth: for the wicked doth compass about the righteous; therefore, wrong judgment proceedeth.

In this chapter through the spirit of God in Christ we will delve into what law really is. Beginning with the premises 98% of people that walk into a court room automatically assume that law is on the table because those people that purport to use law use legalese words or words of art which is colorable law. It is not law. That which colorable resemble something that it is not. Law is that which is laid down, ordained, or established.

I contend that 99% of the people are slaves today inside of a Matrix that they thought was just a movie. In 1863 by way of the Emancipation Proclamation the so-called black slaves were supposed to be set free. Since most people suffer from aphasia allow me to help you over stand the words.

What is EMANCIPATION?

The act by which one who was unfree. or under the power and control of another, is set at liberty and made his own master. Fremont v. Sandown, 50 N. H. 303.

What is Proclamation? The act of causing some state matters to be published or made generally known. A written or printed document in which are contained such matters, issued by proper authority. 3 Inst 162; 1 Bl. Comm. 170. The word "proclamation" is also used to express the public nomination made of any one to a high office. Knowing thus it should be now obvious that proclamation Is not a law, its merely a public announcement and not a law. It because clear that we have been lied to and that the Emancipation Proclamation did not free any slaves. Essentially this provided a standard for which other nations around the world emulated to create nation states to reduce their people from a sovereign capacity to subjects by means of these nations' states. Thereafter they would be able to create rules, Acts, codes, statutes, resolutions on them. A code, a statute, an act is not law. It is a corporate policy that was created by the corporate wards of the commonwealth of Virginia incorporated which is a nonprofit. U. S Codes, U.S. statues are not law even if they are used in the supreme court it is not law, they are exactly what they claim to be, codes, statutes, acts, rules. A parking ordinance for entertainment purposes is not law.

The reason that these things are not law is because the only people that can issue laws are those people in a sovereign status. Euro Gentiles (Edomites) cannot be sovereigns in a foreign land know as America and they are not Americans, and if they want to be sovereigns, they must return home to Europe. The judges, and lawyers and folks that hold public office are members of a corporate ward, and so as long as you have a 1040 form on file, a birth certificate, an SSN etc., you belong to the chattel slave holders and are a corporate word by way of these contracts known as the birth certificate, SSN,1040 etc. You belong to the policy makers and this is known as slavery. If you are a me member of a corporate ward state known as The United States then you are a citizen, resident, or have an address which is a fictitious number associated with a designation issued by a corporate ward. This places you under the jurisdiction of those public servant which are also corporate wards yet also slaves' holders. Therefore, if you are operating under the said capacity then laws do not apply to you because you are a corporate ward and their statutes, codes resolutions apply to you of the nonprofit corporation.

Positive affirmation: except who you are and choose to let the world see the real you. Embrace your destiny, your identity and the freedom that comes with it. Promise today to be an original and stay true to you, to who you really are.

**Self-assessment questions.**
why do I feel such a need to have the acceptance of others?
Do I dress the way that I dress because I think that is what the world expects of me, or do I like it?

Who knows the real me?
What does it feel like when I am being honest to myself?

What time in the past have I shown my true colors?

How would my life improve if I showed more of the real me?

**Today's prayer:** I pray today, Father God for the strength and courage and boldness to display my identity. Please help me to be

comfortable with who I am. God move me away from anything that is not aligned with the original version you made of me in Ya-

Yahawashi name I pray amen.

**Successful quotes.**

when you are content to be simply yourself, and do not compare or compete everyone will respect you.

Do not compromise yourself you all that you have.

Do not dilute yourself for any person or any reason. You are enough be unapologetic.

Always be a first-rate version of yourself and not a second-rate version of someone else. Judy Garland's

Your action steps:

write down a list of times in your life when you felt most authentic.

Write down a list of your personal strengths.

Write down a list of the ways that you can build more of your life around your answers for the above.

Acknowledge and accept the person God designed you to be.

Examine your dreams and goals to make sure that they are really yours and not just borrow from someone you admire.

Audit your dress code to see if what you are wearing every day is aligned with who you really are.

**Inspiration for victory:**

when you are playing the role that God designed you to be you are invincible and unstoppable.

# 9 BORN: THE ILL MIND OF A CREDITOR

Bible Verse: Romans 8:28 And we know that for those who love God all things work together for good, for those who are called according to his purpose.

Average is defined in Webster's New World College dictionary fourth edition as the results obtained by dividing the sum of two or more quantities by the number of quantities.

Average is also defined in maritime law as a loss incurred by damage to a ship at sea or to its cargo; the equitable division of such laws among the interested parties a charge arising from such laws any various small charges paid by the master of a ship.

However, average is also defined acts being intermediate in value rate normal or ordinary such as an average student. Average is a fatal illness that has plagued the minds of most of the people upon the earth. 99% of the people are affected by the plague of being average and settled with being infected by the disease of average. Too many this is known as adjustment, I defined it as failure and lack of willpower, and an indomitable spirit. You must be extremely cautious and walk circumspectly into rooms because most of the people therein will be infected with the disease of average and this disease is highly contagious.

This disease is more widespread than cancer, leukemia, the HIV plague. It is a pandemic crushing the goals, therefore be careful not to be around those that are average or will be infected by this plague. You could be exposed to this disease and contaminated merely by being in the same room with one of the people that is infested with the sickness, the disease called average. It will affect a small portion of your brain and then it will start to spread and tell you of negativity thoughts until it grows and expand and occupies your entire mentality and body with mediocrity.

Once this disease enters a small portion of your life, it will grow and manipulate your thinking until it reduces you to mediocrity and you settle with being average and contend this is what now is known as adjustment. Just look at the guy next to you, just look at your neighbor, it is a pandemic that has spread throughout the earth just about everyone that you encounter it is affected with the disease of average. It is so crafty that it will work its way down into your subconscious until you begin to consciously act it out and it would spread to other people all the way down into your genes and into your children. The antidote or the vaccine is to bring a demise to the thinking that gives birth to the disease of average is as a man think it in his heart so is, he.

Some may say Tazadaq, most people are successful extremely successful, but most people are successful at being average. Average has no place within the life or the minds of wonderful warrior mentality as Tazadaq. It has no place in the life of a champion. If there is anything that a warrior or a successful person is at peace of failing at, is failing at being average. Something to ask yourself are these very imperative questions; how bad do you want to be successful? How bad do you want to be great? How bad do you want to be extra ordinary? Action is a direct answer for a corresponding mindset. My question that I had to you if you were on trial right now would you be convicted for being average?

Or is there enough evidence in your life is there enough proof in your life that if trial before a jury of 12 would you be convicted of found guilty of being successful? There is nothing about the creator that is average that is nothing about the creator this mediocre, and you were made in the image and likeness of the creator. Stop placing limitations on God Psalms 82 verse 6 did I not say that you are God's.

Anything that is average in mediocre will make you sick if you have the mind of God. Stop just reading about success, stop just talking about success, and be great. Any book, any manual, any person, any friend, any spouse that tells you that you are average is a damn liar. The mind will go as far as you could push it, stop placing limitations on God. Most people are to content, too comfortable with being average or even with being good, to be sensational or great. Therefore, most of the people on earth sit passively as time passed by waiting to discover who they are waiting to reach for their dreams, but the successful people preciously and ferociously drive for their dreams and become great.

Nevertheless, I am going tell your love story, about a man and a woman that grew up in a small town named mediocrity. Some people refer to town as average town USA. The woman's name was Yapah Kimberly Desire, and the man's name was Tazadaq Determination. It appears as if from the inception of the process of being born it was as if the creator had taken a rib from Determination and created Desire. Thus, Determination was always searching for his Desire to accomplish his goals and his dream. Desire always had a passion to be great, but she lacked determination. So, one day they encounter each other on a higher plane known as

destiny. As it stands Yahawah put these two souls that became mates together, and it was love at first sight. Although they faced struggles, they face hardships, they face difficulties, but despite of all these challenges they did not grow apart they grew even stronger together in a bond that became inseparable. So, when you looked at determination you always saw desire within determine-nation and determination was consistent now because he had a strong desire.

Once Determination was with Desire they were driven and consistent and became blessed and unstoppable. You see as they began to soar and grow, they became too huge, too big for that small town called mediocrity in average USA. Once they had their minds in the right place, they decided that it was time to graduate from that school, and overcrowded congested town called mediocrity and average. They made a pact between themselves; they drew up a verbal covenant between each other, that they would move away from that small town called mediocrity. So eventually Determination became engaged with Desire and because of their consistency took on the bond of marriage, and they moved away from that small town of mediocrity also known as average USA where the people was content at being normal. See Determination and Desire came to an unequivocal agreement that normality was just as deadly as the disease known as average, and therefore they moved away from that small town of mediocrity and average. They moved to a big urban environment the greatest city on earth, called success that was filled with goals, dreams, and greatness.

They built a mansion and other real estate on their legal property known as perseverance Avenue and hard work corner. It was not easy, they did not do it overnight it required some time and burning the midnight oil, but they accomplished their dreams and de-termination impregnated desire, and they had a beautiful baby that was named success, greatness, blessed, and unstoppable. Now even though they receive many letters, phone calls, comments, and emails from the naysayers back in that small town called mediocrity and average, to bring them back down to average; they rejected the offers. It was as if that small town known as mediocrity had never existed. Why did it appear to never exist? It is because determination and desire had a strong why. So, I ask you to listen to me right now, what is your why? What is your reason? You see determination and desire never went back to that small town referred to as mediocrity and average therefore if you want to get out of that small town you must have a why.

**Positive affirmation**: I will surround myself with those wiser than I. I will not do selective listening but will heed to advice. I am ill-equipped for the life of success that I desire. I am so grateful for the wise experience and honest people I have around me.

**Self-assessment question**:
what is one thing today I can do to begin assembling my peer group?
Who are the wisest and most intelligent people I know?
Who do I know that can give me wise counsel?
When in the past have, I learned from mentor ship?
who has the most integrity that I know?
Who would be a great mentor for me to study under?
In what areas of my life do I need to seek advice?
Today's prayer: I think you dear father God for surrounding me with wise counsel. Provide me the strength to

humble myself and have a meek spirit to enable me to follow the advice of these mentors you have sent me. I pray for you to help me assemble people of your righteous character to guide me in every area of my life.
In Christ's name I pray amen.

**Successful quotes:**
many receive advice only the wise profit from it.
Surround yourself with the best people you can find, delegate authority, and do not interfere if the policy you decided upon is being carried out.
Whatever you do in life, surround yourself with smart people who are you with.
A single conversation across the table with a wise man is worth much study of books. Nothing is impossible for those who act after wise counsel and careful thought. A full despises good counsel, but a wise man takes it to heart.
**Your action steps:**
within the next three days identify the top three people within your fill, contact them and see if they would be open to mentor and you. Each week sort for more and more ways to connect with smart, talented, and experienced veterans who already doing what you want to do.
**Inspiration for victory:**
God is sending all the right people into your life to assist you with fulfilling your divine goals.

chapter nine text here. Insert chapter nine text here. Insert chapter nine text here. Insert chapter nine text here. Insert chapter nine text here. Insert chapter nine text here. Insert chapter nine text here. Insert chapter nine text here. Insert chapter nine text here. Insert chapter nine text here.

# 10 ACKNOWLEDGE KNOWLEDGE CIPHER

Bible verse: Jeremiah 29: 11 to 13 for I know the plans I have for you declares the Lord, plans to prosper you, and not harm you, plans to give you hope and a future. Then you will call on me and come and pray to me and I will listen to you. You will seek me and find me when you seek me with all your heart.

The highest has plans for you having that which you desire. Many of you desire an awesome body; however, you do not have the willpower and discipline to school your body into that which you desire. I have witnessed many people in the gym day after day, week after week, month after month. These folks are dedicated to coming to the gym, but they are not dedicated to training their bodies because their minds are not discipline enough to do so. Some encounter me and ask. How can I get my body to look like yours?

I reply, first train your mind. Many of these people are very wealthy, therefore they hire personal trainers to try and assist them with losing weight, they pay large sums of money, but they will not train their minds to stop eating the bad foods. One should not expect to have a warrior's body with a feeble mind. You must first train your mind to be discipline enough not to contaminate your body with bad eating. You must have the discipline not to eat the bad food, not to eat late at night. You are what you eat, that aphorism is worth repeating to yourself. If you eat drunk you should not expect your body to be healthy despite how much you train. You must eat good fruits and vegetables, drink plenty of water get adequate sleep and stay away from the simple sugars, the process food, and negative people that will encourage you to eat poorly.

Once you train your mind, once your mind is disciplined enough to eat clean, to put healthy fruits and vegetables into your temple and once you have a good work out ethic in the gym you will be unstoppable. I therefore need you to commit this moment to not putting any more confined sugars, processed foods such as Ramen noodles, ice creams, Entenmann's, cakes, cookies, even processed meats into your temple. These will only hinder you in the future you and prevent you from having the body that you desire.

At the gym I am approached by the male and female that is devoted to come into the gym, but they come to the gym to jaw a chat. These people seem to have a goal of coming to the gym and working the jaw muscles. One would think that they had already been overworking the jaw muscles at the table, because of their weight in the way that the bodies look. It does not take a rocket scientist to conclude how I have created the body that I have. It requires hard work, Dedication, discipline, and perseverance. I come to the gym I work out to get that burn, and once I get that burn, I do not allow the fire to go out until I leave the gym. Because once that fire is burning my body is like the clay that I can mold into the shape that I desire. This is the gym; you do not talk here you perform in here. Hence, when you go outside you still do not have to talk because your body will speak for you. Look at yourself in the mirror of truth, and say the old me is dead, the new me is here to stay. Within your mind tell the old you to get the hell out of your thinking, there is a new me that is here and the new me is taken over and this is a permanent takeover.

If you want a warrior's body, you must have the warriors mind state. You are not seeing any results in the gym or in life, or on your job's, because you are not pushing yourself as you should. You are to content with being average. You have not given your body or your mind the opportunity to grow because you were not pushing it beyond what you have been told is normality. The weight considers normality as living are considered as death.
In the gym, on the job, and your relationship, or in life stop jaw chatting! In the gym stopped taking four minutes, or five minutes between sets because you are allowing the fire to go out; your recovery period is too long. Do not allow the burn to go out. In the draw up, and your relationship, and in life you must do the work now you speak with your actions, you teach by example, allow your actions and your dedication and devotion to speak volumes for you.
You must have the ability, or develop the ability, to have the self-discipline to do with when you do not feel like doing it or do not want to do it, it is then when you must do it harder and push through the temptation of not doing it. When you are doing the things that you do not feel like doing, that you detest doing on the other side of your slackness is greatness, going get it!

This current world, this present society are designing weak, complacent unmotivated people. 99% of the people are so weak that they cannot tolerate any wrong which occurs within their lives. As soon as they experience a little difficulty, they are given a prescription, but this does not fix the problem this disguised the problem, it places a mass over the problem and the problem lays dormant behind the fact gave of the drug prescription. Of the soft lying words. But I get strategies. to strengthen your mind. I speak truth, and I tell them as I am telling you right now you have allowed your life to get to this point. You are responsible for your failures; you are responsible for your shortcomings. It is not my full, it is not your mother's full, it is not because her father left, it is not.

because you may have been right, it is you and you are thinking that is at fault for your failures in life.
It is time to take responsibility, assume responsibility within this moment and develop the commitment to learning why you feel as you feel. What is the scientific facts of why you feel the way that you feel what can you do to strengthen it? The moment that you offer corrective criticism, instead of evaluating the criticism for truth or prove those wrong that have criticized you, instead you just give up. Because you are weak! You are feebleminded, and a product of a degenerate society.

You defend the criticism with useless polemics, you are a polemics extraordinaire. You never defended with definitive action, but with useless arguments. The moment you are challenged you crumble, so God has sent me as a messenger to tell you that you have greatness within you. God told me to tell you when things get difficult, you can no longer declare defeat or say it is not meant to be, or it must not be for me. I am the messenger sent to you to warn you as Jeremiah, that God says stop making excuses and make solutions. I am the messenger sent by the highest to tell you that he has planned for you, but you must stop saying, if it was not been for someone else. I would had made it; if they did not criticize me, I would have done it. Stop it now!

You are just weak feeble and unmotivated. You must tell yourself the truth, investigate the mirror of your soul and acknowledge the weakness. And acknowledge that you are the problem you will always be prone to failure, two being weak. You will never be able to grow into the person that can achieve all your goals and dreams. Until you admit that you are the problem, and the only problem you will never get those things that you genuinely want.
Your mind state is the problem, your negative attitude is the problem. It is not my fault, it is no one else's fault it is your fault. You are the problem if you want to be great you also the solution to accomplishing that greatness. You and only you must do this if there is any character within you whatsoever that previous statement, I just made will change your life. However, if you have no character you will remain an average, complaining, negative, cynical degenerate person. You will be a hater like most of the people that hate to see others aspire to be great. You are your only problem, and you are your only solution.

Absolutely, there are more problems that will arise, and you will face more difficulties, but you must not be so weak that difficulties destroy you. Some of you are so feebleminded, so weak that you are one cookie away from overindulging back into bad eating, you are one job loss away from committing suicide; you are one argument away from a mental breakdown; you are one relationship breakup away from an emotional depression. One more argument will ruin your entire year. Get your mind right King, get you mind right queen. This is not how you are supposed to live. The king does not fall to weakness he overcomes it with strength. Despite wat the challenge may be, if you have perspective, if you know who you are, if you really appreciate everything you have, and believe everything is as it should be, all those problems will be handled much better.
If you just lost someone to death, know that your loved one would want you to be happy and to live on. If you aspire to have an awesome body, know that people are secretly rooting for you but they are hating on you verbally. But there is a thin line between love and hate, the fact that they are expressing jealousy reveals that they have a secret love because they see you are driven. If you have been wronged by someone, living in pain, and holding onto resentment is allowing that person that done you wrong to win. You must relax, let go live your life and love your life, that is how you express with actions that I will not allow your perception of me define who I am any longer. I will not allow you to own any piece of my mind and spirit any longer.

That is the correct mentality, that is mental strength, that is being driven, and that is true courage. I am not suggesting that you should abort pain, or avoid pain, or not to suffer; these are all part of life's experience that enhances your development toward success. We all suffer on some level; some suffer worse than others but there is some that decide to live in that pain permanently and wreck their lives; but others use that pain and struggle as a growth process. Your mental strength should come from the struggles, it is born from pain. You must refuse to give up when most people would, your strength grows when you keep going, you keep pushing forward, when things seem impossible. Push one more time beyond what you assumed was a limit. That is a warrior's mentality, that is true mental strength. Excuses are for the feebleminded, weak people that have no heart. You must assume re-possibility for where you are at this moment and commit to do something that will ensure that your future is better. You can make excuses, or you have a choice to do better. You can make an excuse to stay where you are, or you could take responsibility, act, and get where you need to go and where you deserve to be what path you choose.

Positive affirmation: I am utterly focus, and purposely driven. I refuse to get distracted by things that do not move me towards my calling. Daily I will review my goals to ensure I stay on the path to achieving them.

**Self-assessment questions:**

Which things in my life are most important?

Where should I place most of my focus?

In which area of my life am I currently most focus?

In which area of my life in my most distracted?

Why am I giving so much time and energy to that which sabotage my success?

What is one of my most productive activity?

What one thing should I dedicate my life to accomplishing?

What are my least productive activities?

Do I review my goals each day?

If I spent most of my time on perfecting my craft how great what I be?

How does successful people stay focused?

**Today's prayer:**

I pray Father God for your help me to stay focused on the most important things in life. Thank you for guiding me and keeping my eyes on your plan for me. Please continue to guide me with your spirit so that I can be mentally and spiritually united in Christ's name amen.

**Successful quotes:**

What you stay focused on grows.

You must be single-minded. Try for one thing in which you have decided.

When trouble comes, focus on God's ability to protect you.

With every physical and mental resource focus one's power to sort a problem out.

**Your action steps:**

set the tone for the day by reviewing your life's goals first thing in the morning.

Decide the outcome that need to be accomplished each day that you move towards them.

Rate them in order of impact.

Structure your schedule around accomplishing the most important objectives first.

Make sure every action on your agenda is improving your chances at success. Eliminate all time and energy killers that stop you from your destiny.

Review your life's goals again right before bedtime.

Inspiration for victory:

God has designed you to make a massive impact on the world you must believe.

## 11 ACKNOWLEDGE THE POWER WIHTIN

Bible verse: Colossians 3:19 husband love your wives and be not harsh against him.

Right now, at this moment, you are reading this message and you are being abused, either physically, mentally, or both. Internally you know that this abuse is an injustice, yet for the deprivation of self-love you remain within an abusive relationship. You have become complacent and comfortable with the abuse to the degree that you suffer from Stockholm syndrome. Unaware of the adverse effects that this has on your psyche you attempt to justify the abuses and wrongdoing with internal thoughts, internalize thereby exacerbating the abuse.

There is a war occurring within your thoughts, within your mind. One half of you have wanted to depart from the abuser, but the other half questions the efficacy of your departure, because you fear being incapable of sustaining yourself, in a healthy mental state, and your livelihood. You therefore remain within the abusive relationship. This is killing you, yet you continue to justify the abuse of this evil person. The reason that you are reading this message right now, is because it is the divine will of Yahawah (God) that you do so. It is not coincidental that you are reading this message. This message was written for you to alter your life in your current existence. If you remain under the clutches of the abuser, you are incapable of making rational decisions. Your mind revolves around the abuse, and the fear that if you leave you will be incapable of surviving therefore you stay. When the Bible says in Colossians chapter 3 verse 19 grow not harsh suffer yourselves to be exacerbated. The word is used metaphorically only in this passage literally in Revelation chapter 8 verse 11. While submission is the duty of wives. However, it is submission to a severe Lord but not to a stern tyrant but to her husband who is engaged to an affectionate duty.

Husbands are commanded to love their wives with tender and faithful affection. When one goes to the gym and pushes their muscles beyond what they thought was tolerable the burning sensation in the pain is a healthy type of pain. From this type of pain there was pain that would be a growth, break the muscle down, and rebuild it stronger. However, if you are being verbally, mentally, and physically abused this type of pain will destroy you, will make you feel worthless, and you will suffer from self-loathing. You must break away from this abusive relationship now! When you are about to depart an abusive relationship, your departure may provoke the abuser to become even more violent, therefore it should be done without his or her awareness. You must plan a time that this person, is at work, or away from the home you, must leave at the said time. If it is fear that thundering you, please be mindful that fear is an intangible. Fear is not real, it is akin to a shadow it only appears to exist. Your fear only exists within your mind, you create the fear with your thinking, therefore you can destroy the fear, it is an intangible.

The abuser will often provide a sob story once you have left, they would tell you sweet lies to get you to return. Do not fall for this because eventually if you return the abuse will return and usually become worse. Many lives have been lost by returning to an abusive relationship. If a man absolutely loves a woman, he does not express that love by beating and striking her with his hands, nor verbal abuse. Do not be a Striker. First Timothy's chapter 3 verse 5 reads as thus, not given to wine nor Striker. This is suggesting that a man should not beat his wife, neither shall a woman strike her husband. There is a deluge of relationships where the female abuses the male and gets away with it merely because she is a female. This is utterly wrong, no one should have to undergo physical, verbal, or mental abuse in a loving relationship because that relationship is not loving. With God all things are possible, that's Matthew chapter 19 verse 26. But you sure beheld them and said with man this is impossible but with Yah all things are possible.

Therefore, if you think that you are incapable of surviving without this abusive person you are around. You must change your thinking. It is your thinking that is keeping you enslaved to this abusive person. As a man think so is, he, that is Proverbs 23 and 7. For as he thinks in his heart so is, he. The heart spoken of here is your mind which is the core of your thinking; get your mind right queen, get your mind right King. Whatever you think about most becomes your reality. You will never get positive results from negative thoughts. Likewise, positive thinking does not yield negative results. Although this sounds very trivial it is essential that you comprehend what you think about most you become. The words that you speak from your mouth, you speak them into existence. Henceforth you think positive, and you repeat to yourself daily I love me, I was created to be great. There is greatness within me.

In order to bring this greatness forth you must be disciplined, and there must be consistency. Transforming from an abusive relationship may not be easy, but anything that has real value is never easy. But every transformation always gets worse before it gets better. On the opposite side of that wall of pain, struggle, of difficulty is greatness and success and a peace of mind. Once you are away from the abusive person do not tell them where you are, do not answer any of the emails or phone calls, do not call them despite how bad you may want to. One that has been abused over long periods of time often suffer from Stockholm syndrome.

This means the person that has been abuse feel sympathy for the abuser and is thinking wrong, this can be very detrimental. Now is the time that you must focus on you, what is your passion, what is the one thing that you have always wanted to do in life? Once you figure that out, this is where your focus should be, not upon the past abusive relationship. If you allow your mind to linger on the abuse, or if you hate the abuser, it will destroy you, it will prevent you from being what the most high created you to be. You must forgive the abuser but never returned to them or allow them back in your life. Because without forgiveness you will never heal internally.

When bad memories of the abuse return to your mind, you must replace them with positive thinking. This is no time to be worrying, this is grinding season. You are no longer the sheep being led to a slaughter, instead you have become that lion running up the hill. You do not want to be the lion that is already on the hill. The lion that is on the hill becomes content, and complacent. But the lion running up the hill has an insatiable desire for more. Let success be your prey, let greatness be that which you are chasing. This is a warrior's mentality; you are now in beast mold.

Everyone wants to be a beast, until it is time to do what beast does. This is your freaking time, do not allow anyone to deprive you of it.

**Positive affirmation:** I am utterly clear about what I want to accomplish in my life. Each day, I will move closer to my goals my ambitions and my dreams. I have established a daily routine to effectively achieve what I have set up to accomplish.

**Self-assessment questions:**

Am I clear about what I need to accomplish in each area of my life?

Have I written all my goals down on paper?

Have I established a timeline to accomplish my goals?

Are these goals that I am aiming at really shaping me to become the best me that I could be?

What will I do today that will be working towards my dreams?

Who do I know that has already written down a list of goals and have accomplish them?

Just what are my strategies for accomplishing these awesome ambitions that I have?

**Today's prayer:**

Thank you, Father God, for giving me a complete clear perception over my life. I pray that you help me to stay focus on my dreams, my ambitions, and my goals, that you have planted inside of me. Please assist me in developing the right plans and strategies needed to accomplish these goals. In Christ's name I pray amen.

**Success quotes**

Setting goals is the first step in turning the invisible into the visible. For every God-given goal he gives grace to accomplish it.

Our goals can only be reached through a vehicle of pain in which we must fervently believe and upon which we must vigorously act there is no other route to success.

The greater danger for most of us is not that our aim is too high and missed but that it is too low, and we reach it. Michelangelo

Your action steps:

Decide what you want to accomplish in each area of your life and then write it down.

make sure that your outcomes are clearly defined and measurable.

Ask yourself this question: Are my goals big enough to stretch me and make me better?

Verify that these goals are within your control.

Establish aggressive, yet realistic time limits to reach each one of your goals.

Write your goals on an index card and keep them in front of you so you know what you are working towards every day. It is

inspiration for victory: do not be discombobulated by the deceptions of the world the highest explosive favor will flush you into victory.

The C.O.R.P.O.R.A.T.I.O.N.

(Crooked Officials Robbing People of Rights Against Truth in Our Nation) BOOK TITLE

(Crooked Officials Robbing People of Rights Against Truth in Our Nation) BOOK TITLE

## 12 ELIMINATE DEBTOR HATER CRITICS

Psalms 35:11 "False witnesses did rise up; they laid to my charge things that I knew not."

There are many critics that come against Tazadaq and charge me with things I did not do. I do not know if any of you noticed a critic came in the room last night doing the live stream begging for attention asking, "does he have down syndrome?" They do whatever they can to get some attention from Tazadaq. Lie on me, attempt to plant false charges on me. follow me, tap my phones monitor me on social media. I want you to know family, that if I mysteriously disappear it is because the government have their minions in my phones, monitoring my emails, and following me. Is it any surprise that a tracking device is found on my conveyances? What have I done? I have shown you love by teaching you right knowledge. This makes Tazadaq an extremely dangerous adept. So, they have decided that they want Tazadaq dead; or some really want me locked up in jail for life or dead. You could think I am playing all that you want to, but this is a profoundly serious matter. I do not have time to play I am trying to build this nation that Yahawah has sent me to assemble and teach.

So, I say to the De facto, to the critics, and to all of those that hate me; Galatians 4:16 Am I therefore become your enemy, because I tell you the truth? I mailed a package off with some of my books in it a few days ago and brother Dexter showed me that the package was open, two the books removed, and they sent the one book. This is not the first time that this has happened. So, they are tampering with mail that I send out. See you only see what is on the surface, you do not see I am being harassed behind the scenes. You do not see the Tazadaq that is being threatened. Yet I still stay in the spirit. Every hour that you should be praying and fasting for me you take this as a trivial matter.

There are only a few Israelite brothers that say I love you Tazadaq, but the vast majority detests me, envy me, and hate me because they have not been given a gift to be capable of reaching people the way that the highest is using me to reach his people. Understand this brother, do not hate me Ahch, love your brother. I did not choose this, I did not choose to be a modern-day Moses, I did not choose to be a Jeremiah, I did not choose to be like Ezekiel but the most high talked to me in the spirit of John 15:16 Ye have not chosen me, but I have chosen you, and ordained you, that ye should go and bring forth fruit, and that your fruit should remain: that whatsoever ye shall ask of the Father in my name, he may give it you.. So, you see Mr. de facto I must keep teaching and speaking, or Yahawah will kill me. I am not of this world John 15: [19] If ye were of the world, the world would love his own: but because ye are not of the world, but I have chosen you out of the world, therefore the world hateth you.

Some brothers and sisters have said Tazadaq "I love what you do, don't ever stop doing what you do." And it is those people that give me the inspiration and make me feel as if I am not doing this for nothing that I am changing lives. When I get the testimonies of the sister that says you saved my life, or the brother that told me you stop me from losing my home to foreclosure, or the sister that says you help me win in traffic court. Therefore the de facto do not like Tazadaq.

When they attempt to entrap with me semantics, when they send trolls that come with polemics, when agents monitor my every word, the most high instructs me on what to say in that very moment. Luke 21: [12] But before all these, they shall lay their hands on you, and persecute you, delivering you up to the synagogues, and into prisons, being brought before kings and rulers for my name's sake. [13] And it shall turn to you for a testimony.( this is what wicked men do not comprehend, that when the Lord cause things to go down and they does something to Tazadaq it's for a testimony against the heathens) [14] Settle it therefore in your hearts, not to meditate before what ye shall answer: [15] For I will give you a mouth and wisdom, which all your adversaries shall not be able to gainsay nor resist.

Now tell me, how can you tell me that you believe in the Highest and you falsely think that judgment comes from Esau and his court system? How can judgment come from the enemies of Yah? If you are a true man or women of Yah then you are supposed to know that Yah will destroy this wicked kingdom and you would love Tazadaq, God's man. But when you are a Judas a crooked turn coat, then you take sides with the enemies of Yahawah and Tazadaq. You pray for my downfall to Cesar.

Some say, Tazadaq your videos should be more popular, but they are going to bring you down, arrest you, or kill you before you are even known. Thus, saith the Lord Thy Power Ecclesiastes 7: 8 Better is the end of a thing than the beginning thereof: and the

patient in spirit is better than the proud in spirit.
There is no one like Tazadaq on YouTube today. I am not out here arguing over doctrine, battling Egyptologist, Moors, Muslims, I am teaching right knowledge and truth. I am not running I am facing the enemy.

So, watch the end rather than the beginning beloved, as if Christ were not hated and bought to prison, as if John were not bought prison, as if Peter were not brought to prison. When I tell you, I am not of this world you think I am playing games. I do not know how much longer I will be with you beloved, so spread my message, stand up for the truth with me. None of the wicked will never understand this which is why Yahawashi will have to bring judgement.

They might kill my flush brother and sister, or at least locked me up, because for us Israelites it is no justice for all its just us all, and most of our people are just ice frozen on a dead level, therefore Yah sent me to teach you educational purposes the law of the land.

Zechariah 11:5-7 King James Version (KJV) 5 Whose possessors slay them and hold themselves not guilty. This unjust legal system will not stand much longer. As a Prophet and priest of the Almighty Yah he is using me, Tazadaq as bait to lure in the enemy so he can justify bring down a system that brought no justice to Travon Martin, Mike Brown, Eric Garner, Sandra Bland, Freddie Gray, etc. The list goes on and on.

When you see people come along and talk bad about Tazadaq, "that SPC madness, Tazadaq is this, he a crook", they are sent by the United States and these agents of Satan do not realize it is not them and the United State vs Tazadaq its them and the United States vs Yahawah Was Yahawashi.

So, yah is sending Tazadaq like a modern Moses, telling the De facto Thus saith the Lord Yah of Israel let me people got. If you do not let my people go, I will smite America which is a spiritual Egypt and Sodom, with plagues and destructions thus saith the Lord god.

Rev 11: 8] And their dead bodies shall lie in the street of the great city, which spiritually is called Sodom and Egypt, where also our Lord was crucified.

I say this with great conviction to all people under the sound of my voice that have spoken ills of me. To you that have created lies on me, to you that have badmouth me. How can you stand against a man like me that is speaking out against this de facto, that is oppressing the people and the mass mind, and declare yourself to be righteous? How can you stand, lay down, reset with a clear conscious against a man as me that is the battling with this beast, that is battling with this the factor? You will get your reward from God and it will be a fitting punishment. Now that I have dealt with you trolls, bedbugs, bird brains, and cockroaches let me address the real enemies.

The real enemy is this defacto and that is who the highest has raised me up to stand against this is the real enemy. And you do not realize this because of cognitive dissonance. Their education system has programmed you as voluntary slave. You embraced words that they have placed upon you, like Negro, black, colored, African American, and Indians. The application of the term Indian originated with Christopher Columbus. Later the Americas came to be known as the west Indies. Initially the term Indians was not originally shared by indigenous people, but many over the last two centuries have embraced the identity. You are deceiving why are you deceive? Because of a defacto that you consider government.

The aboriginal Americans Hebrews, Moors or misrepresented as Indians and are in real fact the real Lords, Hebrews Moors. The identity of the Indians or Hebrews, moors or Asiatic. The definition of moor is from Murrells meaning dark a member of any of the Asian or African tort races.

American is defined 1828 as any aboriginal or any one of the various copper-colored natives found on the continent by Europeans Webster's unabridged dictionary 1820 8C. You do not know who you are because the de facto has manipulated your mind. The matrix was not just a movie the matrix is a documentary of your life. It is real which is why you think I am crazy. The definition of a moor again is any dark skin person check, it out in the encyclopedia. So, you do not know this system of law thus, God raised me up as a messenger and a prophet. I am the messenger sent to give the De facto warning; To teach you your nationality that quality of character which arises from the fact of a person belonging to a nation by state. Nationality determines the political status of the

individual especially with reference to allegiance while domicile determines his civil aboriginal means the first original aboriginal people status. Some agents of Satan ignorantly stated, Tazadaq you are not an aboriginal it is because you do not understand words because of the fact of these programs. Aboriginal simply means the first aboriginal people, or the first inhabitants of a country source natural law Webster's 1936 unabridged dictionary.

Each time that the de facto hear Tazadaq speaks, the government itself is shaking because they know that God's man is speaking truth therefore, they want me silence. But I am not afraid and not scared I speak the truth right knowledge Qam Yahsharahla.

Luke 21[16] And ye shall be betrayed both by parents, and brethren, and kinsfolks, and friends; and some of you shall they cause to be put to death. [17] And ye shall be hated of all men for my name's sake. [18] But there shall not a hair of your head perish. [19] In your patience possess ye your souls.

So good brother, my queen, beloved, family if you shall hear about them bringing false charges against me and locking me up without me having a fair trial do not be surprised. They did this to John the Baptist, they did this to Jeremiah, they did this to the apostle Paul, and they did this to Christ and so many of the men that dared to speak the truth. But will you be willing to ride for me? How many of you will stand for me?

**Bible Verse**: Revelation 13: 3 And I saw one of his heads as it were wounded to death; and his deadly wound was healed: and all the world wondered after the beast. 4 And they worshipped the dragon which gave power unto the beast: and they worshipped the beast, saying, who is like unto the beast? who can make war with him?
In Revelation 13:1 (KJV), we see a picture of a beast rise out of the sea, having seven heads and ten horns, and upon his horns ten crowns, and upon his heads the name of blasphemy. Yet in vs 3, we find: And I saw one of his heads as it were wounded to death; and his deadly wound was healed: and all the world wondered after the beast. Since this beast has 7 Heads, which 'Head' was wounded unto death, and healed?

## 13 DIMINISH THE SATAN OF SELF ALL NEGATIVE THOUGHTS

. Bible Verse: Ephesians chapter 5 verse 15 See then that you walk circumspectly, not as fools, but as wise.

The highest has given each of us the same 24 hours within a day. We all have the same 24 hours within a day to allocate as we desire. The sum out of 1440 minutes, or to break it down even more 86,400 seconds. It is essential that you harness each fraction of a second and hold them accountable for your greatness.

People that cannot manage their time are incapable of managing anything else. Each step of the ladder of success requires more and more control over your time. The average person structures their days around hours, but the great, those that are successful, dilapidated their days into blocks of minutes. If you want to be great you will schedule your time more towards your goals and ignore the rest. If you want to be successful in a marriage, if you want to be successful on a job, or successful in life in general it is imperative that you learn to manage your time. Successful time management consists of moving or eliminating the naysayers, and the time wasters out of your life that is not generating positive results. The average person may have a to do list, but a to do list often just render people busy, divert them from their ultimate objective. To become more time efficient, you must allocate your most essential resources towards the things that really matter.

When you have constructed a plan for the day, your actions will be intentional and strategic, resulting in you less likely to be held hostage by the moment. Certainly, situations may arise that you do not anticipate, but having a solid structure in place will help you to navigate the situations more effectively. Part of mastering your time, and controlling your reality is learning the art of saying no. Do not schedule something just to schedule it. Make certain that there is an essential purpose behind the meeting. Successful people, the people that are great in life comprehend the 80/20 rule that states you will get 80% of your results from 20% of your activities.

You must engage in a process of elimination to determine what yields your desired results and build your life around it. The great people, the successful people do not just micromanage their time, they multiply it by eliminating nonessential people and delegating authority to qualified people. Henceforth each night plan out what you are to do the next day. When you arise in the morning praise the highest, and make sure that you have a pre-established attendant. Every second of every minute should be thrusting you in some way towards reaching your goals and your targets. Construct daily routines that allow you to leverage and maximize your time eliminate the time wasters from your life. There is this mathematical equation that determines that we become like the top five people that we affiliate with most. It also suggests that we make somewhere in between the salary of the top five people that we affiliate with most.

Therefore, from today forth you mean be compelled to eliminate people from your life that are losers. It may seem harsh but if you hang around five people, or your affiliate with five people and four of them are losers you are going to be a loser. If you affiliate with five people and three of them only makes $25,000 a year you are more likely to make something close to 25,000 or less. This has been scientifically proven in both mathematically and science. You need to start the process of elimination right now. This goes for family members as well. If you are affiliated with family members that are losers, that overindulge in drugs and alcohol, then their life will be partially responsible for how your life is going. You could ignore this, and you will look back years from now and wonder why you just average, or at worst below average and a freaking loser. Get rid of the negative people now, friends' family or peers. If you want to be successful you must follow the scientific equation.

**Positive affirmation:** From today for our master all my time down to the second. I will plan, and I will properly schedule my day and I was on the day and the day will not only. I shall focus on the top results desired and make sure every one of my actions were effective at bringing them into existence.

**Self-assessment questions:**

what does a successful person schedule look like?

How can I structure my daily routines to be more effective at achieving my goals and dreams?

Which task bring me the most positive result?

Where the biggest time killers in my life right now?

Do I have a clear vision in my mind for how my day should look?

**Successful quotes:**

The bad news is that time flies the good news is that you are the pilot.

We do not manage time we manage activities within time.

Time is the only commodity that is irrevocable invested share it suspended but never wasted.

**Today's prayer**: thank you Father God for showing me how precious my time is. Help me allocate the gift you have given me more.

effectively in every area of my life. Strengthen my wisdom so that I can see ahead of time the things that need to be planned in me.

schedules thank you for assisting me in getting the most out of each day in the name of Christ I pray amen.

Your action steps:

At the beginning of each week write the most important outcomes for each week.

Divide each day's schedule into increments of 20 minutes.

Before you schedule a task on your list, always ask the question is this task leading me towards my goals?

Set a specific time to respond to an answer emails and phone calls.

**Inspirational quote.**

wave goodbye to lack of a scarcity the Almighty's abundant blessing or about to overtake you!

## 14 Be Quick to Listen and Slow to Speak

Bible Verse: Matthew chapter 12 verse 36 But I say unto you, that every idle word that men shall speak, they shall give account thereof in the day of judgment.

The highest has given each one of us the ability, and power to construct with our mouth. The verbiage that we speak sow the seeds of our world. Articulating declarations that are in correspondence with God's truth bring our thoughts, body, spirit, and souls into compliance with this truth. If we want to move in the completeness of God's blessings, we must constantly confess words full of inspiration, victory, and blessings.

What we speak vocally is a direct reflection of the belief that has been embedded into our minds by our teachers, our parents, our peers, and the media propaganda machine. The way we choose to express ourselves whether express by our actions or implied by our actions, or verbally dictate what we attract into our lives. We all can curse, maim, injure, heal, bless, or to destroy each time we state something out of our mouths. Being aware of this transformative power is imperative to constructing a life of success and greatness. Words dictate our outcomes into action in motion therefore it is essential for us to be quick to listen and slow to speak and think before we speak. It is imperative that we always stay disciplined keeping guard over our tongue. When we learn to control our mouth, we take control of our destiny.

Our forefathers, the great kings and rulers never spoke silly words like pheasants, which is why they was able to become kings. Ruling from their thrones they never wished and hope for things to happen, they boldly decreed them. The Royal were totally aware of the power and authority their words contain. Your mouth carries full authority of the room dictating each aspect of your life. Success must be first thought and then spoken into existence. Each syllable, each word, each phrase that we speak is either carrying as closer or further away from our dreams, our goals and our failure or success. Despite if we are encouraging family, friends, establishing our own business, or being the CEO of an organization, each verbal expression sends out a wavelength of energy impacting the environment around us. The words that we state when applied with other natural laws within this book have the power to change the world. If you have faith you can move mountains. During times when you are about to slip into depression.

Your words are your most effective weapon. Despite what challenges you are facing, keep the clearing positive confessions over your life. Eventually you will recap what you have said, please ensure you are planting the type of seeds you want to see grow in your future.

Positive affirmation: I choose today to pronounce strong words of life. I boldly declare the positive things I want to happen with total faith and authority. I asked him for encouraging words of inspiration, motivation into the lives of those around me to enable them to be driven.

**Self-assessment questions:**

Are the words that I am speaking throughout my daily life overflowing with faith, hope, and love?

Are the words that I use daily aligned with the words of the highest?

In which areas of my life must I speak more positive?

Does speaking negative about myself or other people help bring my dreams alive?

Would using a better selection of words help my relationships?

Am I truly verbally articulate with words to express love for my friends and family?

Today's prayer: Thank you Father God, for helping me over stand the true power of speaking your words. Please provide me with the divine awareness so that I can speak your blessings over the people and things around me, and crisis name I pray amen.

**Successful quotes:** the words that come out of our mouth going to our own ears as well as other people is and they drop down into our souls where they give us either joy or sadness, peace or upset, depending on the types of words we have spoken. George Meyer

But the human tongue is a beast that you can master it streams constantly to break out of his cage, and if it is not tame it will turn while in cause your grief. Robert Greene

So, shall my word go forth out of my mouth: it shall not return unto me void, but it shall accomplish that which I please, and it shall prosper in the thing were to I sent it. Isaiah chapter 55 verse 11.

Think twice before you speak, because your words and influence will plant the seed of either success or failure in the mind of another. Napoleon Hill.

**Your action step:** when you start your day in the morning still declaring the most high's blessings and favor over your life. Speak and affirm the positive things you wish to give birth to in your life with energy and expectation. Remember that each word that you speak or seeds of power that set-in motion the destiny that you will inherit. Guard your words throughout the day to make sure the things that you say does not contradict your amazing future.

**Inspiration for victory:** the challenges that you are facing may appear insurmountable but Yahawah (God) still moves mountains.

## 15 It is GRIN SEASON, ALLOW YOUR GRIND TO SPEAK FOR YOU HUSTLE HARDER

Your thoughts ignite your mind to create dreams, but for this to become your reality it must be constantly nurtured with sweat, blood, and tears. Greatness success and victory comes directly off the assembly line of hard work, consistency, and a driven work ethic.

Average or mediocrity effort should not be an option for one who wants to live at their highest capacity. Warriors, champions, and winners do not take days off. The competition is so vast that taking a day off may determine either victory or lost. Those with a warrior mentality must go all out every day, or you are never going to be great or successful. To be driven, with consistency and hard work is the membership fee that filters out the weak and feeble, from the strong and driven. The respect and credibility required for the warrior's mindset in high achievers is so costly that only the rich in the struggle can afford it.

Champions only have one goal which is they aspire to be great. They chisel, they hammer, and they contrast with maximum effort until success become their reality. Put in for this type of relentless pressure allow those with the warrior's mindset to overcome any talent deficiencies that they may have once possessed. If you want to be a legend, we must refuse to give anything less than 100% because that is the only level of effort the legends know. Average, and mediocrity are words in a foreign unspoken language that the warrior mindset and champions do not understand. Good is undesirable because they recognize the greatness of the creator in them. Take the limitations off God, you are made in God's image and likeness, and God breathed the breath of life into you man, and you became a living soul.

Therefore, God is in you. When you place limitations on yourself your place limitations in God. Those with a warrior's mindset holds themselves to the higher standards, because of the mere fact that they are not just doing it for themselves, they are doing it for the glory and honor of the God that represent. Your why, blended with your passion in years of perspiration grants worldwide success. Hustle and grind are universal words respected and admired in every culture in the world. The work ethic of one with the warrior's mindset and champions will carry them places where 99% of the remainder of the world will never go or see.

You must discover the most essential factors that determine success in which ever field of endeavor that you are in and then put all your time, energy, and devotion on it. We must grind all day doing the right things, because grinding all day doing the wrong things will not only get you, but you will end up a failure. You must be driven to outwork the competition in the areas that decide who will be the winner.

Put in 100% towards the things that really matter and stay focused. Most people can give their best for three or four days and perhaps even a week or maybe some even a month. But very few can sustain it for a year, two years, three years, five years, or a decade. The things worth achieving does not arrive overnight, it takes years of dedication and preparation to bring a dream into reality. A victorious business plan is not constructed around wishing, hoping, or sheer luck. It is constructed on a silent structure of discipline, commitment, and hard labor. The one in the arena with his hands held high belongs to the one who purchase it and sweat.

What you accomplish in life will be equivalent to same level of the effort you exerted. There is no dream, no goal, or ambition that can deny the person who masters the art of being driven. Success does not have to be complex, just decide what you want and then grind at the level that is required to get it.

Positive affirmation: My grind and driven work ethnic becomes my weapon. From today forward no one in my field of work will ever outwork me again! My dedication, consistency, hard work and sweat will water my dreams. I will get 100%, day in and day out for as long as it takes to accomplish my goals.

## Self-assessment questions:

How can I increase my work ethnic to a level that will ensure success?

How many hours do I need to grind each day to achieve greatness?

Am I willing to pay the price for the things I want in life?

Am I willing to keep up the intensity day in and day out needed to be successful?

**Today's prayer**: I pray today to God, that you will instill in me the work ethnic required to be successful in life. Provoke me to be driven, increase my endurance, my stamina, and my energy so that I can allocate my all to accomplishing the goals and dreams you put inside me. In Christ's name a man

**successful quotes**: If people knew how hard I had to work to gain my mastery, it would not seem so wonderful. Michel Angelo Great or average? If you want to become great you must pay the price the price the average is unwilling to pay. Eric Thomas. I viewed myself as slightly above average in talent. And where I excel is ridiculous, sickening work ethic. Will Smith

People do not understand that when I grew up, I was never the most talented. I was never the biggest, I was never the fastest. I certainly was never the strongest. The only thing I had was my work ethic, and that is then would has got me this far. Tiger Woods

## The action steps:

Decide if your dream is worth the time, energy and effort required to make it a reality. If it is to make a commitment to yourself right now to get 100% effort every single day from here forward to make it happen. Set the tone for the day by establishing a morning routine of power and purpose. Take ownership of the day by getting into motion. Stay healthy exercise regularly. Remove and eliminate all distractions from your life and negative people. Figure out the amount of the of time required each day to accomplish your goals. Every time someone doubts or criticize you, respond by increasing the level of hours you are putting in towards your dream. Use their negative energy as fuel to grind harder. Stop making excuses, and just do what it takes to get the things you want in life.

Inspirational for victory: The most high's blessing you with power and energy and an incredible work ethic that will make you a thousand times greater.

## 16 THE WISDOM OF THE WORLD IS FOOLISHNESS

Bible Verse: 1st Corinthians 3: 19 For the wisdom of this world is foolishness with God. For it is written, He taketh the wise in their own craftiness.

There are many of you that try to save folks that have no desire to be saved. Some of you attempt to save family members that are wicked and have no desire to learn this truth. Others desperately attempt to save a spouse that is abusive and suffers from borderline personality disorder, narcissistic personality disorder or even both. Such people do not want to be saved, and they do not want to hear the truth that you are providing them with. But the Lord says in first Corinthians chapter 14 verse 38 if any man be ignorant let him be ignorant. You will get divorced raped if you are deranged enough to marry in this system. This system pimps' men like a whore and you will get screwed like one.

It is not your duty to attempt to save someone that has no desire to be saved. King Solomon was perhaps the richest man to ever live, and one of the wisest. He said, and I quote "wisdom is the principal thing; therefore, get wisdom and with all thy getting get understanding "that is the book of Proverbs chapter 4 verse 7. The highest put in place specific laws and principles within the universe that if you would tap into them properly you would be successful, blessed, and invincible.

The process of wisdom is three steps:

The first step is to acquire accurate knowledge.

The second step is to gain full revelation and comprehension of the knowledge that one has acquired. The third step is to properly implement and apply what you have learned to your life.

Searching for knowledge is a lifelong journey. To successfully and properly ascertain wisdom the adept must be patient, humble, open-minded, and more sensually open to learning. Daily we still strive to become better than we were the day prior. We can achieve this by dedicating and disciplining ourselves daily to study in the word of the highest. True wisdom is practical, call it accurate knowledge comprehend and consistently apply It. An essential key that will lock any door within the universe that you have a desire to truly open up by musing and meditating on the Scriptures we are blessed with divine revelation of the way the world works and how God wants us to conduct ourselves. The word of God is the greatest book of knowledge ever constructed!

The Bible is the official guide to prosperity, happiness, winning, and having the mind of a warrior. Construct your life around it and success and blessings will follow wherever you go.

Never more than today have the aphorism readers are leaders in truth, been true. The man that consistently fell to upgrade his knowledge and skills will eventually become unimportant and obsolete. Despite with your master's degree, your BS degree, your PhD., to be successful is work hard. When you study the minds of the greats, such as Mohammed Ali, Einstein, Aristotle etc. it provides you with direct insights into their mindsets, the principles, and the techniques that they used to gain such a mindset. The more analytical you are of their daily habits, routines, and processes the more you will uncover their secrets and achievements.

Studies reveal that those that earn thousands read on an average two books per month. The important fact here is that they read on a consistent basics and are therefore immersing their minds with a type of knowledge and material that allows them to improve themselves. How many books have you read this month? To become a true warrior a true champion you must be driven and possess a warrior's mentality. You must master the art of observing and dissecting and analyzing greatness. First from the Bible second from self-help books, third from videos or seminars such as my seminars. One quickly should spot the pattern and strategies being applied that determine success, then seek ways to implement them.

Incorporating the wisdom, you have learned from the greats into your life will help you replicate the results and thrust you to a higher level.

Positive affirmation:

Each day is a new opportunity for me to educate and improve my mind and self. I have become a sponge and constantly soak up information of the great men and women that I encounter. The more that I apply what I have learned the more awesome I become.

in life!

**Self-assessment questions:**

What books do I need to be reading?

How much of my time and my allocating for learning and self-improvement each day?

Why is self-education so important in today's fast-changing world?

What books are champions, millionaires, and other phenomenally successful people reading?

In which ways can I learn to read faster?

What is the difference between knowledge and wisdom?

Which person has taught me the most about life?

Why are the greatest leaders in life all dedicated reader?

**Today's prayer:**

Therefore, dear God, I pray that you increase my wisdom, knowledge, and understanding 300-fold. Provide me the strength and discipline, and consistency to apply what I have learned more effectively. Help me to stay humble and always seeking to learn and grow in Christ's name I pray amen.

**Successful quotes:**

Keep this book of the law always on your lips; meditate on its day and night, so that you may be careful to do everything written in it. Then you will be prosperous and successful. Joshua chapter 1 verse 8.

I do not think much of a man who is not wiser today than he was yesterday Abraham Lincoln.

Prepare for the unknown by studying how others in the past have dealt with the unforeseeable and unpredictable George S Patton.

Any fool can know. The point is to understand Albert Einstein.

A wise man will make more opportunities than he finds Francis Bacon.

There is a wisdom of the head, and there is a wisdom of the heart Charles Dickens, where wisdom range, there is no conflict between thinking and feeling C G John.

**Your action steps:** The greatest success and leadership resources ever written in the annals of history are in the book of Proverbs of the Bible. It is precisely divided up into 31 chapters 1 chapter for each day of the month in my opinion. Any person who is serious about success should discipline him or herself to reading one chapter from it each day just as I have suggested that you read one chapter of this book each day. Immersing yourself in the undefinable wisdom of the wises and riches came to ever live King Solomon will truly transform your life.

**Inspiration for victory:**

This is your moment of preparation. The highest is equipped and you with everything you need to be a winner last and invincible.

17 LIVE IN THE NOW NOT YESTERDAY OR TOMORROW

James 4 :14 Yet you do not know what tomorrow will bring. What is your life? For you are a mist that appears for a little time and then vanishes.

If there is one thing I would like to emphasize to start this chapter is that the past is not real anymore, and neither is the future. A dear friend of mine wanted to call me by an old name Tank. I politely asked her can you not call me that because that guy is dead. I stressed to her that I buried him in a mental grave. However, like most debtors she insisted that she was still calling me that name and became somewhat irate and disrespectful. Her tone altered like a chameleon. The phone call ended with her being really upset.

Prior to the call ending I tried to get her to grasp the reality that the past is not real anymore, and that it only exists within her mind. And she said, "where did you get this concept, who said that? "Where is it written? I attempted to explain to her that it was my personal moto which I utilize to control my reality and remain positive. I was unable to fully explain to her because she was busy talking over me suggesting that what she had to say was much more important. I proceeded to ask how can I explain anything if your behavior is like a three-year-old interrupting me, being disrespectful, and showing no etiquette? I asked her question to which she had no answer proving that the past was no longer real. However, because she was busy jaw japing chatting, she never grabs the concept of what I was saying. I asked her if the past is real could you please go back into the past right now and change an event that occurred between, she and I?

She ignorantly responded with how would you know if I went back to change the past because were living in the now? I said within your abyss of ignorance you have proven my point without even being consciously aware, that the past is not real.

Brothers and sisters, time have three dimensions, the future, the past, and the present. Never forget this fact, the future and the past only exist within your mind and have absolutely no power by themselves. They are both intangibles. The only power lies within the now, and that is all that essentially exists. Like my friend living deeply rooted in the past sows' seeds of depression and anxiety. I asked her to live in the past how is that working out for you? She immediately hung up the phone and proceeded to text me explaining how I hurt her by asking the question. The question that she needed to ask herself, because her life is at a standstill and she is utterly depressed. Yet she still results to the same insane thinking, doing the same thing over and over.

 I also explained to her that living too much in the future cause the mind to manufacture more stress, worrying, and anxiety. True contentment and peace of mind comes only from awakening to the present which is the now. Living in this moment it is how true enlightenment is obtained in the highest level of satisfaction. However about 10% of your day should consist of planning and envisioning your future but you should not live there. The other 90% should be living in the present which is the now. The Holy Spirit, your divine guidance could only behave in the now.

When you focus on the now, the distracting noise of depression, chaos, and confusion will dissolve into nothingness. Barriers that previously existed will be shattered right before your eyes. True faith can only exist in the now which is the present moment. You become impregnable when you are firmly planted in this very moment, for the present is where God is and always will be. Opening your mind to this state of mental consciousness is truly empowering. Do not allow the past and future to the start your dreams or your life. All the elements and tactics that you could use resides in the now and can only be maximized in this state of awareness.

Your mind is in a constant state of motion. To control it you must be the driver behind the steering will. You must become more aware of your thoughts only then will you be capable of recognizing of the precise dimension your mind is currently inhibiting. By being the driving force of your mental energy, you can drive back to the now where it is most effective, you will be fully capable of handling any situation that arises. Only the now will allow you to see clearly and to capitalize on all the wonderful opportunities that the highest has prepared for you.

Living in the present is the most conducive state for healing your body. It allows you to meditate on the word of God in a way that.

gives divine revelation. No disease can conquer you. Disease can only sustain itself when the mind is in a state of misalignment. Once you truly align with the present it will call the body back into perfect balance. Illness and disorder cannot continue to coexist when you rise above the level that you are one into higher consciousness. The present will starve these weaker states annihilating them utterly. The level of happiness that you experience on earth will be centered around the amount of the present that you conquer. Tapping into the power of the president will increase your awareness and will allow you to enjoy every ounce of sensation that this life has to offer.

Too many people, allow the future and the past to rule their own realms while you only can control and command the current moment. Only then will you truly feel alive, the most joy, and the most love. The quality of your life will drastically improve when you live in the present and cherish to give of the now for without it you cease to exist. Your merely like is equal to 37-chapter dry bones in the Valley. I have attempted to get K.O. Snowden to get this she claims to, but I see that she does not. Each time that I have attempted to explain something she always have a comeback. How many of you know people like that who cannot contain their emotions enough to hear the message?

Positive affirmation: less all your attention into the now except the powerful feeling of living in this beautiful moment. I lack nothing because everything that I need is in the now.

## Self-assessment questions:

when does my mind most will render away from the now?

When stress or anxiety attempts to come on me, where is my focus?

What are some ways to bring my mind and thoughts back into the present?

What does live in the present mean to me?

How would my help improve if I chose to live in the now?

What does be present feel like internally?

How would living in the moment improve my life?

## Today's prayer:

father God, I pray today for you to make me more aware of when my mind is not fully present. God me and steering my thoughts back to the now to enable me to be more productive. Lord help me to surrender the past and future to you so that I can fully function in the gift of the present moment in Christ name a man.

## Successful quotes:

Realize deeply that the present moment is all that you have. Make the now the primary focus of your life.

you can take all the pictures you want, but you can never relive the moment same way.

Whatever you are be there. If you can be fully present now, you know what it means to live.

Forever is composed of knows. Emily Dickinson

if you are depressed, you are living in the past. If you are anxious, you are living in the future. If you are at peace you are living in the present. Lao Tzu

**Your Action Steps:**

Begin today by concentrating on your breathing. While being completely mindful of every that you make. Concentrate on the awareness and energy that your body is radiating. Maintain your concentration firmly rooted in the now. Let all the stress, worrying, and fears just vanish away. Enjoy and Savior every ounce of peace that this moment has to offer. Meditating like this for 5 to 10 minutes will empower you, bring you into balance, and set the tone for the rest of your day.

Inspiration for victory: amazing Grace is from God, and it will replenish your power. True or your peace and energy from the creator.

That talk that Nazi don't want simps to hear. Tuesday Nights 9:30 PM est. YouR Host Taz talking that talk

## EMPLOY YOUR SOVEREGINTY STAND LIKE A MAN

Bible Verse: Luke 10:19 - Behold, I give unto you power to tread on serpents and scorpions, and over all the power of the enemy: and nothing shall by any means hurt you.

If you ever wondered where Esau gets his fictional superhero characters from its biblical verses such as the one above. If you keep the laws statutes and commandments of the highest, if you have faith you will be blessed with superpowers as a superhero. The Almighty clearly express that I will give unto you power over all your enemies and nothing shall by any means hurt you. This is a real superhero.

With Yahawashi (Christ) the law of animal sacrifice is over, as he became the ultimate human sacrifice. His death granted you mercy and grace to accomplish your divine will. You have that power if you believe. The highest has provided you with the power and ability to excel. You have been anointed with the spirit of the Lord to be great. He has placed the seed of greatness inside of you. Even the smallest of you, does not think that you are nothing has his greatness within you. With this anointing all things are possible. So, the Scriptures read I could do all things through Christ that strengthens me Philippians 4 verse 13.

Once you become fully awake to this invincible power and where it resides, you will become unstoppable. I am a star seed, not of this world, my soul comes from the ninth galaxy. I was birth through the womb of a woman, but my soul did not come from this world. The highest does not want his ambassadors walking around on earth without money, and degenerate. There is no blessing for the highest in that. The most high created you to prosper in every way, so that you could give a beacon testimony to the world of his greatness. With each blessing, accomplishment that you experience is designed in some way to put you in position to minister to the failure of others. The highest has employed you and empower you to succeed so that you can have greater access to bigger and better platforms to pronounce his glory before the world.

You are a warrior not just a soldier in the mighty army of God Almighty. No great general or commander would deploy his warriors or troops out into battle without proper instructions, weapons, and armor to defend themselves. God Almighty has fully equipped you to have a warrior mentality and be a winner. Your weapons are faith and an indomitable spirit, a powerful mind, and the spoken word. You are fully equipped with the most powerful weapons in existence and no one or nothing can stand successfully against them. These are the same weapons that the Messiah perform all his miracles with, and you have complete access to them. The Scriptures read John 14 verse 12 verily verily I say unto you he that believe it on me, the works that I do shall he do also; and greater works than these shall he do because I go unto my father.

The highest has granted true believers, the power and spiritual authority to command into fruition all the works of Christ. The wicked one's techniques have always been to deceive you into believing that you are at the mercy of your circumstances. This is deception and a trick you have full sovereignty over all devices of the devil and his agents. To truly walk in this state of empowerment you must shift from having a mere faith in God to having the faith of God. Every transformation always gets worse before it gets better. Knowing thus, when you transition to this higher state of mind all the powers of heaven's is at your disposal according to your faith. If you believe, you have the capacity to lay hands on the sick and help them. The highest still heals today if you are truly anointed use that anointing to express the abundance of this life, the glory of God, in the fullness of the Almighty.

Apply it to those things that are from a positive perspective and of outstanding report in which you cause no harm to other people. Live it out in love, through patients, the mercy, through gentleness, and with self-control.

You have the capacity to show all the doubters, the naysayers, here on earth a glimpse of what heaven looks like. Good brother, dear sister, use this anointing and it will join and attract others to the kingdom of the highest. You must believe were full confidence that wherever you are God is with you. If the word of the highest promise you anything, then you can best believe in full faith that you will have. This power is lying dormant within you arise and change the world with it!

Positive affirmation: I am blessed with the authority, the might, and the power inside of me to fulfill the destiny that the highest.

created me to do. I will use this anointing to display the power and the glory of my heavenly father in every fill of endeavor. The more successful I am the greater opportunities I will possess to testify of the greatness of God.

**Self-assessment questions:**

how can I use my victories to bring glory to God?

How can I use the power and still within me to help others be blessed?

If the highest is in me can anything stand effectively against me?

How does it feel inside to know I have been given the essential give up power and authority over evil?

what does be blessed really mean?

Does not God's way word say he have placed the power to within me to help others?

Today's prayer: dear father God I sincerely thank you for granting me the capacity, the power, the sovereignty to overcome all the obstacles within my path. Make me the greatest steward of the power that you have bestowed on me through the Messiah. Bless me to use this power to glorify your name each day. In Christ name I pray amen

**successful quotes:**

power resides only remain believe it resides George Martin.

very truly I tell you whoever believes in me will do the works I have been doing and they will do even greater things than these because I am going to the father John 14 verse 12.

it is our faith that activates the power of God Joe Alstyne

for God have not given us the spirit of fear, but the power and of love and of a sound mind second Timothy is one verse seven.

the action steps:

you must accept the Messiah into your heart completely.

Repent confess all your sins and atone.

Praying every area of your life into alignment with the word of God.

You must believe that you are blessed with the power and authority that the Bible says you have.

Give praises to the highest in Thanksgiving be certain to make your supplications known to God Almighty.

Pray in the name of Yahawashi. With absolute unwavering faith.

Trust the highest to interject on your behalf and it will happen.

**Inspiration for victory:**

no weapon formed against you will prosper everywhere you go you will excel.

The amount of success and greatness that you attain will be correlative and attach directly to the type of people that you affiliate with. The people that you associate with will have a tremendous impact on the way that you think, speak, and behave. The people can be family and friends that you choose to be around will ultimately determine the outcome of your destiny. The highest has commanded his chosen ones to go into the world and speak the truth, preach the gospel, for salvation. However, you must be extremely selective of the people that you decide to surround yourself with on a regular basis. Second Corinthians 6 verse 14 be ye not unequally yoked together with unbelievers: for what fellowship hath righteousness with unrighteousness? And what communion have a light with darkness?

Recent studies have indicated that your annual salary will be the average of the five people that you spend most of your time with. The principle behind the list of these five mandates that sooner or later you will become who you affiliate with. This rule applies to your family members, to your peers, just as much as it does to your best friends. Their views on homosexuality and lesbianism, and politics, their social views, their religious views, will all become contagious and a part of your character. Their perspective on money, on marriages, on eating will directly influence your thinking, that is why it is so important to examine whether your circle of five or aligned with your goals and dreams. It is therefore bull crap when you have friends that are not following Yahawah's laws. You are a liar!

Your primary focus should be detaching from those relationships that are reaching your energy and draining your power. Once you begin to spend less time with negative unproductive degenerate thinking people, the more your life will begin to improve. The more that you affiliate with winners and champions the more their influences and habits will become part of your character. Success is a team effort; you must select your companions of wisdom. Avoid those with questionable character, for to be unequally yoked is inviting destruction and failure. Have you ever heard the story about the guy that almost made it? No, no one else has either. The only people that are remembered are the people that is great and successful. You must partner up with people who have dreams, vision, goals and are driven and ambitious as you are. Associate with people who are being prospers and the relationships, in their marriages, on their jobs so that you can learn as much as you can from them.

Construct a strong support system of friends, associates, mentors, and members that bring the best out of you. There is greatness within you develop it and bring it out. The determining factor for adding or subtracting members from your inner circle should be that you get stronger in some sort of a way because of their presence. You must limit the amount of time that you give to anyone that does not support your goals your dreams and your visions. Greatness and success are determined not just by those that you associate with, but also with those that do not. Your circle of these five people will speak volumes about you in your future, so do everything within your power to surround yourself with positive motivated driven people.

Positive affirmation: Be certain to associate with those of higher quality who inspire and encourage you to be driven to chase your goals and dreams. From this moment forth, the people that I allowed in my inner circle must in some way improve my chances at success. My circle of five will consist of nothing but winners and champions with a warrior mentality that exemplifies greatness.

**Self-Assessment:**

Am I spending most of my time with positive people?

The five people that I affiliate with most, do they improve or hinder my chances toward success?

Do the people that I affiliate with believe in God Almighty and have the type of core values that I represent?

Are those five people ambitious and driven?

Are these people successful or making the type of money that I would like to make?

Do the five people I affiliate with months encourage me to chase my dreams.

How many books have I read this month?

Which friends do I need to spend less time with?

Which members of my family discouraged me the most?

Today's prayer:

Father God help me to affiliate myself with people that are driven and of a stronger character. Please display to me the people I need to spend less time with and who I should associate with more. Place me around a devoted group of encouraging, talented, loving, people who will assist me in reaching my new goals in Christ's name I pray amen.

Success quotes

Surround yourself with people who are smarter than you, pick people who are interested in what you are interested.

We gain nothing by being with such as ourselves, we encourage one another. I am always longing to be with men more excellent than myself. Charles Lamb

You are the average of the five people you spend most of your time with Jim Rohm the next best thing to being wise oneself is to live in a circle of those who are CS Lewis.

Keep away from people who try to belittle your ambitions. Small people always do that, but the great make you feel that you too can become great. Mark Twain

Your action steps: evaluate the five people that you associate with most of the time and determine whether they are increasing or diminishing your chances to be successful. Determine the impact on your life on a scale from 1 to 51 being the most negative and five representing the most positive. Begin to immediately distance yourself from anyone who grades out 1 to 2. If they rank is a three which is neutral find a way to improve the dynamic of the relationship or begin to limit the time that you spend with them. When the sum of your team of five finally grades out at 20 or better you build a strong inner circle of positive and trustworthy people who can achieve success.

Inspiration for victory do not he discourage for God Almighty will supply you with extreme favor with the people needed to help you achieve your goals.

NEVER QUIT OR GIVE INTO BEING AVERAGE

Bible Verse: Joshua chapter 1 verse 9. have I not commanded you? Be strong and courageous. Do not be frightened, and do not be dismayed, for the Lord your God is with you wherever you go.

There is no secret to success, the key factor is refusing to quit. Endurance transforms mediocrity and everyday people into those with a warrior mentality as a result a champion is born. Despite what your goals may be, in your dreams and life there will always be massive difficulties, times that you fall, setbacks, and heartbreaking disappointments. Each time that you fall, each circumstance will disguise itself as failure. If you genuinely want to be great, if you have a desire to be successful you must reject the thought that this is failure and continue towards your goals, your ambitions, with even more determination.

Difficult times require a strong reason and purpose to excel and prevail. The more troublesome and challenging that your obstacles are to overcome, the more you must keep your reason for succeeding before you. Life will knock you down, you will fall, you must stand back up with an even greater hunger to be that lion running up the hill to succeed. Long-suffering, endurance, and perseverance is the key to successful relationships, successful businesses endeavors, and being successful in your spiritual walk with God. Resilience and determinations arise out of the depths of your thinking, as you think in your mind which is your heart so will you be. If your talent is mediocre or ordinary, your persistence and work ethnic must become legendary. If you desire to bring your goals and dreams to life you must carry perseverance in the back of your mind they end and day out. Endurance is faith proven day by day. True believers in the highest can endure because they believe in him, a God that will not fail them. True faith provokes them to develop deeper and conquer their own negative thinking and doubts and fears. Each step they keep pressing towards the gift, the prize. The possibilities are limitless to what you can achieve expect the ones you do not believe. Average leads to a life of mediocrity and bondage while optimism leads to a life of freedom and greatness. To be a super achiever you must raise your standards, believe for more and trust that God will bring it about.

On the road to success, there will be many times when you feel like you have been devastated, an energetic, exhausted, and abandoned. You may be tempted to lay down and give up or tap out, but it is the mighty warrior that you must arise to the occasion. Your choices doing these soul-searching moments will ultimately define who you are. You must refuse to be a victim and claim the crown of glory by way of persistence and determination. Keep applying the pressure until the universe. Your demands. You must have faith, stand strong and press forward for with God you are blessed and invincible.

**Positive Affirmation:** I would never quit on my dreams and goals. I possess a warrior's mentality. I am a champion. I am blessed invincible and unstoppable. I have been anointed by the highest, to be great to succeed and therefore I am blessed, and invincible.

Self-assessment questions:

If I consistently quit when things become challenging, will I ever be the man that God created me to be?

Do I use my faith to strengthen me during difficult times?

Does anyone I know helped me to persevere when I encounter difficulties?

Do I know anyone now that is struggling and could use my assistance?

Why do I want to be successful and succeed in life?

**Today's prayer:** Dear father God, please provide me with the strengths to overcome all obstacles in my life. Help me endure even.

when things seem impossible. I can fully understand that there is nothing that I will face is greater than you. May the mercy of Christ always be in me. In Yahawah's name I pray amen.

Successful quotes: It does not matter how slowly you go if you do not stop. Confucius

I am not concerned that you have fallen and concerned that you arise Abraham Lincoln.

Most of the important things in the world have been accomplished by people who kept on trying when there seem to be no hope at all. Dale Carnegie

The difference between a successful person and others is not the lack of strength, not the lack of knowledge, but the lack of will Vince Lombardi Junior

It is not that I am so smart, it is just that I stay with the problem longer. Albert Einstein. We will either find a way to make a way. Hannibal

It always seems impossible until it has done. Nelson Mandela

When you start living the life of your dreams, there will always be obstacles doubters' mistakes and setbacks along the way. But with hard work and perseverance and self-belief you can be successful. There is no limit to what you can achieve. Roy T. Bennett

Victory is always possible for people who refuse to stop fighting. Napoleon Hill.

Your action steps: Recall your reason and remember why you must succeed.

Create an environment that build's perseverance. Delete failure and giving up and anything synonymous from your vocabulary. Stop focusing on how big your problems are and pinpoint in on what needs to be accomplished now.

**Inspiration for victory.** I am a survivor. I am the most high's most prized possession. I know he will never leave me nor forsake me.

## TAKE THE LIMITATION OFF YAHAWAH AWAKEN THE RUACH HA QADAH WITHIN

Bible verse: revelations 3: verse 8. I know that works, behold, I have set before thee an open door, and no man can shut it.

The phrase ruach hakodesh (also transliterated ruach ha-Kadesh) is used in the Tanakh and other writings to refer to the Holy spirit of inspiration. It is the Divine Presence among the Hebrew Israelites, also known as the Shechinah. n English we say The Holy Spirit or Holy Ghost. The Spanish and Brazilians say Espíritu Santo. The French say Espirt Saint. The Germans say Heiliger Geist and in Sweden it is Helig Ande. Here in Israel the Hebrew name for the spirit of YHVH is Ruach HaKodesh. Let us look at what those Hebrew words mean.

Spirit in Hebrew is the word Ruach, which also means "breath" or "wind". It is the Life that God Almighty himself breathed into Adam. I contend that if God uses the same Hebrew word for spirit and breath there must also be a spiritual connection between man and God when man walk in his laws, statutes, and commandments. When Yahawah created Adam, he did so I am his own image and likeness, an amazing form, but he was not a living being until The Almighty put His breath or spirit into the body and Adam became a living soul (Genesis 2:7). When babies are born, they are not living independent of their mother's resources until they take their first breath. When I ask our people where in their bodies is the spirit? Most people point to their lower chest area, why is that? I beg to differ; the scriptures are noticeably clear. Leviticus 17:11 we read that "the life of the flesh is in the blood".

We know that it is our Ruach or breath (spirit) that keeps us alive, so it is noticeably clear to me that the spirit is in the blood and is present throughout our entire body, wherever the blood flows to. This explains why some people can see an 'aura' around me Tazadaq and other star seeds on your planet. They are seeing the visible spiritual force that is flowing through the veins of I, man. When I breathe, the breath or the spirit comes into my lungs and from there, it is absorbed into my blood. It is the same for you beloved. I surmise the reason why you feel that your spirit is in the lower chest is that the largest quantity of blood in one place in your body is in the heart. This explanation is not from the Bible, rather it is just what I believe may be the case. Now allow me to explain the remainder of the name of the Holy Spirit in the original Hebrew: Ha is the easy part as it simply means "the". Kadesh is the noun from the adjective Kadesh, which does mean Holy. The word holy in English and most other languages also means sacred, saint, saintly, hallowed, blessed, sit apart. May the Yahawah God the Father fill you with His Ruach HaKodesh, to comfort you with the comforter HaMashiyach Yahawashi. Keep the laws for they will teach you and lead you and empower you to be the person He created you to be.

We are the way to salvation through Ha Mashayach Us

radio show that airs every Tuesday at 8:30 pm Est, you will find out that this knowledge cannot be found anywhere else on this earth unless you engage an Israelite camp, school or organization that is ordained by Yahawah wa Yahawashi to teach the truth. We teach the true light of Yash's word Jer 3: [15] And I will give you pastors according to mine heart, which shall feed you with knowledge and understanding. (This is what occurs each time you tune into this show by True Disciples of Christ Right Knowledge Radio on Talkshoe.com

Romans 3: [1] What advantage then hath the Jew? (What advantage is it to be an Israelites that keep these laws) or what profit is there of circumcision? (what does it truly profit you for being of Yahsharahla and keeping the laws) [2] Much every way: chiefly, because that unto them were committed the oracles of God. So, each week that you tune in to this show and learn who you are and how to understand this bible and common law and contact law these are major advantages.

2nd Esdras 16: 74 Hear, O ye my beloved, saith the Lord: behold, the days of trouble are at hand, but I will deliver you from the same. [75] Be ye not afraid neither doubt; for God is your guide.

Rev 12: [12] Therefore rejoice, ye heavens, and ye that dwell in them. Woe to the inhibiters of the earth and of the sea! for the devil is come down unto you, having great wrath, because he knoweth that he hath but a short time. Having knowledge of this gives us an advantage. The Highest is allowing you to prepare for it by listening Tazadaq the men you have set up on this show that teach the truth.

All the other nations are doomed. And you Israelites that teach salvation of the nations need to get with us or one of those others.

camps out there that teach the truth because if you are teaching salvation of the nations unless you repent you will not make it. If you want to be mad at someone be mad at the Highest. Isaiah 30: [15] For thus saith the Lord GOD, the Holy One of Israel; In returning and rest shall ye be saved; in quietness and in confidence shall be your strength: and ye would not. There are top demons that come on this show each week and top evil things in the room because they hate the name Yahawah wa Yahawashi, they hate when we say the name and that we know the name.

Jer 16: 16] Thus saith the LORD, stand ye in the ways, and see, and ask for the old paths, where is the good way, and walk therein, and ye shall find rest for your souls. But they said, we will not walk therein. These nations are mad that you so-called black Hispanics and natives Americans are the chosen people of God. You got women coming on face book talking about the chart if wrong. But when I ask them to justify their accusation they shut up. These are top demons that want to stop this truth. We are not wasting time anymore to teach someone that do not want to be taught. We will teach those that want to teach the truth.

When you are in these churches or even many of these Israelites camps with 501 c3 status the government gives you what you want. You get your vain glory; you mislead members throughout states. You get what you want. But Christ separated himself from the government and he will return to destroy this government and all of you joined on to the whore with your 501 c3 status. Isa 9: 6] For unto us a child is born, unto us a son is given: and the government shall be upon his shoulder: and his name shall be called Wonderful, Counsellor, The mighty God, The everlasting Father, The Prince of Peace.

[7] Of the increase of his government and peace there shall be no end, upon the throne of David, and upon his kingdom, to order it, and to establish it with judgment and with justice from henceforth even forever. The zeal of the LORD of hosts will perform this.

"A son will be given to us" implies the Savior's deity. He existed before His birth as the : "Although He existed in the form of God, did not regard equality with God a thing to be grasped, but emptied Himself, taking the form of a bond-servant, and being made in the likeness of men" (Philippians 6] Who, being in the form of God, thought it not robbery to be equal with God: [7] But made himself of no reputation, and took upon him the form of a servant, and was made in the likeness of men: He came as the Son of God-God in human flesh-to conquer sin and death for Israel. But look at many of these Israelites. Many will not support this truth. You are supposed to be donating to the priest and prophets of Yahawah. You make it seem something great you donated a few hundred dollars. Or you say I gave $1000 to become a secured party creditor and feel as you did Tazadaq a favor not realizing the reward you receive if you just would do the things suggested. How much have you invested in this world? You better donate on a regular. You are supposed to donate to the priest of the Highest. The government will rest on His shoulders" affirms His lordship. This verse looks to a time still in the future when Christ will reign over a literal, earthly, geopolitical kingdom that encompasses all the kingdoms and governments of the world. Daniel 2: 44] And in the days of these kings shall the God of heaven set up a kingdom, which shall never be destroyed: and the kingdom shall not be left to other people, but it shall break in pieces and consume all these kingdoms, and it shall stand for ever.

Zechariah 14: 9] And the LORD shall be king over all the earth: in that day shall there be one LORD, and his name one. We speak so badly because we know this is the truth and we do not care who do not believe. Like the days of old when miracles were worked many Israelites still did not believe so many of you will not accept this truth. As God incarnate, Christ is the source of all truth. Jesus said, "I am the way, and the truth, and the life" (John 14:6). No politician can match that! It is He to whom we must ultimately turn and trust His loving rule of our lives. Many of our politicians turn everywhere else for counsel. They go to one another; they listen to special interests; they have their own psychologists, psychiatrists, analysts, philosophers, spiritual advisors, gurus, astrologers, and other human counselors. But the King of kings keeps His own counsel. After all, "Isa 40: [13] Who hath directed the Spirit of the LORD, or being his Counsellor hath taught him?

**Positive affirmation positive.**

Man is only limited to his thoughts within his mind, the world is mind. If you can change your thinking you can change the world around, you. The world is mind!

**Self-assessment questions:**

Since Christ died for you. Are you at least willing to give some your time to improve the lives of others?

Am I surrounded by people, and am I doing things that will attract the success in my life that I desire?

Your seeds of thought are akin to a garden of fruit. Your mind fields are determined by thoughts "the world is mind".

How amazing have you felt since you have extricated negative people and negative thoughts from your life? Am I making it a great day, or am I sitting around hoping that my day be great?

Today's prayer:

Please heavenly father gives me the strength to resist any temptation that arise before me, for I know of God can overcome them. all. I will not let the devil win, in the name of Christ, I pray amen.

**Successful quotes:**

From an infant to age 7 we are program by the things that we are exposed to, 95% of what we do for the remainder of our lives is determined by the information that we have been program with up to age 7 unless we break the program. We must stop and step outside of the box and become the people of Zion no longer living within the matrix.

Your mind is your paintbrush, your thoughts are your canvas your spirit is the artist. You could choose the paint heaven, or you could paint hell, just to not blame those around you. Your future is determined by your mind, the world is mind.

**Your action steps:**

I will no longer do the things that have hindered me in my past. I will resist the things that were against my spirit and my goals, I will persevere and overcome all opposing thoughts and people.

Inspiration for victory:

this is the beginning of my new forever. This is a revolution of my mind complete constructive change the world is mind.

**Bible Verse:** Matthew 6:24 No one can serve two masters. Either he will hate the one and love the other, or he will be devoted to the one and despise the other. You cannot serve both God and Money.

**Positive Affirmation:** I would never quit on my dreams and goals. I possess a warrior's mentality. I am a champion. I am blessed invincible and unstoppable. I have been anointed by the highest, to be great to succeed and therefore I am blessed, and invincible.

Self-assessment questions:

if I consistently court, when things become challenging, will I ever be the man that God created me to be? Do I use my faith to strengthen me during difficult times?

Does anyone I know helped me to persevere when I encounter difficulties?

Do I know anyone now that is struggling and could use my assistance?

Why do I want to be successful and succeed in life?

Today's prayer: dear father God please provide me with the strengths. To overcome all obstacles in my life. Help me endure even when things seem impossible. I can fully understand that there is nothing that I will face is greater than you. May the mercy of Christ always be in me. In crisis name I pray amen.

Successful quotes: is does not matter how slowly you go if you do not stop. Confucius I am not concerned that you have fallen and concerned that you arise Abraham Lincoln.

Most of the important things in the world have been accomplished by people who kept on trying when there seem to be no hope at all. Dale Carnegie

the difference between a successful person and others is not the lack of strength, not the lack of knowledge, but the lack of will Vince Lombardi Junior

it is not that I am so smart, it is just that I stay with the problem longer. Albert Einstein. We will either find a way to make a way. Hannibal

it always seems impossible until it has done. Nelson Mandela

when you start living the life of your dreams, there will always be obstacles doubters' mistakes and setbacks along the way. But with hard work and perseverance and self-belief. There is no limit to what you can achieve. Roy T. Bennett

victory is always possible for people who refuse to stop fighting. Napoleon Hill.

**Your action steps** recall minding your reason and remember why you must succeed.

Create an environment that bird's perseverance. Failure and giving up in anything synonymous from your vocabulary. Stop focusing on how big your problems are and pinpoint in on what needs to be accomplished now.

**Inspiration for victory**. I am a survivor. I am the most high's most prized possession. I know he will never leave me nor forsake me.

## 21 MARRIAGE ACCORDING TO YAHAWAH

Bible verse: Hebrew 13:4 Marriage is honourable in all, and the bed undefiled: but whoremongers and adulterers God will judge.

The first union of Husband and Wife

Marriage appears to be a dying institution. The media and society in general seem to look down upon the married. Many say I do not know any happy married people. People have become so abased and sexually perverted that it is not uncommon for modern man and woman to label that which Yah considers abominable and unclean adultery as an affair. God says that the punishment for adultery is severe. How than can man say, it ok's it is normal to have an affair. This tremendous gulf between man and Yah has cause man to emulate beast. Man now strive from his physical lower plan instead of spiritual and mentally. Marriage is ordained by the Highest. When a man goes and has intercourse with a man's wife or a woman with a woman's husband that is killing that man and woman and it destroys family. When we destroy a family, we destroy our nation that is why God says both shall be put to death. Let us allow the words of Yah Himself to go forth. Exo 20:14 "Never commit adultery.

Lev 20:10 "If a man commits adultery with another man's wife or with his neighbor's wife, both he and the woman must be put to death for their adultery.

Deut 5:18 "Never commit adultery. The Father says never commit adultery you are therefore never justified in an affair.

Pro 6:32 "Whoever commits adultery with a woman has no sense. Whoever does this destroy him". Destroyed because God condemns it.

Pro 30:20 this is the way of a woman who commits adultery: She eats, wipes her mouth, and says, "I haven't done anything wrong!" And this is what most of you tell yourselves today to be able to look in the mirror.

Jer 29:23 "They have done shameful things in Israel. They committed adultery with their neighbors' wives and spoke lies in my name. I did not command them to do this. I know what they have done. I'm a witness, declares the LORD".

Mat 5:27 "You heard that it was said: 'You will not commit adultery.' [Exod 20:14; Deut 5:18]

Mat 5:28 "But I say to you, every [one] looking on a woman in order to lust after her already committed adultery [with] her in his heart" One can clear see that God takes this adultery business very seriously. God is nothing to play with. Sometimes he even punishes us through our children parents or those we favor most to hurt us deeply. No one will escape his wrath. Here we have God that gave man authority over all on the earth now look ho woman has shown his lewdness.

Genesis 1:26 Then God said, "Let Us make man in Our image, according to Our likeness; let them have dominion over the fish of the sea, over the birds of the air, and over the cattle, over all the earth and over every creeping thing that creeps on the earth." The Farther created man to be in his image and likeness. We are to be like God not a degenerate. We have failed God. We as men have failed and resulted to beast like creatures in human form as slithery as snake, making a crooked path wherever we walk. The poison of asp is coming out of our mouth so "there is none that is righteous no, not one."

Genesis 2:7 And the Lord God formed man [Adam] of the dust of the ground and breathed into his nostrils the breath of life; and man became a living being.

Genesis 2:19-24 Out of the ground the Lord God formed every beast of the field and every bird of the air and brought them to Adam to see what he would call them. And whatever Adam called each living creature that was its name. So, Adam gave names to all cattle, to the birds of the air, and to every beast of the field. But for Adam there was not found a helper comparable to him. And the Lord God caused a deep sleep to fall on Adam, and he slept; and He took one of his ribs and closed up the flesh in its place. Then the rib which the Lord God had taken from man He made into a woman, and He brought her to the man. And Adam said: "This is now bone of my bones and flesh of my flesh; she shall be called Woman, because she was taken out of Man." Therefore, a man shall leave his father and mother and be joined to his wife, and they shall become one flesh.

But we are not as one. Most of us do not know what to do with and how to properly treat a woman. We therefore cannot bring out of her what God put in her which is peace and contentment of mind. To being this out of her we must resemble God, we instead catch hell because we do not reflect God in our conscious. We as men allowed evil to tempted woman the weaker vessel and allowed her to tempt us.

Genesis 3:2-6 And the woman said to the serpent, "We may eat the fruit of the trees of the garden; but of the fruit of the tree, which is in the midst of the garden, God has said, 'You shall not eat it, nor shall you touch it, lest you die.'" And the serpent said to the woman, "You will not surely die. For God knows that in the day you eat of it your eyes will be opened

65

and you will be like God, knowing good and evil."

So, when the woman saw that the tree was good for food, that it was pleasant to the eyes, and a tree desirable to make one wise, she took of its fruit and ate. She also gave to her husband with her, and he ate. It was not Adam that was deceived but the woman who misled her husband. Eve made a covenant with Satan and her punishment is the pain of childbirth. She can escape the wrath of Yah if she keeps the laws and live righteously.
Genesis 3:16 to the woman He said: "I will greatly multiply your sorrow and your conception; in pain you shall bring forth children; your desire shall be for your husband, and he shall rule over you."

The C.O.R.P.O.R.A.T.I.O.N.

(Crooked Officials Robbing People of Rights Against Truth in Our Nation) BOOK TITLE

(Crooked Officials Robbing People of Rights Against Truth in Our Nation) BOOK TITLE

# Contact =Law = Contract

# Kahan Tazadaq making Creditor Moves Stop being a DEBTOR

## 22. WHAT THEY DON'T WANT US TO KNOW ABOUT UCC

The first order of law is Natural Law. These are Universal Principals which so necessarily.

agrees with nature and state of man, that without observing their inherent maxims, the peace

and happiness of society can never be preserved. Knowledge of natural laws may be attained.

merely by the light of reason, from the facts of their essential agreeableness with the

constitution of human nature. Natural Law exists regardless of whether it is enacted as positive.

law.

When law began to emerge into human consciences, thought, word and deed we come to the

next order of law on this planet. The most fundamental law of all human law has to do with

survival which is a Universal Principal. It has to do with human interactions, of any kind, any.

relationships, buying, selling, or trading or relating in any way. It is based upon treating or

dealing with others the way that you would like to be treated or dealt with. This is the Law of

Commerce. The Law of Commerce has been in operation since man interacted with each.

other starting many thousands of years ago through the Sumerian/Babylonian era where it was.

codified and enforced. Ancient artifacts dating over 6,000 old reveals that the system was so.

complex it even included receipts, coined money, shopping lists, manifestos and a postal

system with the medium being in baked clay.

As a derivative of Commercial law, being removed from natural law, and therefore inferior, is.

Common Law (common [L co together + minis service, gift, exchange] to exchange together).

This emerged, basically, in England out of disputes over a portion of the earth in allodium.

(sovereign ownership of land) and was based on "common" sense. So, common law is the law.

of the earth. Common law gave rise to the jury system and many writs and processes which.

governments have absorbed and strategized and made into rules and regulation processes in

courts.

Common Law procedures were based on the opportunity "to face your accuser or the injured.

party" in front of witnesses to sort out the problem directly. This process was never intended to.

include "lawyers, attorneys or judges construing their own law", as these "titles" are all based.

upon the fiction of "representation" which can never "be the real thing".

After common law come governments, and their laws and legislative regulations, ad infinitum.

of the organic republics of the states. The only "laws" that the state can create is to "allow.

commerce to flow more efficiently WITHIN the state". The only "law" the central government,

United States of America could create was to "allow commerce to flow more efficiently.

BETWEEN the states. " It was never intended to regulate people – the sovereigns.

Below that, the "garbage froth," more or less, is politics and the private copyrighted company.

policy of foreign corporations such as UNITED STATES, THE STATE OF…, THE COUNTY

OF…, THE CITY OF…, etc. The purpose of these "municipalities" [L minus service, gift,

exchange + capere to take; to take service and exchange] is to "govern" fictitious entities such.

as JOHN DOE and K-MART – not to regulate people. Remember back when you thought that.

YOU were JOHN DOE because that is how it is written on your driver's license?

One of our problems is that when we engage with government, municipalities and other such.

elements, in all our dealings in the law when have been conditioned to interact on and in

THEIR level. We have never risen to the level where the base of law is, where the reality, the

power, the solidity and the pre-eminence exist - THE SOVERANS LEVEL. But now, we can

function in this powerful level. This is Check mate. This is the end of the game. THIS IS THE

REMEDY

Commerce

The principles, maxims and precepts of Commerce Law are eternal, unchanging and

unchangeable. They are expressed in the Bible, both the Old Testament and the New. We

learned in the second course how the law of commerce has plagued us for more than 6000.

years. This law of commerce, unchanged for thousands of years, forms the underlying.

foundation for all law on this planet and for governments around the world. It is the law of

Nations and everything that human civilization is built upon. This is why it is so powerful. When?

you operate at this level, by these precepts, nothing that is of inferior statute can overturn or

change it or abrogate it or meddle with it. It remains the fundamental source of authority and

power and functional reality.

The Affidavit

Commerce in everyday life is the vehicle or glue that holds, or binds, the corporate body politic.

together. More specifically, commerce consists of a mode of interacting, doing business, or

resolving disputes whereby all matters are executed under oath, certified on each patty.

commercial liability by sworn affidavit, or what is intended to possess the same effect, as true,

correct, and complete, not misleading, the truth, the whole truth and nothing but the truth.

This affidavit is usually required for an application for a driver's license, and IRS form 1040, a

voter's registration, a direct Treasury Account, a Notary's "Copy Certification" or certifying a

document, and on nearly every single document that the system desires others to be bound or

obligated. Such means of signing is an oath, or Commercial Affidavit, executed under penalty.

of perjury, "true. Correct, and complete". Whereas in a court setting testimony (oral) is stated in

judicial terms by being sworn to be "the truth, the whole truth, and nothing but the truth, so help.

my God."

In addition to asserting all matters under solemn oath of personal, commercial, financial, and

legal liability for the validity of each and every statement, the participant must provide material.

evidence, i.e., ledgering, or bookkeeping, providing the truth, validity, relevance, and verifiably.

of each particular assertion to sustain credibility. Commerce is antecedent to and

more fundamental to society that courts or legal systems, and exists and functions without

respect to courts or legal systems. Commercial Law, the non-statutorily variety as presented.

below in maxims 1 through 10, is the economic extension of Natural Law into man's social.

world and is universal in nature. The foundational, invariant, necessary, and sufficient

principles or "Maxims of Commerce"

Commercial Law

This phrase designates the whole body of substantive jurisprudence, i.e., the Uniform.

Commercial Code, the Truth in Lending Act, applicable to the rights, intercourse, of persons

engaged in commerce, trade, or mercantile pursuits. Blacks 6th.

Commercial Law maintains the commercial harmony, integrity, and continuity of society. It is

also stated as "to maintain the peace and dignity of the State." Over the millennia these

principles have been discovered through experience and distilled and codified into those ten.

fundamental Maximums listed above. There is no legal issue or dispute possible which is not a

function of one or more of these principles. The entirety of world commerce now functions in

accordance with the Uniform Commercial Code (UCC), the UNITED STATES' corporation

version of Commercial Law.

Collection, and How to Calculate Your Damages

Now, here is another aspect of your affidavits. In commerce there is the Assessment aspect,

which is who owing who, and what, why, how and for what reasons; and there is the Collection?

aspect.

The collection aspect is based in International commerce that has existed for more than 6000.

years. Again, this is based on Jewish Law and the Jewish grace period, which is in units of

three; three days, three weeks, three months. This is why you get 90day letters from the IRS.

Commercial processes are non-judicial. They are summary processes (short, concise-without

a jury).

The IRS creates the most activity of Commercial Collection in the entire world. The collection

process is relatively valid, although the IRS is not registered to do business in any state. Did

you understand what you just read? The IRS is NOT REGISTERED TO DO BUSINESS OR

PERFORM COMMERCIAL MATTERS IN ANY STATE. So how do they get all the money they?

get? ANSWER: because you give it to them without requesting a proof of claim from them or

even if they were "licensed" to give you offers based on "arbitrary" estimations.

However, this is where things get remarkably interesting. The other phase of matters is the

assessment phase: THERE IS NO VALID ASSESSMENT. The IRS has, and never can, and

never will, and never could, EVER issue a valid assessment lien or levy. It is not possible.

First of all, in order for them to do that there would have to be paperwork, a True Bill in

Commerce. There would have to be sworn Affidavits by someone that this is a true, correct.

and complete and not meant to deceive, which, in commerce is, essentially "the truth, the

whole truth and nothing but the truth" when you get into court. Now, nobody in the IRS is going.

to take commercial liability for exposing themselves to a lie, and have a chance for people to

come back at them with a True Bill in Commerce, a true accounting. This means they would.

have to set forth the contract, the foundational instrument with your signature on it, in which.
you are in default, and a list of all the wonderful goods and services that they have done for.

you which you owe them for; or a statement of all the damages that you have caused them, for

which you owe them.

To my knowledge, no one has ever received goods or service from the IRS for which they owe.

money. I personally do not know of anyone that has damaged anybody in the IRS that gives.

them the right to come after us and say that "you owe us money because you damaged me".

The assessment phase in the IRS is non-existent, it is a complete fraud. Wait a minute, there is.

one definition of "service" that actually applies to the IRS.

Service. The act of bringing a female animal to a male animal to get *&%$#@ so that the

owner of the animals may "enjoy the product of this union."

Gives you a warm fuzzy feeling inside doesn't it?

This is why these rules of Commercial Law come to our rescue. T. S. Eliot wrote a wonderful

little phrase in one of his poems: "We shall not cease from exploration, and the result of all of us.

exploring will be to arrive at the place at which we began and know it for the first time."

This is the beginning, and this is the end. This closes the circle on the process.

One reason why the super-rich bankers and the super-rich people in the world have been able.

to literally steal the world and subjugate it, and plunder it, and bankrupt it and make chattel.

property out of most of us is because they know and use the rules of Commercial Law and we

do not.

Because we do not know the rules, nor use them, we do not know what the game is. We do not

know what to do. We do not know how to invoke our rights, remedies, and recourses. We get lost.

in doing everything under the sun except the one and only thing that is the solution.

No one is going to explain to you what and how all this is happening to you. That is never.

going to happen. These powers-that-be have not divulged the rules of the game. They can and

do get away with complete fraud and steal everything because no one knows what to do about it.

SOLUTION.

Well, what CAN you do about it? YOU NEED TO ISSUE A COMMERCIAL AFFIDAVIT. You do not have to title it that, but that is what it is. You can assert in your affidavit, "I have never. been presented with any sworn affidavits that would provide validity to your assessment. It is. my best and considered judgment that no such paperwork or affidavit exists." At the end of this document, you put demands on them. They must be implicit and then you state, "Should you? consider my position in error . . ."

You know what they have to do now, don't you? They must come back with an affidavit which. rebuts your affidavit point for point, which means they have to provide the paperwork with the real assessment, the true bill in commerce, the real sworn affidavits that would make them.

assessment or claims against you valid.

No agent or attorney of a fictitious entity can sign an affidavit for the corporation. How can they? swear as fact that the corporation has done or not done ANYTHING? They do not have the standing. They cannot and never will provide you with this. This means your affidavit stands as truth in commerce.

You can even make it more interesting if you like. You go to all their laws like Title 18 and you. tabulate the whole list of crimes they have committed against you in lying to you, foreclosing. and selling your home and issuing liens and levies. This could be quite an impressive list.

If you tabulate the dollar amounts of the fines involved in these offenses, you could take just. Title 18 section 241 alone which is a $10,000.00 fine on any public official for each offense. That means for every single violation of the Constitution, or commercial law, there could be 35. or 40 of these just in Title 18. You are looking at $300 to $400 thousand. When they start adding up, they become very impressive.

Now you attach this accounting, the criminal accounting to your affidavit and you file it as a criminal complaint with the State Attorney. This is like putting the fox in charge of guarding the hen house. However, more about this will be outlined later in this course.

For now, just attach your affidavit and your criminal complaint to a commercial lien. But wait! There is even a more effective way of getting you equity back – Involuntary Bankruptcy! These procedures will be detailed in Course 5.

The reason you go through this criminal complaint is because by their own laws and value.

system and penalties, they have hung themselves. They have already discerned and

formulated the dollar amount involved in each of the various offenses. When your lien them for

those amounts, they can't come back and say: "Well, these are out of nowhere. They are

unreasonable. Where did you get this?" Right out of your own codes.

COMMERCIAL PROCESSES ARE NON-JUDICIAL, PRE-JUDICIAL, AND ARE MORE

POWERFUL THAN JUDICIAL PROCESSES.


valid and enforceable against them. And they find that things become more and more.

uncomfortable with each passing day. Judges even think all this does not matter because they

can get another judge to remove all your paperwork against them. Other agents of the

government think they can hide behind the sovereign immunity of the Government, behind all.

the power and prestige, all their attorneys and all their capacity to get the courts to do whatever.

the wish is going to save them. None of these have any effect on your process.

It has no effect because there is only one way that they can be saved and that is to come in.

with their own affidavit that rebuts your affidavit point by point and prove you wrong. If they did

get this into court or jury that is not going to do them any good because the same battle still.

exists.

All this means is that the conflict between affidavits is now fought out in the open. And that is.

embarrassing to them because they are not going to change anything. All this will simply do

them more harm.

The third way to settle your claim is for them to pay it. If they do not satisfy your claim you give

them a grace period, at the end of 90 days you transform the Secretary of State into your

Accounts Receivable Office. Legal Title of all their real and personal property has now passed.

to you. You now file the correct paperwork with the Secretary of State, and you serve this on

the Sheriff and say, "I want to take possession of my property." Things begin to get interesting.

If you send a criminal complaint on a public official to the Insurance Commissioner of the State,

it becomes instantly and automatically a lien against the bond of the official, the judge or

district attorney and he is dead. He cannot function without bonding. This is held in suspension.

until the issue is resolved.

Now, all of a sudden, we find ourselves, simply by going back to what we've wanted all along,

which is truth, rightness, and a remedy, that we have, by going back in this and finding the rules?

that pertain to it, a way to have more power than they do, since we are sovereign.

No one, not a judge, jury, or anyone else can overturn this or change this process.

To do so would be to dissolve the world immediately into chaos. This would be the end of all.

law, all order, all standards, for all civilization.

It is not possible. They are stuck. This forms the underpinnings of philosophy, in tangle.

practices, of the way to put power on your side and against those agents of government who.

violate your being, injure you all in violation of their oath of office.

That is how, through their own process, we can use the rules of the game in OUR favor instead.

of remaining in ignorance and being taken forever as slaves. This applies to everything, not.

just the government. This forms a valid foundation for your life, and it forms a basis for any kind.

of dealings with government. What most people do not even consider is that governments do not

have and cannot have anything to support an affidavit of truth to support their actions.


Governments invent all the regulations and statutes to impose on you, affecting your life and

commercial/economic standing. And no one is taking any liability, responsibility nor

accountability. They may have some kind of bonding. But in most states this bonding is only for

about $5-10 million for the entire state and all its employees. However, you can tabulate a

simple traffic ticket into more than $5 million if you so choose.

Uniform Commercial Code

The National Conference of Commissioners on Uniform State Laws together with the American

Law Institute drafted Nation-wide Uniform Laws and each state has now adopted these laws.

These laws govern commercial transactions, including sales and leasing goods, transfer of

funds, commercial paper, bank deposits and collections, letters of credit, bulk transfers,

warehouse receipts, bills of laden, investment securities, and secured transactions. The UCC

has been adopted in whole or substantially by all states. Blacks 6th. The UCC is a code of laws.

governing various commercial transactions -- sale of goods, banking transactions, secured

transactions in personal property, and other matters, that was designed to bring uniformity in

these areas to the laws of the various states, and that has been adopted, with some.

modifications, in all states, including the District of Columbia and the Virgin Islands. Barron's

3rd. Unless displaced by the particular provisions of this code, the principles of law and equity,

including the law merchant and the law relative to capacity to contract, principle, and agent, estopple, fraud, misrepresentation, duress, coercion, mistake, bankruptcy, or other validating

or invalidating cause shall supplement its provisions. UCC 1-103.

To paraphrase the third definition above, the UCC is the supreme law on the planet, and all.

other forms of law are encompassed by it and included in it (accept you as a sovereign, of

course). Pennsylvania was the first state to adopt the UCC (July 1954), and Louisiana the last

(January 1, 1975).

The following is a quote from the BANK OFFICERS HANDBOOK OF COMMERCIAL

BANKING LAW WITHIN THE UNITED STATES, sixth edition, paragraph 22.01(1) and pertains.

to certain types of transactions:

"There are twelve transactions to which the UCC does not apply. They are as follows:

"1. Security interests governed by federal statutes . . .

"2. Landlord liens . . .

"3. Liens for services or material provided . . .

"4. Assignment for claims for wages . . .

"5. Transfers by government agencies . . .

"6. Certain isolated sales of accounts or chattel paper.

"7. Insurance Policies . . .

"8. Judgments . . .

"9. Rights of setoff . . . (see setoff)

"10. Real Estate interests . . .

"11. Tort Claims . . .

"12 Bank accounts . . ."

UCC-104 states: "Construction against implicit repeal. This code being a general act intended.

as a unified coverage of its subject matter, no part of it shall be deemed to be impliedly.

repealed by subsequent legislation in such construction be reasonably avoided".

Nothing in the UCC has ever been repealed, nor can it ever be. In the event of conflict between

a deleted section and a current section, the deleted section controls. If this is examined one

will see that it cannot be the other way. Potentially countless commercial transactions can be.

consummated based on the current UCC at any time. To "cancel" any portion of the UCC at a

later point is to throw into upheaval and chaos all commercial agreements that were based on.

the deleted portion, an act that would carry unimaginably astronomical liability to the many actors who attempted to effect such change.

Now, we must define the United States. This was covered in course number 2. But for

purposes in this particular area, we must define it for a better understanding applied to this.

procedure.

Commercial Lien

A commercial lien is a non-judicial claim or charge against property of a Lien Debtor for

payment of a debt or discharge of a duty or obligation. A lien has the effect of permanently.

seizing property in three months, ninety days, upon failure of the lien debtor to rebut the

Affidavit of Claim of Lien. The commercial grace of a lien is provided by the three-month delay.

of the execution process, allowing resolution either verbally, in writing, or by jury trial within the

90-day grace period. A Distress (to be defined in Blacks 6th) bonded by an affidavit of

information becomes a finalized matured commercial lien and accounts receivable ninety days.

from the date of filing. The Lien Right of a Lien must be expressed in the form of an Affidavit.

sworn true, correct, and complete, with positive identification of the Affiant. The swearing is.

based on one's own commercial liability.

A commercial lien differs from a true bill in commerce only in that ordinarily a true bill in

commerce is private, whereas a lien is the same bill publicly declared, usually filed in the office.

of the County Recorder, and, like all such declarations, when uncontested by categorical point-for-point rebuttal of the affidavit, is a Security (15 USC) and an accounts-receivable.

A commercial lien differs from a non-commercial lien in that it contains a declaration of a one to-one correspondence between an item or service purchased or offenses committed, and a

debt owed. A commercial lien does not require a court process for its establishment. However,

a commercial lien can be challenged via the Seventh Amendment jury trial but may not be.

removed by anyone except the Lien Claimant or a jury trial, properly constituted, convened, and concluded by due process of law. It cannot be removed by summary process, i.e., a judge.

discretion. A commercial lien (or distress) can exist in ordinary commerce without dependence.

on a judicial process, and is therefore not a common law instrument unless challenged in a

court of common law, whereupon it converts to a common law lien. A commercial lien must

always contain an Affidavit in support of Claim of Lien and cannot be removed without a

complete rebuttal of the Liens Claimant affidavit point-by-point, in order to overthrow the one to-one correspondence of the commercial lien. Also, no common law process can remove a

commercial lien unless that common law process guarantees and results in a complete rebuttal.

of the lien claimants Affidavit categorically and point-for-point in order to overthrow the one-to one correspondence of the commercial lien.

What is a True Bill in Commerce?

This is a ledgering or bookkeeping/accounting, with every entry established. This is your first.

Affidavit, certified and sworn on the responsible party's commercial liability as true, correct, and

complete, not meant to mislead. It must contain a one-to one correspondence between an item.

or service purchased or offenses committed, and the corresponding debt owed. This

commercial relationship is what is known as "Just compensation" (5th Amendment to the

Constitution), in relationship between the Government and the American people, a true bill is.

called a warrant (4th Amendment to the Constitution), and the direct taking of property by

legislative act, (e.g., IRS and the like) is called a "Bill of Pains and Penalties" (Constitution, Art.

I, Section 10, Clause I, and Article I, Section 9, Clause 3 -"Bill of Attainder).

There is one other matter we must define before we start putting all these pieces of the puzzle.

together into a workable tool for our benefit. That is the Uniform Commercial Code itself.
To my knowledge, no one has ever received goods or service from the IRS for which they owe.

money. I personally do not know of anyone that has damaged anybody in the IRS that gives.

them the right to come after us and say that "you owe us money because you damaged me".

The assessment phase in the IRS is non-existent, it is a complete fraud. Wait a minute, there is.

one definition of "service" that actually applies to the IRS.

Service. The act of bringing a female animal to a male animal to get *&%$#@ so that the

owner of the animals may "enjoy the product of this union."

Gives you a warm fuzzy feeling inside doesn't it?

This is why these rules of Commercial Law come to our rescue. T. S. Eliot wrote a wonderful

little phrase in one of his poems: "We shall not cease from exploration, and the result of all of us.

exploring will be to arrive at the place at which we began and know it for the first time."

This is the beginning, and this is the end. This closes the circle on the process.

One reason why the super-rich bankers and the super-rich people in the world have been able.

to literally steal the world and subjugate it, and plunder it, and bankrupt it and make chattel.

property out of most of us is because they know and use the rules of Commercial Law and we

do not.

Because we do not know the rules, nor use them, we do not know what the game is. We do not know what to do. We do not know how to invoke our rights, remedies, and recourses. We get lost.

in doing everything under the sun except the one and only thing that is the solution.

No one is going to explain to you what and how all this is happening to you. That is never.

going to happen. These powers-that-be have not divulged the rules of the game. They can and

do get away with complete fraud and steal everything because no one knows what to do about

it.

SOLUTION.

Well, what CAN you do about it? YOU NEED TO ISSUE A COMMERCIAL AFFIDAVIT. You

do not have to title it that, but that is what it is. You can assert in your affidavit, "I have never.

been presented with any sworn affidavits that would provide validity to your assessment. It is.

my best and considered judgment that no such paperwork or affidavit exists." At the end of this

document, you put demands on them. They must be implicit and then you state, "Should you?

consider my position in error . . ."

You know what they have to do now, don't you? They must come back with an affidavit which.

rebuts your affidavit point for point, which means they have to provide the paperwork with the

real assessment, the true bill in commerce, the real sworn affidavits that would make them.

assessment or claims against you valid.

No agent or attorney of a fictitious entity can sign an affidavit for the corporation. How can they?

swear as fact that the corporation has done or not done ANYTHING? They do not have the

standing. They cannot and never will provide you with this. This means your affidavit stands as

truth in commerce.

You can even make it more interesting if you like. You go to all their laws like Title 18 and you.

tabulate the whole list of crimes they have committed against you in lying to you, foreclosing.

and selling your home and issuing liens and levies. This could be quite an impressive list.

If you tabulate the dollar amounts of the fines involved in these offenses, you could take just.

Title 18 section 241 alone which is a $10,000.00 fine on any public official for each offense.

That means for every single violation of the Constitution, or commercial law, there could be 35.

or 40 of these just in Title 18. You are looking at $300 to $400 thousand. When they start adding

up, they become very impressive.

Now you attach this accounting, the criminal accounting to your affidavit and you file it as a criminal complaint with the State Attorney. This is like putting the fox in charge of guarding the hen house. However, more about this will be outlined later in this course.

For now, just attach your affidavit and your criminal complaint to a commercial lien. But wait! There is even a more effective way of getting you equity back – Involuntary Bankruptcy! These procedures will be detailed in Course 5.

The reason you go through this criminal complaint is because by their own laws and value. system and penalties, they have hung themselves. They have already discerned and formulated the dollar amount involved in each of the various offenses. When your lien them for those amounts, they can't come back and say: "Well, these are out of nowhere. They are unreasonable. Where did you get this?" Right out of your own codes

Sail together or sink together swimming in America's corporate sea of

commerce.


We serve no one by withholding information. We do not serve ourselves by refusing to investigate. Lack of information never assisted anyone. Accurate information allows us options; we can choose to act based upon it or choose to ignore it, but not knowing does not assist us. So, put aside your preconceived notions, your psychological defense mechanisms, and your prejudices. Take a chance on remembering what could well grant you complete economic, emotional, and spiritual freedom.


Any "Logics" course will teach that we can have a completely logical system which reaches a logical conclusion, yet it is not true because it is based upon a false premise.

to care if it reacts from something that is untrue if it feels certainty. So, the best position from which to learn is from 'uncertainty' - 'being in the question'.

"Can we afford to be so arrogant as to pretend we know something we

don't know, the knowing of which could transform our lives - W. Earhart."


Many people have ruined

their lives when they

could have prevented it

.... but for want of

opening their minds.


Remember my T-shirt, 'QUESTION AUTHORITY'. Everyone said it, yet no one did anything about it. I did; I recognized it. I had known from an incredibly young age that I, and none other, was my own and only authority. It seems I simply spent my life evidencing it. I never, ever, listened to anyone outside myself. The problem was that I also never listened to me. It took me decades to learn to trust my intuition. The most important thing we will ever learn is who we are, and this will require that we change our minds about we think we are. This will require that we throw out everything we think we know and replace it with what we have intuitively always known. We must listen only to what our intuition intends for us.


WHAT HAPPENED

Around 1997 I noticed that my family was getting broker by the month and my fear level

increased exponentially. When I had to pay the telephone bill with a credit card, I knew we were in trouble. I knew that the entire credit card game was a scam due to my having read, back earlier a book called, Truth in Money by Theodore R. Thorin. I also knew from my study cracking the code and read in the Bible about miracles. Believe me family that nothing is as it seems. Still, I did not know what to do about the banks telephoning every day 'payment'. I detected, by the desperation in their voices, that at some subconscious level they also knew that I did not really have to pay any credit card debt. I just did not know how to remove myself from the ostensible obligation. If I had been truly obliged to pay credit card debt, these callers would have been kinder and just asked when and how I might be able to send them part of what was 'owing'. Their rage was the tip-off that they were bluffing.

One day, as I was out riding my road bike in Las Vegas, I burst into internal tears as I was incapable or crying externally special ops left me cold, heatless and a lean mean fighting machine. It was at this point that I was forced to ask my Creator what to do. I

knew, from A Course in Miracles that 'God' would not put $80,000 on the living room table in the middle of the night for me to pay the credit card bills. I also knew that my real problem was not the fact of the matter, rather, how I felt about it. As Krishna murti

said, there are no problems apart from the mind. If I could just change my mind about what seemed to be a problem, I felt certain I could resolve it. At this point I thought up the concept "the world is mind". If I can control my thinking within my mind, I can change my world.

So, I found myself asking the Holy Spirit, et al, to change my mind about me.

circumstances. Seek not to change the world; seek only to change your mind about the world.

The next day a Malik Davis called talking about how income taxes are were taken for back child support.

His anxiety was that the IRS had been confiscating his refunds to settle back child support 'debt' with them. All I could tell Malik, from my years of studying $$$, taxes, etc. was, "You know there is no law compelling you to pay tax on your income in the first place." He said I know! I was delighted. I also told son, "If it makes you feel any better, you're not alone - the credit card banks, and car loan bank think I owe them $60,000. I know that I don't really owe them, I just don't know how to prove it."

Praise be Yahawah he said, "You just send the sons of bitches letters." I leapt from number 2 train on to the 5 at Franklin Avenue and headed back to Brooklyn. Blessed is the God of Israel - my prayer had indeed been answered - ask and ye shall receive. She then produced a series of letters, the drift of

which was to request the bank to provide me with three things:

1. validation of the debt (the actual accounting).

2. verification of their claim against me (an affidavit or even just a signed invoice); and,

3. a copy of the contract binding both parties.

I was to write that, as soon as I received these three documents, I would be happy to pay any financial obligation I

might lawfully owe.

I suddenly realized that the banks cannot validate the debt because they never sustained a loss; they cannot verify any claim against me because I am not the NAME, they are billing. They cannot produce.

a copy of the contract because one does not exist. What exists is an unenforceable unilateral contract. What the banks refer to as 'your contract with us' is not a valid bilateral agreement since the four requirements of a lawful, binding contract were not met on the credit card 'application', namely:

1.  Full Disclosure (we are not told that we are creating the credit with our signature).

2.  Equal Consideration (they bring nothing to the table; hence they have nothing to lose).

3.  Lawful Terms and Conditions (they are based upon fraud); and

4.  Signatures of the Parties (corporations cannot sign because they cannot contract - they are legal fictions). Credit cards, bank loans, mortgages are win/ win for the banks and lose/ lose for everyone else - it is the slickest con game on earth.

My writing the letters worked for all but one account. The bank filed suit. I poured over all kinds of legal nonsense, none of which matters - how we handle banks now works beautifully, yet back in 2009, we were still fumbling - and so, since the card was in a NAME like that of me.

sons' mother, the bank came after her. She did not want to go to court and since I regarded this as research, not to mention adventure, I went in his place. (If you are not living on the edge, you are taking up too much space. Get out of my way I am trying to eat!) When the administrator (aka 'judge') called her name, I stood up and

said, "I'm here about that matter." A year prior I had used a similar tactic when I went to court over a 'traffic violation' and was promptly thrown into jail for stating that my name was nowhere on the ticket or the summons. I learned from that and realized that you become a debtor if you engage in polemics in court. Never argue1 Debtors argue and lose. Although I was accurate, I did not know the next step. This time I knew what I was doing. The District Court 'Judge' asked me my name. I responded,

"If answer that, will I have entered into a contract with you?" He became irate. I knew I was onto something. I pulled his whore card now I was about to pimp this trick as he pimped thousands of others. But I will pimp him with Right Knowledge. He furiously said, "I'm going to ask you again; what is your name?" I said the same.

thing again and was literally, bodily tossed from court. On my way out, I told the bailiff, and the 5 others the removed me "I believe I hit a nerve." I was ecstatic.

As it turned out, I had indeed hit on the only issue which matters. CONTRACT IS LAW AND LAW IS CONTACT. Contract Law is the only law. There is no Constitutional Law, Bill of Rights, Charter of Rights and Freedoms, no codes, rules, regulations, ordinances, statutes, or anything else which most people think of as

'law' which applies to free, sovereign people or Secured party Creditors. They all apply only to corporate entities. There is only one law which applies to us: the law which protects the life, liberty, rights, and property of all living souls. That which causes us to think that all these 'laws' apply to us is the contracts/

agreements we have made, either wittingly or unwittingly. If there is no contract there is no case. If there is not contact, there is no case. Roger that! That is how we own it!

Contract is the law. Contractual Financial Liability is all that matters; it must be proven.

When I was in grade 4, my teacher was telling us about Columbus the so-called white man, that they claim discovered America with 50 million indigenous people already here in Amexem. This was not particularly difficult for me to accept, and yet, suddenly I sat back in my chair and looked at my fellow students and was hit by the realization, (how could he do that when there were already 50 million people here?)

"She could tell us anything." From then on, I became suspect of everything which might be construed as propaganda or about which my grandfather had warned me, "Consider the source". By that he meant, always look for a vested interest. Question the credibility of the source. Who says so? Quo warranto (by what authority)? Who stands to gain? This is now commonly known as, "Follow the money".

From that day on, I became highly suspicious of the true purpose of my being 'schooled'. For those interested in 'education' I suggest you read John Taylor Gatto and, The Underground History of American Education. Schooling is a huge waste of time, talent, energy, and creativity. There is little to learn, that school offers, until we are out doing what we want to be doing. Apprenticeship worked which is why the PTB (powers-that-be) do not want anyone apprenticing anymore, they want us in gov't-operated schools - to waste our lives learning what no one wants to learn, and what no one needs to know. The entire concept of life is that we learn as we go; schooling is anathema to this natural concept. Gatto wrote, Children allowed to take responsibility and given a serious part in the larger world are always superior to those merely permitted to play and be passive. At the age of twelve, Admiral Far-ragut got his first command. I was in fifth grade when I learned of this. Had Farragut gone to my school he would have been in?

seventh.

A psychologist name Greg once told me, "Don't ever do anything for any male over the age of 10 unless you are specifically asked." We are destroying our children by prolonging childhood. This is by design of the corporate monsters, Kids ought to be out doing what they want by age 13 and we ought to be available ONLY for counsel. I told my boys that in my books, age 15 is the age of majority.

It seems the purpose of the so-called educational system is not to educate us to be free-thinking natural beings, but rather to distort what is really going on in the world and also convince us that we will be happy if we just get a good education in order to get a good job in order to make a lot of money in order to buy as many worthless items as possible, and thereby become dependent upon them, in order to create as much debt as possible, thereby enslaving us on all counts -programming, slave-labor, debt, addiction, and ultimate confiscation of property - the first plank of the Communist Manifesto. Please keep in mind this goal as you read, and it will become clear that not only is this precisely what is going on but also that there is a lawful and spiritual way out of it.


Your peace of mind depends upon it - and isn't this really all we genuinely want?

I knew at age seven, when my parents pulled the "Eat your dinner; there are children starving in Africa" routine, that there was something drastically wrong. Certainly, the mere fact that someone knew that there were starving children meant they had the means to do something about it and I noticed nothing was being done about it - by those with the means. Sure, CARE packages, which depended upon the generosity of the people, were being sent yet I soon learned that the reason the problem continued is because someone wanted it that way. It would have been easy to correct if indeed the PTB wanted it corrected - same as every other 'problem' in the world. But how can they when Donald Duck Trump want to build walls and promote a white agenda?


So, I learned at a very tender age that the entire system is 'designed not to work' and hence, 'things are not what they seem'. At age 9 (born) I experienced my first commercial success. I wanted a weight bench and, on my way, home.

from school I went to the local department store to look longingly at a weight bench, sitting on a shelf. The cost was $59.99. I was shocked and appalled. I told my father, who happened to work in the 'racehorse' business, the cost of the weight bench, and he explained to me that it cost only pennies to make. I returned to the store the next day to stare at it with the thought, 'if only...'. Finally, I said to the store owner, "I really want that bench. I think $59.99 is too much for a child my age to pay." On my way home from school the same day I went in and noticed that he had dropped the price to $29.99 so I bought it. If you do not ask, you do not get.

In 1999 I told my mother, "I don't know what to do with my $$$; I don't trust the banks." I do not know why I might have made this comment because my father thought the banks were great, so I did not get any cues from him. Au contraire, when my brother wrecked his car, he told him, "You just lost $12,000 dollars." Clearly, he saw life as the means to accumulate $$$ and anything which 'went wrong' in life was measured thus. Dear mama looked at me askance at first and then said, "You're probably right. Buy 'things. Every day the value of 'money' diminishes through inflation and pretty soon you will rather have things than valueless money." I think she anticipated another depression. I feel certain she is very aware of the imminent economic collapse. I like to think she might see this as 'good news' as opposed to how most people see it, if indeed they see it at all.

When I was In Las Vegas I worked for a bank. After six weeks I told the other I.T. guy next to me that I figured out how to rob the bank and I described to him my methods. I would tell you, but I do not recall and besides, it would no longer be true due to EFT.

(Electronic Funds Transfer) banking. I thought he would be excited but instead he was clearly horrified and the next day I was given notice to leave. My father always told me, "Get yourself with a good company". This, coming from a man.

whose 'good company' had him working nights when he was aging, fueled my position that we are meant to do what we love to do... and nothing else. I keep telling KO Snowden this I pray she gets it before it is too late.


After I dropped out of college before I went back, I went to work for Mount Sani Hospital. After a month I told a fellow employee who had trained with me that I wanted to get my own place and then asked, "But how will I pay the rent when I no longer have the job?" She told me I was silly to worry about that. Within a month our training class of 5 was laid off. Each of the others was hired back; I was not. I learned later that I had scored too high on the aptitude test. Some hotshot executives had discovered that I was not within the 'hiring range' for that job. It is not so much that.

I am brilliant as much as apparently, I am equally left and right braned, which is somewhat uncommon. Most people do well in either the Math or the English part of an aptitude test, but not both, as I had done, and so my score was off the charts. Now I had this expensive apartment. I wished that I had listened to my intuition.

I was always a Maverick. I told a friend, who happened to work as a teacher, that if I ever have children, I will teach them that they are their own authority and never to let any teacher intimidate them. She was aghast and said in no uncertain terms that this was.

the problem in the schools today - no respect for authority. I mentioned that there is no authority outside oneself besides Yaha-wah. I am my own authority besides my creator. I added that teachers are part of the agenda which programs kids into believing that someone else knows what is best for them. There is no limit to the agencies,

professionals, and bureaucrats which exist solely to dictate how we ought to live our lives. Teachers, doctors, government, ministers, and bankers spend time, funds, and effort intending to convince children what to think. I determined that my children would think for themselves. They will know how to think for themselves.

Joseph Chilton Pierce, in his book, Magical Child, advises parents, "Children think their parents are perfect, so use this and be an example. As soon as we go to an 'authority' (doctor, teacher, minister) we lose our power. The child wants to think of us as omnipotent since he knows he can become that ... if we are." If you take nothing else from this message, please remember that family.


I read that J. P. Morgan had said, "I don't want a lawyer to tell me what I cannot do; I hire an attorney to tell me how to do what I want to do." So, I told my boys, "I understand that you don't want me to tell you what you can't do; you hired me to tell you how to do what you want to do." Alas, I have since learned that my boys are too subjected to mind-manipulation (school, TV, friends) to grant me any credibility. (I was a great parent before I had children.) Parenthood is like an 18 to 22-year sentence, except in jail they let you read.

The best thing about having children is finally getting to understand why we (all) felt neglected by our parents. We have, as they had, lives to lead and we children were only a part of it. As children, we presumed we were their entire purpose in life. Feeling the neglect was painful only because we blamed our lack of worth for any inattention. When we have our own children and realize, that as much as we love our children, they still are not our entire lives although for a while we are theirs. It allows us to see it was-not our lack of worth which kept our parents from focusing on us 100% of the time, it was that they had a life of which we were only a part. About 21 years ago I heard man say, on a talk show, "Try not paying your taxes and find out who owns your house." My eyelids flew open like Venetian Blinds and I suddenly knew that I knew this and somewhere hidden in my psyche was the entire story.

As a youth, I worked for both corporations and smaller, privately-owned companies. Never conscious of it until much later, I noticed that while working for a small firm or real living souls, I would faithfully put one dollar into the jar for drinks when doing so was based upon the 'honor system'. The goods belonging to the privately-owned company were not mine until I compensated them in some way. Much later I realized that when I had worked for corporations, I would rob them to the extent of my ability. I think intuitively I knew that anything a corporation ostensibly 'owned' was already mine, because I had pre-paid everything (more on this later). For a while I put it down to anonymity, but it was not that; it was the fact that I knew it was mine ... and I was accurate. Again, my intuition was correctly guiding me, and therefore I never felt any.

guilt. This was Yahawah (God) talking within.

In the early 1990s I was in the car with my father and brother. My father was telling my brother to put the 'maximum allowable' into RRSP as it was a great investment as he will not pay tax on that amount until he takes it from the account. I am surprised my father did not see the problem with this since he was so acutely aware of the insidious graduated income tax not to mention the worst tax of all - inflation. My bro would pay much more tax later than he ever would then.

Again, I recall sitting back and looking out the window and intuitively knowing that not only would he never see any of his RRSP investments but also, he would never see any of his company pensions. If you think I am inaccurate, because you are already receiving yours, you must be older than I am. We will not see our pensions at age 65. If you feel fear from reading that, be certain to recognize that your fear is not about your future; it is about your belief in your powerlessness. Why would you think that there being no government financial security in your future has anything to do with who you are?

and what you can do?

In 2007 my friend told me she was my pension. I told her she will never see it. She dismissed me with a wave of her hand. All the property of this country now belongs to the state and will be used for the good of the state. - FDR, 1933

For you Canadians who are feeling smug that this is not happening in Canada, consider that Canada is the 13th Federal Reserve.

District. Both USA/ CA, the corporations, are subject to the jurisdiction of the Crown/ Vatican. Can/Am is not 'a free country'. We are not free until we realize 'who we are'. What I write applies either to America (Canada and the United States) or to USA/ CA (corporations). There are certainly differences in our cultures but do not kid yourself about jurisdiction.

I always attributed to my cynicism these intuitive glimpses into the future until I learned that in 1993, in Canada, Bill C-124 was passed which states approximately: In order to pay the national debt (as if there were any national debt) the government might be required, and now has the legislation in place, to confiscate the pensions, RRSPs, investments, property, and all other tangible assets of the people.

This scheme is a ruse. I will explain later how the Feds will legally (not lawfully) be able to do this. Right now, though, remember, the entire raison deter of the government is to confiscate your property under the guise of your having lost it because you could not pay your 'debts'.

Unfortunately, most people have fallen for this and most will continue to do so until they have nothing left which, I will explain later, is not as horrific as you might think ... so lighten up. Living souls cannot have 'debt'. There is nothing to fear about the imminent collapse of the global financial prison. -

David Icke

When I was working in the I. T department, I went into the psyche ward to fix a computer, there was patient called Bruce, who had been diagnosed "paranoid schizophrenic". I had always thought schizophrenics simply interpreted the illusion of life on this planet a bit more accurately than the rest of us and that there was nothing 'wrong' with them; au contraire, there might be something wrong with someone who would label another as 'paranoid schizophrenic'. My supervisor asked.

one morning, "Tazadaq, tell us about the patient; what's wrong with Bruce?" "Nothing is wrong with Bruce. He is a typical 17-year-old - a few drugs, a few problems .... nothing wrong." He was incensed by my attitude and raged, "Of course there is, or he would-not be here." I did not have to take this nonsense, so I got up and left the room.

On my way out, I wondered what I was intending to do. Ah! - I will look through his chart for 'evidence' that there is "nothing wrong with Bruce". Just as I went for his chart, I noticed that a doctor was writing in it. I said, "Just the man I want to see! What exactly is wrong with Bruce?"

He answered, "Nothing; I've just discharged him." Do I have horseshoes on my penis, or what? So, I said, "Will you go and tell my supervisor this; he thinks I'm being contrary. And he did. I was a big hit with my fellow coworkers. I realized just how important my timing had been. When another incident re-enforced this, I vowed to act accordingly from then on.

After 8 years of the frustrating nonsense of a Mount Sani - Idealism is what precedes experience; cynicism is what follows. - D Wolf - I was bored and thought I ought to resign.

I wanted with no fear of failure. Alas, the fear had been so ingrained over the years that I

regarded that episode as a fluke rather than an example of the possibility for all circumstances in which I found myself. All I had to do is remember who I am. I notice that when there appears to be any struggle at all to do anything, I feel compelled to do or accomplish, I can count on the timing being off. When I just "do what's next", everything works out.

I worked as a Computer network Administrator, on and off for yea10 yrs. ... 'on' when I needed the cash, and 'off' when I was bored and frustrated by the unethical nature of it all.

In the early 90's I was earning $22 (USD) an hour. When the IRS sent me a bill for a tax

they thought I owed; I smelled a rat. We have all heard horrendous IRS stories. Since we are programmed to fear, these stories can influence our behavior, however, if we are aware that fear itself is the killer ("do not take counsel from your fears") then we can notice it and behave in a manner which works for us. So, I challenged them. I noticed that they could not support their claim. I also noticed that the amount they claimed I owed rose dramatically with each letter and for no apparent reason other than they added penalties, late fees, interest, etc. The higher the amount, the clearer their scheme became to me. I also noticed that every letter came not only from a different entity but also with no signature, thereby rendering it an invalid commercial instrument. All invoices, in order to be valid, must be signed by someone able to bind the corporation in contract. We are not lawfully bound to pay anything which is unsigned. Think of all the 'statements' you receive which read 'amount due' yet have no clout as they are incomplete.

I shall not outline my interim steps, yet here is the drift about what allowed me finally to deal with the IRS. I admit it took years, however it is interesting that of all the people with whom I not only chatted about the IRS but also treated for anxiety over the IRS, I noticed they all had one thing in common: the IRS sent them a bill, the amount of which was above and beyond anything credible. Anyone with a brain can see that this is what blows their cover. If they sent a bill for $3,000, one might be inclined to pay it. But a bill for $33,000 when one earns only $40,000 is simply laughable. It is this which gets people to declare they will never file or pay again. There are now over 45 million people in the USA who are no longer filing 1040s. Those who file 1041s can get back all the tax they have ever paid. I am just now learning about this. I am sure there is something similar, that of filing for a 'Trust', in Canada. IRS agents now openly admit that they have what is termed, "fishing expeditions" whereby they send out a few million "Notice of Assessment" just to see who bites. The amount is not enough to create so much angst as to get questioned on it yet enough to make it worth their while. Most people will figure that a $3,000 bill from the IRS is not worth fighting and/or going to jail over.

so, they pay it. If the bill were $35,000 all hell would break loose. Imagine $3,000 from several million unquestioning taxpayers: wow.

I began to suspect that IRS agents, at some unconscious level, want to expose their own fraudulent activities - clear their conscience, so to speak, and therefore they send out these inane letters. Yet, as David Icke says, "Those at the top of the pyramid are the manipulators of human consciousness. They are sentient programs with no soul." So, there is not one iota of divine intervention at the IRS/CRA; rather this is a case of four things; 1. they are desperate,

2. they are surreptitious,

3. they get a percentage of the $$$ they recover,

4. they require our fear in order to stay alive. They think the extortive 'total amount owing' frightens us when in fact it is

laughable.

1. They are so desperate that they will do weird things which blow their cover. The IRS/CRA for those in Canada is so frantic about collecting cash in order to pay the interest on the loan from the World Banksters that it will even behave in a self-defeating manner. It frantically sends out statements from every remotely conceivable source - have you ever noticed that you never get one from the same person/ office more than once? This is because they are scrambling, and no one knows what anyone else is doing, not to mention that the name at the bottom of the statement is the name of the computer which generated the letter. There is no living soul behind the letter. The timing is ludicrous, and the

92

wording is ridiculous as letters are based upon an IRS Manual called How to Write a Non-Response Response. Take a look at some of their letters and you'll realize that they have been composed by a group of Doo birds, not unlike those whom Christ Rock describes in his skit, An Infinite Number of

Doo doo birds. "If you take an infinite number of Doo doo birds and an infinite number of computers, over an infinite period, they will ultimately type all the great works. Needless to say, there would have to be people hired to monitor what the Doo doo birds were turning out. Here is a day in the life of one of these monitors: 'Oh, Taz, I think we might have something here!

"To be ... or not ... to be...............that is the       Plan.'"' Next time you get a letter.

from the IRS/CRA, just picture this same scene in your mind and you will know with whom you are truly dealing. The world is mind!

2.      What the IRS/CRA want is for you to create a controversy. They want you to argue because debtors argue and lose. They make this 'amount owing' so 'off the charts' that you will either telephone or write to them about this 'outrage' thereby creating a contract with them. This is all they need to enforce their nonsense. I do not contract with thugs. They are worse than loan sharks. If you argue, then you as a debtor have created a

controversy and the entire issue can go to court in order to be adjudicated. If you conditionally accept their offer, where is the controversy? What is there to judge? The only reason any matter ever goes to court is because the officers of the court know that at some point you will unwittingly grant them jurisdiction over you. Until you do this, they cannot hold you – no matter what you think you might have done. The world is mind, that is how we own it!

Call it the blessing of Yahawah, but one day I got a (signed) letter from some slick Willie at the IRS stating that my account is 'paid in full' and apologizing for any inconvenience. The only explanation I can think of is that I never testified, argued, or contracted further with them; I only asked questions. Brother Stomach had this same victory in California, after he did not back down the IRS took the lien off his business. You might have read recently about the Brother Loan or Somsach in Cali who won against the IRS in Federal 'court'. he won because he had documented that she had continually asked the IRS to.

provide the law compelling him to pay tax on his business income and they had failed to respond. His affidavits proved they had defaulted so the judge ruled in his favor.

3.      Each agent is vicious because he stands to receive personally a percentage of the funds, he recovers from you. Do not fall for his intimidation. Know that he is as frightened for his job as you might be about losing your $$$.

4.      About 5 years ago, a friend received from the IRS, a letter saying they intended to audit him. He was very frightened and intimidated. An IRS agent came to his house since this is where he claimed to have his office. I told him he was not required by law to let her into his house and he ought to demand by what authority she intended to

93

investigate his business. He immediately transformed into bitch mode and he said, "If I'm co-operative and courteous, she will be reasonable." His allowing her into his house.

was deemed his acquiescence thereby granting her jurisdiction. He thought it

would end quickly yet it only allowed IRS to know they had another wimp

who fell for their bluff.

The IRS hounded him for another eight years until they levied his bank account and confiscated his 'pay checks' from his clients. Realizing they would put him out of business, he left the country. It was fear which gave them this incredible control over his

life. Had he turned around and looked at the monster chasing him in his dream, he would have seen that it was not what he thought. The nonsense ended only after I wrote the IRS a check (on the private side of my closed bank account EFT) for $154,000.00. The son of a Ahch I know was fleeced by the IRS who confiscated from his bank account.

$5,000. I suggested that he write them a letter which included five (5) questions. The IRS agent invited him to his office in order to answer his questions. At the time of the meeting the IRS agent returned to his account the $5,000. You might want to know what the five questions were. He asked for answers to the following to be made under penalty of perjury: the law requiring Americans to pay income tax, their regulatory authority and delegated authority to address him, the law which made the IRS part of the Constitution, the agent's oath of office, and the contract with both signatures on it. Since NONE of these exists, his $5,000 was refunded. Since an oath of office by any 'public official' is their swearing to uphold our rights, we accept their oath of office into

the matter at hand and they are bound to honor their oaths and stop attacking us. I am about to tell you something that no other sovereign soul has told you and that is, we are not bound to respond to anyone who has no oath of office. This Oath of Office limits those who are in the biz of confiscating our rights and freedoms. Always ask for it and if you do not get one be sure to issue your own orders to them on what you want them to do. Remember who you are. King, Queen a sovereign soul

One of my most memorable experiences was when I asked an IRS agent, in person, to show me in the Internal Revenue Manual, which is about 5 inches thick - all of it bogus - where it is written that I must pay a tax on my income. He pointed to the book and said, "In there." "I believe that you think it is 'in there'; show me were." This time he pounded the book and then fluttered the pages and again, this time more forcefully said, "In the manual!" "I see ... where exactly?" Now he got even more violent with his beloved manual at which point my friend and I burst out laughing and just left him spluttering in his office. Do not take these threats too seriously.

Call their bluff.

To those in Canada, CRA sent my friends a Notice of Assessment wherein they told him they had over-paid him and he was to return some $$$. This was due to their having confiscated funds from his 'paycheck', without his permission, when I showed him How I sent them a Bond to discharge their debt and settle and close the account. Sure, I received a few subsequent letters from unknown entities. Since I had sent my Bond to the CFO, I was not about to correspond with anyone but him. He did not seem to have any complaint about my bond. I told me My friend to return all the CRA correspondence, 'acceptance denied for cause without dishonor', since their letters were immaterial. He has not heard from them in months. If indeed he really 'owed' them something, me.

experience has taught me that they would confiscate, with impunity, the entire contents of my bank account. They did not. There was nothing wrong with my bond. We cannot pay for anything; there is nothing with which to pay if we are secured party creditors.

One day I was on my dirt bike. I again heard my intuition, the voice of god "Put down both feet at STOP sign.". However, a few blocks later, I was stopped by a cop. When I asked why he stopped me he said that I had not stopped at the STOP sign. I responded (this was before I learned never to testify or argue the facts) that indeed I had stopped. He said, "You didn't put down both feet at the STOP sign." I was stunned! I had been told precisely what to do by some Yahawah (God) who could foresee what was about to occur and cared enough to warn me - verbatim. I was shaken that I had not trusted my intuition since the subsequent ramifications became a bureaucratic nightmare.

I became aware of many other times I had intended to warn myself about one thing or another and had ignored my intuition. Clearly my lesson in life was to trust myself - to BE my own authority. I had blatantly failed to behave according to what I knew to be true. I vowed always to listen to only me.

About 5 years ago, I received one of those in the mail credit cards "Here's $3,000 (USD) for a Happy Christmas .... simply make certain that you sign the back of the card you are preapproved I was ecstatic. I headed on down to the Apple store and was handed a brand-new Mac Book Pro. They were almost right; I did have a happy Hanukkah that year. When they sent me a statement about a month later, trying to collect.

something from me which not only did not exist, but also did not cost them anything other than postage and printing, I requested proof of their loss. They were irate. You may say Tazadaq that is wrong. I say corporations are Crooked Officials Robbing People of Rights Against Truth in Our Nations; They did not lend me.

anything. Do you Understand that banks do not 'qualify' you in order not to lose $$$, they 'qualify' you in order to gain $$$; they don't want to lend to deprogramed and enlightened customers. How can they lose something they never lent? I sent them a conditional acceptance telling them to piss off. I can where your alter ego just took you ... 'Tazadaq, you got something for nothing'. I say be quiet slave and learn step outside of the box. The Matrix was not a science fiction movie it was a documentary of your life and you are the best type of slave because you are unaware that you are confined within your mind. The world is mind!

I did not get anything for free, the MAC Book Pro was not free, I sold my signature for $2,700 - a good price back in 5 years ago. All I got was a piece of plastic that they claimed was with $3000 in worthless FRNs. Since then, I have done the math. My signature is now worth 10 billion dollars. Someone call Floyd Mayweather and tell him out should be part of the Money Team we all should be if we are creditors.

Then they got crafty and sent me threatening letters. It is not what they say it is what they do. I asked that they show me their loss. What loss could that corporation possibly have sustained? Is my bank out any $$$? No, its books are balanced since they were electronically credited by the 'other' bank (there is only one bank).

Is the other bank out any $$$? No, the returned credit card statement with my signature was their credit. So, their books were balanced. Were my books balanced? Of course! My debit was my signature, and my credit were how I got the MAC Book Pro. It is all just bookkeeping entries. Who owes what to anyone? The transactions are complete. It was simply an exchange of debit/ credit. Why would I give them anything more than what I already gave them - my signature, which is by the way, by far more valuable than $3,000 because they will lend funds against my signature many times, earning them, depending upon the rate of interest, at least 10 times that amount. This is called 'fractional.

reserved banking' Rothchild and the other top 12 bloodlines and they're not apprising me of this is called 'bank fraud'. So, in fact I did them a huge favor by selling them my signature. They informed me that I had not 'repaid my loan'. This is.

called 'double billing'. It is fraudulent. And this is how we own it! Do you understand, do you understand?

The 'money' the banks issue is merely bookkeeping entries. It costs them nothing and is not backed by their wealth, efforts, property, or risk. From 1913 until 1933 the U.S. paid 'interest' with more and more gold. The structured inevitability soon transpired - the Treasury of the United States' government was empty, the debt was greater than ever, and the U.S. was forced into involuntary bankruptcy. This means that the Crown laid claim to everything. This is how the Banksters who are really Illuminati took over America and the world in this One world order. The United States used the Federal Reserve Notes. In exchange for using notes belonging to bankers who create them out of thin air, based on our credit, we are forced to repay in substance - our labor, property, land, productivity, businesses, and resources -in ever-increasing amounts.

At that time, I did not know what I know today and so they did put a smudge upon my credit record, yet it was worth it because at that point, with a black mark anyway, I figured that I might just as well ring up all the credit cards and ask the same question. The upshot was that I lived about 5 years without credit but since I came away with about $80,000 USD worth of credit along with the education on how not to re-pay more than double for something I never received,

it was well worth it. Meanwhile, the process has improved, and I intend there to be only temporary black smudges on my credit record. I am still working on this.

My signature is worth whatever I say it is at any given instance. I signed for $10,000 credit with Chase Bank. They sold my signature for who knows how much. After I used all the credit I had created, I discharged their debt. Yes, their debt; I allowed them to use my credit, via my signature, and they created the debt in order to balance their books. Now they wanted me to send.

them over $11,000. I asked them to send me a copy of the contract between 'TAZADAQ' (the name in upper case letters) and MBNA. I guess they could not find it ... maybe because it never existed.

I also asked them for validation of the debt (record of their accounting) and verification of their claim against me since what I am called (Tazadaq) was nowhere on the alleged contract. They began to telephone asking me to send them $$$ yet never put anything in writing. What does this tell you? They had no valid claim. I told them I was very willing to pay any obligation I might owe if they could provide proof of their claim. They could not.

They were incapable of substantiating their claim. I never received anything from them.

suggesting that the way I had paid them was insufficient, unacceptable, improper, or failed to discharge the debt. Besides, I did pay them; in fact, I paid them more than double. They had my original signature and I also sent them another signature attached to the final amount they claimed I owed them, not to mention a few hundred I sent while I was busy ringing up the card, so they made a killing off me. If they had a legal leg to stand upon, they most certainly would have written to me, not to mention sent their 'legal counsel' after me, which they did threaten, by the way, but only over the telephone, never on paper. Idle verbal threats have no lawful clout.

I never stiffed anyone. The 'contract' they believe I had with them was invalid because there was no full disclosure - one of the requirements of a valid contract. It was not spelt out to me that they were in the business of perpetrating fraud upon unsuspecting people. Since most people are willing to have their funds fraudulently confiscated, they generally leave people like me alone.

By incite through observation we can deduce how most things function. I am Tazadaq Shah and if you allow this information to enter your subconscious mind you can alter your life and the false perception of reality that is present to you by, mainstream media, educators, parents, and peers. The information in this book need to go around to world to break the spell that has been cast on the mass mind. Below are the 10 rules of commerce that must be applied whenever one is involved in commerce to be effective.

1.   You can only control that which you create. (Pro Create a son or daughter not a child it is a fiction or corporation)

2.   You cannot control that which you did not create. (State has no control over son or daughter)

3.   All of commerce is based on Title. (Birth certificate, MSO, copyright)

4.   The only true Title to anything is the MSO Manufacture Statement of Origin. (Genesis 1 verse 1)

5.   When you register anything anywhere you give up Title. (Car, Child, vote)

6.   There is no Money just fiat currency. (Only credit in circulation Public, and private)

7.   There is no involuntary Servitude. (You must consent, and you have a right to contract, Amistad, Joseph)

8.   First in line is first in time. (Recorded into public record at county)

9.   Do not interfere with commerce.

10.   Allow nothing to come between you and your Creator. (Eliminating paganism) (Examples) A. My Divorce B. Biker Billy Lane C speeding with MCO Applying these rules can help us to understand and even master commerce.

One cannot investigate history and right out the children of Yah. When we examine the history of Commerce as we know it, we find it in Babylon; we see how commerce began with Daniel's interpretation of king Nebuchadnezzar's dream. In my attempt to teach many Hebrew Israelites in the early 2001's they rejected it because they lacked the comprehension to grasp the concept how commerce is imperative in their lives under this system.

The king's dream is about a body and the body is clad in various metals from head to toe, each metal represents a world

Empire from Babylon, Persian and Medes, Greeks, Romans to America which is an extension of Rome. Why is this important Tazadaq? Why are you talking about a dream and the body, or corpse? A dead body is a corpse (corps) which is short for corporation. Corporations are dead, they have no life they do not think, feel, or see.

The body has to do with all of commerce as we know it, that is a phrase worthy to be repeated, Corporations are dead bodies. I can just picture reptile Banksters all fighting each other for a bigger piece of the body. Commercial rules are in Probate because dead bodies, dead corporations are all in probate. (All commercial contracts are in Probate (except) a will is the only commercial agreement that survives death. The Banksters reptile minds creates an illusion of a shortage and sells the solution at an exorbitant price.

There are millions of people that have an interest in Real estate dreams of owning a home or rents one. An example of selling an interest in real estate. "New York apartments"

I am not just fabricating lies I will now explain how the rules of commerce work in probate and apply to Real estate, the buying and selling of interests in Land begins with a landing, and then a survey, and finally a selling of an interests in the survey, and never has anything to do with the Earth. Do you understand?

The typical commercial transaction in real estate starts with an offer to buy, next is a purchase and sale agreement. For most of us this leads to a "Pretend Lender" who is allegedly going to loan us public credit to satisfy our obligation, created by the signature on the purchase and sale agreement. Then lend us nothing our signature created the promissory note, and we are the lenders.

You may think I am deranged because you are programmed to think as such, but your signature creates all the energy your tender is your pen.

There is no requirement to use public credit, or a lender/ servicer. You can always use your private credit and anyone trying to force you to do business with a third party in order to do business with them is in violation of RICO. This is known Racketeering in Collusion Operation

I am giving right knowledge for those who have a mortgage, deed of trust. Examine what the contract says. If you are conveying your fee simple interest at closing, when, and how did you acquire this interest? You do not know so allow me to further explain. With the signature on the promissory note, you discharged / set off or settled the

indebtedness that was created with the signature on the purchase and sale agreement. Have you ever stopped and thought of why your signature does everything? What if I told you that you can conduct all your commerce privately with just your signature?

Private commerce in real estate have fun ravishing you, but the banks / courts are even having more fun. If you knew contract/ law, then you would know that you can create all the energy that you would ever need or want. Let us look at how I once purchase REO properties with my private credit.

For informational and educational purposes only. I am not giving legal advice.

The following are the steps that I take to complete the process successfully.

1.    I find property, I like high end bank owned or REO, and there are a lot to choose from.

2.    Make an offer to buy make sure that you do not offer earnest money because of payment in like kind. Ok to offer a promissory note for full or partial amount.

3.    I sign purchase and sale agreement.

4.    I sign a promissory note and a bond to back say note.

5.    I record the contract, promissory note, and bond. A quit claim deed or warranty deed is just an agreement to sell. I just purchased an REO using only my private credit.

The C.O.R.P.O.R.A.T.I.O.N.

(Crooked Officials Robbing People of Rights Against Truth in Our Nation) BOOK TITLE

I do not just shoot the breeze I facilitate right knowledge and arise up every morning and see how I can create more love and positive energy. But on the contrary most people have been programmed to wake up and plan and scheme and desire to get more FRNs, and people we end up with debt because we are creators and may create everything that we envision.

A few days ago, an unlearned slave told me that we will soon go into a national emergency. What is ironic is that most people assume that they know what is going on and have no ideal. I love our people, so I politely stated brother we have been in a national emergency since 1933 under FDR. He looked at me in anger and awe. Then I asked him as I am asking you the reader, "did you know that every two years they renew this national emergency to keep us under a national emergency?" Do not believe me do your own research. There are many people that will give you bits and pieces of information and have you doing Affidavits, but they are not totally clear on what to do. They sell you information and do not know the full process. Then there are those of you that want to be free, but you do not want to do the work. You do not want to put in the time that is required to study, research, and learn. You will never have rights unless you get back in the Bible and realize that the rights given by Yah is given to you at birth by the creator. If you read the scriptures, you will realize that rights are correlative to duty. You must obey Yah's laws to have those rights. If you do not keep the laws Yah punish you and you do not get the rights. This is what has happened to the children of Israelite.

If you want to be sovereign, you must read your bible and get back to these God given rights and demand them. You cannot allow government to deprive you of your rights given by the creator. Just look at the Declaration of Independence, it lets you know that man is given certain inalienable rights that cannot be taken from him and even if the government that gets its power from the people attempt to deprive the people of their rights the people should abolish that government. I did not make that up just read the Declaration of Independence. Many do not know this because you have never read the Declaration of Independence. Read it and use it against this government to force it to acknowledge your rights. If you want the people to rule this country, you return to God then have faith and read that bible because you will learn that your rights come from the creator not government. Since government did not give you rights, they cannot take them away. Are you going to stand for the Highest or stand for democracy?

You must read that Constitution and you must read and learn that Declaration of Independence. Abortion is ungodly, it is wicked. In a world where they tell you it is illegal to talk God in school or at work it is easy to encourage abortions. It is okay too many to be homosexuals and lesbians, 2nd chronicles 7:14 Return to Yahawah people!

You are all sinners right now because you all have a SIN which is social insurance number now known as social security number. It is a SIN. You are a person and the only person known to law is a corporate fiction. In Law human is also known as monsters which is one that cannot inherit property. All you persons go to the human resource department because you are a resource. You are a commodity. At the human resources to seek employment. Well, I discovered that to be two words, me= for and ploy = deceit. Employment is for deceit. Because job is official public business for private dishonest gain. We know to get a job that want you to have a SIN Social Insurance Number.

103

We have been lied too about darn near everything. We must learn laws of our creator and not allow anyone to take away our rights. These words that they use to deceive us sound awful. So, I have learned to acquire legal documents because I must combat people like Woodrow Wilson that signed into existence the Federal Reserve Act. And to those of you that do not know your federal reserve notes have a hidden lien attached. If I sold you a car and there was a lien attached that car could be taken from you unless the lien was satisfied. Prior to 1933 a birth certificate was not required. It was created to register you as property and put a lien against you.

If you are smart you will purchase my book "The Infliction of Commerce" and "The Real Hebrew Israelites vs Edom and Khazaria". Not only will you be supporting me, but you will be gaining a wealth of wisdom knowledge and understanding. I was raised by the creator to teach. I am not an ordinary man. I am a vessel that the spirit of truth speaks through. Those that love the truth hear my voice and recognize god in me.

But too many of you trust in oppression. You trust Donald Trump or Hillary Clinton. The United States government is a Defacto, there are two United states.

The United States of America was made up of a union of what is now fifty sovereign States, and a three-branch (legislative, executive, and judicial) republic known as The United States of America, or as termed in this article, the Continental United States. Its citizens live in one of the fifty States, and its laws are based on the Constitution, which is based on Common Law. It has become an administrative (bureaucratic, military tribunal) legislative democracy via the obligation of contract being extended by duplicity and deception. Remember we all have a Right to contact Article 1 Section 10 Clause 1. Less than one hundred

fifty years after this united state took the land from my native forefathers became a nation, a loophole was discovered in the Constitution by deceptive lawyers in league with the international bankers. They created a separate nation, by the same name, that Congress had created in Article I, Section 8, Clause 17. This "United States" is a Legislative Democracy within the Constitutional Republic and is known as the Federal United States. It is confirmed in their 28 USC 3002 Sub section 15b. It has exclusive, unlimited rule over its Citizens, the residents of the District of Colombia, the territories, and enclaves (Guam, Midway Islands, Wake Island, Puerto Rico, etc.), and anyone who is a Citizen by way of the 14th Amendment (naturalized Citizens). If you are a citizen of these nation States, you are essentially a slave. You do not have rights. You contracted your rights away as you have a right to contact. This explains why you need a gun permit. A man does not ask another man for aa right to defend his life that right is given at birth by the creator. The writers of the Constitution knew the potential of mankind to want to assume a public office then become a despotic figure and manipulate the people that granted them to the power that they now have. Judges, lawyers, and most of the current judicial system has become an autocratic system. This has been able to occur by violating one law at a time. By slowing depriving the people of the Constitution. Most people celebrate the 4th of July but have never read it. If they did, they would be aware that therein, if government oversteps its boundaries then that government is to be replaced. Watch this,

"We hold these truths to be self-evident, that all men are created equal,"

From the inception we see that this was a click of criminal because the time that was written many of these men had slaves and therefore knew the potential of their own people to do wickedness and go against the very laws they were establishing and therefore had to write this in their books.

Now let us read one, "that they are endowed by their Creator with certain unalienable Rights," It should be clear that man is born with rights from Yah. A few examples it hats man has the rights to defend their lives, (bear arms 2nd amendment) a right to freedom of speech (1st amendment) a right to travel (fourth amendment). "that among these are Life, Liberty and the pursuit of Happiness. --That to secure these rights, Governments are instituted among Men, deriving their just powers from the consent of the governed," If one would only read this, they would realize that all government gets it power from the people, from man.

Therefore, man in his proper capacity has authority over the judge, the lawyers the politician etc. Therefore, it is important to know the bible because this system of law is built on the foundation of biblical law. Genesis 1:26 "And God said, let us make man in our image, after our likeness: and let them have dominion over the fish of the sea, and over the fowl of the air, and over the cattle, and over all the earth, and over every creeping thing that creepeth upon the earth". We clearly see that the creator gave manpower over all so if I go into a court I go in as a man not as a person which is a fiction. I go in the image of my creator. I am the authority unless I have violated the law. No one is above the law. Now back to the Declaration "That whenever any Form of Government becomes destructive of these ends, it is the Right of the People to alter or to abolish it, and to institute new Government," It just clear expressed that government should be abolished if it becomes destructive. Now my question is having the court system and government of the United States become destructive? If the answer is yes does not the people have the right to abolish it and alter it?

This now takes us back to my point that there are two United States. I must point out that Both United States have the same Congress that rules in both nations. One "United States," the Republic of fifty States, has the "stars and stripes" as its flag, but without any fringe on it. You must remember this if you ever enter a court room and see a flag with a fringe on it. You must remember that the Federal United States' flag is the stars and stripes with a yellow fringe, seen in all their colorable courts today. Have you ever stopped to think why? No! because you are programmed not to think but to agree. The abbreviations of the States of the Continental United States are, with or without the zip codes, Ala., Alas., Ariz., Ark., Cal., etc. The abbreviations of the States under the jurisdiction of the Federal United States, the Legislative Democracy, are AL, AK, AZ, AR, CA, etc. (without any periods). The latter Is not an abbreviation it invokes federal jurisdiction and make you a party to the jurisdiction. Under the Constitution, based on Common Law, the Republic of the Continental United States provides for legal cases.

"THE WORLD IS A DANGEROUS PLACE.

NOT BECAUSE OF THE PEOPLE WHO ARE EVIL,

BUT BECAUSE OF THE PEOPLE WHO DON'T DO ANYTH! NG ABOUT! T." ∞ ALBERT EINSTE! N

Order my books, " The Infliction of Commerce", "Commercial Warfare", Red Pill Right Knowledge, and the Real Hebrew Israelites vs Edom and Khazaria.

## The C.O.R.P.O.R.A.T.I.O.N.

### (Crooked Officials Robbing People of Rights Against Truth in Our Nation) BOOK TITLE

I By Tazadaq Shah Bey. The long awaited well needed books that teaches you how you can learn to handle Swim in a Sea or Commerce and not drown in debt or jail. Learn how to end Credit Card Debt, Traffic stops, how to write A Conditional Acceptance, how to end Property Taxes, also learn what are the positive effects of being a Secured Party Creditor and so much more. Many talks it but, Tazadaq has lived the lifestyle for years and has coached many of people that assumed they had no hope to freedom and a new life. Learn to stand as a man today or continue to be a slave. Many do not believe that it is possible to see corrupt judges fleeing the courtroom and corrupt prosecutors leaping to their feet to withdraw the charges against you? Tazadaq has experienced this firsthand. The knowledge contained in this book can help you do just that.

Do you want to remain a fictional legal entity (the "strawman") that was created without your consent when you were born, through your birth certificate? Some of you may know that this entity is a corporation, but did you also know that it is a trust? And that YOU are the beneficiary of the trust? Beneficiaries have the most power of anyone involved with the trust - they can terminate or dissolve it if they want. If there is no trust, there is no charges and no case! Learn how to apply this knowledge in court and get your case dismissed! The choice is yours. Learn how to defend yourself in court, successfully escape unlawful fines, fees and citations, stop foreclosure and more. Remember, Government only gets its power from the consent of the governed. You can choose to withdraw that consent at any time! These books maybe your answer. Order now on www.truedisciplesofchrist.org.

Now let get back to business. Under the Constitution of the Republic, which was essentially based on Common Law, the Republic of the Continental United States provides for legal cases at Law. It also has what is known as Equity, and Admiralty which is a Military Tribunal. What is law? Law is the collective organization of the individual right to lawful defense. It is the will of the majority, the organization of the natural right of lawful defense. It is the substitution of a common force for individual forces, to do only what the individual forces have a natural and lawful right to do: to protect people, liberties, and properties; to maintain the right of each, and to cause justice to reign over us all. Since an individual cannot lawfully use force against the peoples, liberty, or property of another individual, then the common force -- for the same reason -- cannot lawfully be used to destroy the people, liberty, or property of individuals or groups. Law allows you to do anything you want to, if you do not infringe upon the life, liberty, or property of anyone else. Law does not compel performance.

Today's so-called laws (codes, ordinances, statutes, acts, regulations, orders, precepts, etc.) are often erroneously perceived as law, but just because something is called a "law" does not necessarily make it a law. It is color of law, but it Is not law and is only enforceable because the people keep consenting. Did you know that there is a difference between "legal" and "lawful? " Anything the Defacto/government does is legal, but it may not be lawful. Keep that in mind the next time you get an offer from a colorable court. Next is Equity, which is the jurisdiction of compelled performance (for any contract you are a party to) and is based on what is fair in a situation. The term "equity" denotes the spirit and habit of fairness, justness, and right dealing which would regulate the intercourse of men with men. You have no rights other than what is specified in your contract. Equity has no criminal aspects to it. It is important to remember that. Finally, we have what is known as Admiralty, which is compelled performance plus a criminal penalty, a civil contract with a criminal penalty.

By 1938 the gradual merger procedurally between law and equity actions (i.e., the same court has jurisdiction over legal, equitable, and admiralty matters) was recognized. The nation was bankrupt and was owned by its creditors (the international bankers) who now owned everything -- the Congress, the Executive, the courts, all the States and their legislatures and executives, all the land, and all the people. Everything was mortgaged in the national debt. We had gone from being sovereigns over government to subjects (slaves) under government. What most do not know because of lack of research is that using negotiable instruments we can discharge our public debts with limited liability, instead of paying our debts at common law with money which is gold or silver coin. I will explain how this happened, where we are today, and what remedy we must protect ourselves from this system. Our Present Commercial System of "Law" and the REMEDY Provided for Our Protection. There is a remedy.

What you may know today as the present commercial system of " color of law" has replaced the Laws of Yah (God) and the Common Law upon which this nation was founded. I will reveal the legal thread which brought we the indigenous people from sovereigns' souls over government to subjects under a Defacto government, using negotiable instruments known as Federal Reserve Notes. What is hidden in plain sight is that one can discharge public debts with limited liability instead of paying public debts at common law with gold or silver coin. This can be proven by reading House Joint Resolution 192 and Public Law 73.10

The wolves have changed this nation's system of law from public law to private commercial law which was recognized by the Supreme Court of the United States in the Erie Railroad vs. Thompkins case of 1938, after which case, in the same year, the procedures of Law were officially blended with the procedures of Equity.

If one look back prior to 1938, all U.S. Supreme Court decisions were based upon public law which was a system of law that was controlled by Constitutional limitation. Since 1938, all U.S. Supreme Court decisions are based upon what is termed public policy. When you go into a public venue known as a court you assume that law is on the table, but it is Public Policy. Do not believe me, please do your own research. Public policy concerns commercial transactions made under the Negotiable Instrument's Law, which is a branch of the international Law Merchant. This has been codified into what is now known as the UCC (Uniform Commercial Code), which system of law was made uniform throughout the fifty States through the cunning of the Congress of the United States (which "United States" has its origin in Article I, Section 8, Clause 17 of the. The

The information that I Tazadaq introduce to many is often too much weight for one's brain to tolerate at once due to past programming. I therefore suggest you read this book twenty times to enable it to be embedded into your subconscious mind. Only a fraction of people will properly receive this information and apply it. Others will too be afraid to even dare step into a colorable court and face the fraud. People have been trained to think a certain way and if you introduce new information to them if it conflicts with their belief, they will reject the information even if what they have previously learned is false and what I am introducing is the absolute truth. This can be supported by the fact that today is September 11,2016. There is a memorial for those that died on 911.

2001, and no one is saying forget it even though it was fifteen years ago. But when a so-called black man or woman speak of the horrors that a terrorist that was given a title settler invaded our lands and murdered us and enslaved us, we are often charged with living in the past. Where is the memorial or the millions of so-called black victims?

How can this be a just system when she continues to ignore these atrocities? How can white men design a Declaration of Independence yet still have the so-called black man and woman in slavery yet consider it a system of justice.? The children of those that enslaved my and your forefathers are still in power today and there is a hidden hand causing that same oppression. Only a few token negroes can shine to enable Esau to justify stating that we all have equal rights. Because I have stated these facts those that are guilty of these crimes will label me a racist. But what do I care about angering you if it will make my people from their sleep? Now let us return to the matter at hand.

It is an absolute fact that the Constitution, as distinguished from the "United States," which is a Union of the fifty States. This is not a misprint, yes there is two United States. Did you know that the offering of grants of negotiable paper (Federal Reserve Notes) which the Congress gave to the fifty States of the Union for education, highways, health, and other purposes, Congress bound all the States of the Union into a commercial agreement with the Federal United States (as distinguished from the Continental United States)? These union states are now controlled by the Federal Corporation known as the United States according to 26 USC 3002 Subsection 15B. The fifty States accepted the "benefits" offered by the Federal United States as the consideration of a commercial agreement between the Federal United States and each of the corporate States. Knowing thus if you are a state citizen of the union states then you are a federal baby, and the president is your daddy. The insurance company is not playing when they say, "state farm", because you are like livestock on a farm. Your birth certificate bond is sold on the stock market. God and research, it yourself you will find that everything I am stating is truth.

The corporate States are obligated to obey the Congress of the Federal United States and to assume their portion of the equitable debts of the Federal United States to the international banking houses, for the credit loaned. The credit which each State received, in the form of federal grants, was predicated upon equitable paper.

This sewer (system) of negotiable paper binds all corporate entities of government together in a vast system of commercial agreements and is what has altered our court system from one under the Common Law to a Legislative Article I Court, or Tribunal, system of commercial law. Those persons brought before this court are held to the letter of every statute of government on the federal, state, county, or municipal levels unless they have exercised the REMEDY provided for them within that system of Commercial Law whereby, when forced to use a so-called "benefit" offered, or available, to them, from government, they may reserve their former right, under the Common Law guarantee of same, not to be bound by any contract, or commercial agreement, that they did not enter knowingly, voluntarily, and intentionally.

This is exactly how the corporate entities of state, county, and municipal governments got entangled with the

Legislative Democracy, created by Article I, section 8, Clause 17 of the Constitution, and called here The Federal United States, to distinguish it from the Continental United States, whose origin was in the Union of the Sovereign States. The same national Congress rules the Continental United States pursuant to Constitutional limits upon its authority, while it enjoys exclusive rule, with no Constitutional limitations, as it legislates for the Federal United States. With the above information, we may ask: "How did we, the free People of the Sovereign States, lose our guaranteed inalienable rights and be forced into acceptance of the equitable debt obligations of the Federal United States, and also become subject to that entity of government, and divorced from our Sovereign States in the Republic,

which we call here the Continental United States?" We do not reside, work, or have income from any territory.

subject to the direct jurisdiction of the corporation that was crafty enough to name itself the Federal United States. These are.

questions that have troubled me and other Hebrews, here in North Amexem for many years. Our lack of knowledge concerning the cunning of the legal profession is the cause of that divorce, but a knowledge of the truth concerning the legal thread, which caught us in its net, will restore our former status as a free man or womb-man of the Republic. The answer follows: What is I told you that the national Congress works for two nations foreign to each other, and by legal cunning both are called The United States? One is the Union of Sovereign States, under the Constitution, termed in this article the Continental United States. The other is a Legislative Democracy which has its origin in Article I, Section 8, Clause 17 of the Constitution, here termed a corporation or the Federal United States. Knowing thus how many people ask, when they see some "law" passed by Congress, "Which nation was Congress working for when it passed this or that so-called law?"

Or few ask, "Does this particular law apply to the Continental people of the Republic, or does this particular law apply only to residents of the District of Columbia and other named enclaves, or territories, of the Democracy called the corporation or the Federal United States?" Since these questions are seldom asked by the uninformed people of the Republic, it was an open invitation for "cunning" political leadership to seek more power and authority over the entire population of the Republic through the medium of "legalese." Congress deliberately failed in its duty to provide a medium of exchange for the people of the Republic, in harmony with its Constitutional mandate. Instead, it created an abundance of commercial credit money for the Legislative Democracy, where it was not bound by Constitutional limitations. Then, after having created an emergency situation, and a tremendous depression in the Republic, Congress used its emergency authority to remove the remaining substance (gold and silver) from the medium of exchange belonging to the Republic and made the negotiable instrument paper of the Legislative Democracy which is the corporation of the Federal United States a legal tender for Continental United States people to use in the discharge of debts. At the same time, Congress granted the entire citizens of the two nations the "benefit" of limited liability in the discharge of all debts by telling the people that the gold and silver coins of the Republic were out of date and cumbersome. The citizens were told that gold and silver (substance) was no longer needed to pay their debts, that they were now "privileged" to discharge debt with this more "convenient" currency, issued by the Federal United States.

Consequently, everyone was forced to "go modern," and to turn in their gold as a patriotic gesture. The entire news media complex went along with the scam and declared it to be a forward step for our democracy, no longer referring to America as a Republic. From that time on, it was a falling light for the Republic. This is when the deception really began to be effective and a beacon light for Franklin Roosevelt's New Deal Democracy, which overcame the depression, which was caused by a created shortage of real money. There was created an abundance of debt paper money, so-called, in the form of interest-bearing negotiable instrument paper called Federal Reserve Notes, and other forms of paperwork credit instruments. When money is defined to clearly states it does not embrace notes!

Since all contracts since Roosevelt's time have the colorable consideration of Federal Reserve Notes, instead of a genuine consideration of silver and gold coin, all contracts are colorable contracts, and not genuine contracts. [According to Black's Law Dictionary (1990), colorable means "That which is in appearance only, and not in reality, what it purports to be, hence counterfeit, feigned, having the appearance of truth."]. Now you know why If you watch my videos, I refer to them as colorable courts, colorable laws etc.

Eventually, a new colorable jurisdiction, called a statutory jurisdiction, was created to enforce the contracts. Soon the term colorable contract was changed to the term commercial agreement to fit circumstances of the new statutory jurisdiction, which is legislative, rather than judicial, in nature. Do you understand? This jurisdiction enforces commercial agreements upon implied consent, rather than full knowledge, as it is with the enforcement of contracts under the Common Law. Therefore, I suggest you order my book, "The Infliction of Commerce" if you do not have it already.

All of theirs courts today sit as legislative Tribunals, or Military Tribunals and the so-called "statutes" of legislative bodies being enforced in these Legislative Tribunals are not "statutes" passed by the legislative branch of the three-branch Republic, but as "commercial obligations" to the Federal United States Corporation for anyone in the Federal United States or in the Continental United States who has used the equitable currency of the Federal United States and who has accepted the "benefit," or "privilege," of discharging his debts with the limited liability "benefit" offered to him by the Federal United States.

There is hope and remedy for those who availed themselves of the remedy within this commercial system of law, which remedy is today found in Book 1 of the Uniform Commercial Code at Section 207/308. When used in conjunction with one's signature, a stamp stating "Without Prejudice U.C.C. 1-207/308" is sufficient to indicate to the magistrate of any of our present Legislative Tribunals (called "courts") that the signer of the document has reserved his Common Law right. He is not to be bound to the statute, or commercial obligation, of any commercial agreement that he did not enter knowingly, voluntarily, and intentionally, as would be the case in any Common Law contract. That is however not enough you should email me right now at creditorsdebtorscon-tracts@yahoo.com and become a SPC (Secured Party Creditor). You can also visit the website www.creditorsdebtorscontractsincommerce.org.

Furthermore, pursuant to U.C.C. 1-103, the statute, being enforced as a commercial obligation of a commercial agreement, must now be construed in harmony with the old Common Law of America, where the tribunal/court must rule that the statute does not apply to the man who is wise enough and informed enough to exercise the remedy provided in this new system of law. One can retain one's former status in the Republic and fully enjoys his inalienable rights, guaranteed to him by the creator and reserved by the Constitution of the Republic, while those about him "curse the darkness" of Commercial Law government, lacking the truth needed to free themselves from a slave status under the Federal United States, even while inhabiting territory foreign to its territorial venue. Editor's note: the following excerpts are from letters in which Tazadaq Shah Bey further clarifies the REMEDY, as given to us in UCC 1-207/308, and the distinctions between Public Policy and Public Law:

"Allocution".

Shalom: "There is an important "right" available to you. The name of the right is "Allocution". It is

111

presumed to have been waived if it is not requested! The purpose in demanding it is to preserve the "legal issues" brought up in the case and overruled by the trial court. Otherwise, one's appeal from a criminal conviction to a higher Court will only be a review of the "Fact Issues" decided in the lower Court, the Law Issues of the case are presumed to have been waived by the accused, unless those issues have been preserved though the right of "allocution."

There is more that can follow one's exercise of that right, and I will cover that, but first, let me explain what allocution is. Once the Court, or a Jury, has found you guilty of disobedience to a commercial statute demanding, or prohibiting, performance in a specified manner, you, the accused, have the right of "Allocution", which right, consists of having the Court (Judge) ask you on the record of the case (be sure that the Court Reporter is including this in the case transcript) "Is there any reason why this Court should not sentence you at this time?" Being asked that question by the Court, in the Court Record is all there is to your right of Allocution, but a proper response upon the Court Record by the accused shows that same has not waived dispute upon the legal issues of the case, which were overruled by the trial Court, and now those issues may be brought up on appeal.

The proper response of the accused upon being confronted with this question from the Judge, which allocution requires of him, is "Your Honor, the accused, in this criminal case, coming as it does from a colorable jurisdiction over his person and property, does object to being sentenced by this court at this time, because conviction in this case has been based upon The Facts of the case, while the Law Issues are still in dispute - namely - the Courts' Colorable Jurisdiction in this Criminal charge, which lacks the essence of a substantial claim by a damaged party." At this point, your right of Allocution has preserved for you your right to bring Law Issues into your Appeal. Now, I will bring to your attention an additional benefit of exercising your right of Allocution, which I alluded to earlier in this letter: After you have placed the above response to the Judge's question in the record, I would suggest that you continue on in the following manner: "Your Honor, the accused in this case would like to put this Court ON NOTICE, that if it DOES pronounce sentence at this time, over the OBJECTIONS of the accused, that the accused will formulate his objection, before a higher Court, IN THE NATURE OF A WRIT OF ERROR (see Supervisory Control in Black's 5th Law Dictionary)." The reason for the remark above is that the Court will tell you that WRITS OF ERROR have been done away with in modern Courts. In that situation, point out to the Judge that you do NOT intend to file a GENUINE WRIT OF ERROR, which is not recognized in colorable Jurisdictions, but that you stated on the record of the court that your OBJECTION to being sentenced at this time on FACT ISSUES while the LAW ISSUES of the case are still in dispute would be: IN THE NATURE OF A WRIT OF ERROR which is a Colorable Objection recognized under the name of Supervisory Control in Black's 5th.

The advantage of an objection in the nature of a writ of error is that the Judge (not you) must bring forth the Transcript, or Record, of the case to the higher panel of Judges, and, the burden of proof is upon that Judge to show that the Jurisdiction that he exercised over your person and property existed AS A FACT OF LAW, and further, he must show the legal basis for EACH RULING ON ISSUES OF LAW that the Transcript shows that an objection thereto was made by the accused. Now you know the benefit of stating your objection a Writ of Error, over making an appeal, wherein the expense of bringing forth the transcript is on you, as well as,

the burden of proof on all the law issues in dispute." Sincerely, Tazadaq

## 23 HOW TO LIVE TOTALLY FREE AS AN AMERICAN NATIONAL

Get Person Out of Prison

For Entertainment Purposes Only Not Legal Advice You will need the following:

1.      A Birth Certificate –and Social security Number for Each Pearson You Want Out

2.      The Docket (s) for each person (Court Case # - If Appealed – Appellate Court Case # And Docket - Inmate # for each person)

3.      Prison Name and Address (not PO Box) where person (s) is currently incarcerated

4.      Warden's Address (PO Box Acceptable)

5.      Person who will serve as Power of Attorney for the person (s) incarcerated

6.      Money to cover costs of filing and verification paperwork - about $200 to $600.

Order of Filing

(No Staples – Only Paper Clips Accepted)

Forms must be filed in the court that has jurisdiction to act on them, which is where the case was heard. That is the court that issued the bonds that you want to pay off.

1.      STANDARD FORM 28 AFFIDAVIT OF INDIVIDUAL SUERTY

2.      POWER OF ATTORNEY

3.      OPTIONAL FORM 90 RELEASE OF LIEN ON REAL PROPERTY

4.      OPTIONAL FORM 91 RELEASE OF PERSONAL PROPERTY FROM ESCROW

5.      STANDARD FORM 24 BID BOND

6.      STANDARD FORM 25 PERFORMANCE BOND

7.      STANDARD FORM 25A PAYMENT BOND

8.      a. COPY OF BIRTH CERTIFICATE – ATTACHED (WITH PAPERCLIP) TO FORM 25A Write copy across colored copy of Birth Certificate diagonally in red ink – if not A copy but an original BC – do not write anything on it.

9.      COPY OF THE DOCKET

First Form SF 28 (Two Pages)

STANDARD FORM 28 AFFIDAVIT OF INDIVIDUAL SURETY (Front Page)

(2 Pages – Front and Back – do not staple but use paper clip)

The C.O.R.P.O.R.A.T.I.O.N.

(Crooked Officials Robbing People of Rights Against Truth in Our Nation) BOOK TITLE

STATE OF: (State where Notary is from – best to use a notary from the state where the person is incarcerated). If you are filling out the forms for someone else, you can use a notary by your home – you are only verifying your signature as Power of Attorney.

COUNTY OF: (Where it was notarized)

SS.: Leave blank

1.    NAME

GEARLD DOVE PAYNE - Must be the name on the Birth certificate. If the

Person has no middle name on the Birth Certificate you must put NMN between The First and Last Name. E.g.- ERALD NMN PAYNE

2.    HOME ADDRESS:

Since the person is in prison – you must use their prison address.

The PRISON NAME and PRISON ADDRESS must be in all CAPS.

Example: FMC ROCHESTER

FEDERAL MEDICAL CENTER 2110 EAST CENTER STREET ROCHESTER, MN 55904

3.    TYPE AND DURATION OF OCCUPATION: SUERTY/LIFETIME

4.    NAME AND ADDRESS OF EMPLOYER The prison name and address – all caps.

FMC ROCHESTER

FEDERAL MEDICAL CENTER 2110 EAST CENTER STREET ROCHESTER, MN 55904

5. NAME AND ADDRESS OF INDIVIDUAL SUERTY BROKER USED:

Box 4 – United States

c/o 55 Water Street, New York City, New York 10041-0099

6. TELEPHONE NUMBER: HOME: N/A

BUSINESS – N/A

7. THE FOLLOWING IS A TRUE REPRESENTATION OF THE ASSETS I HAVE PLEGED TO THE UNITED STATES IN SUPPORT OF THE AT-

TACHED BOND:

(a)    See CRIMINAL CASE NUMBER: 8:05-cv-259-T-JDW #38293-018, C-1

(If an appeal then types in: See APPELLATE CASE #      )

See attached OPTIONAL FORM 90 RELEASE OF LIEN ON REAL PROPERTY

See attached OPTIONAL FORM 91 RELEASE OF PERSONAL PROPERTY FROM ESCROW

See attached STANDARD FORM 24 BID BOND

See attached STANDARD FORM 25 PERFORMANCE BOND

See attached STANDARD FORM 25A PAYMENT BOND

(b)      Leave Blank In no Appeal. If Appeal, then type in both Original Criminal Case # and type in the Appellate Case # as well.

8. IDENTIFY ALL MORTGAGES, LIENS, JUDGMENTS, ETC.:

Type in the Criminal Case #; (Type in Appellate Case # if appealed); Then type in the Inmate #

Example: 805-CV-259-T-JDW    #38239-018-C-1

9. IDENTIFY ALL BONDS, INCLUDING BID GUARANTEES, ETC.:

Type in Case # (Appellate Case # - if one exists) Inmate Number Remember to type Forms in proper order.


See attachment OPTIONAL FORM 90 RELEASE OF LIEN ON REAL PROPERTY

See attachment OPTIONAL FORM 91 RELEASE OF PERSONAL PROPERTY FROM ESCROW See attachment STANDARD FORM 25A PAYMENT BOND

See attachment STANDARD FORM 24 BID BOND

See attachment STANDARD FORM 25 PERFORMANCE BOND

DOCUMENTS OF THE PLEDGED ASSET MUST BE ATTACHED

10.      SIGNATURE: Gerald Dove Payne by John Doe as POA

The Signature must be in blue ink – signed by the person who has Power of Attorney.

11.      BOND AND CONTRACT TO WHICH THIS ADDIDAVIT RELATES:

OPTIONAL FORM 90 RELEASE OF LIEN ON REAL PROPERTY

OPTIONAL FORM 91 RELEASE OF PERSONAL PROPERTY FROM ESCROW

12. SUBSCRIBED AND SWORN TO BEFORE ME AS FOLLOWS:

Notary: It is best to use a Notary from the State where the person is incarcerated. If you are filling out the forms for someone else and must use a Notary who lives close to you then that is okay but not the best.

Back Page: Leave blank but attach to Front Page with a Paper Clip (No Staples)

Second Form (Power of Attorney)

The C.O.R.P.O.R.A.T.I.O.N.

(Crooked Officials Robbing People of Rights Against Truth in Our Nation) BOOK TITLE

Third Form – OF 90 - Two Pages:

OPTIONAL FORM 90 RELEASE OF LIEN ON REAL PROPERTY

(TWO PAGES – FRONT AND BACK)


Whereas GERALD DOVE PAYNE, (STRAWMAN in all caps)

Of __STATE (IF #NOT HYPENATED) / birth certificate # (Place of Residence)

by a bond for the performance of U.S. Government Contract Number ____ (Person who is in prison Social Security #)

and recorded this pledge on _____CRIMINAL Court Case Number) (If Appeal Use that #) ____ (Inmate #) _____

in the FEDERAL MEDICAL CENTER of MINNESOTA

(Locality – Name of prison where person is held) (State – where prison is located)

Whereas I Gerald Dove Payne by John doe as POA

Notary Notarizes (The notary must be in the same county where the person last lived)

Gerald Dove Payne by John Doe as POA

No Notary        [Signature]

Seal

Thumb Print (Red Ink) of person who has Power of Attorney.

Back Page: Leave Blank – attach to front page with paper clip.

Fourth Form OPTIONAL FORM 91

OPTIONAL FORM 91 RELEASE OF PERSONAL PROPERTY FROM ESCROW


(2 Pages – Front and Back)


Whereas GERALD DOVE PAYNE, of STATE & Birth Certificate number Hyphenated,

(Name) (Place of Residence)

STRAWMAN

For the performance of U.S. Government Contract Number __ (Social Security Number)

In Account Number        Most Recent Case Number        Inmate Number

Located at address of prison No PO Box

(Address of Financial Institution)

Whereas I, Gerald Dove Payne by John Doe as POA (Name of natural person in prison)

Claims arising therefrom:

Criminal Case Number (Appeal Case # if applicable)

See STANDARD FORM 28 AFFIDAVIT OF INDIVIDUAL SURETY See OPTIONAL FORM 90 RELEASE OF LIEN ON REAL PROPERTY NAME OF FINANCIAL INSTITUTION: Type in Name of Prison

Name of Financial Institution: Type in Name of Prison

Example: FMC ROCHESTER

FEDERAL MEDICAL CENTER 2110 EAST CENTER STREET ROCHESTER, MN 55904

Notarized No Notary Necessary (TK says have it notarized – KH says it is not necessary)


[Date]????????


[Signature] Gerald Dove Payne by John Doe as POA

Seal: The person who is Power of Attorney must put their thumb print in red ink - to right of Seal in blank space.

Back Page: Leave Blank and attach to the front page with a paperclip.

Fifth Form STANDARD FORM 24TANDARD FORM 24 BID BOND

(2 Pages – Front and back)

DATE BOND EXECUTED: Arraignment Date - Example: January 30, 2005

PRINCIPAL: GERALD DOVE PAYNE – The All-Capital Letter Person as it appears on Social Security Card. If no middle name put NMN between 1st and last name.

Under the name in all caps put the current PRISON NAME in all CAPS:

Example:      GERALD DOVE PAYNE

FMC ROCHESTER

FEDERAL MEDICAL CENTER 2110 EAST CENTER STREET ROCHESTER, MN 55904


TYPE OF ORGANIZATION: Check - INDIVIDUAL

(Crooked Officials Robbing People of Rights Against Truth in Our Nation) BOOK TITLE

STATE OF INCORPORATION: Type in the Birth Certificate Number and STATE WHERE BORN (ALL CAPS)

SURETY(IES): GERALD DOVE PAYNE

55 Water Street

New York, New York 10041

PENAL SUM OF BOND: Leave blank - if you desire all who were convicted to get out.

BID DATE: Type in Arraignment Date

INVITATION NO.: Type in Case Number

CONDITIONS: Leave blank

WITNWSS: You need the Notary or someone who is in their office sign off as a witness and date it.

(Today's Date)

PRINCIPAL: 1. SIGNATURE(S) Gerald Dove Payne by John Doe as POA

1. NAMES AND TITLES TYPED: GERALD DOVE PAYNE by John Doe as POA

Leave 2. & 3. blank POA's have put their thumb print in red in space 2. before (Seal)

Corporate Seal: The person who is POA must put their thumb print in red ink over this Corporate seal.

INDIVIDUAL SURETY(IES)

1. SIGNATURE(S): Gerald Dove Payne by John Doe as POA [Red Thumb Print of POA] 1. NAME(S) & TITLE(S): GERALD DOVE PAYNE by John Doe as POA

Leave 2. & 2. blank

CORPORATE SURETY(IES): Leave all blank.

PAGE BOTTOM: Do not notarize.

Back Page: Leave Blank and attach to front page with paperclip)

Sixth Form – Standard Form 25

STANDARD FORM 25 PERFORMANCE BOND

DATE BOND EXECUTED: Type in Arraignment date.

PRINCIPAL: Type in STRAWMAN NAME – GEARAL DOVE PAYNE

(Crooked Officials Robbing People of Rights Against Truth in Our Nation) BOOK TITLE

Under the name type in all CAPS the PRISON where the person is and the prison's address.

TYPE OF ORGANIZATION: X the box labeled INDIVIDUAL.

STATE OF INCORPROATION:

Type in Birth Certificate number – if B.C. number is not Hyphenated then just type in the State Name in all Caps.

SURETY(IES): Type in: DEPOSOITOTY TRUST COMPANY55 Water Street

New York, New York 10041 PENAL SUM OF BOND: Leave blank – so everyone in the group can get out. CONTRACT DATE: Type in Arraignment Date Contract NUMBER: Type in the Case Number OBLIGATIONS: (Leave Blank) CONDITIONS: (Leave Blank) THEREFORE: (Leave Blank)

WITNESS: Have the Notary or someone in their office sign off as witness.

PRINCIPAL:

SIGNATURE(S) 1. Gerald Dove Payne by John Doe as POA Leave 2. & 3. Blank

NAMES(S) & TITLES: GERALD DOVE PAYNE by John Does POA

Leave 2. & 3. Blank

Corporate S                    eal: The person who is POA must put their thumb print in red ink right over the Corporate Seal.

INDIVIDUAL SURETY(IES)

SIGNATURE(S) 1. Gerald Dove Payne by John Doe as POA

Leave 2. Blank

NAMES TYPED: 1. GERALD DOVE PAYNE by John Doe as POA

Leave 2. Blank

SEAL: The person who is POA must put their thumb print in red ink right over the Seal

CORPORATE SURETY(IES): Leave everything blank in this section.

NOTARY: The bottom of this page must be Notarized by a Notary living in Seventh Form 25A

STANDARD FORM 25A PAYMENT BOND

DATE BOND EXECUTED: Type in Arraignment Date

PRINCIPAL: Type in STRAWMAN NAME – GERALD DOVE PAYNE PRISION NAME (ALL CAPS)

PRISION ADDRESS (ALL CAPS)

The C.O.R.P.O.R.A.T.I.O.N.

(Crooked Officials Robbing People of Rights Against Truth in Our Nation) BOOK TITLE

TYPE OF ORGANIZATION: Place an X in the box in front of INDIVIDUAL.

STATE OF INCORPORATION: Type in the Birth Certificate Number and STATE WHERE BORN (ALL CAPS)

SURETY(IES): 55 Water Street

New York, New York 10041

PENAL SUM OF BOND: Leave blank - if you desire all who were convicted to get out.

CONTRACT DATE: Type in Arraignment Date

CONTRACT NO.: Type in Case Number

OBLIGATION: Leave Blank

CONDITIONS: Leave blank

WITNWSS: You need the Notary or someone who is in their office sign off as a witness and date it.

(Today's Date)

PRINCIPAL: 1. SIGNATURE(S) Gerald Dove Payne by John Doe as POA

1. NAMES AND TITLES TYPED: GERALD DOVE PAYNE by John Doe as POA

Leave 2. & 3. blank

Corporate Seal: The person who is POA must put their thumb print in red ink over this Corporate seal.

INDIVIDUAL SURETY(IES)1. SIGNATURE(S): Gerald Dove Payne by John Doe as POA

1. NAME(S) & TITLE(S): Gerald Dove Payne by John Doe as POA


Leave 2. & 3. blank


CORPORATE SURETY(IES): Leave all blank.

PAGE BOTTOM:

Notarize bottom by Notary who lives        ?

Affidavit of reservation of rights UCC 1-308/1-207 Sovereign Authority Public        First-Middle: Last,sui juris
THIS IS A PUBLIC COMMUNICATIONTO ALL All rights reserved UCC 1-308/1-207    Notice to agents is
notice to principles c/o Address  Notice to principles is Notice to Agents    City,  State a republic near [zip code]
        Applications to all successors and assigns  Phone: [ XXX XXX-XXXX ] All are without excuse
        Non-domestic without the United States Let it be known to all that I, First-Middle: Last explicitly

121

reserves all of my rights. See UCC 1-308 which was formally UCC 1-207. "§ 1-308. Performance or Acceptance Under Reservation of Rights. (a) A party that with explicit reservation of rights performs or promises performance or assents to performance in a manner demanded or offered by the other party does not thereby prejudice the rights reserved. Such words as "without prejudice," "under protest," or the like are sufficient." I always retain all of my rights and liberties and in all places, Nunc pro tunc (now for then) from the time of my birth and forevermore. Further, I retain my rights not to be compelled to perform under any contract or commercial agreement that I did not enter knowingly, voluntarily, and intentionally. And furthermore, I do not accept the liability of the compelled benefit of any unrevealed contract or commercial agreement. I am not ever subject to silent contracts and have never knowingly or willingly contracted away my sovereignty. Further, I am not a United States citizen or a 14th amendment citizen. I am a State Citizen of the republic and reject any attempted expatriation. See 15 United States statute at large, July 27th, 1868 also known as the expatriation statute Violation fee of my liberty is $250,000 per incident or per 15 minutes or any part thereof. Wherefore all have undeniable knowledge. AFFIDAVIT Affiant, First Middle: Last, sui juris, a natural born Citizen of (Your state here) in its Dejure capacity as a republic and as one of the several states of the union created by the constitution for the United States of America 1777/1789. This incidentally makes me an American national and a common man of the Sovereign People, does swear and affirm that Affiant has scribed and read the foregoing facts, and in accordance with the best of Affiant's firsthand knowledge and conviction, such are true, correct, complete, and not misleading, the truth, the whole truth, and nothing but the truth. Signed By: sui juris, This Affidavit is dated    NOTARY PUBLIC State         County

        Subscribed and sworn to before me, a notary Public, the above signed First-Middle: Last, This         day of        ,        year.


Notary Public

MY COMMISSION EXPIRES:

5 Reasons Why Hebrew Israelites or Moors Should Not Obtain a State Marriage License

Every year thousands of people amble down to their local county courthouse and obtain a marriage license from the State in order to marry their future spouse. They do this unquestioningly as programmed subjects. They do it because their, parents or pastor has told them to go get one, and besides, "everybody else does. This section attempts to answer the question - why should we not get a marriage license?

1.      The definition of a "license" suggest that we not obtain one to marry. Black's Law Dictionary defines "license" as, "The permission by competent authority to do an act which without such permission, would be illegal." We need to ask ourselves- why should it be illegal to marry without the State's permission? More importantly, why should we need the State's permission to participate in something which Yahawah (God) instituted (Gen. 2:18-24)? We should not need the De facto State's permission to marry nor should we grovel before state officials to seek it. What if you apply and the State says "no"? You must understand that the authority to license implies the power to prohibit. A license by definition "confers a right" to do something. The State cannot grant the right to marry. It is a

Yah (God) -given right.

2.      When one marries with a marriage license, you grant the Defacto State jurisdiction over your marriage. When you marry with a marriage license, your marriage is a creature of the State. It is a corporation of the State! Therefore, they have jurisdiction over your marriage including the fruit of your marriage. This means your

children. What is the fruit of your marriage? Your children and every piece of property you own. There is plenty of case law in American jurisprudence which declares this to be true.

In New York State, parents were upset here in New York City because a test was being administered to their children in the government schools which was very invasive of the family's privacy. When parents complained, they were shocked by the school bureaucrats who informed them that their children were required to take the test by law and that they would have to take the test because they (the government school) had jurisdiction over their children. When parents asked the bureaucrats what gave them jurisdiction, the bureaucrats answered, "your marriage license and their birth certificates." Judicially, and in increasing fashion, practically, your state marriage license has far-reaching implications.

3. When you marry with a marriage license, you place yourself under a Colorable law which is immoral. By obtaining a marriage license, you place yourself under the jurisdiction of Family Court which is governed by unbiblical and immoral laws. Under these laws, you can divorce for any reason. Often, the courts side with the spouse who is in rebellion to Yahawah and castigates the spouse who remains faithful by ordering him or her not to speak about the Bible or other matters of faith when present with the children. This is the truth about your so-called American apple pie.

As a Hebrew Kahan (priest), I cannot in good conscience perform a marriage which would place people under this colorable immortal body of laws. I also cannot marry someone with a marriage license because to do so I must act as an agent of the State! I would have to sign the marriage license, and I would have to mail it into the State. Given the State's demand to usurp the place of Yaha-wah (God) and family regarding marriage, and given its unbiblical, immoral laws to govern marriage, it would be an act of treason for me to do so. Israelites should ask the Hebrew Israelites that have accepted the 501-C3 grants do they submit their do this to their members?

4. The marriage license invades and removes Yah (God)-given parental authority. When you read the Bible, you see that Yahawah intended for children to have their father's blessing regarding whom they married. Daughters were to be given in marriage by their fathers. This is real law that this system of colorable law ignores. (Dt. 22:16; Ex. 22:17; I Cor. 7:38). We have a vestige of this in our culture today in that the Hebrew Israelites takes his daughter to the front of the altar and the priest.

asks, "Who gives this woman to be married to this man?"

Historically, there was no requirement to obtain a marriage license in America prior to Esau's invasion. When you read the laws of the Torah and then our ancestors, you see only two requirements for marriage. First, you had to obtain your parents' permission to marry, and second, you had to make a public notice of the marriage by way of the ceremony.

Notice you had to obtain your parents' permission. Back then you saw a government of Yahawah displayed in that the State recognized the parent's authority by demanding that the parents' permission be obtained. Today, the all-encompassing wicked, ungodly State demands that their permission be obtained to marry.

By issuing marriage licenses, the State is saying, "You don't need your parents' permission, you need our permission." If parents are opposed to their child's marrying a certain person and refuse to give their permission, the child can do an end run around the parent's authority by obtaining the State's permission and marry anyway. This is an invasion and removal of the Highest Yahawah -given parental authority by the State.

5.        When you marry with a marriage license, you are like a Sinner from the State's point of view, when you marry with a marriage license, you are not just marrying your spouse, but you are also marrying the State. Better state you become property of the state.

The most blatant declaration of this fact that I have ever found is a brochure entitled "With This Ring I Thee Wed." It is found in county courthouses across Ohio where people go to obtain their marriage licenses. It is published by the Ohio State Bar Association. The opening paragraph under the subtitle "Marriage Vows" states, "Actually, when you repeat your marriage vows you enter into a legal contract. There are three.

parties to that contract. 1.You; 2. Your husband or wife, as the case may be and 3. the State of Ohio."

See, the State and the lawyers know that when you marry with a marriage license, you are not just marrying your spouse, you are marrying the State! You are like a slave to the state thereafter. You are not just making a vow to your spouse, but you are making a vow to the State and your spouse. You are also giving undue jurisdiction to the State. Then you get a court case and ignorantly argue jurisdiction.

When Does the State Have Jurisdiction Over a Marriage?

It should never unless you consent. Yahawah never intended the State to have jurisdiction over a marriage. The Torah is to be applied in the event of a divorce. Unfortunately, the State now allows divorce for any reason, and it does not prosecute for adultery. The system is wicked. When will you wake up?

In either case, divorce or crime, a marriage license is not necessary for the courts to determine whether a marriage existed or not. What is needed are two witnesses just as in Matthew 18:15. Therefore, you have a best man and a maid of honor. They should sign the marriage certificate in your family Bible, and the wedding day guest book should be kept.

Marriage was instituted by Yahawah; therefore, it is a Yah -given right. According to Scripture, it is to be governed by the family, and the State only has jurisdiction if you consent to a license.

History of Marriage Licenses in America

If George Washington was married without a marriage license, why do you feel that you need one? So, how did we come to this place in America where marriage licenses are issued?

Let us look a racist America that man so-called white pretends never exist or just want the Indigenous people to forget.

Historically, all the states in America had laws outlawing the marriage of so-called blacks and so-called whites. In the mid-1800's, certain states began allowing interracial marriages or miscegenation as long as those marrying received a license from the state. In other words, they had to receive permission to do an act which without such permission would have been illegal.

Black's Law Dictionary points to this historical fact when it defines "marriage license" as, "A license or permission granted by public authority to persons who intend to intermarry." "Intermarry" is defined in Black's Law Dictionary as, "Miscegenation; mixed or interracial marriages."

Give the State an inch and they will take your life, not long after these licenses were issued, some states began requiring all people who marry to obtain a marriage license. In 1923, the Federal Government established the Uniform Marriage and Marriage License Act (they later established the Uniform Marriage and Divorce Act). By 1929, every state in the Union had adopted marriage license laws. Are you surprised?

What Should We Hebrew Moors Do?

Hebrew Israelites/ Moors should not be marrying State marriage licenses, nor should priest, deacons or anyone be marrying people with State marriage licenses. Some have said to me, "If someone is married without a marriage license, then they aren't really married." Given the fact that states and Supreme Court has legalize same-sex marriages, we need to ask ourselves, "If a man and a man marry with a State marriage license, and a man and woman marry without a State marriage license - who's really married? Is it the two men with a marriage license, or the man and woman without a marriage license? This contention that people are not really married unless they obtain a marriage license simply reveals how Statist we are in our thinking. We

need to think biblically. (As for homosexuals marrying, outlaw sodomy as Yahawah's law demands, and there will be no threat of sodomites marrying.)

You should not have to obtain a license from the State to marry.

someone any more than you should have to obtain a license from the State to be a parent, which some in academic and legislative circles are currently pushing to be made law.

When I marry a couple, I always buy them a Family Bible which contains birth and death records, and a marriage certificate. We record the marriage in the Family Bible. What is recorded in a Family Bible will stand up as legal evidence in any court of law in America. Early Americans were married without a marriage license. They simply recorded their marriages and birth's in their Family Bibles. So, should we Yahsharahla.

Hebrew Israelites should refuse to marry couples with State marriage licenses.)

ACCEPTANCE FOR VALUE

To understand "Acceptance for Value" you must first understand contracts. For this purpose, we will stick with the basics. There are two types of contracts: Simple and Adhesion.

## SIMPLE CONTRACTS

A simple contract is one in which two parties negotiate an agreement. It is bilateral in that each party gives up something and gets something of equal value in return. It normally is purely up to the parties' discretion as to what the value is. If a dispute develops over the interpretation of the contract, the courts will weigh the evidence, and whichever way the scale tips (however small the tip), then the heavier side wins the game.

## ADHESION CONTRACTS

An adhesion contract is also bilateral, but it is offered on a "take it or leave it" basis, with no opportunity for negotiating the terms. Insurance and lease contracts are good examples of adhesion contracts. To protect the offeror, every detail of the contract must be specified. If a dispute develops over the interpretation of the contract, the courts will decide all points in the contract in favor of the offeror and will decide all points not covered in the contract to be in favor of the offeree.

Let us say that you hire someone to paint your house. You have specified that it will be painted yellow, that the job will be finished in three days, and that the painter will notify you when it is done. The specifications are not negotiated because you offered to the painter the contract on a take-it-or-leave-it basis.

The painter accepts the contract and paints the house exactly as specified, within three days, and notifies you that it is finished as specified.

Then...he presents his bill. It is for 3 times as much as you were expecting. You decide to go to court.

The court looks like the contract and notes that the adhesion contract was completed according to specification but has nothing in it about the value. Because you, the offeror, failed to specify the value, the value decision must be in favor of the painter, no matter what is fair. The painter accepted your contract for the value he perceived, and you pay.

If the contract has been a negotiated contract instead of an adhesion contract, the court would have listened to both sides equally, then decide as to what would have been a fair value to pay.

## TRAFFIC TICKETS ARE ADHESION CONTRACTS

When a traffic ticket is offered by the State through its officer, it is an adhesion contract offered on a take-it-you-can't-leave-it basis. The terms are specified, and you have no opportunity to negotiate: You must perform to their specification and satisfaction.

That is their side of the deal. Lucky for you, in their enthusiasm to specify what you must do and give up, they failed to specify what they must give up (i.e., pay) for the privilege of commandeering your life. You accept their offer for the value that it has, and you now specify that value because they failed to specify it in their adhesion contract.

## EVERY CONTRACT HAS TWO SIDES

When you accept the contract for value, both sides must fulfill their obligations. In the case of a traffic ticket, you MUST pay the fine, get a driver's license, fix the license plate, or whatever it calls for. On the other hand, the State must pay you the value you placed on the ticket, whatever that value may be. Failure by either side to perform its obligation constitutes an actionable breach of contract.

The C.O.R.P.O.R.A.T.I.O.N.

(Crooked Officials Robbing People of Rights Against Truth in Our Nation) BOOK TITLE

Administrative Remedy staying out of Public court.

Today's lesson will come from Matthew 18: chapter. Matthew 18: 15]" Moreover if thy brother shall trespass against thee, go and tell him his fault between thee and him alone: if he shall hear thee, thou hast gained thy brother.

[16]     But if he will not hear thee, then take with thee one or two more, that in the mouth of two or three witnesses every word may be established.

[17]     And if he shall neglect to hear them, tell it unto the church: but if he neglects to hear the church, let him be unto thee as a heathen man and a publican.

[18]     Verily I say unto you, Whatsoever ye shall bind on earth shall be bound in heaven: and whatsoever ye shall loose on earth shall be loosed in heaven.

[19]     Again I say unto you, that if two of you shall agree on earth as touching anything that they shall ask, it shall be done for them of my Father which is in heaven.

[20]     For where two or three are gathered together in my name, there am I during them".

Administrative remedy is constructing documents without going to court. We are to handle this without argument. Henceforth after this lecture you will only go to court for problems that you cannot resolve out of court. Again, The Father said through his


Spirit Matthew 1815] "Moreover if thy brother shall trespass against thee, go and tell him his fault between thee and him alone: if he shall hear thee, thou hast gained thy brother... The principles of contract law determine which agreements will be enforceable by the courts. Contract law is based on case law, statutes, and tradition subject to slight variation from state to state. Common Law contracts include employment agreements, and other contracts involving services, leases and sales of real property, loan agreements, stock purchases agreements settlement agreements and joint venture agreements. Commercial transactions involving the sales of goods that are moveable property are governed by article 2 of the Uniform Commercial Codes ((UCC) Article 2.

What is a contract? A contract is a legally enforceable promise or set of promises. If the promise is broken the person to who the promise was made which is the promise has certain rights against the person who made the promise which is the promisor. If the promisor fails to carry out its promise, the promise may be able to recover money damages, or it may be able to get an injunction which is a court order forcing the promisor to perform promise. The formation of a valid contract requires four basic elements 1) There must be an agreement between the parties by offer and acceptance. 2) The party's promises must be supported by something of value, known as consideration. 3) The parties must have the capacity to enter into t a contract which in means in legal term that a person ability to understand the nature and effect of the agreement. And 4) The contract must have a legal purpose meaning contracts that acre contrary to statute or public policy are illegal and considered void that is they are not valid contracts.

For administrative remedy, all documents that you send will be sent proof of service and registered or certified mail to get evidence, in doing so it will stand up in a public court. In the upper left-hand corner, you will put the case number, on the proof of service by mail form the list all the documents that you are mailing off on this day. The person who is sending this cannot be a party to the case and you really do not want it to be a spouse, but a brother or neighbor is fine. The person that does this you will call as a witness in court. The service date is the date that you put it in the mail. The addressee is the person that you are sending it to. The executed-on date is the date that the person sending it for you send it. We send it certified or registered because the post office can prove that they delivered it. The opposing party cannot say they did not get it. Along with this I would submit an Affidavit and a self-executing contract. Always make copies of your documents for your records. The person that performed this proof of service for you can be called as a witness if need be in a public court which is why I would have a good notary send it its akin to it coming from the secretary of state.

In Administrative remedy you reach an agreement simply from letter writing it is not like court remedy. Let us say officer unfriendly pulled me over and threaten me if I do not sign a citation for yielding a red light. I sign without prejudice all rights reserved ucc1-308 by Tazadaq. This enables me to reserve all my rights and now if I do not appear in court, I cannot be charged with failing to appear because I reserved my right. The judge may order me to appear but within 72 hours I am going to send the citation back with refused for cause or no plea written at a 45-degree angle across the citation. Per UCC1-308. Then make a copy for my records. I will also send my Affidavit Denial Traveling in commerce. If you need help with that contact, we via our web site or help2creditorsdebtorscontractsincommerce.org If the court fails to rebut my Affidavit it stands as the truth. I would I also send a letter of conditional acceptance regarding the citation. On the conditional acceptance put a 3-cent stamp in the upper right-hand corner, sign your name across the state and date it. This cancels the stamp and makes you postmaster general and proves you are a living soul and not a corporation. Corporations are not alive them cannot sign. Thus, you get the proof of service and send the conditional acceptance, the citation and the Affidavit to the DA and a copy to the court certified mail and I would wait 21 days. If they do not respond send in a notice of default and notice of Estoppel to prevent them lawfully and legally from coming back against you because they have agreed to your contract.

If you go to public court thereafter you now have a record of default and proof of mailings and he will have to dismiss. If you try to get you to contract for educational purposes do not agree or consent to anything. You stand firm on that you want a dismissal since they have no lawful cause of action. After 21 days wait 7 days and send a notice of default by way of proof of service. If they do not respond wait 7 more days and send the final notice of default by way of proof of service, they are done. They get 3 chances.

How to get documents on public record when the clerk has been told not to file your Affidavits and other documents. The De Facto does not want the county recorder to put your docs on record. They do not want you on record as a sovereign. One way is to get them on public record is to submit them to the republic of Texas to the national republic registery.com. They will record your documents for all to see and will be in the public record. They put them in pdf format. Or try writing "file on demand" at the top of the documents and give them to the county clerk or recorder of deeds. When you write file on demand, they should file it. Have at least one witness and a voice recorder. If the county recorder refuse, have to them write a statement saying they have the authority to refuse to put your documents of evidence into the record then have them sign it and date it. Then ask them for a copy of the bond they are operating under. All public official is bonded. The head clerk has a bond. If he or she violate the term of his/her job the bond is revoked and thereafter can no longer work for the county.

The county recorder, the head clerk of the court the judges etc. are all bonded by a public hazard bond which is to protect the public against unlawful actions on the part of the public servant. Yes, I said servant because they provide public service, but you go in like a scared dog with your tail between your legs scratching where you do not itch. /Stand up and be a man damns it! You act like a debtor expects to be treated as such. These public servants are required to show evidence of their bonds and if they violate the terms of their job their bond can be awarded to cover damages to the public. In layman's terms you can sue them, and the money will be paid out of that bond. If they lose their bond, they are unemployable by the state and county and will be fired because all employees must be bonded. This is the method that I use to ensure my brother does his duty. This is not legal advice. I would not give you legal advice I am not in the legal profession and have no such desire.

Never discus anything with an opposing party over the phone. Simply advise them you only respond in writing or answer in writing. Now remember you are not a resident or a citizen. I discussed that before. If you are then you are not sovereign a resident and citizen are subjects not sovereigns. When you request for a manager and the clerk or person refuse you can sue the manager and owner because they are responsible under the "respondent superior rule" The owner is responsible for the decision of his subordinates. This same rule applies to the county. If a court clerk does not accept your documents without getting a manger, they are assuming responsibility which is not theirs to take. It is their superior which is the named clerk. They are making a legal determination which is against the law. They are damaging you under your declaration of independence rights quote to claim right to life, liberty, and pursuit of happiness. By what authority can they claim that you are injuring another by filing your paperwork unless I can be proved to be fraud? By their act are they not accreting that they more equal than you in status? But in truth they are in a public servant position and are therefore less than you in status as you are sovereign, they are there to serve you.

A check is a promise to pay a check is not payment it is a promise to pay. You assume that it comes from your bank account by way of your payment for FRN's, but the Notes are just a promise to pay that you accept. Just as that check my signatures on a a4v is a promise to pay as per HJR 192. Do you understand? My signature is the energy, my signature is what they desire. If I do not sign the freaking check it of no use my signature is the real energy.

Courts of Record

And the Common Law in State Constitutions and State Statutes

Black's Law Dictionary, 4th Ed., 425, 426

COMMON LAW ACTIONS are such as will lie on the particular facts, at common law, without the aid of a statute. - Black's Law Dictionary 5th Edition

COURT OF RECORD

A "court of record" is a judicial tribunal having attributes and exercising functions independently of the person of the magistrate designated generally to hold it, and proceeding according to the course of common law, its acts and proceedings being enrolled for a perpetual memorial. Jones v. Jones, 188 Mocap. 220, 175 S.W. 227, 229; Ex Parte Glad hill, 8 Metc. Mass., 171, per Shaw, C.J. See, also, Ledwith v. Rosalsky, 244 N.Y. 406, 155 N.E. 688, 689.

CLASSIFICATION

Courts may be classified and divided according to several methods, the following being the more usual:

COURTS OF RECORD and COURTS NOT OF RECORD. The former being those whose acts and judicial proceedings are enrolled, or recorded, for a perpetual memory and testimony, and which have power to fine or imprison for contempt. Error lies to their judgments, and they generally possess a seal.

Courts not of record are those of inferior dignity, which have no power to fine or imprison, and in which the proceedings are not enrolled or recorded. 3 Bl. Comm. 24; 3 Steph. Comm. 383; The Thomas Fletcher, C.C.Ga., 24 F. 481; Ex parte Thistleton, 52 Cal 225; Erwin v. U.S., D.C.Ga., 37 F. 488, 2 L.R.A. 229; Heininger v. Davis, 96 Ohio St. 205, 117 N.E. 229, 231.

"Inferior courts" are those whose jurisdiction is limited and special and whose proceedings are not according to the course of the common law." Ex Parte Kearny, 55 Cal. 212; Smith v. Andrews, 6 Cal. 652

"The only inherent difference ordinarily recognized between superior and inferior courts is that there is a presumption in favor of the validity of the judgments of the former, none in favor of those of the latter, and that a superior court may be shown not to have had power to render a particular judgment by reference to its record. Ex parte Kearny, 55 Cal. 212. Note, however, that in California 'superior court' is the name of a particular court. But when a court acts by virtue of a special statute conferring jurisdiction in a certain class of cases, it is a court of inferior or limited jurisdiction for the time being, no matter what its ordinary status may be. Heydenfeldt v. Superior Court, 117 Cal. 348, 49 Pac. 210; Cohen v. Barrett, 5 Cal. 195" 7 Cal. Jur. 579

"The judgment of a court of record whose jurisdiction is final, is as conclusive on all the world as the judgment of this court would be. It is as conclusive on this court as it is on other courts. It puts an end to inquiry concerning the fact, by deciding it." Ex parte Watkins, 3 Pet., at 202-203. [cited by SCHNECKLOTH v. BUSTAMONTE, 412 U.S. 218, 255 (1973)]

CONCLUSION

Courts of Record must proceed according to the course of the common law, without the aid of a statute.

Courts which proceed according to statutory jurisdiction are inferior courts, and may be sued directly, without appealing. Courts designated as courts of record may act as statutory courts unless the parties to a case object.


Kimberly Snowden

xxxxxxxxxxxxxxxxxxxxxxxxx apt

Anywhere, Maryland [21061-6679]

Peroutka, Miller, Klima & Peters, P.A. 8028 Ritchie Highway, Ste 300 Pasadena, Maryland 21122

June 27th, 2018

Re: Acct #

Case Number xxxxxxxxxxxxxxxxxxxxxxxxxx

Dear Peroutka, Miller, Klima& Peters, P.A.

The C.O.R.P.O.R.A.T.I.O.N.

(Crooked Officials Robbing People of Rights Against Truth in Our Nation) BOOK TITLE

I am in receipt of your noticed dated on May 25th, 2018 attached herewith. Please also find attached a debt validation letter which was mailed to you via certified mail number 7xxxxxxxxxxxxxxxxxxx dated April 12th, 2018 to which you failed to answer on a point by point basic. This is a letter is notice of fault to which you have ten days (10) to respond to this notice on a point by point basic; acquiescence is agreement. Failure to respond within the allotted 10 days confirms that this debt is sit off, settled, and closed.

I just pulled my credit report and noticed "closed account" by an alleged Capital One account. This is a second notice requesting validation of this debt. I am requesting proof that I am indeed the party you are involved with this debt, and there is/was some contractual obligation which is binding on me to pay this debt. Your action to collect on an alleged debt that is already, sit, off, settled and closed might constitute defamation of character, fraud, negative marks on my credit report harming my credit and prevent me from enjoying all the benefits of good credit. I am sure your company being legal staff will agree that non-compliance with this request could put your company in serious legal trouble with the FTC and other state or federal agencies.

I conditionally accept your offer to pay this alleged debt upon proof of claim that,

Complete payment history, the requirement of which has been established via SPEARS vs. BRENNAN 745 N.E. 2d 862 and Agreement that bears the wet ink signature of the alleged debtor wherein he/she agreed to pay the original creditor.

Letter of sale or assignment from the original creditor to your company. (Agreement with your client that grants you the authority to collect on this alleged debt.)

Intimate knowledge of the creation of the debt by you, the collection agency Proof this account is mine.

I am sure you know, under FDCPA Section 809 (b), you are not allowed to pursue collection activity until the debt is validated. You should be made aware that in TWYLA BOATLEY, Plaintiff, vs. DIEM CORPORATION, No. CIV 03-0762 UNITED STATES DISTRICT


COURT FOR THE DISTRICT OF ARIZONA, 2004, the courts ruled that reporting a collection account indeed is considered collection activity. Why are you pursuing collection activity on an account that is sit off, settled, and closed in the first place? You may be guilty of harassment and in violation of the FDCPA under 15 USC 1962e:

That you are not guilty of false representation or implication that the consumer committed any crime or other conduct in order to disgrace the consumer.

In addition, according to the information given to us on the credit report, the date of last activity by the original creditor is June 15th, 2018. The SOL on this alleged debt, even if it was mine, is 3 years in the state of Maryland.

I am sure you are aware of the provisions in the Fair Debt Collection Practices Act (FDCPA). However, I would like to point out that your firm has violated provisions of the FDCPA in the following respects:

(a)     by using deceptive or misleading representation for collection of the alleged debt and therefore violating 15 USC 1692e

(b)     by falsely representing the legal status of the alleged debt and therefore violating 15 USC 1692e(2)(A).

I am sure your legal staff will agree that non-compliance with this request could put your company in serious legal trouble with the FTC and other state or federal agencies. Under the FCRA and the FDCPA, each violation is subject to a $1000 fine, payable to me.

Kimberly Snowden

Monique Free

c/o 0000 South 49th Street

Philadelphia, Pennsylvania [nondomestic 19143] Attornatus Privatus

UCC FILING OFFICE

P.O. BOX 9660

Olympia, Washington98507- 9660

Filed:

Clerk or Deputy Clerk:

ORDER TO SECETARY OR CLERK OF COURT TO PERFORM SPECIFIC DUTIES

Comes now the above-entitled court and orders as follows, DISCUSSION AND CONCLUSION OF LAW

The Clerk of the Court or Clerk at this office is a ministerial position not having authority of a tribunal. As such it is required to carry out its duties without acting as a tribunal, but by merely performing the duties authorized by the court. One of those is a duty owed to the plaintiff to file documents presented for the record. Failing to file a document for the record is a criminal offense.

A document is considered filed once it is received.

The clerk of the court, like a recorder, is required to accept documents filed.

The Federal Rules of Civil Procedure was the agreed format for the court proceedings. A paper is filed upon delivering it (A) to the clerk. FPRC 5(d)(2)

The job of the clerk of the court "is to file pleadings and other documents, maintain the court's files and inform litigants of the entry of court orders." Sanders v. Department of Corrections, 815 F. Supp. 1148, H49(N.D. Ill. 1993). (Williams v. Pucinski, 01C5588 (N.D.Ill. 01/13/2004).)

The duty of the clerk is to make his record correctly represent the proceedings in the case. Wetmore v. Karrick, 27 S. Ct. 434, 205 U.S. 141 (U.S. 03/11/1907 Failing to file documents presented and reflect the documents on the docket is a failure to perform the ministerial duties of the Clerk of Court.

It is hereby the ordered as a matter of law of record that the Clerk of the UCC filing Division fulfill its obligations under the authority of law and file any documents presented for said purpose.

The C.O.R.P.O.R.A.T.I.O.N.

(Crooked Officials Robbing People of Rights Against Truth in Our Nation) BOOK TITLE

Monique Free

Attornatus Privatus

(a) Whoever willfully and unlawfully conceals, removes, mutilates, obliterates, or destroys, or attempts to do so, or, with

intent to do so takes and carries away any record, proceeding, map, book, paper, document, or other thing, filed or deposited with any clerk or officer of any court of the United States, or in any public office, or with any judicial or public officer of the United States, shall be fined under this title or imprisoned not more than three years, or both.

(b) Whoever, having the custody of any such record, proceeding, map, book, document, paper, or other thing, willfully and unlawfully conceals, removes, mutilates, obliterates, falsifies, or destroys the same, shall be fined under this title or imprisoned not more than three years, or both; and shall forfeit his office and be disqualified from holding any office under the United States. As used in this subsection, the term "office" does not include the office held by any person as a retired officer of the Armed Forces of the United States. 18 USC § 2071

it is settled law that delivery of a pleading to a proper official is sufficient to constitute filing thereof. United States v. Lombardo, 241 U.S. 73, 36 S. Ct. 508, 60 L. Ed. 897 (1916); Milton v. United States, 105 F.2d 253, 255 (5th Cir. 1939). In Greeson v. Sherman, 265 F. Supp. 340 (D.C.Va.1967) it was held that a pleading delivered to a deputy clerk at his home at night was thereby "filed." (Freeman v. Giacomo Costa Fu Adrea, 282 F. Supp. 525 (E.D.Pa. 04/5/1968).)

The clerk of a court, like the Recorder is required to accept documents filed. It is not incumbent upon him to judicially determine the legal significance of the tendered documents. In re Halladjian, 174 F. 834 (C.C.Mass.1909); United States, to Use of Kinney v. Bell, 127 F. 1002 (C.C.E.D.Pa.1904); State ex rel. Kaufman v. Sutton, 231 So.2d 874 (Fla.App.1970); Malinou v. McElroy, 99 R.I. 277, 207 A.2d 44 (1965); State ex rel. Wanamaker v. Miller, 164 Ohio St. 176, 177, 128 N.E.2d 110 (1955.).) (Daniel K. Mayers Et Al., v. Peter S. Ridley Et Al. No. 71-1418 (06/30/72, United States Court of Appeals for the DC Circuit.) [emphasis added.]

Counterclaim filed October 7th, 2016, Paragraph 17, page 4.

Traffic tickets

Contract contract contract! http://youtu.be/8oLCnTHkXNM

What to know who to handle traffic offer (tickets) watch this entire video. If you need further assistance, I require donations for my time and energy I am exhausted.

THUS, CONTRACTS FOR JURISDICTION and JURISDICTION BY CONTRACTS was the only way they could trick us into their scheme of being a slave to them. This is not legal advice I do not offer legal advice if you need legal advice see yourself a competent consul and be advised,

Note I take donation for my time and energy please Donate cash, me/$tazadaqshah or paypal.me/tazadaq
TRAFFIC TICKETS:

These are always offering to contract. We then have 3 days for rejecting this offer of contract under the Truth in Lending and return-ing their contract-torn in half-back to the Municipal Court Collection Plate. Or if you are in a state that may charge you with dam-aging their property Reject it by doing the following .... Write across the CONTRACT OFFER (ticket) the following: Your offer of CONTRACT is.

hereby Rejected and Returned to you unsigned in full accord with Truth in Lending. Any further correspondence from the signer of the document and heirs, agents, assigns must be done under the penalty of perjury. If you are representing Me or assuming that

you represent Me, you are FIRED! Take the ticket to the location where you pay ticket in your state. Also take two witnesses. Tell the clerk that you are here to set off settle and close the charging instrument. They will tell you that it is not yet in the system. What they do not tell you is that you have 72 hours to set off the debt. You are not told this because ignorance of the law is no excuse. So, you then have your tow witness make an affidavit stating that they witness you trying to settle the debt.

If you wait past the 3 days, you must call and set a court date. You must go into court as a man or woman never as defendant. You also need to require that it be a court of record with a jury. Then put an Affidavit into the court records attached to the ticket-writing across your rejection. The affidavit would be about the Policeman --- i.e., he/she did not have a Contract with you for stop-ping you and violating your right to travel and your right for Privacy, the Policeman did not have a License to practice law and was committing a Commercial Crime. Show up on the day of the hearing and the Policeman would not dare show up. Most do not show up anyways. If he /she shows up, make "for the record if anyone here has a claim against me it must be done under oath and affirmation.

This principle applies to each and all CONTRACTS with the UNITED STATES COPORATION and ALL OF THE UNINCORPORATED PART OF THIS SCHEME.

1. Write across the CONTRACT OFFER the following: Your offer of CONTRACT is.

hereby Rejected and Returned to you unsigned in full accord with Truth in Lending. Any further correspondence from the signer of the document and heirs, agents, assigns.


must be done under the penalty of perjury. If you are representing Me or assuming that you represent Me, you are FIRED!

2.      Remember that any further correspondence not signed under the penalty of perjury

concerning #1 is Returned and answered the same way.

What Tazadaq did when a UCC Clerk / Secretary refused to file my Documents, acquiesce is never an option

Sometimes a court clerk might refuse to file a document because it does not meet certain form guidelines. For educational purposes only, A clerk is not permitted to refuse filing a document for form as required by rule 5. (d)(4) of the Federal Rules of Civil Procedures specifically state,

5.(d)(4) Acceptance by the clerk.

A clerk must not refuse to file a paper solely because it is not in the form prescribed by these rules or by a local rule or practice.

This is an important rule especially for those who are preceding in a court of record. Although a court of record proceeds according to common law, the creditor or sovereign can choose the Federal Rules by which to proceed. This is one of the ways I used to get a clerk to do his/her job. Since law is the decree of the creditor or sovereign, creditors or sovereigns can decree that some statutes apply in his case.

First and far most, a court clerk does not have the authority to make any decisions. His duties are ministerial and not tribunal. The tribunal is who gets to make the decisions regarding the quality of a paper. Therefore, if at first a clerk did not file my papers. I Simply stated politely that he files them on demand. When that failed, I presented the clerk with an order from the court of record. I mailed it by registered mail to get the clerk to comply.

As you will see in my template, I have typed for educational purposes only, the anyone who removes a document from the record can be punished for up to three years in prison according to.

18 USC § 2071

(a)      Whoever willfully and unlawfully conceals, removes, mutilates, obliterates, or destroys, or attempts to do so, or, with intent to do so takes and carries away any record, proceeding, map, book, paper, document, or other thing, filed or deposited with any clerk or officer of any court of the United States, or in any public office, or with any judicial or public officer of the United States, shall be fined under this title or imprisoned not more than three years, or both.

(b)      Whoever, having the custody of any such record, proceeding, map, book, document, paper, or other thing, willfully and unlawfully conceals, removes, mutilates, obliterates, falsifies, or destroys the same, shall be fined under this title or imprisoned not more than three years, or both; and shall forfeit his office and be disqualified from holding any office under the United States. As used in this subsection, the term "office" does not include the office held by any person as a retired officer of the Armed Forces of the United States.

There is also case law that specifies that a document is filed once it is delivered to the clerk. It does not have to be stamped and sign. That is done merely to designate a time of filing. In one case, the court opined that a document is filed even if delivered to a deputy clerk at night at his home.

it is settled law that delivery of a pleading to a proper official is sufficient to constitute filing thereof. United States v. Lombardo, 241 U.S. 73, 36 S. Ct. 508, 60 L. Ed. 897 (1916); Milton v. United States, 105 F.2d 253, 255 (5th Cir. 1939). In Greeson v. Sherman, 265 F. Supp. 340 (D.C.Va.1967) it was held that a pleading delivered to a deputy clerk at his home at night was thereby.

"filed." (Freeman v. Giacomo Costa Fu Adrea, 282 F. Supp. 525 (E.D.Pa. 04/5/1968).)

Read the rest of the Order to the Clerk that I will cover hereto. It has good information regarding the duties of the clerk.

I always remember, do not argue with a deputy clerk or anyone because you go in dishonor. Nobody ever wins an argument. The deputy clerk is not someone who you debate law with. They are simply paper warehouses and do not usually comprehend such things. I always send my order directly to the clerk along with a letter explaining the crime being committed by the deputy clerk and he will usually perform his duties as the law requires.

.

The C.O.R.P.O.R.A.T.I.O.N.

(Crooked Officials Robbing People of Rights Against Truth in Our Nation) BOOK TITLE

The C.O.R.P.O.R.A.T.I.O.N.

(Crooked Officials Robbing People of Rights Against Truth in Our Nation) BOOK TITLE

24 A CREDITOR IN COMMERICAL WARFARE

AFFIDAVIT DENIAL

TRAVELING IN COMMERCE

I, Roosevelt Tankard , Principal with an Address

Correction c/o 175 Willis Avenue apartment 4C, Bronx, New York being duly affirmed, deposes, and says under penalty of perjury.

I, _____ Roosevelt Tankard , a natural living soul man/woman competent to testify to the accuracy of this.

affidavit, do hereby attest to the

following:

I, _____ Roosevelt Tankard am not a CORPORATION, CREATED FICTION, or FRANCHISE.

ROOSEVELT TANKARD

175 WILLIS AVE 4C, BRONX, NY 10454

IN THE MAGISTRATE COURT; COUNTY OF BRONX; THE STATE OF NEW YORK; US; UNITED STATES; IRS, DOROTHY K BUMBLE-CLERK; BENNY J JUDD-JUDGE are CORPORATIONSIFICTIONS/FRANCHISES and I, _____, (Roosevelt Tankard) _ do hereby declare that they do NOT exist.

I, _____ Roosevelt Tankard , do hereby affirm that I did not drive or operate a

Motor Vehicle on (date you received ticket).

I, _____ (Your name) , do hereby affirm that I was not engaged in Commerce on any public road or highway on

(date you received ticket).

I, _____ Roosevelt Tankard , do hereby affirm that I did not carry passengers,

goods, or merchandise for hire or compensation in my private truck or private automobile on (date you received ticket).

Furthermore, I will defend against and seek remedy for "deprivation of any rights, privileges, or immunities secured by the Constitution and laws of the New York Republic against all guilty parties.

This document was prepared by Roosevelt Tankard _____, Principal.


Roosevelt Tankard

Affirmed to before me a notary public this the _____ day of 2012.

SEAL

The C.O.R.P.O.R.A.T.I.O.N.

(Crooked Officials Robbing People of Rights Against Truth in Our Nation) BOOK TITLE

Notary Public - State of New York My Commission expires

ROSIE THERMAL, A Third-Party Debt Collector, this is Notice that your July 29, 2002, received. July 31, 2002 offer of contract for Subject Matter Jurisdiction and Summary Judgment are hereby Rejected and Returned unsigned in full accord with Truth in Lending.

Any further correspondence from ROSIE THERMAL, DEPUTY COURT CLERK, heirs, agents, assigns must be accompanied with the Original Contract upon which you are making your CLAIM against Me, Jack Rabbit Patriot, or a copy of your bond card, your bond number, and the name of your bonding company or write to Me, Jack Rabbit Patriot, under the penalties of perjury-

If you ROSIE THERMAL, DEPUTY COURT CLERK, heirs, agents, assigns think or assume you are representing Me, Jack Rabbit Patriot or JACK R PATRIOT or any derivative thereof, you are FIRED!

In LAW MERCHANTS or LAW OF CONTRACTS, equality under the Law is paramount. My Summary Judgment to you ROSIE THER-MAL is for you to Cease and Desist in this matter or ROSIE THERMAL prove up your Judgment. Where did you get a CLAIM against Me and are you holding the Bond against this CLAIM?

ROOSEVELT TANKARD

By, Roosevelt Tankard, Principal, Agent Attorney in Fact


Affidavit

To all to whom these presents shall come, greeting,

I, Me, My, Myself, Affiant, One, living, breathing man with an address correction c/o Roosevelt Tankard 175 Willis Avenue Apartment C, Bronx, New York commonly known as Bronx, County , being of sound mind, and over the age of twenty-one, whose advocate is , the Christ, reserving all rights, and who has no bar attorney, and does not waive counsel, knowingly and willingly Declares and Duly affirms, according to law, in special appearance, in good faith, with no intention to delay or obstruct, and with full intent to preserve and promote the public confidence in the integrity and impartiality of the judiciary, that the following statements and facts, in the matter (s) of C02-1999-C1, and any matter relating to this, are of my own first-hand knowledge, and are the truth, the whole truth, and nothing but the truth, with a belief in a life hereafter having rewards and punishments, so help me Yahweh.

1.      I, Affiant, inhabitant

the address Roosevelt Tankard, and speaks only for Roosevelt Tankard, and speaks for no other person, entity, individual, group, organization, association, order, or society, whether incorporated or not, and is not misrepresenting herself, and has not duly granted, sold, or donated any power of appointment, special power of appointment, general power of appointment in trust, or any general or special franchise of her name, character, or living body to any other.

2.      Affiant States that I am not, and my name is not ROOSEVELT TANKARD

, TANKARD, ROOSEVELT, R TANKARD, nor ROOSEVELT nor am I associated with ROOSEVELT TANKARD, TANKARD, ROOSEVELR, R TANKARD. Roosevelt, nor related to, and have no contact, nor contract, franchise, donation to, nor automatic, nor pre-existing arrangement, duly certified or not, with any such person, nor entitlements of any such person.

3.      Affiant states that I, am not responsible now, nor have I ever been responsible for any/all debts or encumbrances of ROOSEVELT TANKARD, TANKARD, ROOSEVELT, R TANKARD.

4.      Affiant states that I, am not a corporation, nor a body corporate, nor am intending or undertaking to become a body corporate.

5.      Affiant states that neither what is commonly known as the STATE OF NEW YORK, nor State of New York, nor NEW YORK nor NY, or any derivative thereof; the UNITED STATES OF AMERICA, UNITED STATES, the United States of America, United States, nor USA, nor their agents, representatives, assigns, or contacts, have or have had custody or have been donated custody, by Me, of any of My documents, personal effects, or property, or living body, either express or implied, or automatic, or by pre-existing arrangement, or entitlement, or donation, duly certified or not;

6.      Affiant states that I neither have, nor had any contact,

contract, association, express or implied, or franchise "to be" or "to do", or automatic pre-existing arrangement, donation to, or entitlement, duly certified or not, with either what is commonly known as the STATE OF NEW YORK, nor State of New York, nor NY, or any derivative thereof; the UNITED STATES OF AMERICA, UNITED STATES, the United States of America, United States, nor USA.

7.      Affiant states that I have made a fundamental Mistake, shown by the following facts:

8.      Affiant states that I submitted a Notice of Understanding and Intent and Claim of Right against "Clark" who after investigation I have learned that the correct name is "Calvin" a personal trainer at Bally's Total Fitness 1915 Third Avenue, New York, New

York. Please refer to registered mail number RR50903201BUS or Certified Mail Receipt number 7011 3500 0001 2707 6576 Who's aggressive behavior and threatening body language caused me to suffer Intentional Infliction of Emotional Distress. as results of nearly assaulting me by violation my personal space. Please see attached.

9.      Affiant mistakenly presumed, because of asking another trainer the name of the person that had conducted himself in such a manner. that his name was "Clark" which is incorrect the correct name is "Calvin", and I apologize and correct the mistake.

10.     Affiant used the name "Clark" by mistake, and which to correct it with the right person which is "Calvin"

11.     Affiant used the name "Clark" in the foregoing documents, by mistake.

12.     Affiant is unschooled in law and has been without benefit of counsel or an attorney, and never been represented by an attorney, and has not acted pro se, nor accepted for myself, nor in propria persona, and have never with knowledge and approval, or by express or implied consent, express or implied agreement or promise, duly authorized any attorney to act in my behalf or for my benefit, since aforesaid document was mailed to your organization.

13.     Affiant wrote and sent Notice of Understanding and Intent and Claim of Right

14.    I have just realized my mistake: the name on the previously mailed document was incorrect the correct name is "Calvin".

15.    I apologize to all for any inconvenience or hardship my mistake has caused, and I ask forgiveness.

In witness whereof, I have hereunto set my hand, this the fifth day of the seventh month, in the year of our Lord, two thousand twelve, Gregorian,

Roosevelt Tankard

state of _____New York_____ ss:

____Bronx      county

Be it remembered that on this ___5__ day of the  7_____ month in the

Year of _____2017___, before me , who being by me duly

sworn did say that he is Roosevelt Tankard, the Affiant in the foregoing Affidavit, and that said instrument was signed by Roosevelt.


Tankard by authority and said Roosevelt Tankard acknowledged to me that he as such, executed the same in my presence. The Affiant also acknowledged the signing thereof to be his own voluntary act and deed.

Notary Public

Seal:

Address

my commission expires:


with God all things are possible


COPYRIGHT INSTRUCTIONS

This document is especially important in that it gives you control over who can and cannot use your "STRAWMANS " name.

Fill it out and file it into the county records along with your POWER OF ATTORNEY IN FACT.

Notice anyone who would write to you using your COPYRIGHT name and gentle enforce upon them that they are in violation by sending them a copy.

From that day forward-anyone who would write to you in violation of your COPYRIGHT should immediately receive an Invoice for $1,000,000.00 per violation per person involved. Take these to the county and file them into the county and mail them out.

Anyone who would seek to enrich themselves from the unauthorized use of your COPYRIGHT should receive an Invoice for $1,000,000.00 per person per violation.

After 10 days, Mail them a Default letter. After 30 days when the Invoice becomes Law-send them another letter-make out an order for the COUNTY JUDGE-take it to him/her and have them enforce your order.

TRUTH AFFIDAVIT IN THE NATURE OF SUPPLEMENTAL

RULES FOR ADMINISTRATIVE AND MARITIME CLAIMS RULES C (6)

In the matters for commerce, all commerce operated in truth, demand for truth is made by all party for full disclosure=who are you? Who do you represent and who is the real party of interest? Is the real party of interest the Commonwealth for Britain, the British Crown, the Queen for England, the Holy See? Is the United States flying the Queen's Banner Flag? What city does the Flag in the United States and State Court Houses, the House and the Senate, State and Federal and the oval office's State and Federal represent? Have you desecrated our Flag for Liberty old Glory the lawful Flag for the United States defined by 4 USC J~?

Verified Declaration in the Nature by an Affidavit for Truth in Commerce and Contract by Waiver for Tort Presented by me, me, my, myself, addressee, Roosevelt Tankard, living soul, one for We the People under Original Common Law Jurisdiction by the New York and united states of America Contracts, the Constitutions.

Republic and one by the)

several united states        ) ss

New York        )

in America        )

For: Whom it may concern: In the Matter for ROOSEVELT TANKARD; (and all derivatives thereof):

I, Me, My, Myself, addressee, Roosevelt Tankard, (herein after Title Owner) the undersigned for one We the People, Sovereign, natural born living souls, the Posterity, born upon the land in the one for several counties within the one for the several states united for America, the undersigned Posterity, Creditors, Claimants and Secured Party, herein after "I, Me, My, Myself, Title Owner" do hereby solemnly declare, say and state:

1.        I, Me, My, Myself, the Title Owner am competent for stating the matters set forth herewith.

2.        I, Me, My, Myself, the Title Owner have personal knowledge concerning the facts stated herein.

3.        All the facts stated herein are true, correct, complete, and certain, not misleading, admissible as evidence, and if stating I, Me, My, Myself, the Title Owner shall so state.

Plain Statement of Facts

A matter must be expressed for being resolved. In commerce, truth is sovereign. Truth is expressed in the form for an Affidavit.

The C.O.R.P.O.R.A.T.I.O.N.

(Crooked Officials Robbing People of Rights Against Truth in Our Nation) BOOK TITLE

An Affidavit not rebutted stands as Truth in commerce. An Affidavit not rebutted, after thirty (30) days, becomes the judgment in commerce. A Truth Affidavit, under commercial law, can only be satisfied: by Truth Affidavit rebuttal, by payment, by agreement, by resolution, or by Common Law Rules, by a jury.

I, Me, My, Myself, the Title Owner, am expressing truth by this Verified Declaration in the Nature for an Affidavit of Truth in Commerce and Contract by Waiver for Tort Presented by me, addressee, Title Owner, living soul, one for We the People under Original Common Law Jurisdiction for the New York and United States of America Contracts, the Constitutions.

WHEREAS, the public record is the highest evidence form, I, Me, My, Myself, Title Owner, am hereby timely creating public record by Declaration with this Verified Declaration in the Nature for a Truth Affidavit in Commerce and Contract for a Tort Waiver Presented by Me, addressee, living soul, the Title Owner, one for under We the People under Original Common Law Jurisdiction for the New York and United states of America Contracts, the Constitutions.

1.      Fact: The person known as ROOSEVELT TANKARD, (and all derivatives thereof) is fiction without form or substance, and any resemblance for any natural born body living or dead is entirely intentional in commercial fraud by Genocide acts for We the People for New York by the alleged Government officials and agents for the Commercial Corporation and Commercial Courts for the disfranchising purpose, We the People for New York from our Life, Liberty, Property, and Happiness Pursuit, among other Rights, for their self-enrichment using their New York Rules of Civil Procedure, outside the law authority and our Courts by original jurisdiction.

2.      Fact: I have placed a copyright on the Fiction issued for Me without My Permission or consent by assent known as ROOSEVELT TANKARD or, TANKARD, ROOSEVELT (fiction) and all derivatives thereof, is now My private property and cannot be used without My prior written consent and then only under the terms set out in this contract.

3.      Fact: The Fiction is My perfected securities and registered by contract with me and with the Secretary under State of New York as such for five years and is My recorded copyright Fiction by this declaration under original common law jurisdiction for one hundred (100) years and is My private property, the Secured Party, for My Estate protection, My Life, and My Liberty. This Truth Affidavit of Copyright is Nunc pro tunc to December 8, 1965.

4.      Fact: Using My Fiction on any document associated in any manner with My Estate or Me, the holder in due course, Secured Party, Exempt from Levy, without My written prior consent is strictly forbidden and chargeable against each user and issuer in the amount, the sum certain for one thousand (1,000.00) dollars, silver specie, in lawful coinage for the united states of America per user and per issuer per Fiction.

5.      Fact: Using My Fiction for the intended gains for themselves (the issuers or users) or for others for any of My Rights, my private property or any part about my Estate without full disclosure and my written prior consent is strictly forbidden and chargeable per each user and issuer, in the amount of the sum certain for one million (1,000,000.00) dollars silver specie in lawful coinage for the United States of America as defined under Article I, Section 10 of We the People's Contract/Constitution for the United States of America per using Fiction including any past, present, or future use.

6. Fact: Using My Fiction on any document associated in any manner with my Estate or me, the holder in due course, Secured Par-

ty, and Exempt from Levy, without my written prior consent is all the evidence required for enforcing this agreement/contract and evidence that all users and issuers are in full agreement and have accepted this agreement/contract under the condition and terms so stated and set forth herein and is due and payable under the terms and conditions set forth herein by this agreement/contract.

I, Me, My, Myself, the Title Owner, am not an expert in the Law, however I do know right from wrong. If there is any human being that is being unjustly damaged by any statements herein, if he/she will inform me by facts, I will sincerely make every effort and amend my ways.

I, Me, My, Myself, the Title Owner, hereby and herein reserve the right for amending and make amendment for this document as necessary in order that the truth may be ascertained and proceeding justly determined.

If any living soul has information that will controvert and overcome this Declaration, since this is a commercial matter, please advise me IN WRITING by DECLARATION/AFFIDAVIT FORM within ten (10) days from recording hereof, providing me with your counter Declaration/Affidavit, proving with particularity by stating all requisite actual evidentiary fact and all requisite actual law, and not merely the ultimate facts and law conclusions, that this affidavit by Declaration is substantially and materially false sufficiently for changing materially my or the Fiction's status and factual declaration.

Your silence stands as consent, and tacit approval, for the factual declarations here being established as fact as a law matter and this affidavit by Declaration will stand as final judgment in this matter; and for the sum certain herein stated and will be in full force and effect against all party, due and payable and enforceable by law.

The criminal penalties for commercial fraud are determined by jury, by law, the monetary value is set by me for violation against my rights, for breaching the law, the contract, the Constitutions in the sum certain amount as stated herein for dollars specie silver coin lawful money for the United States of America as defined by Article I, Section 10 under the Constitution, by We the People for the United States and will be due and payable on the eleventh day or any day thereafter as use occurs after filing by Me, in the public records for the county of Bronx, New York, under this declaration.

The Undersigned, I, Me, My, Myself, the Title Owner, holder in due course for original, do herewith declare, state, and say that I, Secured Party, issue this with sincere intent in truth, that I, Me, the undersigned Secured Party, am competent by stating the matters set forth herein, that the contents are true, correct, complete, and certain, admissible as evidence, reasonable, not misleading, and by My best knowledge, by me undersigned addressee.

Notice for the agent is notice for the principal applies under this notice.

Notice for the county clerk for the county Bronx, New York, and record court for original jurisdiction, is notice for all.

I sign this document on this date, Nunc pro tunc to the date of December 8, 1965 of the creation of the FICTION(S).

Addressee signature, holder in due course, the Title owner


Temporary mailing location

The C.O.R.P.O.R.A.T.I.O.N.

(Crooked Officials Robbing People of Rights Against Truth in Our Nation) BOOK TITLE

c/o 175 Willis Avenue apartment 4C

Bronx, New York

Roosevelt Tankard

Addressee, Title owner

## DECLARATION OF INDEPENDENCE BY PUBLIC NOTICE

I, Me, My, Myself, a man and a living Soul, a sovereign with an addressee correction c/o Roosevelt Tankard - Bronx, New York does hereby notice the public and all public officials of the UNITED STATES and the STATE OF New York, under the authority of rights given by Almighty God, said rights being protected, enumerated, and excepted from government intrusion in the National Constitution of New York, 1836, of the following:

1.      I am not a citizen or subject of GREAT BRITAIN, ENGLAND, the BRITISH CROWN, the HOLY SEE, the UNITED STATES, the STATE OF NEW YORK or any other governmental entity.

2.      I am not a party to the Constitution for the United States of America; Therefore, I am not a citizen under the terms of the 14th amendment to the Constitution for the United States of America.

3.      I, am not a party to or subject of, and denies the compelled performance of, the Judge's Chambers, the private copyrighted laws, statutes, ordinances, rules, regulations, codes, rules of court used by GREAT BRITAIN, ENGLAND, the BRITISH CROWN, the UNITED STATES, the STATE OF NEW YORK or any other

governmental entity.

4.      I am a man and a living Soul, and am NOT a legally created person, legal entity, corporation, trust, or artificial entity of any kind, and is NOT a surety for or representative of the fiction ROOSEVELT TANKARD or any I any derivation of an all-capitalized entity and is not res of any constructive public trust created by any governmental entity. I deny consent by assent for the use of all capital letter name by any administrators, officers, agents, fiduciaries, objects of any and all trusts.

5.      I, am the Donee and having Power, hereby releases, refuses acceptance of, extinguishes, and renounces all schemes and artifices for defrauding, including but not limited by, any and all instruments creating any estate(s), use(s), trust(s), however created, constructive, implied, involuntary, direct or other, and terminates all rights and interests under any and all estate(s), use(s), trust(s) affecting the Substantive, Inherent, and Private Rights, and any

and all Private Property Rights of Me. Release is retroactive to      (December 8, 1965).

6.      I, hereby release, refuse acceptance of, extinguish, and renounce all schemes and artifices for defrauding, including but not limited by, any and all instruments creating any implied or adhesion contract(s), and terminates all obligations of I, Me, My, Myself under any and all implied or adhesion contract(s). Release is retroactive to

(December 8, 1965).

7.      I, hereby release, refuse acceptance of, and extinguish any and all trusteeship(s) of any and all administrators, agents, objects, and fiduciaries claiming any interests in the Private Property, Inherent, and Substantive Rights of Me

Release is retroactive to   (December 8, 1965).

8.      I, hereby denies consent by assent and refutes all assumptions and presumptions of the Inherent, Substantive and Private Rights and Private Property being acquired by Me that are the rest of any and all estate(s), use(s), trust(s), and hereby denies and refuses the trespass of any and all administrators, agents, objects, and fiduciaries on the Private Property and Private Rights of Me.

9.      The use of all Bills of Credit in any form is done inebriates non-assumpsit, with all rights reserved, and

without recourse, by the Law of Necessity.

Roosevelt Tankard, Addressee, a man and a living soul, a sovereign Date

Witness Witness

Notice for Competency and Incompetence, Revocation of Power of Attorney and Firing all Persons below and Demand to cease and desist.

Roosevelt Tankard

175 Willis Ave 4C

Bronx, New York [10454]

To all Agents, Administrators, acting as third party titled persons.

Equality under the Law is PARAMOUNT, and Mandatory by law.

I am competent to handle my own affairs. A sovereign cannot be tried in his/her court.

I am accepting all documented matters as recorded by the below listed, present or future with the person named ROOSEVELT TANKARD or any other derivative and everything in them as true. I am returning all documented recorded past, present and future matters to you for discharge and closure.

To all BAR members and 3rd party agents acting in/and for the following.

1.THE CROWN OF ENGLAND et. al.

2.      THE UNITED NATIONS et. al.

3.      THE UNITED STATES et. al and/or the United States of America.

4.      THE TREASURY OF THE UNITED STATES et. al.

The C.O.R.P.O.R.A.T.I.O.N.

(Crooked Officials Robbing People of Rights Against Truth in Our Nation) BOOK TITLE

5.      THE FEDERAL RESERVE et. al.

6.      THE INTERNAL REVENUE SERVICE et. al.

7.      THE BUREAU OF ALCOHOL AND FIREARMS et. al.

8.      THE FEDERAL BUREAU OF INVESTIGATION et. al.

9.      THE UNITED STATES POSTAL SERVICE et. al.

10.    THE FEDERAL BUREAU OF PRISONS et. al.

11.    THE FIFTH U.S. ARMY et. al.

12.    THE STATE OF NEW YORK et. al.

13.    THE STATE OF NEW JERSEY et. al.

14.    THE STATE OF DELEWARE et. al.

15.    THE STATE OF MARYLAND et. al.

16.    THE STATE OF VIRGINIA et. al.

17.    THE STATE OF NEVADA et. al.

18.    THE STATE OF FLORIDA et. Al

I, Roosevelt Tankard, now and forever, declare all the 3rd party Agents for the above so named as incompetent and I presently and permanently revoke their power of attorney for representing or making any legal determinations for me in any of my affairs. You are now Fired. Return the voucher to me immediately.

It is hereby Demanded and ordered by the Sovereign, Roosevelt Tankard, that all parties Cease and Desist all future actions and those trespassing on the Land of New York without specific permission from the people's Certified Republic Government are demanded to leave this Land or be subject to the Sovereign New York people's courts.

This the _____ day of    2012 by me        seal:

owner, principal surety

Witness Witness

CERTIFIED MAIL 7003 3333 0005 7777 8888    January 19, 2012

NOTICE TO COUNTY CLERK

The minute you receive any affidavit, it is recorded. Should you refuse to record My affidavits, once deposited with you, you are committing a crime against justice under Statutes at Large Sec. 5403 and it is punishable by up to a $2000 fine and 3 years imprisonment. If your county attorney told you not to file any documents like mine, you are still responsible, as I do not accept any third-party interveners. Any attorney, district attorney, or anyone from the lawyering craft are all third parties and do not have a license to make a legal determination in this matter as they do not represent Me and you, the county clerk, do not have the authority to represent Me.

Title LXX.---CRIMES. --- CH. 4. CRIMES AGAINST JUSTICE

(Destroying, &c., public records.)

SEC. 5403. Every person who willfully destroys or attempts to destroy, or, with intent to steal or destroy, takes and carries away any record, paper, or proceeding of a court of justice, filled or deposited with any clerk or officer of such court, or any paper, or document, or record filed or deposited in any public office, or with any judicial or public officer, shall, without reference to the value of the record, paper, document, or proceeding so taken, pay a fine of not more than two thousand dollars, or suffer imprisonment, at hard labor, not more than three years, or both: [See §§ 5408,5411,5412.1]

Title LXX.---CRIMES. --- CH. 4. CRIMES AGAINST JUSTICE

(Conspiracy to defeat enforcement of the laws.)

SEC. 5407. If two or more persons in any State or Territory conspire for the purpose of impeding, hindering, obstructing, or defeating, in any manner, the due course of justice in any State or Territory, with intent to deny to any citizen the equal protection of the laws, or to injure him or his property for lawfully enforcing, or attempting to enforce, the right of any person, or class of persons, to the equal protection of the laws, each of such persons shall be punished by a fine of not less than five hundred nor more than five thousand dollars, or by imprisonment, with or without hard labor, not less than six months nor more than six years, or by both such fine and imprisonment. See §§ 1977-1991, 20042010, 5506-5510.1

Title LXX.---CRIMES. --- CH. 4. CRIMES AGAINST JUSTICE

(Destroying record by officer in charge.)

SEC. 5408. Every officer, having the custody of any record, document, paper, or proceeding specified in section fifty-four hundred and three, who fraudulently takes away, or withdraws, or destroys any such record, document, paper, or proceeding filed in his office or deposited with him or in his custody, shall pay a fine of not more than two thousand dollars, or suffer imprisonment at hard labor not more than three years, or both-, and shall, moreover, forfeit his office and be forever afterward disqualified from holding any office under the Government of the United States.

To Whom It May Concern:

Please kindly correct your records to show that I am located at:

NON-DOMESTIC

C/O 402 East 105 street apartment 2A

The C.O.R.P.O.R.A.T.I.O.N.

(Crooked Officials Robbing People of Rights Against Truth in Our Nation) BOOK TITLE

New York, New York

Zip code exempt (DMM 122.32), As Amended

Since the use of Zip codes is voluntary (see Domestic Mail Service Regulations, Sections 122.32), the U. S. Postal Service cannot discriminate against the non-use of ZIP codes, pursuant to the Postal Reorganization Act, Section 403 (Public Law 91-375).

The federal government attempts to assert jurisdiction by, sending letters with ZIP codes, when jurisdiction would otherwise be lacking. The receipt and "acceptance " of mail with ZIP codes is one of the requirements for the Internal Revenue Service to have jurisdiction to send notices. In fact, the IRS has adopted ZIP code areas as "Internal Revenue Districts ". See the Federal Register, Volume 51, Number 53, for Wednesday March 19, 1986.

The federal government cannot bill a New York State Citizen because such a Citizen is not within the purview of the District of Columbia, its territories, possessions, or enclaves. As a group, these areas are now uniquely and collectively identified as "the federal zone", as explained in the book entitled, The Federal Zone: Cracking the Code of Internal Revenue, San Rafael, Account for Better Citizenship, 1992. Your immediate cooperation in this matter will be most appreciated.

Signed with explicit reservation of all My Rights and without prejudice to any of My rights.

Roosevelt Tankard, Agent

Roosevelt Tankard, state Citizen


(Nonresident Alien with respect to The Federal Zone D.C., its territories, possessions, and enclaves)


THE TRUE BIRTH

VERIFIED BY THE CREATOR GOD

IN ORDER A DECLARATION BY AFFIDAVIT CONFIRMING

THOSE THINGS MOST SURELY BELIEVED

(Luke 1: 1-4)

NOW THE BIRTH INVOLVING Roosevelt Tankard WAS ON THIS WISE

AT THE TIME APPOINTED

I, Roosevelt Tankard, BEING LEGAL AGE, MAKE THE FOLLOWING STATEMENTS AND DECLARE THAT ON GOD'S PERSONAL WORD AND KNOWLEDGE, THEY ARE TRUE

AT THE TIME LIFE BY GOD WAS BIRTHED On the Land, Northampton County, Virginia (Roosevelt Tankard's Birthdate)

(Genesis I8: 10-14)

SIGNED ACCORDINGLYBY GOD'S WORD ON Roosevelt Tankard's Birthdate) (Holy Scripture)

(Picture)

ROOSEVELT TANKARD, GRANTOR Roosevelt Tankard, Agent

The C.O.R.P.O.R.A.T.I.O.N.

(Crooked Officials Robbing People of Rights Against Truth in Our Nation) BOOK TITLE

SECURED PARTIES SIGNATURE          Attorney in Fact, Autograph

175 WILLIS AVENUE

BRONX, NEW YORK [10454-9998]

Witness Witness Witness

## 25 CONTROL THE COPRORATION

Dealing with fear

Shalom, Islam, Hotep, Peace,

I want to deliver a spiritual message through the spirit of Yahawah ba ha sham wa Yahawashi. Because many of our people fear that some awful event will take place when they get an offer in the mail from a bill collector, or they get subpoena for court. You fear that the worst will happen and usually does because you succumb to your fear. The intent here is to enable you to transcend fear and stand on your square with the truth. When Justice walked the earth, he taught his disciples how to deal with fear by allowing him to watch him pray and to enable them to be capable of dealing with their fears by watch his example. Fear is a natural emotion that if not controlled it will master you. We must learn not to yield to the fear of our emotions. In the book of Job, the Highest Power Abanawa, demands Job to stand up like a man and be strong, knowing thus I encourage you to stand on your square like a man and be totally undaunted. Let us get it.

Job 38: [3] "Gird up now thy loins like a man;" The Father Yah is demanding that we face our fears. If you do not face your fear, they will master you. If Yah is with you who can be against you and win? Many can be against, but they cannot win. Stand up like a man, do not punk out, If I am with you man, you cannot lose with the stuff I use.

Now let us look at how Justice/Christ/ Yeshua taught the apostle to deal with fear. I would fist like to turn your attention to Luke 22: [39] "And he came out, and went, as he was wont, to the mount of Olives; and his disciples also followed him.

[40] And when he was at the place, he said unto them, pray that ye enter not into temptation. [41] And he was withdrawn from them about a stone's cast, and kneeled, and prayed, [42] Saying, Father, if thou be willing, remove this cup from me: nevertheless, not my will, but thine, be done. [43] And there appeared an angel unto him from heaven, strengthening him. [44] And being in an agony he prayed more earnestly: and his sweat was as it were great drops of blood falling down to the ground".

Now lets us examine why did Justice pray this prayer? Why did he ask the Father to move this cup away from him? Was Christ afraid to die? Why did the angel appear to Christ to give him strength? He was so was so afraid that his sweat was dripping like blood, heat pounding, oh my gosh I am about to die, the hour has arrived! But he overcame this fear and said you know what Father not my will, but your will be done. I got this I am going to overcome this fear and gird up my lions like a man. Justice was with the apostles a lot and one of the things he taught them was to overcome fear. This pray was an example to teach the apostles how to deal with fear. He trained them how to overcome fear Peter, James and John needed extra attention thus he was with them more teaching them to overcome fear let look at it. The scriptures say to prove all things so allow me to prove my point.

John 7: [33] "Then said Jesus unto them, yet a little while am I with you, and then I go unto him that sent me. (Here Justice is teaching them that I must go away back to the Father that sent me, and you will have to go on without me come on read on)

[34] Ye shall seek me and shall not find me: (you will look for me but will not find me) and where I am, thither ye cannot come".

We see Christ is preparing them for the day that he will have to leave the apostles. He is preparing them for his departure and how to deal with their fears. Of facing the government and Pharisees alone.

John 16: 1] These things have I spoken unto you, that ye should not be offended.

[2]     They shall put you out of the synagogues (expressing more reasons why they will be afraid those pharisees will throw you out of the synagogues read on) yea, the time cometh, that whosoever killeth you will think that he doeth God service. (they will swear they are doing the will of the Highest)

[3]     And these things will they do unto you, because they have not known the Father, nor me.

[4]     But these things have I told you, that when the time shall come, ye may remember that I told you of them. And these things I said not unto you at the beginning, because I was with you.

[5]     But now I go my way to him that sent me;( I got to leave you, now I have to go my way to him that sent me) and none of you asked me, whither goest thou?[6] But because I have said these things unto you, sorrow hath filled your heart. (Because I have told you these things you have because sad and sorrow has filled your hearts. You are sad because I told you these things)

Luke 21: 8] And he said, take heed that ye be not deceived: for many shall come in my name, saying, I am Christ; and the time draweth near: go ye not therefore after them. (justice is going into the signs of the end of this world ruler ships and those false prophets out there he said do not follow them) [9] But when ye shall hear of wars and commotions, be not terrified: for these things must first come to pass; but the end is not by and by.

[10]     Then said he unto them, Nation shall rise against nation, (this is speaking about race wars) and kingdom against kingdom:

[11]     And great earthquakes shall be in divers' places, and famines, and pestilences; and fearful sights and great signs shall there be from heaven.

[12]     But before all these, they shall lay their hands on you, and persecute you, delivering you up to the synagogues, and into prisons, being brought before kings and rulers for my name's sake.( For Justice name sake for Christ name sake because this is Satan's time so all the demons of the world is against you when you are teaching about Justice) Read on 13] And it shall turn to you for a testimony.

[14]     Settle it therefore in your hearts, not to meditate before what ye shall answer:

[15]     For I will give you a mouth and wisdom, which all your adversaries shall not be able to gainsay nor resist.

[16]     And ye shall be betrayed both by parents, and brethren, and kinsfolks, and friends; and some of you shall they cause to be put to death. (some of you will be put to death. Imagine someone telling you this today. That your father and mother will betray you and you will go to jail or be put to death.) Now let us go back to Luke and break it on down.

Christ knew that the apostles would be afraid after he left that is what the prayer in the garden was all about. Let go back and break it down. to Luke 22: [39] "And he came out, and went, as he was wont, to the mount of Olives; and his disciples also followed him. [40] And when he was at the place, he said unto them, pray that ye enter not into temptation. [41] And he was withdrawn from them about a stone's cast and kneeled and prayed.

Why did Christ only go a stone's cast? It is suggesting that he went a short distance. Why did he go a short distance? Because he wanted the disciples to hear him and see him when he prayed because this is not how he taught the apostles to pray he said to pay in private. You say Taz that is bs and speculation. No, it is not Christ taught the disciples to pray in private not near other. Let prove it. Luke.11: [1] And it came to pass, that, as he was praying in a certain place, when he ceased, one of his disciples said unto him, Lord, teach us to pray, as John also taught his disciples. (So, Christ taught them how to pray now take note he was praying in a certain place not to be seen by others he was not around the disciples when he prayed. [2] And he said unto them, when ye pray, say, Our Father which art in heaven, hallowed be thy name. Thy kingdom comes. Thy will be done, as in heaven, so in earth." But we read earlier he only went away a stone's cast which is not far." Let see how he taught the disciples to pray.

Matthew 6: [5] And when thou preyed, thou shalt not be as the hypocrites are: (do not be like the hypocrites when you pray) for they love to pray standing in the synagogues and in the corners of the streets, that they may be seen of men. (they like to be seen by men so other can see them) Verily I say unto you, they have their reward. (their reward is others looking at him saying oh look at him he is praying.) [6] But thou, when thou prayeth, enter into thy closet, (do not pray around others to be seen pray in secret this is why the scriptures read when he was done praying in a certain place) and when thou hast shut thy door, pray to thy Father which is in secret;( so why did Justice pray only a stone's cast away from the apostles in the garden? Because he wanted to be heard and seen. This was his last lesson before he was to be taken. It was his last hour and he knew this. This prayer was for the apostles and not for the father he wanted them to hear him to prepare them to deal with their fears. As he dealt with his Let us go back to Luke

Luke 22: 41] And he was withdrawn from them about a stone's cast, and kneeled, and prayed, (he went only a stone's cast because he wanted to be seen and heard by the apostles) 42] Saying, Father, if thou be willing, remove this cup from me: nevertheless, not my will, but thine, be done. (Now why did Christ say this? Was he against the will of the father? No, this prayer was for the disciples to hear him he wanted them to hear this prayer that is why he only went a stone's cast.

Matthew 16: 21] From that time forth began Jesus to shew unto his disciples, how that he must go unto Jerusalem, and suffer many things of the elders and chief priests and scribes, and be killed, and be raised again the third day. (Christ had been teaching the disciples about the day and hour when he would pray in the garden)

[22]     Then Peter took him, and began to rebuke him, saying, be it far from thee, Lord: this shall not be unto thee. (Peter said listen we are not going to allow this to happen to you Lord. Peter grabbed him and began to correct him but watch this he rebuked Christ)

[23]     But he turned, and said unto Peter, get thee behind me, Satan (He called Peter Satan because Peter took on the spirit of Satan because he went against the plan and will of God which was for Justice to die on the cross to redeem Israel from their sins. You are going against the plan of my father Peter for my purpose of being born was to die for the forgiveness of sins) Read on

Matthew 16: [13] When Jesus came into the coasts of Caesarea Philippi, he asked his disciples, saying, whom do men say that I the Son of man am?

[14]     And they said, some say that thou art John the Baptist: some, Elias; and others, Jeremias, or one of the prophets.

[15]    He saith unto them, but who say ye that I am?

[16]    And Simon Peter answered and said, Thou art the Christ, the Son of the living God.

[17]    And Jesus answered and said unto him, blessed art thou, Simon Barona: for flesh and blood hath not revealed it unto thee, but my Father which is in heaven.

18] And I say also unto thee, that thou art Peter, and upon this rock I will build my church; and the gates of hell shall not prevail against it.

[19]    And I will give unto thee the keys of the kingdom of heaven: and whatsoever thou shalt bind on earth shall be bound in heaven: and whatsoever thou shalt loose on earth shall be loosed in heaven.

[20]    Then charged he his disciples that they should tell no man that he was Jesus the Christ.

[21]    From that time forth began Jesus to shew unto his disciples, how that he must go unto Jerusalem, and suffer many things of the elders and chief priests and scribes, and be killed, and be raised again the third day.

[22]    Then Peter took him, and began to rebuke him, saying, be it far from thee, Lord: this shall not be unto thee.

[23] But he turned, and said unto Peter, Get thee behind me, Satan: ( now after all that power he gave Peter he called him Satan because Peter's will was against the plan of God so Christ had to check peter hold on Peter you are out of line, contain your emotions this is the plan of my Father) thou art an offence unto me ( yeah you are offending me Peter get behind me with that spirit of Satan, read on) for thou savourest not the things that be of God, but those that be of men.( You worried about how you feel about me peter you are dealing with emotions Peter that's how you feel about me but the plan of God must go forth. This is to show you Justice was never against the plan of Yah and he was not going to allow anyone to come between Yah's plan and what he had to accomplish on earth.

Let get again.

Luke 22: [42] Saying, Father, if thou be willing, remove this cup from me: nevertheless, not my will, but thine, be done. It is important to remember this because the lesson we are dealing with today that Christ wanted the will of God to be done not his will. Christ was not afraid to die he was not against the purpose of him being born. Get

John 12: [23] And Jesus answered them, saying, the hour is come, that the Son of man should be glorified. (Christ knew the exact hour that he would be taken he know that his time had arrived) Luke 22: [27] Now is my soul troubled; and what shall I say? (he is getting your attention and asking the question what I should not allow the will of my father to go forth?) Father save me from this hour (am I supposed to punk out and say save me from this Yah?) but for this cause came I unto this hour (this was my reason for being born was for the forgiveness of sins. I got to die this is. Fall back I got this; this is why I was born for this hour). 28] Father, glorify thy name. Then came there a voice from heaven, saying, I have both glorified it, and will glorify it again.

[29]    The people therefore, that stood by, and heard it, said that it thundered: others said, An angel spake to him.

[30]     Jesus answered and said, this voice came not because of me, but for your sakes. ((this voice came for you to hear it not for my sake but for you to hear that people.)

Let further prove that Christ was not afraid to die to carry out the plans of the father. Because he overcame fear.

Matthew 10: 28] And fear not them which kill the body but are not able to kill the soul: (do not fear them that can only kill your body but him that can kill both your body and soul) but rather fear him which is able to destroy both soul and body in hell. He is teaching the disciples how to deal with fear. Now does this sound like one that is afraid.

Matthew 26: 51] And, behold, one of them which were with Jesus stretched out his hand, and drew his sword, and struck a servant of the high priest's, and smote off his ear. (Peter was so nice with his swords that with great precision he chopped off the man's ear)

[52]     Then said Jesus unto him, put up again thy sword into his place: for all they that take the sword shall perish with the sword.

[53]     Thinkest thou that I cannot now pray to my Father, and he shall presently give me more than twelve legions of angels? (man, I do not need you peter I can pay to my father want too if I need back up my father when send me a legion of angels wipe these men out, chill Peter fall back I got this I do not need you Peter)

[54]     But how then shall the scriptures be fulfilled, that thus it must be? (this got to happen. Now this do not sound like a man that is scared. He is teaching them how to deal with fear).

John 19: [7] The Jews answered him, we have a law, and by our law he ought to die, because he made himself the Son of God.

[8]

[9]     When Pilate therefore heard that saying, he was the more afraid.

[10]     And went again into the judgment hall, and saith unto Jesus, Whence art thou? But Jesus gave him no answer. (Christ ignored

him)

[10]     Then saith Pilate unto him, Speakest thou not unto me? knowest thou not that I have power to crucify thee, and have power to release thee?

[11]     Jesus answered, thou couldest have no power at all against me, except it were given thee from above: (Christ said hold up wait a minute I got to say something now you are going too far Christ said look man you are not got no power over me man. At first Christ said nothing but he had to let this fool know you do not have power over me I am letting you do this to me. Now does this sound like a man that is afraid.

John 10: [17] Therefore doth my Father love me, because I lay down my life, that I might take it again.

[18] No man taketh it from me, but I lay it down of myself (they have no power over me man I am back by God, I can get a legion of angels right now, I am not afraid I am doing this thing on my own free will). I have power to lay it down, and I have power to take it again. (so, what is there to be afraid of?)

Matthew 26: [36] Then cometh Jesus with them unto a place called Gethsemane, and saith unto the disciples, sit ye here, while I go and pray yonder.

[37]     And he took with him Peter and the two sons of Zebedee and began to be sorrowful and very heavy.

[38]     Then saith he unto them, my soul is exceeding sorrowful, even unto death: tarry ye here, and watch with me.

[39]     And he went a little further, and fell on his face, and prayed, saying, O my Father, if it be possible, let this cup pass from me: nevertheless, not as I will, but as thou wilt.

[40]     And he cometh unto the disciples, and findeth them asleep, and saith unto Peter, What, could ye not watch with me one hour?

[41]     Watch and pray, that ye enter not into temptation: the spirit indeed is willing, but the flesh is weak.

[42]     He went away again the second time, and prayed, saying, O my Father, if this cup may not pass away from me, except I drink it, thy will be done.

[43]     And he came and found them asleep again: for their eyes were heavy.

[44]     And he left them, and went away again, and prayed the third time, saying the same words. (he went and prayed 3 times saying the same words the same words why did he pray in repetition because he was trying to teach them to overcome their fears)

Matthew 6: 7] But when ye pray, use not vain repetitions, (Christ used repetition because he was teaching the disciples to deal with fear) mas the heathen does: for they think that they shall be heard for their much speaking.

[8] Be not ye therefore like unto them: for your Father knoweth what things ye have need of, before ye ask him.

Matthew 26: [44] And he left them, and went away again, and prayed the third time, saying the same words. (he went and prayed 3 times saying the same words the same words)

He was teaching the disciples that there will be times you will be afraid, but you must deal with that fear.


Mark 14: 32] And they came to a place which was named Gethsemane: and he saith to his disciples, sit ye here, while I shall pray.

[33]     And he taketh with him Peter and James and John, and began to be sore amazed, and to be very heavy.

[34]     And saith unto them, my soul is exceeding sorrowful unto death: tarry ye here, and watch.


[35]     And he went forward a little, and fell on the ground, and prayed that, if it were possible, the hour might pass from him.

[36]     And he said, Abba, Father, all things are possible unto thee; take away this cup from me: nevertheless, not what I will, but what thou wilt.

[37]    And he cometh, and findeth them sleeping, and saith unto Peter, Simon, sleepest thou? couldest not thou watch one hour? He was teaching them how to deal with fear he was demonstrating fear.

Hebrew 5: [7] Who in the days of his flesh, when he had offered up prayers and supplications with strong crying and tears unto him that was able to save him from death and was heard in that he feared;( The apostle needed to hear Christ in fear praying and demonstrating fear to the apostles so they would know how to deal with their fear).

Shalom, Islam.

How to apply the Constitution

After this lecture you should be capable of presenting yourself in a public as your own consul.

When stopped by a policeman keep in mind that the party is armed thus you will render respect in a polite manner and will not display any rapid movements or disrespectful language. Be cognizant of your rights and render respect. You will need to read the Federalist papers which can be found as a free download on our site. It is by Madison Hamilton and jay. The Supreme court ruled in Choen vs Virginia record in 6 Week reporter volume 2 in 1821 that the Federalist Papers is the exact record of the intent of the framers of the Constitution and that the intent of the law makers is the law. So, we encourage you to read the Federalist Papers. I am going to also suggest that you purchase "To keep and bear arms by Joyce Lee Malcolm."

Many of you have received offers that are referred to as tickets and have not successfully defended your right to travel because you have been told that you were driving while you were traveling but you were not aware of this. God down to your law library and ask for a set of books known as the Federal Digest and it will show you ever Supreme Court case regarding the Right to Travel. Now the States do not want you to exercise your right to travel knowing thus you must be capable of defending that. How do I do that Taz? Well let me ask you a serious of questions to bring this out.

1)    Can a State arbitrary and eventually convert a secured liberty (the right to travel) into a privilege and issue a license and a fee for it? No, who said so? Murdock vs Pennsylvania no state can convert a secured liberty into a privilege. Does everyone see how I was able to apply that? You must be able to think or you will not get this law stuff Does the state require you to have a license to exercise that right? No, we just proved that. Do you understand do you understand? Does everyone see that?

2)    What happens if the state requires you to have a license? Shuttlesworth vs Birmingham Alabama, you can ignore the license and engage into the right impunity meaning they cannot punish you for it.

3)    What happens if the officer pulls you over and writes you a ticket? You will fight it in court later. Your constitution Right is superior to any law that the De facto will put down. You have a right to travel and they cannot pass a law to take away that right. Next if they do it is unconstitutional and 3rd no state can convert a secured liberty into a privilege and issue a license and a fee for it and if they do you can ignore the license and fee and engage in the right with impunity, Shuttles Worth's vs Birmingham Alabama. And since you have committed not wrong and done nothing evil you have the perfect defense for willfulness, thus you cannot be charged with willfulness not going to get a license. Do you understand? Do you understand? You have a perfect defense United States vs Bishop 412 US 346 Defines willfulness as an evil motive or intent to avoid a known duty or tasks under law with a moral certainty. This is not what you did now was it? You relied on previous decision of the supreme court, and your constructional right to travel.

After you present you counteroffer, My Honor if it please the court I would like to move to court to motion dismiss the case for failure to state a cause of action upon which relief can be granted. I also would like my cost and fees for having to defend this frivolous case. You have a right to collect your time for going to court people. But do not overdo it just for your court cost. Submit your bill and proposed order. You fill out your own proposed order that will speed up your case and you will intimidate the prosecutor when you do your own order.

Right to travel one can support by the 1st Amendment and 5th Amendment and Superior Vs Thompson case

as a fundamental right is the right to travel freely among the states. It is important to realize that international travel is not a fundamental right. The right to travel among the states, however, is more than simply the right to physically move freely. In fact, frequently at issue are state laws that classify state citizens based on the length of their residence. For example, a state cannot deny welfare to citizens who have lived in the state for less than a year if they are otherwise qualified and if the state grants such assistance to citizens who have resided in the state for more than a year. See Shapiro v. Thompson, 394 U.S. 618 (1969).

Generally, the Fourteenth Amendment's Equal Protection Clause prevents states from limiting the rights of newly arrived citizens. While there is some overlap with the subject matter of the Privileges and Immunities Clause (see Chapter 2), the Equal Protection Clause, in the context of travel, is meant to protect new citizens of a state against discrimination by their new home state, while the Privileges and Immunities Clause is meant to ensure that citizens of a one state do not have their rights limited by another state. Note that here, as in other fundamental rights Equal Protection cases, it is not the classification which concerns us. Classifying citizens based on how long they have been in a state is neither a suspect classification nor a quasi-suspect classification. Strict scrutiny is applied here only because the classification is being used to burden their right to travel among the states. If the classification were used to determine who could wear red shirts and who could wear blue shirts, mere rational basis review would apply.

It is imperative that we do not enter a plea, I do not intend to answer in the form demure of such as I do not acquiesce to quasi jurisdiction because that an issue to be brought up in my pleadings and brief to be filed with the court.

What is nationality?

By Black's Law Dictionary 4th Edition, nationality is that quality or character which arises from the fact of a person's belonging to a nation or state. Nationality determines the political status of the individual.

What is the difference between nationality and naturalization?

The difference between nationalizing yourself is that you are claiming the nation you belong to and naturalization means you are adopting a foreigner allegiance and receiving the privileges of citizenship under that allegiance. When you nationalize you claim what already belongs to you, and when you naturalize you claim what belongs to another and are given the privilege under its rules.

Who can nationalize?

According to the Declaration of The Rights of a Child -1959, Principle Three of this document states, the child shall be entitled from his birth to a name and a nationality. The Universal Declarations of Human Rights – 1948 in Article 15 states that everyone has the right to a nationality, no one shall be arbitrarily deprived of his nationality nor denied the right to change his nationality. To answer this question, ANY child can nationalize.

Why is it important to nationalize?

It is important to nationalize to claim who you are. To separate yourself from the servitude and the 3/5 man / 14th amendment citizenship you have received under the labels of slave, colored, Negro, black, Afro-American, and African American.

NOTICE AND DEMAND TO LAW ENFORCEMENT:

.

[AMERICAN NATIONALS]

ARE NOT REQUIRED

.

TO SHOW IDENTIFICATION

TO A POLICE OFFICER!

.

The Police Officer swears by Oath to uphold the United States Constitution as an Officer of Law. Supreme Court Decisions are Considered the Law of the Land in Regard to Constitutionally Protected Rights, and they cannot be interpreted, or re-interpreted, as they are 'stare decisis' (already reviewed and clearly described as Law).

.

SUPREME COURT CASE:

Kolender v. Lawson (461 U.S. 352, 1983) in which the United States Supreme Court ruled that a police officer could not arrest a citizen merely for refusing to present identification.

THERE IS NO SUCH THING AS "FAILURE TO IDENTIFY"

YOU CAN SUE THE POLICE FOR AN ILLEGAL ARREST AND RESIST ARREST WITH IMPUNITY!

.

"An illegal arrest is an assault and battery. The person so attempted to be restrained of his liberty has the same right to use force in defending himself as he would in repelling any other assault and battery."

(State v. Robinson, 145 ME. 77, 72 ATL. 260).

"Each person has the right to resist an unlawful arrest. In such a case, the person attempting the arrest stands in the position of a wrongdoer and may be resisted using force, as in self- defense."

(State v. Mobley, 240 N.C. 476, 83 S.E. 2d 100).

"One may come to the aid of another being unlawfully arrested, just as he may where one is being assaulted, molested, raped or kidnapped. Thus, it is not an offense to liberate one from the unlawful custody of an officer, even though he may have submitted to such custody, without resistance."

(Adams v. State, 121 Ga. 16, 48 S.E. 910).

"These principles apply as well to an officer attempting to make an arrest, who abuses his authority and transcends the bounds thereof by the use of unnecessary force and violence, as they do to a private individual who unlawfully uses such force and violence."

Jones v. State, 26 Tex. App. I; Beaverts v. State, 4 Tex. App. 1 75; Skidmore v. State, 43 Tex. 93, 903.

One of the people

When I speak now, I try to stay within the bounds of legal language. I do such because when you talk in common parlance in a public court or in slang, they are setting up traps. When you are caught in these traps by consent or acquiesce the laches occur, and you fall deeper into the traps. If you do not know legal language or legalese, then for education purpose keeps your words to a minimum in a public court. If ask something refer them to the record. It is all on the record. If you are in court and have nothing on the record, then why are you in court? If you have nothing on the record what do expect to get?

We are not searching for ways around the system people, but we are looking for a way to make the system work, ISLAM. Folks" if you don't want to argue a point do not bring it up", so said Abraham Lincoln who happened to be an attorney. The courts do not consider anything that has not been brought up.

Are you one of the people or a citizen of the United States? According to the Constitution a citizen is one born or naturalized and subject to the jurisdiction. I am not subject to the jurisdiction; I am a National which is one of the people in a sovereign capacity. Sovereign is Authority and Authority is Sovereign. The government gets its power from the people; thus, I am being one of the people is the true source of power. If anyone causes me an injury I am entitled to redress.

Knowing thus, I am being one of the people and not a citizen am in my sovereign capacity contrary to what many of these Moorish sheiks are saying. I am one of the people and I am only a citizen for certain purposes when I choose to do so.

Are you one of the people or one of the citizens or persons? The citizens and or persons are wards of the state as one of the people the state is my ward. I am one of the people under the common law where there is a remedy for every wrong unlike the statutory law.

I do not go around calling myself sovereign because that provoke people to want to debate or argue and that is the status of a debtor. So, I therefore just say I am one of the people and not a person and they gladly accept me as one of the people. But if I say I am sovereign they want an argument, so I quail it by simply saying I am one of the people as is used in the Constitution.

Inter revenue code 7806 section 26 says that title 26 is not law. It is not law and since it is not law, I am not obligated to it.

I was filling out a form that requested a social security number and the form had a warning that if you do not tell the truth on this form then you could be fined or serve jail time. I wrote on the form exempt as per internal revenue code 7806 because 7806 says title 26 is not law, and if it is not law, I am not obligated. I ask the IRS what your authority is they said the Internal Revenue Code.

To all my Muslim brothers and sisters that is listening, to all the moors I want you to hear me clearly. The American system of law

was established based on the Bible, the ten commandments and so on and so forth We did not establish the system based on Quran, Buddhism, etc. its was established based on the bible something that you all should consider.

Hence forth one should know that contract is law and law is contract. You must be capable of doing some contracting. When you go into a public court you are usually facing a contract law expert. How will you fair if you are a novice? If according to 27 CFR 72.11 all crimes are commercial, why not know the contract I mean study some law. / Take you and a few of your friends and go into a public court and observe what occurs.

PRINT AND CARRY

PUBLIC SERVANT'S QUESTIONNAIRE

Public Law 93-579 states in part: "The purpose of this Act is to provide certain safeguards for an individual against invasion of personal privacy by requiring Federal agencies...to permit an individual to determine what records pertaining to him are collected, maintained, used, or disseminated by such agencies." The following questions are based upon that act and are necessary in order that this individual may make a reasonable determination concerning divulgence of information to this agency. Fill out the form completely. If any question does not apply, mark the answer with "N/A" or "Not applicable." Do not leave any question blank.

Public Servant Information

1.      Full Legal Name:

2.      Residence Address

City      State _____ Zip

Department Information

3.      Name of department, bureau, or agency by which public servant is employed:

City      State _____ Zip

Supervisor's name:

4.      Mailing address

City      State _____ Zip

Public Servant Duty

5.      Will public servant uphold the Constitution of the United States?


6.      Did public servant furnish proof of identity?

7.      What was the nature of proof?

8.      Will public servant furnish a copy of the law or regulation which authorizes this? Investigation?

9.      Will the public servant read aloud the portion of the law authorizing the questions he will ask?

2

Nature of Investigation

10.     Are the answers to the questions voluntary or mandatory?

11.     Are the questions to be asked based upon a specific law/regulation, or are they being used as a discovery process?

12.     What other uses may be made of this information?

13.     What other agencies may have access to this information?

14.     What will be the effect upon me if I should choose not to answer any part or all? these questions?

Basis for Investigation

15.     Name of person in government requesting that this investigation be made.

16.     Is this investigation 'general' or is it 'special'?


17.     Have you consulted, questioned, interviewed, or received information from any third party relative to this investigation?

18.     If so, the identity of such third parties:

Expected Results of Investigation

19.     Do you reasonably anticipate either a civil or criminal action to be initiated or pursued based upon any of the requested information?

Agency Information

20.     Is there a file of records, information, or correspondence relating to me being?

maintained by this agency?        If yes, which?

21.     Is this agency using any information pertaining to me which was supplied by another? agency or government source?

3

22.    May I have a copy of that information?    If not, why not?

If so, how may I obtain a copy of that information?

23.    Will the public servant guarantee that the information in these files will not be used? by any department other than the one by whom he is employed?

If not, why not?

Affirmation

If any request for information relating to me is received from any person or agency, you must advise me in writing before releasing such information. Failure to do so may subject you to possible civil or criminal action as provided by the act.

I swear (affirm) that the answers I have given to the foregoing questions are complete and correct in every.

Printed name:

Signature:

Date:    (month) (day)    (year)

First Witness Printed Name:

First Witness Signature:

Second Witness Printed Name:

Second Witness Signature:

Authorities for Questions:

1,2,3,4 In order to be sure you know exactly who you are giving the information to. Residence and

business addresses are needed in case you need to serve process in a civil or criminal action upon this.

individual.

5 All public servants have taken a sworn oath to uphold and defend the constitution.

6, 7 This is standard procedure by government agents and officers. See Internal Revenue Manual,

MT-9900-26, Section 242.133.

8,9,10 Title 5 USC 552a, paragraph (e) (3) (A)

11 Title 5 USC 552a, paragraph (d) (5), (e) (1)

12,13 Title 5 USC 552a, paragraph (e) (3) (B), (e) (3) (C)

14 Title 5 USC 552a, paragraph (e) (3) (D)

15 Public Law 93-579 (b) (1)

16 Title 5 USC 552a, paragraph (e) (3) (A) 17,18 Title 5 USC 552a, paragraph (e) (2) 19 Title 5 USC 552a,

paragraph (d) (5) 20,21 Public Law 93-579 (b) (1)

22 Title 5 USC 552a, paragraph (d) (1)

23 Title 5 USC 552a, paragraph (e) (10)

If you are using this document and was not authorized by Creditors, Debtors, Contracts in Commerce you agree to pay a fee of

$100,000 U.S. Dollars for each usage. If you email this to others without the consent of the creator, you are in violation of the copy right and agree to pay the said fee. If this is in your email by accident or otherwise, please delete from any computer immediately.

substantive rights (common law rights)

In the American system of law, People have substantive rights (common law rights) that existed before and are protected by the U.S. Constitution. Substantive rights, as such, are not taxable. You may not be taxed for the words you say, for the hands on the ends of your arms, or for the property you own.

For the government to lay a property tax, it first must be certain that the property being taxed is not owned by the possessor.

Having title to your property is not full ownership of your property. Title only proves your right of possession. To have full ownership of your property you must complete the transfer process by obtaining a land patent. Having a land patent proves your allodial ownership of the land. Allodial signifies ownership without limitation.

Once you have allodial ownership of your land, you now can possess it as a matter of common law right. Remember, common law rights may not be taxed.

The government-controlled schools no longer teach about land patents and substantive common law rights. Because so few know about it, the government is now free to define "title" as "evidence of right of possession". The true holder of the allodial title is the government. And like any owner, is entitled to rent the property to the tenants. To avoid revealing all this to the public, the rent is called a property tax.

MEMORANDUM OF LAW HISTORY, FORCE & EFFECT OF THE LAND PATENT

SECTION I

ALLODIAL v FEUDAL TITLES

The C.O.R.P.O.R.A.T.I.O.N.

(Crooked Officials Robbing People of Rights Against Truth in Our Nation) BOOK TITLE

In America today, there is a phenomenon occurring that has not been experienced since the mid-1930's. That phenomenon is the, increasingly, rising number of foreclosures, both in the rural sector and in the cities. This phenomenon is occurring because of the

inability of the debtor to pay the creditor the necessary interest and principal on a rising debt load, that is expanding across the country. As a defense, the land patent or fee simple title to the land and the Congressional intent that accompanies the patent is hereby being presented. In order to properly evaluate the patent in any given situation, it is necessary to understand.

2

what a patent is, why it was created, what existed before the patent, particularly in Common-Law England. These questions must be answered to effectively understand the association between the government, the land, and the people.

First, what existed before land patents? Since it is imperative to understand what the land patent is and why it was created, the best method is a study of the converse, or the Common-Law English land titles. This method thus allows us to fully understand what we are presently supposed to have by way-of actual ownership of land.

In England, at least until the mid-1600's, and arguably until William Blackstone's time in the mid-1700's, property was.

exclusively owned by the King.    In arbitrary governments; the

title is held by and springs from the supreme head--be he the emperor, king, potentate; or by whatever name he is known. McConnell v. Wilcox, 1 Scam (Ill.) 344, 367 (1837).

The king was the true and complete owner, giving him the authority to take and grant the land from the people in his kingdom who either lost or gained his favor. The authority to take the land may have required a justifiable reason, but such a reason could conceivably have been fabricated by the king leaving the diseased former holder of the land wondering what it was that had brought the king's wrath to bear upon him. At the same time the

3

beneficiary of such a gift, while undoubtedly knowing the circumstances behind such a gift, may still not have known how the facts were discovered and not knowing how such facts occurred, may have been left to wonder if the same fate awaited him, if ever be fell into disfavor with the king.

The King's gifts were called fiefs, a fief being the same as a feud, which is described as an estate in land held of a superior on condition of rendering him services. 2 Blackstone's Commentaries, p.105. It is also described as an inheritable right to the use and occupation of lands held on condition of rendering services to the lord or proprietor, who himself retains the ownership in the lands, Black's Law Dictionary, 4th Edition p. 748 (1968). Thus, the people had land they occupied, devised, inherited, alienated, or disposed of as they saw fit, so long as they remained in favor with the King. F.L. Gunshot, Feudalism, P. 113 (1964). at This holding of lands under another was called a tenure and was not limited to the relation of the first or paramount lord and vassal, but extended' to those to whom such vassal, within the rules of feudal law,' may have parted out his own feud to his own vassals, whereby he became the mesne lord between his vassals and his own or lord paramount. Those who held directly to the king were called his Tenants in ... chief.TM 1 E. Washburn, Treatise on The American Law of

166

Real Poverty, Ch. II, Section 58, P. 42 (6th Ed. 1902). In this manner, the lands which had been granted out to the baron's principal lands were again subdivided,

4

and granted by them to sub feudatories to be held of themselves. Id., Section 65, p.44. The size of the gift of the land could vary from a few acres to thousands of acres depending on the power and prestige of the lord. See supra Gasthof at 113. The. Fiefs were built in the same manner as a pyramid, with the King, the true owner of the land, being at the top, and from the bottom up there existed a system of small to medium sized to large sized estates on which the persons directly beneath one estate owed homage to

the lord of that estate as well as to the King. Id. at 114. At the lowest level of this pyramid through at least the 14th and 15th centuries existed to serfs or villains, the class of people that had no rights and were recognized as nothing more than real property. F. Goodwin, Treatise on The Law of Real Property, Ch. 1, p. 10 (1905). This system of hierarchical land holdings required an elaborate system of payment. These fiefs to the land might be recompenses in any number of ways.

One of the more common types 'of fiefs, or the payment of a rent or obligation to perform rural labor upon the lord's lands known as socage, was the crops fief. Id. at 8. Under this type of fief, a certain portion of the grain harvested each year would immediately be turned over to the lord above that fief even before the shares from the lower lords and then serfs of the fief would be distributed. A more interesting type of fief for purposes of this memorandum was the money fief. In most cases, the source of money was not specified, and the payment was simply made.

5

from the fief holder's treasury, but the fief might also consist of a fixed revenue to be.

paid from a definite source in annual.

payments for the tenant owner of the fief to be able to

remain on the property. Gilbert 01 Mons.Chroaique, cc.69 and

115, pp. 109, 175 (ed. Vanderkindere). The title held by such tenant—owners over their land was described as a fee simple absolute. TMFee simple, Fee coinmeth of the French fief, i.e., parading beneficiaries, and legally signified inheritance as our author himself hereafter expounded it and simple is added, for that it is descendible to his hairs generally, that is, simply, without restraint to the heirs of his body, or the like, Feod-um est quod quis tenet cx quacunqtte causa sive sit tenementum sive radius, etc. In Domesday it is called feudom.'~ Littleton, Tenures, Sec. ib, Fee Simple. In Section 11, f cc simple is described as the largest form of inheritance. Id. In modern English tenures, the term fee signifies an inheritable estate, being the highest and most extensive interest the common man or noble, other than the King, could have in the feudal system. 2 Blackstone's Commentaries, p. 106. Thus, the term fee simple absolute in Common-Law England denotes the most and best title a person could have if the King allowed him to retain possession of (own) the land. It has been commented that the basis of

English land law is the ownership of all realty by the sovereign. From the crown, all titles flow. The original and true meaning of the word "fee" and therefore fee simple absolute is the

6

same as fief or feud, this being in contradiction to the term "allodium" which means or is defined as a man's own land, which he possesses merely in his own right, without owing any rent or service to any superior. Wendell v Crandall, 1 N.Y. 4,91 (1848).

Therefore, on Common-Law England practically everybody who was allowed to retain land, bad the type of fee simple absolute often used or defined by courts, a fee simple that grants or gives the occupier as much of a title as the "sovereign" allows such occupier to have at that time. The term became a synonym with the supposed ownership of land under the feudal system of England at cox~aon law. Thus, even though the word absolute was attached to the f cc simple, it merely denoted the entire estate that could be assigned or passed to heirs, and the f cc being the operative word; f cc simple absolute dealt with the entire fief and its

divisibility, alienability, and inheritability. Friedman v Steiner, 107 Ill. 131 (1883). If a fee simple absolute in Common-Law England denoted or was synonymous with only as much 'title as the King allowed his barons to possess, then what did the King have by way of a title?

Moors, Mason, Karthala, Status and Nationality unveiling the 7th seal by Tazadaq Shah Bey

Shalom, ISLAM, Hotep, peace adepts,

It is essential that we express to you that will never get reparations as a so-called black man, colored woman, Negros or African American. You can stop asking and you will understand why at the conclusion of this lecture. I would like the ask the questions what advantage does a 33rd degree black mason have over a black thug? What advantage does an African with a PhD has over an African American that quit school in the 6th grade and sold illegal drugs and made millions like Alpo, Fat Cat, Or Nicky Barnes? What advantage does a colored man with his master's degree in or an engineer degree have over the colored man that has mastered being a hustler in the streets? The answer is that neither has an advantage over the other. They are all nation less and flag-less, they are all Negros, black, colored, or African American and are still slaves to their European counter parts. If it sounds as if this lecture will offend you then I encourage you to stop listening now. Negros, blacks, colored and African American are terms that were created to steal your birthright. This is one of the great secrets of masonry. You can study as much masonry as you want so-called Blackman if you still think you are a black man you are still mentally dead. This issues of given these name or titles to you as a people was indeed an act of European psychology that subjects you to being inferior to them. These name, Negros, blacks, colored and African American are inferior to white. White is purity, and that which is good. Black, represents, bad, evil.

Watch this. A Polish man belongs to Poland that is his nation, A German belongs to Germany, a Japanese belongs to Japan, what is the name of the Nations that a Negros, black or colored man belongs to? There is not color ride o, Or Negros geria, or Backland. You cannot say American because a Negros, blacks, and coloreds are the property of those that want you to believe that they are American when in fact those that coined these terms are not Americans themselves. This was a plot to steal your birthright. An American according to Webster's 1828 American Dictionary of the English language is defined as thus "American: n. an Aboriginal or one of the various copper-colored natives found on the American Continent by the Europeans; the original application of the name". Knowing thus brothers and sisters calling one's self Negro, black, colored African American separates you from your heritage and renders you in an inferior status. What is your status you 33rd degree black masons? Let me help you out, you are a damn slave!

Our people never used nor embrace these by words Negros, black, colored African American prior to contact with the so-called white man and I say so-called white man because you that call yourselves Negros are the real white man. What? Taz have you lost your damn mind? I challenge any of you Jakes or Ishaw or anyone to show me any contemporary source where those that have been branded Negro, black, colored, and African America ever called ourselves black prior to contract with Europeans. If this upsets you then so be it the truth need no apology; you have the option to stop listening now. My creator granted me the freedom to speak and I intend to use it for something more than a low-down rap song degrading mother earth. My question to you so-called blacks is why do you accept these terms when you have never descended from a nation called black? I surmise that my cousin Malik is listening, and I ask you Cousin Malik if you are black from which nation do you descend? What is your nation if you are a so-called black man? There is no nation called black. That renders your nation less. One can never be free being the property of another. To the Egyptologist, Kamet means black land and it pertains to the Nile region and the people of that region of Egypt however the excuse that Kamet means black Is mute because Egypt is only one of the many great empires of copper colored skin people and it was not the start of the many great empires of the copper-colored skink people. We had many great nations of people with copper colored skin but not one of them were named black.

Now I want to address you masons very briefly. Do not worry I am not going to tell your secret just expose you a little. But first and far most I would like to say to my Moorish brothers and sisters that are listening, ISLAM. Brothers and sisters, we got to talk, do not throw your shoe at your computer yet, if this cuts you a little just eat this truth like a cold cut hero or hoagie. Many moors like to fly the red flag with the 5-pointed green star in the center which is of morocco. That is not your flag. Moors do you not realize that Morocco and a Moor are not one and the same? Let us get your mind right. I am a moor. I am Israel also. Morocco never cared for you moors they sold you into slavery under a Muhammad's rule and a religion know as Islam. They refer to themselves as Arabs which derives from a word araba which means a person that move from place to place like a nomad it has nothing to do with a nation. An Arab is a nomad. These people that call themselves Muslim today has stolen the birth right and heritage of the true descendant of the Ishmaelite people who were of a dark copper skink because their father was Abraham (Ibrahim) and a dark skink Egyptian woman Hagar. If you saw here today, you would call her a nigga and he as well. Nevertheless, those that claim to be Muslim today sold you moors into slavery. These Moroccan people who are really from the Ottoman Empire that come to your land ravish the women and created what is now called Arabs or Muslims. They sold you moors into slavery in 1786.

Let me tell you a bit about, George Washington a 33rd degree mason the 9th president under the British rule and coined the 1st president of the United States under reconstruction history. And as far as you so-called black men that call yourselves masons. Stop, stop, stop, you have been deceived. You can never be a freemason; you are a damn joke and again in an inferior status. When I see you blacks calling yourselves Manson, I know you are still sleeping that is why you have only 33 degrees on knowledge. With 33 degrees you are not even upright you need at least 90 degrees to be upright, is that correct? Do the knowledge to my wisdom god. ISLAM. SHALOM. Watch this; a real mason, a western free mason must be pale skin, age 21 with a sound mind and body. That are the true criteria of being a western free mason. Thomas Jefferson was a mason; George Washington was a mason. You say Taz that is BS, okay let us prove all things.

The C.O.R.P.O.R.A.T.I.O.N.

(Crooked Officials Robbing People of Rights Against Truth in Our Nation) BOOK TITLE

The revolutionary war was essentially about a battle between two Masonic lodges over land that neither was the rightful owner. The York right order. The land is Amexem or as you say America. Now there was a wicked man by the name of Christopher Columbus that they teach you in the public fool system discovered a land that already had over 50 million people on this land, yet he discovered it. Yeah, I know brother and sisters, I know but that is the lie, but we will clear up the lies with truth.

Know I want you to listen. Masonry in the west was established for one sole purpose and that was to enslave the entire continent of what is now called Africa. Do you hear me? That is the sole purpose of masonry in the west. Now do not you miss quote me. I said western masonry. Not Masonry. The true origin of masonry comes out of the grand lodge of Lexes which is in Egypt, which taught you to master yourself. That is what true masonry is, it is the mastery of one's self. The more you master yourself and understand yourself the more you become god. Psalm 82:6. Once you embrace the mind of god it connects you with the original source. Thus, you become as god in human form. To understand what I am saying you must escape your female or many bodies because they do not have the ability to think or reason. You must break the gender line, Peace god!! I self-lord am master (ISLAM). Shalom.

To all of you so-called black mean that are calling yourselves mason in the west and you moor you are assisting in the enslavement of your own people this is what westerly masonry is all about. Let me talk to you about 3 brothers, the Jubilee brothers. Jubilee, below and jubelum. Hah ha-ha. You say how this nigga know this stuff Taz are you a mason. Now I am god! 16-5-1-3-5. Know thy self, I am the self-savior. Only you can save yourself. Ok back to the brothers. Jubilee, jubilee and jubilee, France, Britain, and the United States... jubilee hit you in the head Yahsharahla, he hit you moors, then carried you on a westerly course and buried you in a shallow grave. And therefore, you act like a bunch of damn fools, Oh I am from the house of David, I am from Israel united in Christ, I am from we got next. And if you are not in this camp you do not have the truth. I am a moor and if you are not in this temple you do not have the truth., I am a Christian I am a Muslim. You been hit in the head and you keep fighting each other and you cannot come together. Their power is in your division. Jubilee hit you in the head with a blow of death. You got some truth, but you are just.

cannot seem to get it right because you are divided and weak. Who are you? France and Britain hurt you also so, but the blow of death was from the united states, Judah you got it the worst.

After they killed you, they planted an Acadia tree over your casket and put a 5-pointed star on it in a shallow grave. George Washington dug the grave to put the coffin in it. He was the first in the west. Georgie did not trust anyone but mason. Everyone that signed the Declaration of independence were masons except for 2. Out of the 56 signer all except for two were mason you say coincidental. I say you are delusional! Because not one of them had copper colored skin not one like mine. You are in a comma state; thus, you are not responsible for what you do not know. I cannot blame you mason because you were in a comma like state when you went into these lodges. If you do not know who you and your status and nationality you are not free. How are they saving you if they hoodwink and blind folded you moor?

How can you have a nation with all this division? Over 3 million that think they are black incarcerated, over 6 million on probations or has been warned they will be locked up if they commit another offense, and almost 14 million homes headed by single parents that think she is negro, black, or colored.

A Blackman, African American, colored man has never been free. You cannot be free under their jurisdiction or if you are the property of another. The strongest Blackman is weak as hell because a black man is a slave? Did you

170

hear me? To those that are listening stand up for a second, we are going to play a little grammar school game of nationality. If you know your nation, I want you to have a seat when I state your nationality. For the sake of this lecture, we are going to label your chair as your nation. So, you will sit down on your nation. Now if You are French your chair is called France, have a seat, if you are Chinese your chair is China have a seat, if you are of any other nationality that have a nation have a seat. Where are you blacks and African Americans going to sit? There are no nation nations called black or African America? I did not say American I said African America, so you can stand up for the remainder of this lecture and I hope you wake up because you have slept far too long. You see how this name and status is essential to nationality? The people that made Negros, blacks, and colored have jurisdiction over them. DMX asked a question where my dogs at. Well, if you have a dog you can give that dog any name that you desire. You can name your dog Negro, black or colored. It is your dog. It works the same way with persons you can call your persons Negros, blacks, coloreds, or African Americans they are your dogs or slaves.

Your shallow grave is the 14th amendment you are a black slave. Now I am talking to you so-called white people also, you are black slaves. In 1865 the United Stated abolished slavery, it did not free any of you it just abolished the system of involuntary servitude, but voluntary servitude is totally legal. In 1863 Lincoln wrote the emancipation proclamations. A proclamation is that which is proclaimed, it frees no one. He tried to save the union he wrote this proclamation against his enemies not to render you blacks free. 2 years later congress wrote the 13th amendment to abolish slavery in 1865. 3 years later these western masons came together and constructed the 14th amendment enslaving so-called whites with these so-called blacks who were moors and Jakes; in 1868 under the United Sates congress. I ask you so-called black masons why did you not partake in the creation of the kuku? It damn sure came out of the Masonic lodge. The constitution read In Article 1"section 1. "All persons born or naturalized in the United States, and subject to the jurisdiction thereof, are citizens of the United States and of the state wherein they reside".

A person is a corporation, a fiction, a corporate construct, and Commercial property. When George Washington was in office owned 400 slaves that called themselves Negros, blacks or coloreds who were moors. Think about that and he was president of the United States. Does your birth certificate have your states seal on it? Does that not take you back to the 14th amendment "All persons born or naturalized in the United States, and subject to the jurisdiction thereof, are citizens of the United States and of the state wherein they reside" If you are a citizen you are property of the united states or the state in which you were born. Now you had better learn your heritage you are the mothers and fathers of civilizations. You cannot go into any University and learn the truth about you. They will not teach you the truth about you. Who are you? What is your status? What is your nationality? You can file all the damn freedom papers you want if you are listing yourself as a Negros black or colored you are still a slave. You are in a


shallow grave.

The older birth certificate stated that your parents where both Negros, but the deceivers has stated to use coded numbers, and this was started with the social security number. These codes tell you which race or nationality they are identifying you as. Because they realized that many moors were waking up therefore, they codified it. Black is a slave name it is not a nationality. You need to be in Propria persona. You must be in proper status. Do understand that these colorable courts own you if you go in as negro, black, colored, or African American according to their law the 14th Amendment. But if you are one of the indigenous people if the Moorish empire, they have absolutely no jurisdiction over you. So, if you are in Propria persona which is your proper status you always challenge the jurisdiction of the court and they have none unless you violated a part of the treaty which pertain to you which is article 6 of the constitution of the Federal republic. Once you are in your proper status and you realized that you were denationalized by way of the birth certificate then you charge the united stated with the denationalization of a people. Stay out of these de facto courts brothers and sisters challenge the jurisdiction when they offer you to come in.

Federal Directive 15 states 1. Definitions

The basic racial and ethnic categories for Federal statistics and program administrative reporting are defined as follows:

a.        American Indian or Alaskan Native. A person having origins in any of the original peoples of North America, and who maintains cultural identification through tribal affiliation or community recognition.

b.        Asian or Pacific Islander. A person having origins in any of the original peoples of the Far East, Southeast Asia, the Indian subcontinent, or the Pacific Islands. This area includes, for example, China, India, Japan, Korea, the Philippine Islands, and Samoa.

c.        Black. A person having origins in any of the black racial groups of Africa. (It is clear here that they know there are different nations that they refer to as black

d.        Hispanic. A person of Mexican, Puerto Rican, Cuban, Central or South American or other Spanish culture or origin, regardless of race.

e.        White. A person having origins in any of the original peoples of Europe, North Africa, or the Middle East. (How many so-called whites have an origin in north Africa that you know? Do you see the deception here?

This has nothing to do with skin tone it has do with a social political construct class and status. White is the highest class and black is the lowest class of people. There is no such thing as a white people are a black people these are social status. You need to get up out of these graves. This has nothing whatever so ever to do with skink tone. You consent to being black by way or a son, a birth certificate and 1040, a passport. Do you understand? Do you understand? Color in law means false. Did you know that? Let us show and prove god.

What is COLOR? What is COLOR? definition of COLOR (Black's Law Dictionary) "An appearance, semblance, or simulacrum, as distinguished from that which Is real. A prima facie or apparent right. Hence, a deceptive appearance; a plausible, assumed exterior, concealing a lack of reality; a disguise or pretext. Railroad Co. v. All free, 64 Iowa, 500, 20 N. W. 779; Berks Count v. Railroad Co., 107 Pa. 102, 31 Atl. 474; Broughton v. Haywood, 01 N. C. 383".

To all of you that called black that claim yourselves Israelites but are not in your proper status you are still a slave as well. I do not care how much bible you teach if you got a driver's license, a birth certificate, a 1040 tax form I do not care how much you think you are an Israelite if you have not changed your status on public record you are still a slave on the record and you will find it out once you go into one of these colorable court.


Oh, you can hate me but I am telling you the truth. So can call yourselves Yahsharahla, we got next, GMS, Israel united if you have not changed your status that is just a claim but, on the record, they still have you as a slave and this goes for you in the nation of Gods and earth also if you call your self-Born god and you still have referred to as Clarence on public record you are powerless. Let me see these a black man will never get reparations. Because you are property.

What is wrong are you mad? 1779 you were legally brand as Negros black and colored. So, you can stand on the corner and talk about Esau all day what it has changed for your people. Of you call him Esau now what? What has it done for your people? You still in the ghetto, you still the first fired and last hired. You still getting arrested You see until you change this status until you claim your nationality your preaching is no threat to them because you can call yourselves Israelites all day long until you change your status on the record and before for the world you are still a slave. You got people like brother Farrakhan, Jessie Jackson and other so-called black leaders that think they can get reparations but in a legal sense you can only get reparations as a nation not as individuals and black Is not a nation. When the United Stated paid reparations to the Seminole they had to get rid of those that wanted to call themselves black prior to getting reparations because black is not a nation. I know I know you guys are mad. You say Taz this goes against everything I was taught I know it hurts. Fulfilling the scriptures again. Psalms 83: 4 "They have said, Come, and let us cut them off from being a nation; that the name of Israel may be no more in remembrance." "Web's fee all" "lord web's free" They say praise god and it an image of Cesar Borgia in their heads and on their walls. You are not black, Negros or colored or African American they are social political constructs. Not even Africans that those from Senegal, or Ethiopia called themselves African American.

Affidavit vs. Motions

We deem it of essential importance to comprehend that you must title everything you submit in writing with "Affidavit of Fact", because the sewer (system) can, and often do deny a "Motion", as motions are discretionary and applicable to their colorable courts, ordinances, statutes, and codes, that you assume is law but are often not LAW. Might I note that it applies to corporate fiction, corporation, 14 amendment Citizens, or colorable persons such as negroes, coloreds, and blacks, African American, Afro American, Jamaicans, and Hispanics etc.) because it is a discretionary action that can be and is often denied!

.

Fact: A motion requires a second and can be denied without even being looked at, as these inferior courts often do. An Affidavit of fact cannot lawfully be denied, and must be visited and either answered or rebutted, otherwise it stands as Truth, or, if it requires an answer by the court, it creates an injunction, and the court cannot lawfully move forward until answered. If not answered the matter must be dismissed due to lack of due process of law, lack of prosecution. Knowing thus Affidavit" MUST BE THE ONLY FORM OF COMMUNICATION with the Court by a Sovereign or any people acting in a Lawful manner.

The Corporation

What is a corporation? From Encyclopedia Britannica 2000, corporations as Legal Fictions

What is legal fiction? A rule assuming as true something that is clearly false. An example is Negro, Black, Colored, African American, Afro American, Jamaican, etc.

A fiction is often used to get around the provisions of constitutions and legal codes that legislators are hesitant to change or encumber with specific limitations.

In ancient Rome, where every family needed a male heir the lack of one was overcome through the legal fiction of adoption. In England, when courts handling civil cases were full the court of Queen's (or King's) Bench, a criminal court, could take some of the load by pretending that the defendant in a simple civil suit had been arrested and was in custody.

Almost any legal fiction can be stated in terms of fact. Thus, the fiction that a corporation is, for many purposes, a person separate.

from its members is equivalent to saying that, for those purposes, the law deals with the group as a unit, disregarding for the moment the group's individual members as such.

Again, when we make an affidavit it is sworn to be true before Yah (God), and when any information is contained on the affidavit, such as laws, addresses, assumptions, or anything else not possible to verify by the writer, it nullifies the affidavit, for this reason we keep the affidavit simple and to the point, leaving nothing to chance.

What is the modern name for Amexem? Africa.

The word Moor comes from the Latin word Manures and the Greek adjective Mauro's, meaning dark or black (denoting skin color) Circa 46BC. See: The Oxford English Dictionary (New York, Oxford University Press, 1977, p. `846.)

The status of the descendants of the Moorish Inhabitants of Spain and Portugal on American soil is FREE WHITE PERSONS (natural men and women those that think they are black are white I suggest you define white). This status does not apply to the Caucasian.

Race, Aryan Race, or Indo-European Races under the Naturalization Act (Amended by Act. July 14, 1879), I Stat.103, c.3    See:

Black's Law Dictionary (Fourth Ed. P. 797)

Circa 1676 A.D., The Europeans that arrived in New England (North America) described the Aboriginal-Americans (Moors) to be BLACK AS GYPSIES

(E-GYPTIANS).

Circa 1775 A.D., The first President of the United States of America under the Articles of Confederation was John Hanson, alleged Black-A-Moor, a Maryland Shawnee Native American patriot who fought in the American Revolution. See: Nuragic Moors News¬paper, August 7, 1991.

.

A Moorish-Mason by the name of Ben Bey Emmanuel Mu Ali a/k/a Benjamin Banneker, was the architect who designed the streets of Washington, D.C., with Masonic codes and astrological glyphs. See: Americas Oldest Secret the Talisman, U.S. Mysterious Street Lines of Washington, D.C. by the Signature of the Invisible Brotherhood. The autobiography of Benjamin Banneker.

Circa 1789 A.D., On December 1, 1789. The Ninth President of the United States George Washington apologizes to his Masonic Brother Emperor Mohammed III, for not sending the regular advices (tribute: a payment by one ruler or nation to another as acknowledgement of submission or price of protection, excessive tax). Also,

President Washington asked the Emperor to recognize their newly formed government. The Moroccan Empire (Moors) were the first nation to recognize the thirteen colonies as a sovereign nation. Allegedly the Emperor agreed to their recognition because 25 Moors were members of the first Continental Congress. See: The Writing of George Washington from the Original Manuscript Source 1745—1799, Editor John C. Fitzpatrick, Volume 30, pages 474—476.

Circa 1933 A.D., The city of Philadelphia, Pennsylvania, recognize the Moors domiciling in America and their Moorish Titles: El, Bey, Ali, AL, Dey, etc.

See: House Resolution No. 75 Legislative Journal (Philadelphia) May 4, 1973, page 5759.


I wanted to elaborate on what I taught on YouTube:


"Unilateral rescission on the basis of mistaken identity, duress, coercion, fraud, threat of loss to real time property, or under threat of enslavement ... etc."

-state of California civil code 1689.B.1

- any time the government presents your strawman (person) with an offer it is all voluntary. you have the right to accept it or not, and most of the time unless you have already passed into "silent acquiescence" ::: (after ten days you go from an "offender" to "the defendant," you have "acquiesced") the offer will be still be to your name in all caps; "the strawman," and that by definition is not you... so in California you can use that civil code to rescind the offer.. because it is "mistaken identity, duress, coercion, fraud," etc. any time a L.E.O. gives you a ticket they always give it to your "strawman" and force the "living blood" to accept his debt at gunpoint so it is all of the above. you can also use the "uniform commercial code;" because all crimes are commercial (Title 27 section 72.11) and as such subject to the U.C.C. (U.C.C. 1-103, which clearly states that the purpose of the codes is to make uniform the codes, laws, and customs among the varying "jurisdictions".) after ten days it goes to your "proper person" and so when you appear in court you are there as the name in upper and lower case because you failed to handle it through the "administrative remedy process" or "rescission" within the first ten days. you are there voluntarily because you did not go to the clerk and correct the court as I always do.

to rescind tickets, presentments, offers, etc. (within ten days of receipt)

(if you go after ten days lose the U.C.C. 2-209 reference, it is only good while as an "offender.") (the California code only works in California also)

***(red for the blood of the man, black ink for the body (used on the outside of documents that you rescind without opening., because you can also act as the Sovereign "Patron" of the United states Postal Office established 1781 to 1972 and rescind everything before you ever accept or open it that way as well.) (works good for junk mail) ***

I write the following at a forty-five-degree angle in red ink:

"No Contract- Return to Sender."

The C.O.R.P.O.R.A.T.I.O.N.

(Crooked Officials Robbing People of Rights Against Truth in Our Nation) BOOK TITLE

"Offer signed 'under-duress,' 'coercion,' 'fraud,' 'mistaken identity,' and 'threat of loss to real time property.'" "I do hereby rescind this, and all offers made present."

"California State Civil Code 1689.B.1" (outside of Ca it would be different, a corresponding civil code would need to be found, but still works without this code at all.)

"U.C.C. 2-209" (only good if used within ten days)

"All Rights Reserved"

"Without Prejudice"

"U.C.C. 1-103"

"U.C.C. 1-308"

If you want to rescind (remove all liability) you need to find out who is trying to force contract? Go to that office and read the following.


And remember sometimes it is best to play dumb. so, act like the lamb.

For speeding tickets, court summons, civil summons... etc. go to the clerk of that clerk. bring a witness too.

Go there and ask her if he/she is the clerk of the court. Ask them what their name is.

Make a show of writing it down, note the date and time and any other incidental employees/ witnesses.

Once you have written it down inform them you have something for the court.

they will ask you what you have?

so then hand them the rescinded ticket/offer all marked up in red ink, once they take it...

you read them the following:

"Sir/Ma'am I am simply here to correct a mistake made by this court. I am the "non-title-14," the "non - domestic," the "living flesh and the blood". and I do hereby rescind this, and all offers made present under the laws of the uniform commercial code 2-209, and the state of California civil code 1689.B.1. thank you and god bless."

once you have done that, walk out. your liability is over, do not hang around waiting for an audience. you have just won and sticking around can only result in them attempting to force another contract on you... and most importantly if you are doing this for somebody else, you are simply a "counselor," not a "representative" or an "attorney," simply a "councilor," to really once you drop the documents and read your speech, you should walk fast out of the court after that.

Just remember, be calm and cool, at times you will run into clerks or other personnel who will try to call the bailiffs on you, try to force you to stop and wait for a super, etc... if they stop you, do not let them, keep reading your speech, finish and WALK OUT.

176

and just remember unless you are causing a 'disturbance' you do not have to give a name TO ANYONE even when pushed. I have LEO's all the time that try to force me into contract by talking to them, most of the time I walk away. because even though they sound real intimidating most of the time, they are just asking you a question. WILL YOU PLEASE GIVE ME A NAME? ETC.

HAHA, I was asked one time by a cop if I could: "PLEASE STOP AND TALK TO HIM?" He yelled, so I yelled back "NO! you may not," and kept walking.


He was angry but it worked.

if forced to stop by a cop or bailiff while leaving simply and calmly state you are a common law American or (whatever your nationality may be. "I am a Citizen of the Republic." etc.) and that you wish to go free. the kings wish is enough to enact law... if pressed further say that you "require council present and remain silent."

I wanted this knowledge to get out there because without the government system of fear and intimidation we can change things overnight. this works on taxes too by the way. ANYTHING. I have rescinded everything from civil summons to criminal complaints to the yearly taxes for my manor (the rural farm I own), it works. you can also "accept the deed" and be off the tax rolls completely, as some of us out here have.

By the way.

Under the federal motor carrier's safety act title 383.5 a motor vehicle type class c is defined as 16 or more passengers, a "Non-CMV" is the correct word under the definitions section. under the state of California vehicle code 15210(m) a "non-Commercial Motor Vehicle." I keep a printout of the federal law and corresponding state law as well as keeping a current "foreign agents' statement of registry" document (they have to fill that out prior to all questioning per the 1938 act)

with those documents in hand, as well as knowledge of rescission, I have never had a license plate on my brand-new dodge ram diesel. and I do not get pulled over anymore.

**any knowledge you can pass my way in the way of unlocking the T.D.A. bond would be greatly appreciated. I look forward to hearing what you think of my remedies. We have a group of several hundred across 3 or 4 counties. **

One final thing, if after learning all of this the goobers still insist on coming after you, you should go to the office of Risk Manage-mint in your county and get a "claim for damages form:" a "tort claim form." this process is fantastic, it actually is a claim form made directly against the bond of the agent who harmed you NO matter WHO they are. I recently filed a claim on several directors and a few sheriff's deputies for ten million dollars, it did not go through, but got me a little bit of a name, and the important thing is that an investigation is automatically held and put before the highest officials in the county for a direct vote (all within 45 days in California). So, no more waiting years and years for common law claims that will never go through and payments in bonds you can never cash. the best way is to find direct remedy, no matter what the process, god bless and thank you for speaking with me.


AFFIDAVIT RELIGIOUS EXEMPTION FOR ALL IMMUNIZATIONS

Section 23-7.5 of the Code of Virginia states. Any student shall be exempt from the immunization requirement who objects on the grounds that administration of immunizing agent's conflicts with his/her religious tenets or practice unless an emergency or epidemic of disease has been declared by the Board of Health. Such students must submit a Certification of Religious Exemption (form CRE-1), which may be obtained by contacting the CNU Office of the Registrar.

I/We,   , and   , Free, Natural Flesh and Blood Human Being(s), state Citizen

(s) of the Virginia Republic affirm: Be it known to all courts, governments, and other parties that:

Being a person of Strong Jewish Morals, it is against my/our Deep, Sincerely Held, Religious Convictions to accept the injection of any foreign substance into my Body or the Body of my son(s). This includes, but is not limited to, all, Vaccinations, Shots, Tests for Diseases, Oral Vaccines, Epidermal Patches and in any other way that Live or Killed Bacterium, Viruses, Pathogens, Germs, or any other Microorganisms, may be introduced into or upon my newborn's body.

This written statement to exempt my/our sons from any immunizations, screening, and the Vitamin K shot, because I hold genuine and sincere personal religious beliefs which are inconsistent with these medical procedures & experimentation. The practice of vaccination and the injection or application of any foreign substance is contrary to my conscientiously held religious beliefs and practices and violates the free exercise of my religious principles.

The Hepatitis-B vaccine supposedly protects against a disease that is only transmitted through multiple sexual partners or street IV drug users and therefore usurps my parental authority to condemn such activity in my sons. The acceptance of this vaccine promotes sexual promiscuity and immoral behavior in direct contradiction to the teachings of our faith.

The prescribing information on Vitamin K shot states that fatalities are an adverse reaction according to the Merck pharmaceutical package insert.

http://vaclib.org/chapter/inserts.htm#vitK

"WARNING - INTRAVENOUS USE Severe reactions, including fatalities, have occurred during and immediately after the parenteral administration of AquaMEPHYTON® (Phytonadione)."

A conflict arises because my religious convictions are predicated on the belief that all life is sacred. Yah's (God's) commandment "Thou Shall Not Kill" applies to the practice of injection of carcinogenic substances that can kill.

I John Henry Doe, as the parent (s) /guardian(s)} of Yos Doe and Kim Doe are exercising my rights reserved under the First Amendment of the US Constitution, VA. Code § 32.1-65, § 32.1-64.1. H, and VA. Code Section 23-7.5 to receive Religious Exemption from Vaccination, ALL injections, & testing.

Applicable law has been interpreted to mean that a religious belief is subject to protection even though no religious group espouses such beliefs or the fact that the religious group to which the individual professes to belong may not advocate or require such belief. Title VII of the Civil Rights Act of 1964 as amended Nov. 1, 1980; Part 1605.1-Guidelines on Discrimination Because of Religion.

The Lord YHWH Our Creator are the only source of protection of my body and that of my family that I can accept.

I affirm that vaccination & injections of any foreign substances and proteins conflict with my religious beliefs as stated above. Therefore, I would request that you accommodate my religious beliefs and practices by exempting my child from any vaccinations, injections and testing of any kind.

Rest assured that my family and I do practice a form of immunization that keeps our immune systems strong and is in keeping with Biblical principles.

Further Affiant Saith Not

The use of notary below is for identification only, and such use does NOT grant any jurisdiction to anyone.

Subscribed and sworn, without prejudice, and with all rights reserved, (Print Name Below)

Principal, by Special Appearance, in Propria Persona, proceeding Sui Juris.

Signature of Affiant

ACKNOWLEDGMENT

state of Virginia

county of         :

On this _____ day of , 20__, before me


        personally appeared, to me known to be the person described in and who executed the fore-

going instrument and acknowledged that he executed the same as his free act and deed, for the purposes therein set forth.


(Notary Public)


My Commission Expires , 20____


Affidavit of Fact

Notice of Special Appearance

For the Record, To Be Read into The Record as Evidence

Notice to the Agent is Notice to the Principal- Notice to the Principal is notice to the Agent.

To:

U.S. District Court

For the District of Ohio

Clerk of Court

70 North Union Street

Second Floor

Delaware Territory, Ohio Republic

[43015] United States of America Republic, North America

Petitioner:

Yan Precious Hen Authorized Agent

Aggrieved Woman, In Propria Persona:

All Rights Reserved Without Prejudice: U.C.C. 1-207/1-308; U.C.C. 1-103

c/o 26151 Lakeshore Boulevard Apartment 2117

Euclid, Ohio [44132] Northwest Amexem

Case Number 16TRD00495-A SEATBELT REQUIRED DRIVER

Yan Precious Hen, an aggrieved woman appearing specially not generally, challenging subject matter jurisdiction of The Delaware Municipal Court in response to an improper hearing illegally scheduled at 8:30am on the 20th day of January 2018.

This is a formal request for a certified copy of the "Certified Delegation of Authority Order" issued to The United States District Court for the District of Connecticut and confirmed by Congress.

The 5th Amendment required that all persons within the United States must be given due process of the law and equal protection of the law.

"The Constitution for the United States of America binds all judicial officers at Article 6, wherein it does say, "This Constitution and

the Laws of the United States which shall be made in pursuance thereof, and all Treaties made, or which shall be made under the authority of the United States, shall be the Supreme Law of the Land, and the Judges of every State shall be bound thereby, anything in the Constitution or laws of any state to the Contrary, not withstanding," see Clause 2."

"United States Constitution, Article III, Section II - The judicial power shall extend to all cases, in law and equity, arising under this Constitution, the laws of the United States, and treaties made, or which shall be made, under their authority;--to all cases affecting ambassadors, other public ministers and con-suls;--to all cases of admiralty and maritime jurisdiction;--to controversies to which the United States shall be a party;--to controversies between two or more states;--between a state and citizens of another state;--between citizens of different states;--between citizens of the same state claiming lands under grants of different states, and between a state, or the citizens thereof, and foreign states, citizens or subjects. In all cases affecting ambassadors, other public ministers, and consuls, and those in which a state shall be party, the Supreme Court shall have original jurisdiction. In all the other cases before mentioned, the Supreme Court shall have appellate jurisdiction, both as to law and fact, with such exceptions, and under such regulations as the Congress shall make. The trial of all crimes, except in cases of impeachment, shall be by jury; and such trial shall be held in the state where the said crimes shall have been committed; but when not committed within any state, the trial shall be at such place or places as the Congress may by law have directed.

"The law provides that once State and Federal Jurisdiction has been challenged, it must be proven." Main v. Thiboutot, 100 S. Ct. 2502 (1980)

"Jurisdiction can be challenged at any time." and "Jurisdiction, once challenged, cannot be assumed and must be decided." Basso v. Utah Power & Light Co. 495 F 2d 906, 910.

"Once challenged, jurisdiction cannot be assumed, it must be proved to exist." Stuck v. Medical Examiners 94 Ca 2d 751. 211 P2d 389.

"There is no discretion to ignore that lack of jurisdiction." Joyce v. US, 474 F2d 215.

"The burden shifts to the court to prove jurisdiction." Rosemond v. Lambert, 469 F2d 416.

Where the court is without jurisdiction, it has no authority to do anything other than to dismiss the case." Fontenot v. State, 932 S.W.2d 185 "Judicial action without jurisdiction is void."-Id (1996)

"Criminal law magistrates have no power of their own and are unable to enforce any ruling." V.T.C.A., Government Code sec. 54.651 et seq., Davis v. State, 956 S.W.2d 555 (1997)

Basso v. UPL, 495 F. 2d 906

Under federal Law, which is applicable to all states, the U.S. Supreme Court stated that "if a court is without authority, its judgments and orders are regarded as nullities. They are not voidable, but simply void, and form no bar to a recovery sought, even prior to a reversal in opposition to them. They constitute no justification and all persons concerned in executing such judgments or sentences are considered, in law, as trespassers."

Brook v. Yawkey, 200 F. 2d 633

Elliot v. Piersol, 1 Pet. 328, 340, 26 U.S. 328, 340 (1828)

I, Yaniesha Precious Handing, do not, under any conditions or circumstances, nor by threat, duress, or coercion, waive any Unalienable Rights or any other Rights Secured by the Constitution or Treaty; and hereby request that the Officers of this Court fulfill their Obligations to preserve the rights of this Petitioner (A Moorish American) and to carry out their delegated Judicial Duties with good behavior, and in 'Good Faith'. Agreeable to Article III, Section II of the United States Constitution Judicial Authority is legal in the Supreme Court or a lower court that has a "Certified Delegation of Authority Order" "Proof of Jurisdiction" confirmed by Congress as a lawful and formal Discovery.

Let it be noted for the record, on the record and let the record show a response is required immediately from receipt of this letter. If no copy of the Certified Delegation of Authority Order is received this Affidavit of Fact - Writ of Discovery shall stand as Law affirming that this court does not have Jurisdiction as per Article III, Section II of the United States Constitution.

"Once Challenged, jurisdiction cannot be assumed, it must be proved to exist." Stcuk v Medical Examiners 94 Ca 2d 751.211, P2d 389.

All UNCONSTITUTIONAL Citations – Summons / Ticket – Suits / (misrepresented) Bills of Exchange: Docket Number - SCC   ,

and any other 'Orders' or 'Actions' associated with it or them, to be 'Dismissed', 'Abated' and expunged from the Record; being null on it is face and merits.

Notice to the Agent is Notice to the Principal – Notice to the Principal is notice to the Agent.

Thank You,

I am:

Yan Precious Hen Authorized Representative

Natural Person, In Propria Persona:

All Rights Reserved: U.C.C. 1-207/ 1-308; U.C.C. 1-103

c/o 26151 Lakeshore Boulevard Apartment 2117

Euclid, Ohio [ near 44132] Northwest Amexem]

Non-Domestic

Thank you,

I am:

Yan Precious Hen Authorized Agent

Natural Person, In Propria Persona:

All Rights Reserved Without Prejudice: U.C.C. 1-207/1-308; U.C.C. 1-103

[c/o 26151 Lakeshore Boulevard Apartment 2117

Euclid, Ohio [44132] Northwest Amexem


IN THE CIRCUIT COURT FOR PRINCE GEORGE'S COUNTY, MARYLAND

Plaintiff, ASHLEY R. LAWRENCE

-against-Defendant

(Crooked Officials Robbing People of Rights Against Truth in Our Nation) BOOK TITLE

STEPHEN JONATHAN Washington

CASE # CASR15-38643

ANSWER AND COUNTER-CLAIM

STEPHEN JONATHAN WASHINGTON aggrieved man, answers the complaint of ASHLEY R. LAWRENCE, Plaintiff responding to each numbered paragraph thereof and counterclaiming as follows:

1.      DENIED, STEPHEN JONATHAN WASHINGTON WAS PRESENT BUT NOT ALLOWED TO ENTER COURT ON FEBURARY 23, 2016 AT 1 P.M.

2.      DENIED

3.      Denied,

4.      Denied,

5.      DENIED.

6.      Unaware.

7.      DENIED

8.      DENIED


COUNTER-CLAIM

9.      I conditionally accept your offer upon proof of claim that On or about      FEBURARU 23, 2016, STEPHEN JONATHAN WASHING-

TON Was advised that he could not re-enter the court at 1 P.M. Any man claiming that STEPHEN JONATHAN WASHINGTON was not present at 1 P.M. must claim such under oath or affirmation.

10.     And upon conditions that you prove that the STEPHEN JONATHAN WASHINGTON was not denied due process of law by not allowing him to reenter the court. Virginia.

11.     I conditionally accept your offer upon the condition that you prove that this court does not lack Subject Matter Jurisdiction as the STEPHEN JONATHAN WASHINGTON appeared specially not generally to challenge subject matter jurisdiction. "Once jurisdiction is challenged, the court cannot proceed when it clearly appears that the court lacks jurisdiction, the court has no authority to reach merits, but, rather, should dismiss the action." Melo v. US, 505 F2d 1026.

A judgment rendered by a court without personal jurisdiction over the defendant is void. It is a nullity. [A judgment shown to be void for lack of personal service on the defendant is a nullity.] Samke v. Sramek, 17 Kan. App. 2d 573, 576-77, 840 P.2d 553 (1992), rev. denied 252 Kan. 1093 (1993).

"Court must prove on the record, all jurisdiction facts related to the jurisdiction asserted." Latana v. Hopper, 102 F. 2d 188; Chicago v. New York, 37 F Supp. 150.

183

"The law provides that once State and Federal Jurisdiction has been challenged, it must be proven." Main v. Thiboutot, 100 S. Ct. 2502 (1980).

"Jurisdiction can be challenged at any time." and "Jurisdiction, once challenged, cannot be assumed and must be decided." Basso v. Utah Power & Light Co., 495 F 2d 906, 910.

"Defense of lack of jurisdiction over the subject matter may be raised at any time, even on appeal." Hill Top Developers v. Holiday Pines Service Corp., 478 So. 2d. 368 (Fla 2nd DCA 1985)

12.      I believe to claim STEPHEN JONATHAN WASHINGTON was not present, at 1 P. M. on February 23, 2016 leads me to believe that you may be guilty of fraud.

13.      I require that the case be dismissed because the Plaintiff was present.

14.      STEPHEN JONATHAN WASHINGTON has a right to question the accuser such care is owed to defendant.

15.      Plaintiff negligence in failure to appear is breach of that duty; Plaintiff's negligent conduct resulted in Defendant's loss of rights to question the accuser.

14. Defendant suffered substantial and was denied due process of law and moves the court to dismiss the matter without prejudice.

WHEREFORE ROSEMARY LEBRON, Defendant demands judgment for money damages, with interest from March 12, 2009, together with the cost of this action against NEW YORK HOUSING AUTHORITY, Plaintiff, together with such other and further relief as the Court may deem reasonable and just under the circumstances.

RESPECTFULLY SUBMITTED this 1st March 2016.

STEPHEN JONATHAN WASHINGTON, Defendant


PLAINTIFF ADDRESS:

THIS IS NOT A PUBLIC COMMUNICATION

Notice to Agent is Notice to Principal Notice to Principal is Notice to Agent

Silence is Acquiescence, Agreement, and Dishonor This is a self-executing contract.

Collin county

Texas state

United States of America 1787 AD

NOTICE OF INTERNATIONAL COMMERCIAL CLAIM WITHIN THE ADMIRALTY ab initio ADMINISTRATIVE REMEDY

[28 U.S.C. §1333, §1337, §2461 and §2463]

Certified Mail

Date: 12/10/16

FIRST NOTICE OF DEFAULT

LIBELLANT:

John, ope Trustee, Executive Trustee for the Private Contract Trust known as OPE JOHN

C/O    Notary Witness

Notary Address:

Notary City, State, Zip

LIBELLEE:

HOPE JOHNSON

2355 LEBANON ROAD # 12207

FRISCO, TX 12232

This demand for dismissal is applicable to all successors and assigns.

Libellant is entitled to performance and stipulated damages agreed to by Libellees failure to respond or rebut the DEMAND FOR DISIISSAL FOR LACK OF JURISDICTION AND DENIAL FOR DUE PROCESS OF LAW ab initio ADMINISTRATIVE REMEDY File CERTIFIED

MAIL #       dated    OF CLAIM, hereinafter "ICC".

Additionally, Libellees have failed to respond to the NOTICES OF DEMAND FOR LACK OF SUBJECT MATTER JURISDICTION AND DENI-

AL DUE PROCESS OF LAW THAT WERE DELIVERED BY NOTARY PRESENTMENT dated       OF FIRST NOTICE OF FAULT.

As per Libellees agreement to Silence is Acquiescence amounting to dismissal as you are in dishonor allotted time granted in the said Notice and Demand for Lack of Jurisdiction, as the terms and conditions did clearly manifest, this document is a demand for dismal of the agreed.

Silence is Acquiescence. DEMAND FOR DISMISSAL

Libellant grants Libellee Three (7) days, exclusive of the date of receipt, to answer by certified mail of the claims contained in this document. Failure to settle is a commercial dishonor [UCC3-505]. This is a UCC

CONFIRMATORY WRITING and STATUTE STAPLE and is a perfected Contract upon the completion of this commercial process.

It is mandatory that if Libellee elects to respond to the foregoing, any such response must be done by oath SWEAR UNDER PENAL-TY OF PERJURY THAT THE

INFORMATION CONTAINED IN YOUR DOCUMENTS IS TRUE AND

CORRECT as stated in Libellant's ICC mailing location exactly as shown below:

Johnson, Hope Trustee, Executive Trustee for the Private Contract Trust known as HOPE JOHNSON

C/o     Notary Witness

Notary Address:

Notary City, State, Zip


CONTRACTUAL NOTICE OF DESMISSAL

Libellant is moving for dismissal [U.C.C. 3-501 and U.C.C. Article 9] causing this NOTICE OF DEMAND AND SETTLEMENT service upon the Libellee by certified mail. This is a commercial process within the Admiralty.

Libellee is granted Three (7) days [Truth in Lending Act at Regulation Z at 12 CFR and portions of 15 USC], exclusive of the day of service to respond as stated above and as evidenced in Libellant's Demand for Dismissal.

COMMERCIAL AFFIDAVIT OATH AND VERIFICATION

Collin county     )

) ss     Commercial Oath and Verification

Texas state     )

I, Johnson, Hope Trustee, Executive Trustee for HOPE JOHNSON, under my unlimited liability and Commercial Oath, proceeding in good faith, being of sound mind, having first-hand knowledge, state that the facts contained herein are true, correct, complete and not misleading, under penalty of International Commercial Law. EXPRESS SPECIFIC RESERVATION OF RIGHTS:

I explicitly reserve all my Natural rights as an American under contract Law of the Divine Creator without prejudice and, without recourse to me. I do not consent to compelled performance under any contract that I did not enter knowingly, voluntarily, and intentionally. I do not accept the liability of the benefits or privileges of any unrevealed contract or commercial agreement. By:

By: John, ope Trustee, Executive Trustee for the Private Contract Trust known as OPE JOHNSON


JURAT

Texas state     )

The C.O.R.P.O.R.A.T.I.O.N.

(Crooked Officials Robbing People of Rights Against Truth in Our Nation) BOOK TITLE

) ss

Collin county    )

The above-named Libellant, Johnson, Hope Trustee, Executive Trustee for OPE JOHN appeared before me, a Notary, subscribed, sworn to the truth of this contractual NOTICE OF DEMAND FOR PAYMENT AND SETTLEMENT for closing of the escrow.

under oath this   day of   , 2016.

Notary  SEAL

My Commission expires


Tazadaq Shah

c/o 3319 My Domicile

New York, New York [nondomestic 12345]

Attornatus Privatus

United States District Court Southern District of New York

Filed:    Clerk or Deputy Clerk:

ORDER TO CLERK OF COURT TO PERFORM SPECIFIC DUTIES


Comes now the above-entitled court and orders as follows, DISCUSSION AND CONCLUSION OF LAW

1.       The Clerk of the Court or Clerk at this office is a ministerial position not having authority of a tribunal. As such it is required to carry out its duties without acting as a tribunal, but by merely performing the duties authorized by the court. One of those is a duty owed to the plaintiff to file documents presented for the record. Failing to file a document for the record is a criminal offense.

2.       A document is considered filed once it is received.

3.       The clerk of the court, like a recorder, is required to accept documents filed.

4.       The Federal Rules of Civil Procedure was the agreed format for the court proceedings.

5.       A paper is filed upon delivering it (A) to the clerk. FPRC 5(d)(2)

6.       The job of the clerk of the court "is to file pleadings and other documents, maintain the court's files and inform litigants of the entry of court orders." Sanders v. Department of Corrections, 815 F. Supp. 1148, H49(N.D. Ill. 1993). (Williams v. Pucinski, 01C5588 (N.D.Ill. 01/13/2004).)

7.       The duty of the clerk is to make his record correctly represent the proceedings in the case. Wetmore v. Karrick, 27 S. Ct. 434, 205 U.S. 141 (U.S. 03/11/1907 Failing to file documents presented and reflect the documents on the docket is a failure to perform the ministerial duties of the Clerk of Court.

187

8.     It is hereby the order of this court of record that the Clerk of the Court for the United States District Court Southern District of New York fulfill its obligations under the authority of law and file any documents presented for said purpose.

WITNESS: The SEAL of the COURT this _____ day of , 2018.

THE COURT

Tazadaq Shah

Attornatus Privatus

Tazadaq Legal Brief that he used when Charged with Driving Without a License

The following is Tazadaq Trial Brief used in a Traffic trial case while he was traveling. When the black robe saw what was being discussed in the brief, he had to dismiss the case because he did not want the content to be revealed in the courtroom and that is that the UNITED STATES OF AMERICA (in all caps) is originally incorporated in France so it could never be researched.

Remember, that the Statute of Liberty was given to The United States by 33-degree Masons from France. Have you ever wondered Why?

The application of Knowledge is power when you know how to use it.

Thank you for listening to my brief, please share as it is very educational. Pass it on.


On Thu, May 8, 2015 at 12:50 PM, Tazadaq Shah

I believe I told you that I had received a traffic ticket which I intended to contest. I was required to file a case brief. I did so. When I came home one day a note from the court was on my door ordering me to appear When I came into the court,

the black robe fin-


ished the case, which was before him at the time, and then immediately after called me forward. He said, "I cannot allow your case to be heard in my court. Case dismissed with Prejudice." My brief appears below:

TRIAL BRIEF

IN THE WEST DISTRICT C0URT F0R KLICKITAT C0UNTY IN AND F0R THE STATE 0F WASHINGT0N

STATE 0F WASHINGT0N

Plaintiff< /span>

Vs.

TAZADAQ SHAH Respondent

The C.O.R.P.O.R.A.T.I.O.N.

(Crooked Officials Robbing People of Rights Against Truth in Our Nation) BOOK TITLE

Represented by Tazadaq Shah, Trustee

Respondent claims and alleges that he is innocent of the charge of driving without a license, third degree for the following reasons:

1.       Respondent       agrees that he was not in possession of a valid

State of Washington Driver's License, as the law requires (

RCW 46.20.001

License required — Rights and restriction.

(1)       No person may drive a motor vehicle upon a highway in this state without first obtaining a valid driver's license issued to Washington residents under this chapter. The only exceptions to this requirement are.

those expressly allowed by RCW 46.20.025.

(2)       A person licensed as a driver under this chapter:

May exercise the privilege get upon all highways in this state.

May not be required by a political subdivision to obtain any other license to exercise the privilege; and May not have more than one valid driver's license at any time.

2. Respondent or his representative are aware of no place,

office, location, or other source where such legally required driver's license may legally be obtained from the State of Washington as the statute requires.

3.       Respondent and his representative agree that Defendant was not in

possession of a valid STATE 0F WASHINGT0N driver's license as such is not legally required by State of Washington statute.

4.       The only alleged authority the STATE 0F WASHINGT0N

has over the Defendant been if a contract, adhesive or otherwise, exists between Plaintiff and Defendant? Defendant claims and alleges that no such contract existed at the time and moment of the issuance of the TRAFFIC CITATI0N, nor does any such contract now exist.

5.

Trustee, and TANZADAQ SHAH (the name shown on said citation) are legally three entirely separate and different individuals. TAZA-DAQ SHAH is the cited individual and is a different person from both TAZADAQ SHAH and Tazadaq Shah, Trustee.

6., Tazadaq Shah, Trustee is appearing in this case.

as representative, and as required by the court for the cited party, TAZADAQ SHAH.

Tazadaq Shah, Trustee legally claims and affirms.

there is no obligation, duty, and/or relationship, be it financial, legal, performance, contractual or any other, between himself and TAZADAQ SHAH.

Therefore, because of the circumstances and instances

cited in paragraphs 1 through 7, Tazadaq Shah, Trustee legally disavows and rejects any claim the Court, the Officers of the Court, THE WASHINGTON STATE PATROL, and THE STATE OF WASHINGTON, either individually or collectively, of any alleged legal liability whatsoever in the matter for which TAZADAQ SHAH was issued the WASHINGTON STATE PATROL citation,

The Defendant now cites evidence for the above allegations: 1) "When the Southern states walked out.

of Congress on March 27, 1861, the quorum to conduct business under the Constitution was lost. The only votes that Congress could lawfully take, under Parliamentary Law, were those to set the time to reconvene, take a vote to get a quorum, and vote to adjourn and set a date to reconvene later, but instead, Congress abandoned the House and Senate without setting a date to reconvene. Under the parliamentary law of Congress, when this happened, Congress became "sine die" (pronounced see-na deed-a; literally "without day") and thus when Congress adjourned sine die, it ceased to exist as a exist as a lawful deliberative body, and the only lawful,

constitutional power that could declare war was no longer lawful, or in session.

The Southern states, by virtue of their secession from the Union, also ceased to exist sine die, and some state.

legislatures in the Northern Block also adjourned sine die, and thus, all the states which were parties to creating the Constitution ceased to exist.

President Lincoln executed the first executive order written by any President on April 15, 1861, Executive Order 1, and the

nation has been ruled by the president under executive order ever since. When Congress eventually did reconvene, it was reconvened under the military authority of the Commander-in-Chief and not by Rules of Order for Parliamentary bodies or by Constitutional Law: placing the American people under martial rule ever since that national emergency declared by President Lincoln.

The Constitution for the United States of America temporarily ceased to be the law of the land, and the President, Congress, and the Courts unlawfully presumed that they were free to remake the nation in their own image, whereas lawfully no constitutional provisions were in place which afforded power to any of the actions which presumed to place the nation under the new form of control.

President Lincoln knew that he had no authority to issue any executive order, and thus he commissioned General Orders No. 100 (April 24, 1863) as a special field code to govern his actions under martial law and which justified the seizure of power, which fictionally implemented the provisions of Article.

I, Section 8, Clauses 17-18 of the Constitution beyond the boundaries of Washington, D.C. and into the several states. General Orders No. 100, also called the Lieber Instructions and the Lieber Code, extended the Laws of War and International Law onto American soil, and the United States became the presumed conqueror of the people and the land.

Martial rule was kept secret and has never ended, the nation has been ruled under Military Law by the Commander-in-Chief of that military; the President, under his assumed executive powers and according to his executive orders, Constitutional Law under the original Constitution is enforced only as a matter of keeping public peace under the provisions of General 0rders No. 100 under martial rule.

Under Martial Law, title is a mere fiction, since all property belongs to the military except for that property which the Commander-in-Chief may, in his benevolence, exempted from taxation and seizure and upon which he allows the enemy to reside.

President Lincoln was assassinated before he could complete plans for reestablishing constitutional government in the

Southern States and end the martial rule by executive order, and the 14th Article in Amendment of the Constitution created a new citizenship status for the new expanded jurisdiction. New laws for the District of Columbia were established and passed by Con-

gress in 1871, supplanting those of February 27,1801 and May 3,1802. The District of Columbia was re-incorporated in 1872, and all states in the Union were reformed as Franchisees of the Federal Corporation so that a new Union of the United States could be created. The key to when the states became Federal Franchisees is related to the date when such states enacted the Field Code in law. The Field Code was a codification of the common law that was adopted first by New York, and then by California in 1872, and shortly afterwards the Lieber Code was used to bring the United States into the 1874 Brussels Conference and into the Hague Conventions of 1899 and 1907.

Excerpted from the Introduction of Senate Report 93-549, War and Emergency Powers Acts

2.     THE BUCK ACT

The United States government may not tax those state Citizens who live and work outside the territorial jurisdiction of Article 1, Section 8, Clause 17 or Article 4, Section 3, Clause 2 of the United States Constitution.

In 1940, Congress passed the "Buck Act", 4 U.S.C.S., Sections 105-113. Section 110(e) authorized any department of the federal government to create a "federal area" for imposition of the "Public Salary Tax Act of 1939" 4 U.S.C.S. Sec. 111. The balance of that act is found in the Internal Revenue Code.

4 U.S.C.S. Sec 110(d). The term "State" includes any Territory or possession of the United States.

4 U.S.C.S. Sec. 110(e). The term "federal area" means any lands or premises held or acquired by or for the use of the United States or any department, establishment, or agency of the United States; and any Federal area, or any part thereof, which is located within the exterior boundaries of a NY State, shall be deemed to be a Federal area located within such State.

The legal consequence of that Act was to create 1) Federal areas throughout the 48 constitutional states which overlaid exactly those states, and to illegally convert state Citizens into the status of "Federal citizens", and 2) illegally usurp the Sovereignty of the several states.

3.     Creation of Franchise STATES.

The Federal Areas created under the Buck Act were named by the Federal government with the name of the state included within its borders, but spelled in all capitals, or with specific two letter all- capitals abbreviations.

The C.O.R.P.O.R.A.T.I.O.N.

(Crooked Officials Robbing People of Rights Against Truth in Our Nation) BOOK TITLE

The reason for this is clear since there is a legal rule that two different legal entities may not have the same name, however the legal documentation for this instance has not yet been found in the United States Code, the Code of Federal Regulations, or any other official United States legal publication.

Probably the reason for that omission in United States legal documents and statutes is that "THE UNITED STATES 0F AMERICA C0RP0RATI0N." was created in France shortly after the end of the United States Civil War. The evidence of said incorporation is in French legal archives, so they cannot be found in this country, but inference of that corporation and its activities comes from the highest sources. I quote a letter from President Franklin D. Roosevelt written November 21, 1933 to Colonel Mandell House:

"The thing to find out, and I'm hoping the corporate records.

will show, is who are the shareholders? Who is on the Board of directors of the 'UNITED STATES 0F AMERICA? •••"

That this is this situation is clearly constitutionally both illegal and unlawful is evident as the United States Constitution states in Article IV, Section3, Paragraph 1, "New states may be admitted by the Congress to the Union, but no new state shall be formed or created within the jurisdiction of any other state; nor any state be formed by the junction of two or more states or parts of states, without the consent of the legislatures of the states concerned as well as of the Congress."

That term imposed by the Constitution supersedes any provision of the Buck Act, which is in conflict, and in fact, it will be shown by statute to be such by the Defendant.

Immediately after the Bank Holiday of March 5, 1933, one day after FDR's inauguration he sent a bill to Congress establishing a four day "Banking Holiday," It was passed by Congress and immediately put into effect. A not-generally-recognized fact is that the United States also "declared bankruptcy" at the same time. At that point, the United States government was gradually taken over by

the C0RP0RATE UNITED STATES which certainly was owned by European parties to whom it owed money which it could not pay.

Soon after the establishment of the Buck Act in 1940, the new administrative areas became STATES which were given the status of STATE FRANCHISES by the UNITED STATES 0F AMERICA C0RP0RATI0N.

For example, THE STATE 0F WASHINGT0N is a franchise of the UNITED STATES 0F AMERICA C0RP0RATI0N, and is an entity which is precisely not the Constitutional State of Washington, yet it governs this state and enforces its laws as though it possesses legal Constitutional legitimacy—it legally and lawfully does not.

In like fashion, THE WASHINGT0N STATE PATR0L is a municipal corporate entity under the control of the STATE 0F WASHINGT0N, and in identical fashion is not authorized to enforce any State of Washington law or statute.

As the UNITED STATES 0F AMERICA C0RP0RATI0N is both a foreign and a municipal corporation, the STATE 0F WASHINGT0N is a municipal corporation, and the WASHINGT0N STATE PATR0L is an adjunct to the STATE 0F WASHINGT0N, none have either the United States Constitution or the State of Washington Constitution authority to enforce State of Washington statute. Their collective and only authority extends to parties which are in contractual relationship with them, either individually or collectively actual or adhesive.

Defendant's trustee claims that Defendant and Defendant's trustee are not parties to contracts of any type or sort with the STATE 0F WASHINGT0N or any of its parts. Consequently, Defendant and Defendant's trustee have no legal obligation to any State of Washington law the STATE 0F WASHINGT0N either attempts to enforce or enforces.

Defendant claims The STATE 0F WASHINGT0N has no rights, legal or otherwise, to enforce the statutes of the State of Washington, but illegally and unlawfully does so. That is the case in this specific

instance as well as others, and both the STATE 0F WASHINGT0N and the WASHINGT0N STATE PATR0L, their officers and employees who so act, have committed both the crimes of Treason and Sedition.

Defendant will prove these claims and allegations.

Defendant and Defendant's representative reserve the right to sue the STATE 0F WASHINGTON and the WASH-INGT0N STATE PATR0L, their legal representatives, and their specific officers and employees who are in any fashion or way involved in this case.

Sincerely,

Tazadaq Shah, Trustee and Representative for TAZADAQ SHAH

What Tazadaq did when a UCC Clerk / Secretary refused to file my Documents, acquiesce is never an option

Sometimes a court clerk might refuse to file a document because it does not meet certain form guidelines. For educational purposes only, A clerk is not permitted to refuse filing a document for form as required by rule 5. (d)(4) of the Federal Rules of Civil Procedures specifically state,

5.(d)(4) Acceptance by the clerk.

A clerk must not refuse to file a paper solely because it is not in the form prescribed by these rules or by a local rule or practice.


This is an important rule especially for those who are preceding in a court of record. Although a court of record proceeds according to common law, the creditor or sovereign can choose the Federal Rules by which to proceed. This is one of the ways I used to get a clerk to do his/her job. Since law is the decree of the creditor or sovereign, creditors or sovereigns can decree that some statutes apply in his case.

First and far most, a court clerk does not have the authority to make any decisions. His duties are ministerial and not tribunal. The tribunal is who gets to make the decisions regarding the quality of a paper. Therefore, if at first a clerk did not file my papers. I Simply stated politely that he files them on demand. When that failed, I presented the clerk with an order from the court of record. I mailed it by registered mail to get the clerk to comply.

The C.O.R.P.O.R.A.T.I.O.N.

(Crooked Officials Robbing People of Rights Against Truth in Our Nation) BOOK TITLE

As you will see in my template, I have typed for educational purposes only, the anyone who removes a document from the record can be punished for up to three years in prison according to.

18 USC § 2071

(a)     Whoever willfully and unlawfully conceals, removes, mutilates, obliterates, or destroys, or attempts to do so, or, with intent to do so takes and carries away any record, proceeding, map, book, paper, document, or other thing, filed or deposited with any clerk or officer of any court of the United States, or in any public office, or with any judicial or public officer of the United States, shall be fined under this title or imprisoned not more than three years, or both.

(b)     Whoever, having the custody of any such record, proceeding, map, book, document, paper, or other thing, willfully and unlawfully conceals, removes, mutilates, obliterates, falsifies, or destroys the same, shall be fined under this title or imprisoned not more than three years, or both; and shall forfeit his office and be disqualified from holding any office under the United States. As used in this subsection, the term "office" does not include the office held by any person as a retired officer of the Armed Forces of the United States.

There is also case law that specifies that a document is filed once it is delivered to the clerk. It does not have to be stamped and sign. That is done merely to designate a time of filing. In one case, the court opined that a document is filed even if delivered to a deputy clerk at night at his home.

it is settled law that delivery of a pleading to a proper official is sufficient to constitute filing thereof. United States v. Lombardo, 241 U.S. 73, 36 S. Ct. 508, 60 L. Ed. 897 (1916); Milton v. United States, 105 F.2d 253, 255 (5th Cir. 1939). In Greeson v. Sherman, 265 F. Supp. 340 (D.C.Va.1967) it was held that a pleading delivered to a deputy clerk at his home at night was thereby.

"filed." (Freeman v. Giacomo Costa Fu Andrea, 282 F. Supp. 525 (E.D.Pa. 04/5/1968).)

Read the rest of the Order to the Clerk that I will cover hereto. It has good information regarding the duties of the clerk.

I always remember, do not argue with a deputy clerk or anyone because you go in dishonor. Nobody ever wins an argument. The deputy clerk is not someone who you debate law with. They are simply paper warehousers and do not usually comprehend such things. I always send my order directly to the clerk along with a letter explaining the crime being committed by the deputy clerk and he will usually perform his duties as the law requires.

.

Practical Comprehension of 1099 Forms A Free National 's perspective "taxes."

The Social Security Trust

Our society is structured around the use of Federal Reserve Notes (FRNs) that are loaned to the government at interest by the privately owned Federal Reserve Bank. To get a job, open a bank account, or operate in commerce within the United States, we need to get a Tax Identification Number (TIN) from the Internal Revenue Service (IRS); and most people have contracted with the Social Security Administration (SSA) to be trustees of the Social Security Trust with a Social Security Number (SSN).

194

The C.O.R.P.O.R.A.T.I.O.N.

(Crooked Officials Robbing People of Rights Against Truth in Our Nation) BOOK TITLE

The Social Security Administration (SSA) is one of those Alphabet Agencies created during the New Deal and it is integrally linked to the IRS and the Fed. The IRS was created in 1862 under President Lincoln and was responsible for collecting an income tax enacted to pay expenses of the Civil War under the Revenue Act of 1862. Yet it was not until 1913 that the IRS took on its modern role.

This relationship is more easily understood if you were to imagine the Federal Reserve as being like a giant rental car company with FRNs being the cars owned by the Federal Reserve. Those cars are circulated throughout society, sometimes being deposited in a lot (a bank), and sometimes changing hands. You can use these rental cars to get around or to move personal property, but you must pay for the privilege, or else find another way to deal in commerce (barter, private contract, alternate currency, etc.).

Ultimately, the Fed does not really care who uses the cars, so long as someone pays for their use and pays for any damage done to them or their property. Naturally, no one wants to pull anyone else's weight, so whoever uses the rental car the most ought to pay the most, right? That is only fair. Likewise, you should not have to pay for a car that you are not using; and if you are not going to use it, you ought to let someone else use it who needs it, right? That is only fair. And if you choose not to use a car, then you do not have to pay for it, but your ability to move around is severely limited. You could ask your family and friends if you can borrow their cars, but then you are dependent, rather than independent; and in such a case, your friends and family would have the right to ask you to give up something else in exchange for the use of their rental car. Right?

Many have decided they would rather not pay for this service and so they have created their own money systems, or they live in communal societies. For some, this is a worthwhile trade-off, but for most people, that is not an option. And understandably so since such methods are a pain in the ass and complicate one's personal situation almost as much as having to pay taxes and follow statutes would. So, if we are going to live in this society, it would behoove us to learn as much as we can about this process. To adapt ourselves and work with what we have, rather than trying to upend the whole world. Such is my feeling, at least.

Now, the IRS is so called because it oversees the nation's internal monetary transactions and provides the service of revenue (i.e., changing the location of) that money for us so that we do not have to do it ourselves. Put plainly, the IRS's job is to keep track of who has the FRNs in their possession in any given year and to determine who owes what and to whom and to make sure that those who owe pay those that are owed. The IRS can be thought of as an agency responsible for tracking the Fed's rental cars and figuring out who has been using them the most and who must pay for their use. Because we are using FRNs, we must at least pay the cost of using them. If you are responsible and keep track of your finances, you can report this to the IRS yourself. Otherwise, the IRS must expend resources to figure it out by relying on banks and other agencies to report your use of them. That makes their job harder and makes their employees very disgruntled.


Accounting entails figuring out all the money coming in (income) and all the money going out (expenses) and then determining the difference (balance). Everything else is just details affecting one or the other. And here we get to the various tax forms.

Most people are familiar with the 1040 Form, which is an Individual Tax Return form. This is the basic form in which you take all your account statements and add up the total income it all so suggest that you are a federal employee. Depending on how much you made each year, you pay a certain amount of tax. Most people are familiar with the Income section of the 1040 Form in which they report their income from wages on a W-2 Form. You will probably recognize that there is a box on the W-2 for reporting income earned from employee wages, but there are also boxes in which you can report money that is withheld from you by the employer - i.e., money that does not get added to your income.

We established before how you do not have to pay taxes on non-income (sales tax and others aside for the moment). Recall also that you have an Employee Identification Number (EIN) that is the same as your SSN and this makes you an employee of the State - your job being to act as a trustee and manage the trust that bears a similar name to yours. Instead of getting paid in wages, you get paid in benefits, privileges, and services, cutting out the middleman, which is all money is, really.

Now, if you have a checking account, a savings account, and a credit card account, these are all independent accounts with different numbers, yet you are the creator of all of them. So, they are all part of one system - your system. You might have these accounts vested in different banks, and to the bank, it looks like they are gaining or losing when you move money around, but it is all still under your system. It has not actually left your control. In much the same way, there are many SSNs and EINs, yet they all trace back to the Federal Reserve, the SSA, and the IRS. It is all one system - the State's system. They may have their property in the hands of different persons, and to the individual, it may look like he is gaining or losing money, yet it all remains under the control of the State. It has not really gone anywhere. So, while the rental cars might change drivers, they have not changed owners.

http://youtu.be/zOjKGJy1uKY

When you get a check, what is the first thing you normally do? Deposit that money into the bank, yes? This then appears as income on your bank statement. Most people think they are depositing money into the bank when they do this; but there is no lawful money (no gold and silver), so what is really taking place is an extension of credit from one account to another. The check you deposited is a security that the bank holds onto and adds to its reserves, fractionalizing it and using it as the basis for new loans. The actual security stays with the bank and you are issued a certain amount of credit which becomes the bank's liability. In other words, if lawful money ever returned, this would be how much the bank would owe to you. Similarly, when you write a check, you are issuing a security and the bank then withholds credit from you by diminishing its liability to you. The cycle of how this works can be seen in this diagram.

Recall that the banks are like parking lots in our rental car example. Why would you leave a car in a parking lot? Usually because you just need a safe place to store the car until you need it again. In the same way, banks store our securities and the credit that goes with them until we need that credit again. But how often do you reclaim that credit? How often do you come back for your rental car? Most people do not. They assume they do, since a new car has been made available to them, but it is not the one they originally had. That car was deemed abandoned. But when you park a car, can the owner of the lot automatically assume your car is abandoned? No, it cannot. It must wait a while and then report it to the police and if no one comes to claim it within a reasonable time, then it is abandoned and the first person to come along and lay claim to it can use it. Because the lot owner was the one that reported it, they know of its status and will likely try to claim it for themselves.

In the same way, the banks will hold onto the securities you issued - checks, cash, Electronic Funds Transfers (EFTs), etc. - with the understanding that they belong to you, not the bank. After three years' time, if you do not come and claim those securities (and most people do not), the bank has them declared abandoned and files a form with the IRS to claim those funds and add them to their reserves.

So, you have rental cars sitting in lots that you are not using, but rather than let someone else use them, you are just letting them sit there while you pay a fee for them. Does that sound insane to you, or what? Can you really afford to pay for what you are not using? You are hurting yourself and others needlessly.

How, then, do we remedy this? Well, there exists a form known as a 1099-A. The "A" stands for either "abandonment" or "acquisition," as that is what this form is used for. You can use it to acquire the assets of a loan (e.g., the promissory note) or to declare certain securities as abandoned when you do not intend to get them back, such as when you write a check, use a credit or debit card, or make an electronic funds transfer. Because the various accounts are all part of one system, what the 1099-A does is to help report to the IRS where these securities lie and who is using them.

In the case of a loan, you fill out a promissory note (which is a security and has value) and receive an extension of credit. Why do you have to repay the lender? Because they have an outstanding liability, as evidenced by the promissory note. By filing a 1099-A as an acquisition, you are taking back the security and informing the IRS that you accept possession of these securities and they, in turn, will zero out the liability of the lender for you. This is the form that the bank uses when they acquire your abandoned securities. It would be like if you found a rental car in your driveway one day. You file a 1099-A declaring that you intend to acquire it. If no one else claims it, then you get to use it. Not too bad, eh?

Of course, in doing so, you must pay the rental fee (income tax), so it would behoove you to use it for your purposes and then get rid of it once you are done with it. You might use it once and then no longer need it again. Indeed, no one gets a loan just to have it sit there and do nothing for them. Often, such credit gets spent right away in the purchasing of property or the discharging of debts. So really, the rental car is only staying in your possession for a short time before you abandon it again. In this case, you would file a 1099-A as an abandonment and declare that you are abandoning the car and that it is free for someone else to claim.

So, we return to the 1040 Form and note that all money coming into your accounts gets reported as Income (lines 7 through 22) and all money going out gets reported as either Adjusted Gross Income (lines 23 through 37) or Payments (lines 61 through 71).

Indeed, if we look at line 61, we see that it says, "Federal income tax withheld from Forms W-2 and 1099." But there is nothing on the 1099-A that mentions a withholding. So, what does this mean?

Well, an employer cannot take money from you without cause, but they can withhold wages from you when you do not perform your job correctly, or if you claim certain benefits, or if a law compels them to do so (such as for Social Security) and this gets reported on a W-2 Form. As an employee of the State, when you extend credit from one of your accounts, that credit is withheld from you as well.

This gets reported on a form called a 1099-OID, which stands for "Original Issue Discount." It is so called because, for the purposes of determining taxation, it discounts (does not count) all securities originally issued by you. So, if you wrote $1000 worth of checks within a given year, that $1000 worth of credit that was withheld from you does not count!

Those who have filed tax forms before will know that not all income is necessarily taxable and that the amount you must pay is determined by the amount of taxable income you have. So, depending on your situation, it is possible that you will not have to pay an income tax at all, or even that the IRS owes you a refund.

On the 1040 Form, line 74 states, "Amount you owe. Subtract line 71 from line 60." Line 60 is your total income after considering wages, certain tax credits, exemptions, and the like (everything from line 1 to line 59). Line 71 is your total payments after considering withholdings and certain tax credits (everything from line 61 to line 70). Included in the latter is the total of withholdings from your 1099-OID forms.

Line 72 of the 1040 Form states that, "If line 71 is more than line 60, subtract line 60 from line 71. This is the amount you over-paid." Overpaid. I like the sound of that. So, what this says is that if the amount withheld from you is greater than the amount of taxable income you have, the IRS will refund that credit to you with a nice fat check. Considering most of us spend considerable sums each year, thereby having considerable sums withheld from us, what do you suppose the result would be?

Important Tax Information

Being a creditor means being knowledgeable and responsible, and that means turning in your tax forms on time. If you do not get your forms in on time, you might not get the refund you want (at best) or you might be faced with a late penalty or even jail time (at worst). So here is some information to keep in mind when you file your taxes.

This information is subject to change based on the policies of the IRS, so check back here regularly.

The following forms are for educational purposes only. Do not use these forms as the ones you send into the IRS or you will receive a fine! The real forms all have special ink that can be scanned, which these forms do not have.

1099-A

1099-OID

1096

1040 1040-V

1041 †

4490 ††

† The 1041 is an income tax return for estates and trusts, as opposed to the 1040, which is an income tax return for individuals.

†† The 4490 is difficult to find. It is a proof of claim, signed under penalty of perjury that must precede any attempt to enforce a tax lien against you, according to law.

Dates

Keep in mind the following dates when preparing to file your taxes.

November 1: Earliest day that 1099-A Forms and 1099-OID Forms get processed.

December 31: Last day of the old fiscal year.

January 1: First day of the new fiscal year.

February 20: Recommended date to have 1099-A and 1099-OID Forms in the mail by.

March 1: Last day to file 1099-A Forms and 1099-OID Forms if filing by mail.

March 31: Last day to file 1099-A Forms and 1099-OID Forms if filing online.

April 15: Last day to file 1040 Forms if filing by mail.

April 18: Last day to file 1040 Forms if filing online.

** Do not wait until the last minute to file your forms if you can help it.

** If you do not get your 1099-A Forms and 1099-OID Forms in by the deadline, you will have to wait until November 1 before it gets processed.

** Corrected forms can be sent in later if you already have an original form on file.

Notes

When issued a loan, you must wait at least 30 days before filing a 1099-A Form as an acquisition. This amount gets included in your income.

You need to send in a 1099-A Form as an abandonment before you can send in a 1099-OID Form. Send all 1099-A Forms and 1099-OID Forms before submitting the 1040 Form because you need to include the information from the 1099-A Forms and 1099-OID Forms on the 1040 Form.

When sending in a 1099-A Form or 199-OID Form, you must include a 1096 Form.

When filing 1099-A Forms electronically, there is a wait period of 72 hours between sending in a 1099-A Form and a 1099-OID Form. If sending via mail, it is recommended you wait about a week between sending in a 1099-A Form and a 1099-OID Form. If you do not wait enough time in between each step, the IRS may deem your claim as frivolous, since the necessary credit has not shown up yet on their books - a good incentive to do this process sooner, rather than later.

When sending in your forms by mail, you should consider the time it will take for them to go through the mail, which only counts business days (all days except weekends and federal holidays).

You should file one form per account per year that the account is still open.

For bank accounts, such as checking accounts, you can use December 31 for the date.

Request 1099 OID Court Case

RESPONSE TO:

TAZADAQ SHAH

The C.O.R.P.O.R.A.T.I.O.N.

(Crooked Officials Robbing People of Rights Against Truth in Our Nation) BOOK TITLE

P.O. Box 85384

NEW YORK, NEW YORK 10027

TO:

Judge name and address:

xxxxxxxxxxxxxxxxx 300 E. Walnut St. Pasadena, Ca 91101 Dept. D

Dear Addressees:

As I understand it, the above referenced proceeding is set in a taxable business transaction pursuant to the rules of commerce. Therefore, would your accountant please prepare and file Federal Tax Form 1099 OID (Original Issue Discount) to cover

the eligible issues (products of statutes) in this case # GA081668 STATE OF CALIFORNIA v. JOSHUA GUTIERREZ   (Capitus Diminution Maxima). The eligible issue(s) in this matter consist of:

1)      Appearance Bond

2)      Penal Bond bearing OMB No:9000-0045, Standard Forms 24,25,25A,273,274,275 (Bid, performance, payment, Reinsurance Agreement for A Miller Act Performance, Payment, In Favor of The United States Bonds) (estimated amount shown on 1099 OID forms enclosed)

3)      Any other bonds after and including the True Bill Indictment.

All the above eligible issues listed above (1-3) are all being withheld. Please provide me with my copies of these 1099-OID forms.

All these product(s) in issue is (are) prepaid, and I need information of your business plan to process prepayments in order to facilitate the tax report of the federal withholding to the IRS as taxable income to me. You did not provide me with a check or money order to pay for the product of your withholding which constitutes a dishonor in itself. Any dishonor/denial in this matter on your part admits this settlement to be a tax recovery issue. The IRS will want to know the location of the funds that are being withheld. Please tell me how to proceed to make settlement.

The tax in question is the original issue discount. The filing of the 1099 OID is not mandatory on my part (voluntary), but upon request by me, becomes mandatory upon you, and if not complied with, constitutes tax fraud. You are using my identity and related exemption without my full knowledge and consent, and you are selling securities in my name without my consent. Overall, that is identity theft, as well as sedition against the United States, fraud and embezzlement, theft of public funds, and securities fraud.

The filing of the 1099-OID is to enable the tax charge to return to the source for settlement and closing of escrow in exchange, Treasury Account [ 552672874]. After filing, please return to my possession all the corresponding property that belongs to me. If you do not intend to comply with my request, then please provide me with your tax identification number.

The C.O.R.P.O.R.A.T.I.O.N.

(Crooked Officials Robbing People of Rights Against Truth in Our Nation) BOOK TITLE

Your refusal makes you a participant in an international contract (a small claim), and your name becomes eligible to appear in the tax report as a recipient of the payer, who is identified in the eligible issue/bill/bond/etc. You have knowledge/access to the value and other information to report/file the federal tax form and you are now holding a tax liability until you make settlement, by return to the source (which is what the filing of the 1099 OID does), and that source is eligible for a tax refund. You would become the holder-in-due-course of the eligible issue(s) for the value stated herein, that value being a federal tax liability.

If a response is not received from you within 5 working days of receipt of this letter, the enclosed 1099-OID tax forms will be deemed correct for filing with the IRS. The IRS will calculate the total amount of the tax for which you are liable. The actual filing

of the form will not be made until you are in dishonor of my request.

Thank you for your kind cooperation.

TAZADAQ SHAH©

By: Tazadaq Shah©

Agent, Authorized Representative

CERTIFICATE OF FAXING

On this 22nd      day of October, A.D. 2017, I personally faxed this letter to the above noted addressees, at the default page.

noted fax numbers.

Signature Affidavit to Challenge Jurisdiction KINGS COUNTY CRIMINAL COURT 120 SCHERMERHORN STREET BROOKLYN, NEW YORK

County of Kings Index No.:

COLE CAB CORPORATION

Plaintiff(s)/Petitioner(s)/Claimant(s)        AFFIDAVIT OF FACT

WRIT OF DISCOVERY

-against-

For:

NASSIM ZOULOUECHE        (Relief Requested)

Respondent(s)

State of New York, County of Kings ss: Party

The C.O.R.P.O.R.A.T.I.O.N.

(Crooked Officials Robbing People of Rights Against Truth in Our Nation) BOOK TITLE

I, Nassim Zouloueche, appearing specially not generally an accommodation party for RESPONDENT NASSIM ZOULOUECHE being duly sworn, deposes and says: I am the party named as Defendant/Respondent.

I request that the Court produce a Delegation of Authority in writing I further require that the court prove subject matter jurisdiction or issue an Order for to vacate. If subject matter jurisdiction is not proven the court is denying me due process of law.

Re: Case #_____about Invitation/Suit/Subpoena

This is a formal request for a certified copy of the "Certified Delegation of Authority Order" issued to KINGS COUNTY CRIMINAL COURT and confirmed by Congress.

The 5th Amendment required that all persons within the United States must be given due process of the law and equal protection of the law.

"The Constitution for the United States of America binds all judicial officers at Article 6, wherein it does say, "This Constitution and the Laws of the United States which shall be made in pursuance thereof, and all Treaties made, or which shall be made under the authority of the United States, shall be the Supreme Law of the Land, and the Judges of every State shall be bound thereby, any-thing in the Constitution or laws of any state to the Contrary, not withstanding," see Clause 2."

"United States Constitution, Article III, Section II - The judicial power shall extend to all cases, in law and equity, arising under this Constitution, the laws of the United States, and treaties made, or which shall be made, under their authority;--to all cases affecting ambassadors, other public ministers and con-souls;--to all cases of admiralty and maritime jurisdiction;--to controversies to which the United States shall be a party;--to controversies between two or more states;--between a state and citizens of another state;--between citizens of different states;--between citizens of the same state claiming lands under grants of different states, and between a state, or the citizens thereof, and foreign states, citizens or subjects. In all cases affecting ambassadors, other public ministers, and consuls, and those in which a state shall be party, the Supreme Court shall have original jurisdiction. In all the other cases before mentioned, the Supreme Court shall have appellate jurisdiction, both as to law and fact, with such exceptions, and under such regulations as the Congress shall make. The trial of all crimes, except in cases of impeachment, shall be by jury; and such trial shall be held in the state where the said crimes shall have been committed; but when not committed within any state, the trial shall be at such place or places as the Congress may by law have directed.

"The law provides that once State and Federal Jurisdiction has been challenged, it must be proven." Main v. Thiboutot, 100 S. Ct. 2502 (1980)

"Jurisdiction can be challenged at any time." and "Jurisdiction, once challenged, cannot be assumed and must be decided." Basso v. Utah Power & Light Co. 495 F 2d 906, 910.

"Once challenged, jurisdiction cannot be assumed, it must be proved to exist." Stuck v. Medical Examiners 94 Ca 2d 751. 211 P2d 389.

"There is no discretion to ignore that lack of jurisdiction." Joyce v. US, 474 F2d 215.

"The burden shifts to the court to prove jurisdiction." Rosemond v. Lambert, 469 F2d 416.

Where the court is without jurisdiction, it has no authority to do anything other than to dismiss the case." Fontenot v. State, 932 S.W.2d 185 "Judicial action without jurisdiction is void."-Id (1996)

"Criminal law magistrates have no power of their own and are unable to enforce any ruling." V.T.C.A., Government Code sec. 54.651 et seq., Davis v. State, 956 S.W.2d 555 (1997)

Basso v. UPL, 495 F. 2d 906

Under federal Law, which is applicable to all states, the U.S. Supreme Court stated that "if a court is without authority, its judgments and orders are regarded as nullities. They are not voidable, but simply void, and form no bar to a recovery sought, even prior to a reversal in opposition to them. They constitute no justification and all persons concerned in executing such judgments or sentences are considered, in law, as trespassers."

Brook v. Yawkey, 200 F. 2d 633

Elliot v. Piersol, 1 Pet. 328, 340, 26 U.S. 328, 340 (1828)

Acts more than judicial authority constitutes misconduct, particularly where a judge deliberately disregards the requirements of fairness and due process. *Cannon v. Commission on Judicial Qualifications, (1975) 14 Cal. 3d 678, 694

"Constitutional 'rights' would be of little value if they could be indirectly denied." Gomillion v. Lightfoot, 364 U.S. 155 (1966), cited also in Smith v. Allwright, 321 U.S. 649.644

Supreme Court Justice Field, 'There is no such thing as a power of inherent sovereignty in the government of the United States... In this country, sovereignty resides in the people, and Congress can exercise power, which they have not, by their Constitution, entrusted to it. All else is withheld. Juliard v. Greeman, 110 U.S. 421 (1884)

"Where rights secured by the Constitution are involved, there can be no 'rule making' or legislation which would abrogate them."." MIRANDA v. ARIZONA, 384 U.S. 436 (1966) 491; 86 S. Ct. 1603

"An unconstitutional act is not law; it confers no rights; it imposes no duties; affords no protection; it creates no office; it is in legal contemplation, as inoperative as though it had never been passed." Norton v. Shelby County, 118 U.S. 425 p. 442

"...in our country the people are sovereign, and the government cannot sever its relationship to them by taking away their citizenship." Perez v. Brownell, 356 U.S. 44, 7; 8 S. Ct. 568, 2 L. Ed. 2d 603 (1958)

"When acting to enforce a statue and its subsequent amendments to the present date, the judge of the municipal court is acting as an administrative officer and not in a judicial capacity; courts in administering or enforcing statues do not act judicially, but merely ministerially". Thompson v. Smith 154 SE 583.

Courts in administrative issues are prohibited from even listening to or hearing arguments, presentation, or rational." ASIS v. US, 568 F2d 284.

Ministerial officers are incompetent to receive grants of judicial power from the legislature, their acts in attempting to exercise such powers are necessarily nullities." Burns v. Supp. Ct., SF, 140 Cal. 1.

A response is required within 30 days of receipt of this Writ of Discovery.

I, NASSIM ZOULOUECHE do not, under any conditions or circumstances, nor by threat, duress, or coercion, waive any Unalienable Rights or any other Rights Secured by the Constitution or Treaty; and hereby request that the Officers of this Court fulfill their Obligations to preserve the rights of this Petitioner (An Aggrieved man) and to carry out their delegated Judicial Duties with good behavior, and in 'Good Faith'.

All UNCONSTITUTIONAL Citations – Summons / Ticket – Suits / (misrepresented) Bills of Exchange: Docket Number - SCC ,

and any other 'Orders' or 'Actions' associated with it or them, to be 'Dismissed', 'Abated' and expunged from the Record; being null on it is face and merits.

A RESPONSE IS REQUIRED IN TEN (10) DAYS

A letter, not signed under penalty of perjury, verifying the alleged charges and Delegation of Authority Order, does not constitute a response.

I, Nassim Zouloueche: Ex Rel NASSIM ZOULOUECHE ©, the Affiant, depose, affirm, and certify.

that the foregoing statements made by me are true. I am aware that if any of the foregoing statements made by me are willfully false, I am subject to punishment. I have written the foregoing with intent and understanding of purpose, and that the statements, demands and contents herein, are true correct and complete, commercially reasonable, and just, to the best of my knowledge and ability. If you cannot produce the required Delegation of Authority Order I require the case be dismissed without prejudice. Notice to the Agent is Notice to the Principal – Notice to the Principal is notice to the Agent.

Thank You,

I am:

, 		Nassim Zouloueche

Authorized Representative

Secured Party, In Propria Persona: Ex Relatione NASSIM ZOULOUECHE

All Rights Reserved: U.C.C. 1-207/ 1-308; U.C.C. 1-103

Brooklyn, New York [near] Non-Domestic

Cc: 	United States Justice Department

United States Attorney General Loretta E. Lynch

State of New York Governor Andrew Cuomo

State of New York Attorney General Eric T. Schneiderman

State of New York Secretary of State Cesar A. Perales

United States District Court of Louisiana Judge Jefferson Parish

The C.O.R.P.O.R.A.T.I.O.N.

(Crooked Officials Robbing People of Rights Against Truth in Our Nation) BOOK TITLE

I have some tactics you might like; they are fun to use. 1.Mandatory Judicial Notice under federal rules of Evidence You have no contempt for the Court or anybody in the Court. 2.You are authorized representative and not SURETY. ON and FOR the Record.

3.under the 1951 powers of appointment act, I appoint judge.

as TRUSTEE.to settle the matter.

4.Statement of CLAIM form B-10=they are required to fill out under penalty of perjury.

5.CLAIM form w-10=they are required to fill out under penalty of perjury.

Question: Do you have a claim against me? no. case dismissed for failure to state a CLAIM.

here is where you can get the proper w-10 and B-10 form.

ENJOY and PLEASE share.

Affidavit of Fact

Writ of Discovery

Notice of Special Appearance

For the Record, To Be Read into The Record as Evidence

Notice to the Agent is Notice to the Principal- Notice to the Principal is notice to the Agent.

To:

State of Michigan 86th District Court

Clerk of Court

280 Washington Street

4th Floor

Traverse City, Michigan of Republic 49684

United States of America Republic, North America

Petitioner:

Inty Amaru Torres Authorized Agent

Aggrieved man, In Propria Persona:

All Rights Reserved Without Prejudice: U.C.C. 1-207/1-308; U.C.C. 1-103

c/o 6126 Edmar Drive

Traverse City, Michigan [49686]

The C.O.R.P.O.R.A.T.I.O.N.

(Crooked Officials Robbing People of Rights Against Truth in Our Nation) BOOK TITLE

Case Number 16-g0151946-SI-1

Proof of insurance/registration violation

Inty Amaru Torres, an aggrieved man appearing specially not generally, challenging subject matter jurisdiction of The State of Michigan 86th District Court in response to an improper hearing illegally scheduled at 2:30 am on the 28th day of April 2016.

This is a formal request for a certified copy of the "Certified Delegation of Authority Order" issued to The United States District Court for the District of Connecticut and confirmed by Congress.

The 5th Amendment required that all persons within the United States must be given due process of the law and equal protection of the law.

"The Constitution for the United States of America binds all judicial officers at Article 6, wherein it does say, "This Constitution and the Laws of the United States which shall be made in pursuance thereof, and all Treaties made, or which shall be made under the authority of the United States, shall be the Supreme Law of the Land, and the Judges of every State shall be bound thereby, anything in the Constitution or laws of any state to the Contrary, not withstanding," see Clause 2."

"United States Constitution, Article III, Section II - The judicial power shall extend to all cases, in law and equity, arising under this Constitution, the laws of the United States, and treaties made, or which shall be made, under their authority;--to all cases affecting ambassadors, other public ministers and con-souls;--to all cases of admiralty and maritime jurisdiction;--to controversies to which the United States shall be a party;--to controversies between two or more states;--between a state and citizens of another state;--between citizens of different states;--between citizens of the same state claiming lands under grants of different states, and between a state, or the citizens thereof, and foreign states, citizens or subjects. In all cases affecting ambassadors, other public ministers, and consuls, and those in which a state shall be party, the Supreme Court shall have original jurisdiction. In all the other cases before mentioned, the Supreme Court shall have appellate jurisdiction, both as to law and fact, with such exceptions, and under such regulations as the Congress shall make. The trial of all crimes, except in cases of impeachment, shall be by jury; and such trial shall be held in the state where the said crimes shall have been committed; but when not committed within any state, the trial shall be at such place or places as the Congress may by law have directed.

"The law provides that once State and Federal Jurisdiction has been challenged, it must be proven." Main v. Thiboutot, 100 S. Ct. 2502 (1980)

"Jurisdiction can be challenged at any time." and "Jurisdiction, once challenged, cannot be assumed and must be decided." Basso v. Utah Power & Light Co. 495 F 2d 906, 910.

"Once challenged, jurisdiction cannot be assumed, it must be proved to exist." Stuck v. Medical Examiners 94 Ca 2d 751. 211 P2d 389.

"There is no discretion to ignore that lack of jurisdiction." Joyce v. US, 474 F2d 215.

"The burden shifts to the court to prove jurisdiction." Rosemond v. Lambert, 469 F2d 416.

206

The C.O.R.P.O.R.A.T.I.O.N.

(Crooked Officials Robbing People of Rights Against Truth in Our Nation) BOOK TITLE

Where the court is without jurisdiction, it has no authority to do anything other than to dismiss the case." Fontenot v. State, 932 S.W.2d 185 "Judicial action without jurisdiction is void."-Id (1996)

"Criminal law magistrates have no power of their own and are unable to enforce any ruling." V.T.C.A., Government Code sec. 54.651 et seq., Davis v. State, 956 S.W.2d 555 (1997)

Basso v. UPL, 495 F. 2d 906

Under federal Law, which is applicable to all states, the U.S. Supreme Court stated that "if a court is without authority, its judgments and orders are regarded as nullities. They are not voidable, but simply void, and form no bar to a recovery sought, even prior to a reversal in opposition to them. They constitute no justification and all persons concerned in executing such judgments or sentences are considered, in law, as trespassers."

Brook v. Yawkey, 200 F. 2d 633

Elliot v. Piersol, 1 Pet. 328, 340, 26 U.S. 328, 340 (1828)

I, Indy Amaru Torres, do not, under any conditions or circumstances, nor by threat, duress, or coercion, waive any Unalienable Rights or any other Rights Secured by the Constitution or Treaty; and hereby request that the Officers of this Court fulfill their Obligations to preserve the rights of this Petitioner and to carry out their delegated Judicial Duties with good behavior, and in 'Good Faith'. Agreeable to Article III, Section II of the United States Constitution Judicial Authority is legal in the Supreme Court or a lower court that has a "Certified Delegation of Authority Order" "Proof of Jurisdiction" confirmed by Congress as a lawful and formal Discovery.

Let it be noted for the record, on the record and let the record show a response is required immediately from receipt of this letter. If no copy of the Certified Delegation of Authority Order is received this Affidavit of Fact - Writ of Discovery shall stand as Law affirming that this court does not have Jurisdiction as per Article III, Section II of the United States Constitution.

"Once Challenged, jurisdiction cannot be assumed, it must be proved to exist." Stuck v Medical Examiners 94 Ca 2d 751.211, P2d 389.

All UNCONSTITUTIONAL Citations – Summons / Ticket – Suits / (misrepresented) Bills of Exchange: Docket Number - SCC   ,

and any other 'Orders' or 'Actions' associated with it or them, to be 'Dismissed', 'Abated' and expunged from the Record; being null on it is face and merits.

Notice to the Agent is Notice to the Principal – Notice to the Principal is notice to the Agent.

Thank You,

I am:

Indy Amaru Torres Authorized Representative

Natural man, In Propria Persona:

All Rights Reserved: U.C.C. 1-207/ 1-308; U.C.C. 1-103

The C.O.R.P.O.R.A.T.I.O.N.

(Crooked Officials Robbing People of Rights Against Truth in Our Nation) BOOK TITLE

c/o 6128 Edgar Drive

Traverse City, Michigan [ near49686]

Non-Domestic


Due Process Clause (14th Amendment)

[No State shall] deprive any person of life, liberty, or property, without due process of law.

1.      Show that the government has deprived* you of a non-trivial protected interest, one that the Supreme Court would recognize as falling into one of the three boxes above.

*The deprivation by the government must not be based on simple negligence (e.g., prison officials losing the personal property of an inmate.)

(Note: Critics of this atomistic approach believe that it would be more consistent with framers' intent (and more sensible) to simply require a showing of a governmental deprivation that caused a serious injury.)

2.      Show that your loss of the process you claim is owed you (considering the seriousness of your deprivation and including the added risk of an erroneous deprivation) outweighs the government's interests in not affording the process in question.

Cases

What is a protected "property" interest?

Board of Regents v Roth (1972)

What is a protected "liberty" interest?

Wisconsin v Constantine au (1971)

Paul v Davis (1976)

Vitec v Jones (1980)

The balancing test: What process is due?

Mackey v Monty (1979)

Cleveland Bd. of Educ. v Loudermilk (1985)

NOTICE TO PRINCIPAL IS NOTICE TO AGENT --

NOTICE TO AGENT IS NOTICE TO PRINCIPAL

If you are, or are affiliated with a

Monarchy/Government/Officer/Agency/Employee, foreign or domestic, CFR, UN, the BAR, the Vatican, The Rothschilds/The Rockefellers/J.P. Morgan Chase/ The

(Crooked Officials Robbing People of Rights Against Truth in Our Nation) BOOK TITLE

Warburg's, the IMF, World Bank, and or The Press or in any way affiliated and or

in concert with any of the above, the following pertains to you: If you read any of the contents of My email, YouTube, or website, you agree to pay a user fee of $425,000.00US payable in gold or silver coin, per hour or any fraction thereof, tracked by your IP address. Additionally, If

you use any of the items, context, or images from any of the above emails or

website, you agree to pay a user fee of $145,000.00 US per use, payable in gold or silver coin, per image or paragraph. Get 2 items for only $250,000.00US, payable in gold or silver coin. IN ADDITION: Imaging any web pages, partial or whole, you agree to pay a

per capture fee of $425,000.00US, payable in gold or silver coin. By your use, we mutually agree to this binding contract. All use fees are immediately due and payable upon demand to Tazadaq.

contact Tazadaq.

People's rights vs citizen's rights

Are you one of the People of the United States, as contemplated by the U.S. Constitution Preamble? Or are you one of the citizens of the United States, as defined in the U.S. Constitution 14th Amendment? Just keep in mind that your answer affects the rights you have. If you are one of the People of the United States, then all ten amendments are available to you. You have natural rights If you are a citizen of the United States, then you have civil rights [properly called civil privileges]

COMMON LAW LIEN

RECORDING REQUESTED BY: L Station and wife

Wanita Station

DEMANDANT

HSBC BANK USA NATIONAL ASSOCIATION RESPONDANT

Affidavit of Fact

Notice of Special Appearance

For the Record, To Be Read into The Record as Evidence

Notice to the Agent is Notice to the Principal- Notice to the Principal is notice to the Agent.

To:

U.S. District Court

For the District of Ohio

Clerk of Court

70 North Union Street

Second Floor

Delaware Territory, Ohio Republic

[43015] United States of America Republic, North America

Petitioner:

Yan Precious Hen Authorized Agent

Aggrieved Woman, In Propria Persona:

All Rights Reserved Without Prejudice: U.C.C. 1-207/1-308; U.C.C. 1-103

c/o 26151 Lakeshore Boulevard Apartment 2117

Euclid, Ohio [44132] Northwest Amexem

Case Number 16TRD00495-A SEATBELT REQUIRED DRIVER

Yan Precious Hen, an aggrieved woman appearing specially not generally, challenging subject matter jurisdiction of The Delaware Municipal Court in response to an improper hearing illegally scheduled at 8:30am on the 20th day of January 2018.

This is a formal request for a certified copy of the "Certified Delegation of Authority Order" issued to The United States District Court for the District of Connecticut and confirmed by Congress.

The 5th Amendment required that all persons within the United States must be given due process of the law and equal protection of the law.

"The Constitution for the United States of America binds all judicial officers at Article 6, wherein it does say, "This Constitution and the Laws of the United States which shall be made in pursuance thereof, and all Treaties made, or which shall be made under the

authority of the United States, shall be the Supreme Law of the Land, and the Judges of every State shall be bound thereby, anything in the Constitution or laws of any state to the Contrary, not withstanding," see Clause 2."

"United States Constitution, Article III, Section II - The judicial power shall extend to all cases, in law and equity, arising under this Constitution, the laws of the United States, and treaties made, or which shall be made, under their authority;--to all cases affecting ambassadors, other public ministers and con-souls;--to all cases of admiralty and maritime jurisdiction;--to controversies to which the United States shall be a party;--to controversies between two or more states;--between a state and citizens of another state;--between citizens of different states;--between citizens of the same state claiming lands under grants of different states, and between a state, or the citizens thereof, and foreign states, citizens or subjects. In all cases affecting ambassadors, other public ministers, and consuls, and those in which a state shall be party, the Supreme Court shall have original jurisdiction. In all the other cases before mentioned, the Supreme Court shall have appellate jurisdiction, both as to law and fact, with such exceptions, and under such regulations as the Congress shall make. The trial of all crimes, except in cases of impeachment, shall be by jury; and such trial shall be held in the state where the said crimes shall have been committed; but when not committed within any state, the trial shall be at such place or places as the Congress may by law have directed.

"The law provides that once State and Federal Jurisdiction has been challenged, it must be proven." Main v. Thiboutot, 100 S. Ct. 2502 (1980)

"Jurisdiction can be challenged at any time." and "Jurisdiction, once challenged, cannot be assumed and must be decided." Basso v. Utah Power & Light Co. 495 F 2d 906, 910.

"Once challenged, jurisdiction cannot be assumed, it must be proved to exist." Stuck v. Medical Examiners 94 Ca 2d 751. 211 P2d 389.

"There is no discretion to ignore that lack of jurisdiction." Joyce v. US, 474 F2d 215.

"The burden shifts to the court to prove jurisdiction." Rosemond v. Lambert, 469 F2d 416.

Where the court is without jurisdiction, it has no authority to do anything other than to dismiss the case." Fontenot v. State, 932 S.W.2d 185 "Judicial action without jurisdiction is void."-Id (1996)

"Criminal law magistrates have no power of their own and are unable to enforce any ruling." V.T.C.A., Government Code sec. 54.651 et seq., Davis v. State, 956 S.W.2d 555 (1997)

Basso v. UPL, 495 F. 2d 906

Under federal Law, which is applicable to all states, the U.S. Supreme Court stated that "if a court is without authority, its judgments and orders are regarded as nullities. They are not voidable, but simply void, and form no bar to a recovery sought, even prior to a reversal in opposition to them. They constitute no justification and all persons concerned in executing such judgments or sentences are considered, in law, as trespassers."

Brook v. Yawkey, 200 F. 2d 633

Elliot v. Piersol, 1 Pet. 328, 340, 26 U.S. 328, 340 (1828)

I, Anisha Precious Hendking, do not, under any conditions or circumstances, nor by threat, duress, or coercion, waive any Unalienable Rights or any other Rights Secured by the Constitution or Treaty; and hereby request that the Officers of this Court fulfill their Obligations to preserve the rights of this Petitioner (A Moorish American) and to carry out their delegated Judicial Duties with good behavior, and in 'Good Faith'. Agreeable to Article III, Section II of the United States Constitution Judicial Authority is legal in the Supreme Court or a lower court that has a "Certified Delegation of Authority Order" "Proof of Jurisdiction" confirmed by Congress as a lawful and formal Discovery.

Let it be noted for the record, on the record and let the record show a response is required immediately from receipt of this letter.

If no copy of the Certified Delegation of Authority Order is received this Affidavit of Fact - Writ of Discovery shall stand as Law affirming that this court does not have Jurisdiction as per Article III, Section II of the United States Constitution.

"Once Challenged, jurisdiction cannot be assumed, it must be proved to exist." Stuck v Medical Examiners 94 Ca 2d 751.211, P2d 389.

All UNCONSTITUTIONAL Citations – Summons / Ticket – Suits / (misrepresented) Bills of Exchange: Docket Number - SCC   ,

and any other 'Orders' or 'Actions' associated with it or them, to be 'Dismissed', 'Abated' and expunged from the Record; being null on it is face and merits.

Notice to the Agent is Notice to the Principal – Notice to the Principal is notice to the Agent.

Thank You,

I am:

Yan Precious Hen Authorized Representative

Natural Person, In Propria Persona:

All Rights Reserved: U.C.C. 1-207/ 1-308; U.C.C. 1-103

c/o 26151 Lakeshore Boulevard Apartment 2117

Euclid, Ohio [ near 44132] Northwest Amexem]

Non-Domestic

Thank you,

I am:

Yan Precious Hen Authorized Agent

Natural Person, In Propria Persona:

All Rights Reserved Without Prejudice: U.C.C. 1-207/1-308; U.C.C. 1-103

[c/o 26151 Lakeshore Boulevard Apartment 2117

Euclid, Ohio [44132] Northwest Amexem


IN THE CIRCUIT COURT FOR PRINCE GEORGE'S COUNTY, MARYLAND

x

Plaintiff, ASHLEY R. LAWRENCE

-against-Defendant

The C.O.R.P.O.R.A.T.I.O.N.

(Crooked Officials Robbing People of Rights Against Truth in Our Nation) BOOK TITLE

STEPHEN JONATHAN Washington


CASE # CASR15-38643

ANSWER AND COUNTER-CLAIM

STEPHEN JONATHAN WASHINGTON aggrieved man, answers the complaint of ASHLEY R. LAWRENCE, Plaintiff responding to each numbered paragraph thereof and counterclaiming as follows:

1.      DENIED, STEPHEN JONATHAN WASHINGTON WAS PRESENT BUT NOT ALLOWED TO ENTER COURT ON FEBURARY 23, 2016 AT 1 P.M.

2.      DENIED

3.      Denied,

4.      Denied,

5.      DENIED.

6.      Unware.

7.      DENIED

8.      DENIED


COUNTER-CLAIM

9.      I conditionally accept your offer upon proof of claim that On or about      FEBURARU 23, 2016, STEPHEN JONATHAN WASHING-

TON Was advised that he could not re-enter the court at 1 P.M. Any man claiming that STEPHEN JONATHAN WASHINGTON was not present at 1 P.M. must claim such under oath or affirmation.

10.      And upon conditions that you prove that the STEPHEN JONATHAN WASHINGTON was not denied due process of law by not allowing him to reenter the court. Virginia.

11.      I conditionally accept your offer upon the condition that you prove that this court does not lack Subject Matter Jurisdiction as the STEPHEN JONATHAN WASHINGTON appeared specially not generally to challenge subject matter jurisdiction. "Once jurisdic¬tion is challenged, the court cannot proceed when it clearly appears that the court lacks jurisdiction, the court has no authority to reach merits, but, rather, should dismiss the action." Melo v. US, 505 F2d 1026.

A judgment rendered by a court without personal jurisdiction over the defendant is void. It is a nullity. [A judgment shown to be void for lack of personal service on the defendant is a nullity.] Sramek v. Sramek, 17 Kan. App. 2d 573, 576-77, 840 P.2d 553 (1992), rev. denied 252 Kan. 1093 (1993).

"Court must prove on the record, all jurisdiction facts related to the jurisdiction asserted." Latana v. Hopper, 102 F. 2d 188; Chicago v. New York, 37 F Supp. 150.

213

"The law provides that once State and Federal Jurisdiction has been challenged, it must be proven." Main v. Thiboutot, 100 S. Ct. 2502 (1980).

"Jurisdiction can be challenged at any time." and "Jurisdiction, once challenged, cannot be assumed and must be decided." Basso v. Utah Power & Light Co., 495 F 2d 906, 910.

"Defense of lack of jurisdiction over the subject matter may be raised at any time, even on appeal." Hill Top Developers v. Holiday Pines Service Corp., 478 So. 2d. 368 (Fla 2nd DCA 1985)

12.      I believe to claim STEPHEN JONATHAN WASHINGTON was not present, at 1 P. M. on February 23, 2016 leads me to believe that you may be guilty of fraud.

13.      I require that the case be dismissed because the Plaintiff was present.

14.      STEPHEN JONATHAN WASHINGTON has a right to question the accuser such care is owed to defendant.

15.      Plaintiff negligence in failure to appear is breach of that duty; Plaintiff's negligent conduct resulted in Defendant's loss of rights to question the accuser.

14. Defendant suffered substantial and was denied due process of law and moves the court to dismiss the matter without preju¬dice.

WHEREFORE ROSEMARY LEBRON, Defendant demands judgment for money damages, with interest from March 12, 2009, together with the cost of this action against NEW YORK HOUSING AUTHORITY, Plaintiff, together with such other and further relief as the Court may deem reasonable and just under the circumstances.

RESPECTFULLY SUBMITTED this 1st March 2016.

STEPHEN JONATHAN WASHINGTON, Defendant


PLAINTIFF ADDRESS: THIS IS NOT A PUBLIC COMMUNICATION

Notice to Agent is Notice to Principal Notice to Principal is Notice to Agent

Silence is Acquiescence, Agreement, and Dishonor This is a self-executing contract.

Collin county

Texas state

United States of America 1787 AD

NOTICE OF INTERNATIONAL COMMERCIAL CLAIM WITHIN THE ADMIRALTY ab initio ADMINISTRATIVE REMEDY

[28 U.S.C. §1333, §1337, §2461 and §2463]

Certified Mail

Date: 12/10/16

FIRST NOTICE OF DEFAULT

LIBELLANT:

John, ope Trustee, Executive Trustee for the Private Contract Trust known as OPE JOHN

C/O     Notary Witness

Notary Address:

Notary City, State, Zip

LIBELLEE:


HOPE JOHNSON


2355 LEBANON ROAD # 12207 FRISCO, TX 12232

This demand for dismissal is applicable to all successors and assigns.

Libellant is entitled to performance and stipulated damages agreed to by Libellees failure to respond or rebut the DEMAND FOR DISIISSAL FOR LACK OF JURISDICTION AND DENIAL FOR DUE PROCESS OF LAW ab initio ADMINISTRATIVE REMEDY File CERTIFIED

MAIL #        dated     OF CLAIM, hereinafter "ICC".

Additionally, Libellees have failed to respond to the NOTICES OF DEMAND FOR LACK OF SUBJECT MATTER JURISDICTION AND DENI-

AL DUE PROCESS OF LAW THAT WERE DELIVERED BY NOTARY PRESENTMENT dated        OF FIRST NOTICE OF FAULT.

As per Libellees agreement to Silence is Acquiescence amounting to dismissal as you are in dishonor allotted time granted in the said Notice and Demand for Lack of Jurisdiction, as the terms and conditions did clearly manifest, this document is a demand for dismal of the agreed.

Silence is Acquiescence.DEMAND FOR DISMISSAL

Libellant grants Libellee Three (7) days, exclusive of the date of receipt, to answer by certified mail of the claims contained in this document. Failure to settle is a commercial dishonor [UCC3-505]. This is a UCC CONFIRMATORY WRITING and STATUTE STAPLE and is a perfected Contract upon the completion of this commercial process.

It is mandatory that if Libellee elects to respond to the foregoing, any such response must be done by oath SWEAR UNDER PENAL-TY OF PERJURY THAT THE

INFORMATION CONTAINED IN YOUR DOCUMENTS IS TRUE AND

CORRECT as stated in Libellant's ICC mailing location exactly as shown below:

Johnson, Hope Trustee, Executive Trustee for the Private Contract Trust known as HOPE JOHNSON

C/o     Notary Witness

Notary Address:

Notary City, State, Zip


## CONTRACTUAL NOTICE OF DESMISSAL

Libellant is moving for dismissal [U.C.C. 3-501 and U.C.C. Article 9] causing this NOTICE OF DEMAND AND SETTLEMENT service upon the Libellee by certified mail. This is a commercial process within the Admiralty.

Libellee is granted Three (7) days [Truth in Lending Act at Regulation Z at 12 CFR and portions of 15 USC], exclusive of the day of service to respond as stated above and as evidenced in Libellant's Demand for Dismissal.

## COMMERCIAL AFFIDAVIT OATH AND VERIFICATION

Collin county     )

) ss     Commercial Oath and Verification

Texas state     )

I, Johnson, Hope Trustee, Executive Trustee for HOPE JOHNSON, under my unlimited liability and Commercial Oath, proceeding in good faith, being of sound mind, having first-hand knowledge, state that the facts contained herein are true, correct, complete and not misleading, under penalty of International Commercial Law.

## EXPRESS SPECIFIC RESERVATION OF RIGHTS:

I explicitly reserve all my Natural rights as an American under contract Law of the Divine Creator without prejudice and, without recourse to me. I do not consent to compelled performance under any contract that I did not enter knowingly, voluntarily and in¬tentionally. I do not accept the liability of the benefits or privileges of any unrevealed contract or commercial agreement.

By:

By: John, ope Trustee, Executive Trustee for the Private Contract Trust known as OPE JOHNSON


JURAT

The C.O.R.P.O.R.A.T.I.O.N.

(Crooked Officials Robbing People of Rights Against Truth in Our Nation) BOOK TITLE

Texas state          )

) ss

Collin county      )

The above-named Libellant, Johnson, Hope Trustee, Executive Trustee for OPE JOHN appeared before me, a Notary, subscribed, sworn to the truth of this contractual NOTICE OF DEMAND FOR PAYMENT AND SETTLEMENT for closing of the escrow.

under oath this   day of   , 2016.

Notary  SEAL

My Commission expires

Tazadaq Shah

c/o 3319 My Domicile

New York, New York [nondomestic 12345]

Attornatus Privatus

United States District Court Southern District of New York




Filed:    Clerk or Deputy Clerk:

ORDER TO CLERK OF COURT TO PERFORM SPECIFIC DUTIES

Comes now the above-entitled court and orders as follows.

DISCUSSION AND CONCLUSION OF LAW

1.        The Clerk of the Court or Clerk at this office is a ministerial position not having authority of a tribunal. As such it is required to carry out it is duties without acting as a tribunal, but by merely performing the duties authorized by the court. One of those is a duty owed to the plaintiff to file documents presented for the record. Failing to file a document for the record is a criminal offense.

2.        A document is considered filed once it is received.

3.        The clerk of the court, like a recorder, is required to accept documents filed.

4.        The Federal Rules of Civil Procedure was the agreed format for the court proceedings.

5.        A paper is filed upon delivering it (A) to the clerk. FPRC 5(d)(2)

6.      The job of the clerk of the court "is to file pleadings and other documents, maintain the court's files and inform litigants of the entry of court orders." Sanders v. Department of Corrections, 815 F. Supp. 1148, H49(N.D. Ill. 1993). (Williams v. Pucinski, 01C5588 (N.D.Ill. 01/13/2004).)

7.      The duty of the clerk is to make his record correctly represent the proceedings in the case. Wetmore v. Karrick, 27 S. Ct. 434, 205 U.S. 141 (U.S. 03/11/1907 Failing to file documents presented and reflect the documents on the docket is a failure to per¬form the ministerial duties of the Clerk of Court.

8.      It is hereby the order of this court of record that the Clerk of the Court for the United States District Court Southern Dis¬trict of New York fulfill its obligations under the authority of law and file any documents presented for said purpose.

WITNESS: The SEAL of the COURT this _____ day of , 2018.

THE COURT

Tazadaq Shah

Attornatus Privatus

Tazadaq's Legal Brief that he used when Charged with Driving Without a License

The following is Tazadaq's Trial Brief used in a Traffic trial case while he was traveling. When the black robe saw what was being discussed in the brief, he had to dismiss the case because he did not want the content to be revealed in the courtroom and that is that the UNITED STATES OF AMERICA (in all caps) is originally incorporated in France so it could never be researched.

Remember, that the Statute of Liberty was given to The United States by 33-degree Masons from France. Have you ever wondered Why?

The application of Knowledge is power when you know how to use it.

Thank you for listening to my brief, please share as it is very educational. Pass it on.

On Thu, May 8, 2015 at 12:50 PM, Tazadaq Shah

I believe I told you that I had received a traffic ticket which I intended to contest. I was required to file a case brief. I did so. When I came home one day a note from the court was on my door ordering me to appear When I came into the court, the black robe fin¬ished the case which was before him at the time, and then immediately after called me forward.

He said, "I cannot allow your case to be heard in my court. Case dismissed with Prejudice." My brief appears below:

TRIAL BRIEF

IN THE WEST DISTRICT C0URT F0R KLICKITAT C0UNTY IN AND F0R THE STATE 0F WASHINGT0N

STATE 0F WASHINGT0N

Plaintiff< /span>

Vs.

TAZADAQ SHAH Respondent

Represented by Tazadaq Shah, Trustee

Respondent claims and alleges that he is innocent of the charge of driving without a license, third degree for the following reasons:

1.      Respondent      agrees that he was not in possession of a valid

State of Washington Driver's License, as the law requires (

RCW 46.20.001

License required — Rights and restriction.

(1)      No person may drive a motor vehicle upon a highway in this state without first obtaining a valid driver's license issued to Wash¬ington residents under this chapter. The only exceptions to this requirement are.

those expressly allowed by RCW 46.20.025.

(2)      A person licensed as a driver under this chapter:

May exercise the privile ge upon all highways in this state.

May not be required by a political subdivision to obtain any other license to exercise the privilege; and May not have more than one valid driver's license at any time.

2. Respondent or his representative are aware of no place,

office, location, or other source where such legally required driver's license may legally be obtained from the State of Washington as the statute requires.

3.      Respondent and his representative agree that Defendant was not in

possession of a valid STATE 0F WASHINGT0N driver's license as such is not legally required by State of Washington statute.

4.      The only alleged authority the STATE 0F WASHINGT0N

219

has over the Defendant been if a contract, adhesive or otherwise, exists between Plaintiff and Defendant? Defendant claims and alleg¬es that no such contract existed at the time and moment of the issuance of the TRAFFIC CITATION, nor does any such contract now exist.

5.

Trustee, and TANZADAQ SHAH (the name shown on said citation) are legally three entirely separate and different individuals. TAZA-DAQ SHAH is the cited individual and is a different person from both TAZADAQ SHAH and Tazadaq Shah, Trustee.

6., Tazadaq Shah, Trustee is appearing in this case.

as representative, and as required by the court for the cited party, TAZADAQ SHAH. Tazadaq Shah, Trustee legally claims and affirms.

there is no obligation, duty, and/or relationship, be it financial, legal, performance, contractual or any other, between himself and TAZADAQ SHAH.

Therefore, because of the circumstances and instances

cited in paragraphs 1 through 7, Tazadaq Shah, Trustee legally disavows and rejects any claim the Court, the Officers of the Court, THE WASHINGTON STATE PATROL, and THE STATE OF WASHINGTON, either individually or collectively, of any alleged legal liability whatsoever in the matter for which TAZADAQ SHAH was issued the WASHINGTON STATE PATROL citation,

The Defendant now cites evidence for the above allegations: 1) "When the Southern states walked out.

of Congress on March 27, 1861, the quorum to conduct business under the Constitution was lost. The only votes that Congress could lawfully take, under Parliamentary Law, were those to set the time to reconvene, take a vote to get a quorum, and vote to adjourn and set a date to reconvene later, but instead, Congress abandoned the House and Senate without setting a date to reconvene. Under the parliamentary law of Congress, when this happened, Congress became "sine die" (pronounced see-na deed-a; literally "without day") and thus when Congress adjourned sine die, it ceased to exist as a exist as a lawful deliberative body, and the only lawful, constitutional power that could declare war was no longer lawful, or in session.

The Southern states, by virtue of their secession from the Union, also ceased to exist sine die, and some state.

legislatures in the Northern Block also adjourned sine die, and thus, all the states which were parties to creating the Constitution ceased to exist.

President Lincoln executed the first executive order written by any President on April 15, 1861, Executive Order 1, and the

nation has been ruled by the president under executive order ever since. When Congress eventually did reconvene, it was recon¬vened under the military authority of the Commander-in-Chief and not by Rules of Order for Parliamentary bodies or by Constitu¬tional Law: placing the American people under martial rule ever since that national emergency declared by President Lincoln.

The Constitution for the United States of America temporarily ceased to be the law of the land, and the President, Congress, and the Courts unlawfully presumed that they were free to remake the nation in their own image, whereas lawfully no constitutional provisions were in place which afforded power to any of the actions which presumed to place the nation under the new form of control.

President Lincoln knew that he had no authority to issue any executive order, and thus he commissioned General 0rders No. 100 (April 24, 1863) as a special field code to govern his actions under martial law and which justified the seizure of power, which fic¬tionally implemented the provisions of Article.

I, Section 8, Clauses 17-18 of the Constitution beyond the boundaries of Washington, D.C. and into the several states. General 0rders No. 100, also called the Lieber Instructions and the Lieber Code, extended the Laws of War and International Law onto American soil, and the United States became the presumed conqueror of the people and the land.

Martial rule was kept secret and has never ended, the nation has been ruled under Military Law by the Commander-in-Chief of that military; the President, under his assumed executive powers and according to his executive orders, Constitutional Law under the original Constitution is enforced only as a matter of keeping public peace under the provisions of General 0rders No. 100 under martial rule.

Under Martial Law, title is a mere fiction, since all property belongs to the military except for that property which the Commander-in-Chief may, in his benevolence, exempted from taxation and seizure and upon which he allows the enemy to reside.

President Lincoln was assassinated before he could complete plans for reestablishing constitutional government in the

Southern States and end the martial rule by executive order, and the 14th Article in Amendment of the Constitution created a new citizenship status for the new expanded jurisdiction. New laws for the District of Columbia were established and passed by Con¬gress in 1871, supplanting those of February 27,1801 and May 3,1802. The District of Columbia was re-incorporated in 1872, and all.

states in the Union were reformed as Franchisees of the Federal Corporation so that a new Union of the United States could be created. The key to when the states became Federal Franchisees is related to the date when such states enacted the Field Code in law. The Field Code was a codification of the common law that was adopted first by New York, and then by California in 1872, and shortly afterwards the Lieber Code was used to bring the United States into the 1874 Brussels Conference and into the Hague Con-ventions of 1899 and 1907.

Excerpted from the Introduction of Senate Report 93-549, War and Emergency Powers Acts

2.      THE BUCK ACT

The United States government may not tax those state Citizens who live and work outside the territorial jurisdiction of Article 1, Section 8, Clause 17 or Article 4, Section 3, Clause 2 of the United States Constitution.

In 1940, Congress passed the "Buck Act", 4 U.S.C.S., Sections 105-113. Section 110(e) authorized any department of the federal government to create a "federal area" for imposition of the "Public Salary Tax Act of 1939" 4 U.S.C.S. Sec. 111. The balance of that act is found in the Internal Revenue Code.

4 U.S.C.S. Sec 110(d). The term "State" includes any Territory or possession of the United States.

4 U.S.C.S. Sec. 110(e). The term "federal area" means any lands or premises held or acquired by or for the use of the United States or any department, establishment, or agency of the United States; and any Federal area, or any part thereof, which is located with¬in the exterior boundaries of a ny State, shall be deemed to be a Federal area located within such State.

The legal consequence of that Act was to create 1) Federal areas throughout the 48 constitutional states which overlaid exactly those states, and to illegally convert state Citizens into the status of "Federal citizens", and 2) illegally usurp the Sovereignty of the several states.

3.      Creation of Franchise STATES.

The Federal Areas created under the Buck Act were named by the Federal government with the name of the state included within its borders, but spelled in all capitals, or with specific two letter all- capitals abbreviations.

The reason for this is clear since there is a legal rule that two different legal entities may not have the same name, however the legal documentation for this instance has not yet been found in the United States Code, the Code of Federal Regulations, or any other official United States legal publication.

Probably the reason for that omission in United States legal documents and statutes is that "THE UNITED STATES 0F AMERICA C0RP0RATI0N." was created in France shortly after the end of the United States Civil War. The evidence of said incorporation is in French legal archives, so they cannot be found in this country, but inference of that corporation and its activities comes from the highest sources. I quote a letter from President Franklin D. Roosevelt written November 21, 1933 to Colonel Mandell House:

"The thing to find out, and I'm hoping the corporate records.

will show, is who are the shareholders? Who is on the Board of directors of the 'UNITED STATES 0F AMERICA? •••"

That this is this situation is clearly constitutionally both illegal and unlawful is evident as the United States Constitution states in Article IV, Section3, Paragraph 1, "New states may be admitted by the Congress to the Union, but no new state shall be formed or created within the jurisdiction of any other state; nor any state be formed by the junction of two or more states or parts of states, without the consent of the legislatures of the states concerned as well as of the Congress."

That term imposed by the Constitution supersedes any provision of the Buck Act, which is in conflict, and in fact, it will be shown by statute to be such by the Defendant.

Immediately after the Bank Holiday of March 5, 1933, one day after FDR's inauguration he sent a bill to Congress establishing a four day "Banking Holiday," It was passed by Congress and immediately put into effect. A not-generally-recognized fact is that the Unit¬ed States also "declared bankruptcy" at the same time. At that point, the United States government was gradually taken over by the C0RP0RATE UNITED STATES which certainly was owned by European parties to whom it owed money which it could not pay.

222

The C.O.R.P.O.R.A.T.I.O.N.

(Crooked Officials Robbing People of Rights Against Truth in Our Nation) BOOK TITLE

Soon after the establishment of the Buck Act in 1940, the new administrative areas became STATES which were given the status of STATE FRANCHISES by the UNITED STATES 0F AMERICA C0RP0RATI0N.

For example, THE STATE 0F WASHINGT0N is a franchise of the UNITED STATES 0F AMERICA C0RP0RATI0N, and is an entity which is precisely not the Constitutional State of Washington, yet it governs this state and enforces its laws as though it possesses legal Constitutional legitimacy—it legally and lawfully does not.

In like fashion, THE WASHINGT0N STATE PATR0L is a municipal corporate entity under the control of the STATE 0F WASHINGT0N, and in identical fashion is not authorized to enforce any State of Washington law or statute.

As the UNITED STATES 0F AMERICA C0RP0RATI0N is both a foreign and a municipal corporation, the STATE 0F WASHINGT0N is a municipal corporation, and the WASHINGT0N STATE PATR0L is an adjunct to the STATE 0F WASHINGT0N, none have either the United States Constitution or the State of Washington Constitution authority to enforce State of Washington statute. Their collec¬tive and only authority extends to parties which are in contractual relationship with them, either individually or collectively actual or adhesive.

Defendant's trustee claims that Defendant and Defendant's trustee are not parties to contracts of any type or sort with the STATE 0F WASHINGT0N or any of its parts. Consequently, Defendant and Defendant's trustee have no legal obligation to any State of Washington law the STATE 0F WASHINGT0N either attempts to enforce, or actually enforces.

Defendant claims The STATE 0F WASHINGT0N has no rights, legal or otherwise, to enforce the statutes of the State of Washington, but illegally and unlawfully does so. That is the case in this specific

instance as well as others, and both the STATE 0F WASHINGT0N and the WASHINGT0N STATE PATR0L, their officers and employees who so act, have committed both the crimes of Treason and Sedition.

Defendant will prove these claims and allegations.

Defendant and Defendant's representative reserve the right to sue the STATE 0F WASHINGTON and the WASH-INGT0N STATE PATR0L, their legal representatives, and their specific officers and employees who are in any fashion or way involved in this case.

Sincerely,

Tazadaq Shah, Trustee and Representative for TAZADAQ SHAH

What Tazadaq did when a UCC Clerk / Secretary refused to file my Documents, acquiesce is never an option

Sometimes a court clerk might refuse to file a document because it does not meet certain form guidelines. For educational purpos¬es only, A clerk is not permitted to refuse filing a document for form as required by rule 5. (d)(4) of the Federal Rules of Civil Proce¬dures specifically state,

5.(d)(4) Acceptance by the clerk.

A clerk must not refuse to file a paper solely because it is not in the form prescribed by these rules or by a local rule or practice.

This is an important rule especially for those who are preceding in a court of record. Although a court of record proceeds according to common law, the creditor or sovereign can choose the Federal Rules by which to proceed. This is one of the ways I used to get a

clerk to do his/her job. Since law is the decree of the creditor or sovereign, creditors or sovereigns can decree that some statutes apply in his case.

First and far most, a court clerk does not have the authority to make any decisions. His duties are ministerial and not tribunal. The tribunal is who gets to make the decisions regarding the quality of a paper. Therefore, if at first a clerk did not file my papers. I Simply stated politely that he files them on demand. When that failed, I presented the clerk with an order from the court of record. I mailed it by registered mail to get the clerk to comply.

As you will see in my template, I have typed for educational purposes only, the anyone who removes a document from the rec¬ord can be punished for up to three years in prison according to.

18 USC § 2071

(a)     Whoever willfully and unlawfully conceals, removes, mutilates, obliterates, or destroys, or attempts to do so, or, with intent to do so takes and carries away any record, proceeding, map, book, paper, document, or other thing, filed or deposited with any clerk or officer of any court of the United States, or in any public office, or with any judicial or public officer of the United States, shall be fined under this title or imprisoned not more than three years, or both.

(b)     Whoever, having the custody of any such record, proceeding, map, book, document, paper, or other thing, willfully and unlaw¬fully conceals, removes, mutilates, obliterates, falsifies, or destroys the same, shall be fined under this title or imprisoned not more than three years, or both; and shall forfeit his office and be disqualified from holding any office under the United States. As used in this subsection, the term "office" does not include the office held by any person as a retired officer of the Armed Forces of the Unit¬ed States.

There is also case law that specifies that a document is filed once it is delivered to the clerk. It does not have to be stamped and sign. That is done merely to designate a time of filing. In one case, the court opined that a document is filed even if delivered to a deputy clerk at night at his home.

it is settled law that delivery of a pleading to a proper official is sufficient to constitute filing thereof. United States v. Lombardo, 241 U.S. 73, 36 S. Ct. 508, 60 L. Ed. 897 (1916); Milton v. United States, 105 F.2d 253, 255 (5th Cir. 1939). In Greeson v. Sherman, 265 F. Supp. 340 (D.C.Va.1967) it was held that a pleading delivered to a deputy clerk at his home at night was thereby.

"filed." (Freeman v. Giacomo Costa Fu Adrea, 282 F. Supp. 525 (E.D.Pa. 04/5/1968).)

Read the rest of the Order to the Clerk that I will cover hereto. It has good information regarding the duties of the clerk.

I always remember, do not argue with a deputy clerk or anyone because you go in dsihonor. Nobody ever wins an argument. The deputy clerk is not someone who you debate law with. They are simply paper warehousers and do not usually comprehend such things. I always send my order directly to the clerk along with a letter explaining the crime being committed by the deputy clerk and he will usually perform his duties as the law requires.

Practical Comprehension of 1099 Forms A Free National 's perspective "taxes."

The Social Security Trust

Our society is structured around the use of Federal Reserve Notes (FRNs) that are loaned to the government at interest by the pri¬vately owned Federal Reserve Bank. To get a job, open a bank account, or operate in commerce within the United States, we need to get a Tax Identification Number (TIN) from the Internal Revenue Service (IRS); and most people have contracted with the Social Security Administration (SSA) to be trustees of the Social Security Trust with a Social Security Number (SSN).

The Social Security Administration (SSA) is one of those Alphabet Agencies created during the New Deal and it is integrally linked to the IRS and the Fed. The IRS was created in 1862 under President Lincoln and was responsible for collecting an income tax enacted to pay expenses of the Civil War under the Revenue Act of 1862. Yet it was not until 1913 that the IRS took on its modern role.

This relationship is more easily understood if you were to imagine the Federal Reserve as being like a giant rental car company with FRNs being the cars owned by the Federal Reserve. Those cars are circulated throughout society, sometimes being deposited in a lot (a bank), and sometimes changing hands. You can use these rental cars to get around or to move personal property, but you must pay for the privilege, or else find another way to deal in commerce (barter, private contract, alternate currency, etc.).

Ultimately, the Fed does not really care who uses the cars, so long as someone pays for their use and pays for any damage done to them or their property. Naturally, no one wants to pull anyone else's weight, so whoever uses the rental car the most ought to pay the most, right? That is only fair. Likewise, you should not have to pay for a car that you are not using; and if you are not going to use it, you ought to let someone else use it who needs it, right? That is only fair. And if you choose not to use a car, then you do not have to pay for it, but your ability to move around is severely limited. You could ask your family and friends if you can borrow their cars, but then you are dependent, rather than independent; and in such a case, your friends and family would have the right to ask you to give up something else in exchange for the use of their rental car. Right?

Many have decided they would rather not pay for this service and so they have created their own money systems, or they live in communal societies. For some, this is a worthwhile trade-off, but for most people, that is not an option. And understandably so since such methods are a pain in the ass and complicate one's personal situation almost as much as having to pay taxes and follow statutes would. So, if we are going to live in this society, it would behoove us to learn as much as we can about this process. To adapt our¬selves and work with what we have, rather than trying to upend the whole world. Such is my feeling, at least.

Now, the IRS is so called because it oversees the nation's internal monetary transactions and provides the service of revenuing (i.e., changing the location of) that money for us so that we do not have to do it ourselves. Put plainly, the IRS's job is to keep track of who has the FRNs in their possession in any given year and to determine who owes what and to whom and to make sure that those who owe pay those that are owed. The IRS can be thought of as an agency responsible for tracking the Fed's rental cars and figuring out who has been using them the most and who must pay for their use. Because we are using FRNs, we must at least pay the cost of using them. If you are responsible and keep track of your finances, you can report this to the IRS yourself. Otherwise, the

IRS must expend resources to figure it out by relying on banks and other agencies to report your use of them. That makes their job harder and makes their employees very disgruntled.

Accounting entails figuring out all the money coming in (income) and all the money going out (expenses) and then determining the difference (balance). Everything else is just details affecting one or the other. And here we get to the various tax forms.

Most people are familiar with the 1040 Form, which is an Individual Tax Return form. This is the basic form in which you take all your account statements and add up the total income it all so suggest that you are a federal employee. Depending on how much you made each year, you pay a certain amount of tax. Most people are familiar with the Income section of the 1040 Form in which they report their income from wages on a W-2 Form. You will probably recognize that there is a box on the W-2 for reporting income earned from employee wages, but there are also boxes in which you can report money that is withheld from you by the employer - i.e., money that does not get added to your income.

We established before how you do not have to pay taxes on non-income (sales tax and others aside for the moment). Recall also that you have an Employee Identification Number (EIN) that is the same as your SSN and this makes you an employee of the State - your job being to act as a trustee and manage the trust that bears a similar name to yours. Instead of getting paid in wages, you get paid in benefits, privileges, and services, cutting out the middleman, which is all money is, really.

Now, if you have a checking account, a savings account, and a credit card account, these are all independent accounts with different numbers, yet you are the creator of all of them. So, they are all part of one system - your system. You might have these accounts vested in different banks, and to the bank, it looks like they are gaining or losing when you move money around, but it is all still under your system. It has not actually left your control. In much the same way, there are many SSNs and EINs, yet they all trace back to the Federal Reserve, the SSA, and the IRS. It is all one system - the State's system. They may have their property in the hands of different persons, and to the individual, it may look like he is gaining or losing money, yet it all remains under the control of the State. It has not really gone anywhere. So, while the rental cars might change drivers, they have not changed owners.

http://youtu.be/zOjKGJy1uKY

When you get a check, what is the first thing you normally do? Deposit that money into the bank, yes? This then appears as income on your bank statement. Most people think they are depositing money into the bank when they do this; but there is no lawful money (no gold and silver), so what is really taking place is an extension of credit from one account to another. The check you de¬posited is a security that the bank holds onto and adds to its reserves, fractionalizing it and using it as the basis for new loans. The actual security stays with the bank and you are issued a certain amount of credit which becomes the bank's liability. In other words, if lawful money ever returned, this would be how much the bank would owe to you. Similarly, when you write a check, you are issuing a security and the bank then withholds credit from you by diminishing its liability to you. The cycle of how this works can be seen in this diagram.

Recall that the banks are like parking lots in our rental car example. Why would you leave a car in a parking lot? Usually because you just need a safe place to store the car until you need it again. In the same way, banks store our securities and the credit that goes with them until we need that credit again. But how often do you reclaim that credit? How often do you come back for your rental car? Most people do not. They assume they do, since a new car has been made available to them, but it is not the one they originally had. That car was deemed abandoned. But when you park a car, can the owner of the lot automatically assume your car.

is abandoned? No, it cannot. It must wait a while and then report it to the police and if no one comes to claim it within a reasonable time, then it is abandoned and the first person to come along and lay claim to it can use it. Because the lot owner was the one that reported it, they know of its status and will likely try to claim it for themselves.

In the same way, the banks will hold onto the securities you issued - checks, cash, Electronic Funds Transfers (EFTs), etc. - with the understanding that they belong to you, not the bank. After three years' time, if you do not come and claim those securities (and most people do not), the bank has them declared abandoned and files a form with the IRS to claim those funds and add them to their reserves.

So, you have rental cars sitting in lots that you are not using, but rather than let someone else use them, you are just letting them sit there while you pay a fee for them. Does that sound insane to you, or what? Can you really afford to pay for what you are not using? You are hurting yourself and others needlessly.

How, then, do we remedy this? Well, there exists a form known as a 1099-A. The "A" stands for either "abandonment" or "acquisition," as that is what this form is used for. You can use it to acquire the assets of a loan (e.g., the promissory note) or to declare certain securities as abandoned when you do not intend to get them back, such as when you write a check, use a credit or debit card, or make an electronic funds transfer. Because the various accounts are all part of one system, what the 1099-A does is to help report to the IRS where these securities lie and who is using them.

In the case of a loan, you fill out a promissory note (which is a security and has value) and receive an extension of credit. Why do you have to repay the lender? Because they have an outstanding liability, as evidenced by the promissory note. By filing a 1099-A as an acquisition, you are taking back the security and informing the IRS that you accept possession of these securities and they, in turn, will zero out the liability of the lender for you. This is the form that the bank uses when they acquire your abandoned securities. It would be like if you found a rental car in your driveway one day. You file a 1099-A declaring that you intend to acquire it. If no one else claims it, then you get to use it. Not too bad, eh?

Of course, in doing so, you must pay the rental fee (income tax), so it would behoove you to use it for your purposes and then get rid of it once you are done with it. You might use it once and then no longer need it again. Indeed, no one gets a loan just to have it sit there and do nothing for them. Often, such credit gets spent right away in the purchasing of property or the discharging of debts.

So really, the rental car is only staying in your possession for a short time before you abandon it again. In this case, you would file a 1099-A as an abandonment and declare that you are abandoning the car and that it is free for someone else to claim.

So, we return to the 1040 Form and note that all money coming into your accounts gets reported as Income (lines 7 through 22) and all money going out gets reported as either Adjusted Gross Income (lines 23 through 37) or Payments (lines 61 through 71).

Indeed, if we look at line 61, we see that it says, "Federal income tax withheld from Forms W-2 and 1099." But there is nothing on the 1099-A that mentions a withholding. So, what does this mean?

Well, an employer cannot take money from you without cause, but they can withhold wages from you when you do not perform your job correctly, or if you claim certain benefits, or if a law compels them to do so (such as for Social Security) and this gets re¬ported on a W-2 Form. As an employee of the State, when you extend credit from one of your accounts, that credit is withheld from you as well. This gets reported on a form called a 1099-OID, which stands for "Original Issue Discount." It is so called because,

for the purposes of determining taxation, it discounts (does not count) all securities originally issued by you. So, if you wrote $1000 worth of checks within a given year, that $1000 worth of credit that was withheld from you does not count!

Those who have filed tax forms before will know that not all income is necessarily taxable and that the amount you must pay is determined by the amount of taxable income you have. So, depending on your situation, it is possible that you will not have to pay an income tax at all, or even that the IRS owes you a refund.

On the 1040 Form, line 74 states, "Amount you owe. Subtract line 71 from line 60." Line 60 is your total income after considering wages, certain tax credits, exemptions, and the like (everything from line 1 to line 59). Line 71 is your total payments after considering withholdings and certain tax credits (everything from line 61 to line 70). Included in the latter is the total of withholdings from your 1099-OID forms.

Line 72 of the 1040 Form states that, "If line 71 is more than line 60, subtract line 60 from line 71. This is the amount you overpaid." Overpaid. I like the sound of that. So, what this says is that if the amount withheld from you is greater than the amount of taxable income you have, the IRS will refund that credit to you with a nice fat check. Considering most of us spend considerable sums each year, thereby having considerable sums withheld from us, what do you suppose the result would be?

Important Tax Information

Being a creditor means being knowledgeable and responsible, and that means turning in your tax forms on time. If you do not get your forms in on time, you might not get the refund you want (at best) or you might be faced with a late penalty or even jail time (at worst). So here is some information to keep in mind when you file your taxes.

This information is subject to change based on the policies of the IRS, so check back here regularly.

The following forms are for educational purposes only. Do not use these forms as the ones you send into the IRS or you will receive a fine! The real forms all have special ink that can be scanned, which these forms do not have.


1099-A

1099-OID

1096

1040 1040-V

1041 †

4490 ††

† The 1041 is an income tax return for estates and trusts, as opposed to the 1040, which is an income tax return for individuals.

†† The 4490 is difficult to find. It is a proof of claim, signed under penalty of perjury that must precede any attempt to enforce a tax lien against you, according to law.

Dates

Keep in mind the following dates when preparing to file your taxes.

November 1: Earliest day that 1099-A Forms and 1099-OID Forms get processed.

December 31: Last day of the old fiscal year.

January 1: First day of the new fiscal year.

February 20: Recommended date to have 1099-A and 1099-OID Forms in the mail by.

March 1: Last day to file 1099-A Forms and 1099-OID Forms if filing by mail.

March 31: Last day to file 1099-A Forms and 1099-OID Forms if filing online.

April 15: Last day to file 1040 Forms if filing by mail.

April 18: Last day to file 1040 Forms if filing online.

** Do not wait until the last minute to file your forms if you can help it.

** If you do not get your 1099-A Forms and 1099-OID Forms in by the deadline, you will have to wait until November 1 before it gets processed.

** Corrected forms can be sent in later if you already have an original form on file.

Notes

When issued a loan, you must wait at least 30 days before filing a 1099-A Form as an acquisition. This amount gets included in your income.

You need to send in a 1099-A Form as an abandonment before you can send in a 1099-OID Form. Send all 1099-A Forms and 1099-OID Forms before submitting the 1040 Form because you need to include the information from the 1099-A Forms and 1099-OID Forms on the 1040 Form.

Affidavit of Fact

Notice of Special Appearance

For the Record, To Be Read into The Record as Evidence

Notice to the Agent is Notice to the Principal- Notice to the Principal is notice to the Agent.

The C.O.R.P.O.R.A.T.I.O.N.

(Crooked Officials Robbing People of Rights Against Truth in Our Nation) BOOK TITLE

To:

U.S. District Court

For the District of Ohio

Clerk of Court

70 North Union Street

Second Floor

Delaware Territory, Ohio Republic

[43015] United States of America Republic, North America

Petitioner:

Yan Precious Hen Authorized Agent

Aggrieved Woman, In Propria Persona:

All Rights Reserved Without Prejudice: U.C.C. 1-207/1-308; U.C.C. 1-103

c/o 26151 Lakeshore Boulevard Apartment 2117

Euclid, Ohio [44132] Northwest Amexem

Case Number 16TRD00495-A SEATBELT REQUIRED DRIVER

Yan Precious Hen, an aggrieved woman appearing specially not generally, challenging subject matter jurisdiction of The Delaware Municipal Court in response to an improper hearing illegally scheduled at 8:30am on the 20th day of January 2018.

This is a formal request for a certified copy of the "Certified Delegation of Authority Order" issued to The United States District Court for the District of Connecticut and confirmed by Congress.

The 5th Amendment required that all persons within the United States must be given due process of the law and equal protection of the law.

"The Constitution for the United States of America binds all judicial officers at Article 6, wherein it does say, "This Constitution and

the Laws of the United States which shall be made in pursuance thereof, and all Treaties made, or which shall be made under the authority of the United States, shall be the Supreme Law of the Land, and the Judges of every State shall be bound thereby, any¬thing in the Constitution or laws of any state to the Contrary, not withstanding," see Clause 2."

230

The C.O.R.P.O.R.A.T.I.O.N.

(Crooked Officials Robbing People of Rights Against Truth in Our Nation) BOOK TITLE

"United States Constitution, Article III, Section II - The judicial power shall extend to all cases, in law and equity, arising under this Constitution, the laws of the United States, and treaties made, or which shall be made, under their authority;--to all cases affecting ambassadors, other public ministers and con-suls;--to all cases of admiralty and maritime jurisdiction;--to controversies to which the United States shall be a party;--to controversies between two or more states;--between a state and citizens of another state;--between citizens of different states;--between citizens of the same state claiming lands under grants of different states, and between a state, or the citizens thereof, and foreign states, citizens or subjects. In all cases affecting ambassadors, other public ministers, and consuls, and those in which a state shall be party, the Supreme Court shall have original jurisdiction. In all the other cases before mentioned, the Supreme Court shall have appellate jurisdiction, both as to law and fact, with such exceptions, and under such regulations as the Congress shall make. The trial of all crimes, except in cases of impeachment, shall be by jury; and such trial shall be held in the state where the said crimes shall have been committed; but when not committed within any state, the trial shall be at such place or places as the Congress may by law have directed.

"The law provides that once State and Federal Jurisdiction has been challenged, it must be proven." Main v. Thiboutot, 100 S. Ct. 2502 (1980)

"Jurisdiction can be challenged at any time." and "Jurisdiction, once challenged, cannot be assumed and must be decided." Basso v. Utah Power & Light Co. 495 F 2d 906, 910.

"Once challenged, jurisdiction cannot be assumed, it must be proved to exist." Stuck v. Medical Examiners 94 Ca 2d 751. 211 P2d 389.

"There is no discretion to ignore that lack of jurisdiction." Joyce v. US, 474 F2d 215.

"The burden shifts to the court to prove jurisdiction." Rosemond v. Lambert, 469 F2d 416.

Where the court is without jurisdiction, it has no authority to do anything other than to dismiss the case." Fontenot v. State, 932 S.W.2d 185 "Judicial action without jurisdiction is void."-Id (1996)

"Criminal law magistrates have no power of their own and are unable to enforce any ruling." V.T.C.A., Government Code sec. 54.651 et seq., Davis v. State, 956 S.W.2d 555 (1997)

Basso v. UPL, 495 F. 2d 906

Under federal Law, which is applicable to all states, the U.S. Supreme Court stated that "if a court is without authority, its judg¬ments and orders are regarded as nullities. They are not voidable, but simply void, and form no bar to a recovery sought, even prior to a reversal in opposition to them. They constitute no justification and all persons concerned in executing such judgments or sen¬tences are considered, in law, as trespassers."

Brook v. Yawkey, 200 F. 2d 633

Elliot v. Piersol, 1 Pet. 328, 340, 26 U.S. 328, 340 (1828)

I, Yaniesha Precious Hendking, do not, under any conditions or circumstances, nor by threat, duress, or coercion, waive any Unal-ienable Rights or any other Rights Secured by the Constitution or Treaty; and hereby request that the Officers of this Court fulfill their Obligations to preserve the rights of this Petitioner (A Moorish American) and to carry out their delegated Judicial Duties with good behavior, and in 'Good Faith'. Agreeable to Article III, Section II of the United States Constitution Judicial Authority is legal in the Supreme Court or a lower court that has a "Certified Delegation of Authority Order" "Proof of Jurisdiction" confirmed by Con-gress as a lawful and formal Discovery.


Affidavit of Fact

Notice of Special Appearance

For the Record, To Be Read into The Record as Evidence

Notice to the Agent is Notice to the Principal- Notice to the Principal is notice to the Agent.

To:

U.S. District Court

For the District of Ohio

Clerk of Court

70 North Union Street

Second Floor

Delaware Territory, Ohio Republic

[43015] United States of America Republic, North America

Petitioner:

Yan Precious Hen Authorized Agent

Aggrieved Woman, In Propria Persona:

All Rights Reserved Without Prejudice: U.C.C. 1-207/1-308; U.C.C. 1-103

c/o 26151 Lakeshore Boulevard Apartment 2117

Euclid, Ohio [44132] Northwest Amexem

Case Number 16TRD00495-A SEATBELT REQUIRED DRIVER

Yan Precious Hen, an aggrieved woman appearing specially not generally, challenging subject matter jurisdiction of The Delaware Municipal Court in response to an improper hearing illegally scheduled at 8:30am on the 20th day of January 2018.

This is a formal request for a certified copy of the "Certified Delegation of Authority Order" issued to The United States District Court for the District of Connecticut and confirmed by Congress.

The 5th Amendment required that all persons within the United States must be given due process of the law and equal protection of the law.

Yan Precious Hen, an aggrieved woman appearing specially not generally, challenging subject matter jurisdiction of The Delaware Municipal Court in response to an improper hearing illegally scheduled at 8:30am on the 20th day of January 2018.

This is a formal request for a certified copy of the "Certified Delegation of Authority Order" issued to The United States District Court for the District of Connecticut and confirmed by Congress.

The 5th Amendment required that all persons within the United States must be given due process of the law and equal protection of the law.

"The Constitution for the United States of America binds all judicial officers at Article 6, wherein it does say, "This Constitution and the Laws of the United States which shall be made in pursuance thereof, and all Treaties made, or which shall be made under the authority of the United States, shall be the Supreme Law of the Land, and the Judges of every State shall be bound thereby, any¬thing in the Constitution or laws of any state to the Contrary, not withstanding," see Clause 2."

"United States Constitution, Article III, Section II - The judicial power shall extend to all cases, in law and equity, arising under this Constitution, the laws of the United States, and treaties made, or which shall be made, under their authority;--to all cases affecting ambassadors, other public ministers and con-suls;--to all cases of admiralty and maritime jurisdiction;--to controversies to which the United States shall be a party;--to controversies between two or more states;--between a state and citizens of another state;--between citizens of different states;--between citizens of the same state claiming lands under grants of different states, and between a state, or the citizens thereof, and foreign states, citizens or subjects. In all cases affecting ambassadors, other public ministers, and consuls, and those in which a state shall be party, the Supreme Court shall have original jurisdiction. In all the other cases before mentioned, the Supreme Court shall have appellate jurisdiction, both as to law and fact, with such exceptions, and under such regulations as the Congress shall make. The trial of all crimes, except in cases of impeachment, shall be by jury; and such trial shall be held in the state where the said crimes shall have been committed; but when not committed within any state, the trial shall be at such place or places as the Congress may by law have directed.

"The law provides that once State and Federal Jurisdiction has been challenged, it must be proven." Main v. Thiboutot, 100 S. Ct. 2502 (1980)

"Jurisdiction can be challenged at any time." and "Jurisdiction, once challenged, cannot be assumed and must be decided." Basso v. Utah Power & Light Co. 495 F 2d 906, 910.

"Once challenged, jurisdiction cannot be assumed, it must be proved to exist." Stuck v. Medical Examiners 94 Ca 2d 751. 211 P2d 389.

"There is no discretion to ignore that lack of jurisdiction." Joyce v. US, 474 F2d 215.

"The burden shifts to the court to prove jurisdiction." Rosemond v. Lambert, 469 F2d 416.

Where the court is without jurisdiction, it has no authority to do anything other than to dismiss the case." Fontenot v. State, 932 S.W.2d 185 "Judicial action without jurisdiction is void."-Id (1996)

"Criminal law magistrates have no power of their own and are unable to enforce any ruling." V.T.C.A., Government Code sec. 54.651 et seq., Davis v. State, 956 S.W.2d 555 (1997)

Basso v. UPL, 495 F. 2d 906

Under federal Law, which is applicable to all states, the U.S. Supreme Court stated that "if a court is without authority, its judgments and orders are regarded as nullities. They are not voidable, but simply void, and form no bar to a recovery sought, even prior to a reversal in opposition to them. They constitute no justification and all persons concerned in executing such judgments or sen¬tences are considered, in law, as trespassers."

Brook v. Yawkey, 200 F. 2d 633

Elliot v. Piersol, 1 Pet. 328, 340, 26 U.S. 328, 340 (1828)

I, Yaniesha Precious Hendking, do not, under any conditions or circumstances, nor by threat, duress, or coercion, waive any Unalienable Rights or any other Rights Secured by the Constitution or Treaty; and hereby request that the Officers of this Court fulfill their Obligations to preserve the rights of this Petitioner (A Moorish American) and to carry out their delegated Judicial Duties with good behavior, and in 'Good Faith'. Agreeable to Article III, Section II of the United States Constitution Judicial Authority is legal in the Supreme Court or a lower court that has a "Certified Delegation of Authority Order" "Proof of Jurisdiction" confirmed by Con¬gress as a lawful and formal Discovery.

Let it be noted for the record, on the record and let the record show a response is required immediately from receipt of this letter. If no copy of the Certified Delegation of Authority Order is received this Affidavit of Fact - Writ of Discovery shall stand as Law affirming that this court does not have Jurisdiction as per Article III, Section II of the United States Constitution.

"Once Challenged, jurisdiction cannot be assumed, it must be proved to exist." Stcuk v Medical Examiners 94 Ca 2d 751.211, P2d 389.

All UNCONSTITUTIONAL Citations – Summons / Ticket – Suits / (misrepresented) Bills of Exchange: Docket Number - SCC   ,

and any other 'Orders' or 'Actions' associated with it or them, to be 'Dismissed', 'Abated' and expunged from the Record; being null on it is face and merits.

Notice to the Agent is Notice to the Principal – Notice to the Principal is notice to the Agent.

Thank You,

I am:

Yan Precious Hen Authorized Representative

Natural Person, In Propria Persona:

All Rights Reserved: U.C.C. 1-207/ 1-308; U.C.C. 1-103

c/o 26151 Lakeshore Boulevard Apartment 2117

Euclid, Ohio [ near 44132] Northwest Amexem]

Non-Domestic

The C.O.R.P.O.R.A.T.I.O.N.

(Crooked Officials Robbing People of Rights Against Truth in Our Nation) BOOK TITLE

Thank you,

I am:

Yan Precious Hen Authorized Agent

Natural Person, In Propria Persona:

All Rights Reserved Without Prejudice: U.C.C. 1-207/1-308; U.C.C. 1-103

[c/o 26151 Lakeshore Boulevard Apartment 2117

Euclid, Ohio [44132] Northwest Amexem

IN THE CIRCUIT COURT FOR PRINCE GEORGE'S COUNTY, MARYLAND

x

Plaintiff, ASHLEY R. LAWRENCE

-against-Defendant

STEPHEN JONATHAN WASHINGTON,

x


CASE # CASR15-38643

ANSWER AND COUNTER-CLAIM

STEPHEN JONATHAN WASHINGTON aggrieved man answers the complaint of ASHLEY R. LAWRENCE, Plaintiff responding to each.


numbered paragraph thereof and counterclaiming as follows:

1.      DENIED, STEPHEN JONATHAN WASHINGTON WAS PRESENT BUT NOT ALLOWED TO ENTER COURT ON FEBURARY 23, 2016 AT 1 P.M.

2.      DENIED

3.      Denied,

4.      Denied,

5.      DENIED.

6.      Unware.

7.      DENIED

8.      DENIED

COUNTER-CLAIM

9.      I conditionally accept your offer upon proof of claim that On or about      FEBURARU 23, 2016, STEPHEN JONATHAN WASHING-

TON Was advised that he could not re-enter the court at 1 P.M. Any man claiming that STEPHEN JONATHAN WASHINGTON was not present at 1 P.M. must claim such under oath or affirmation.

10.      And upon conditions that you prove that the STEPHEN JONATHAN WASHINGTON was not denied due process of law by not allowing him to reenter the court. Virginia.

11.      I conditionally accept your offer upon the condition that you prove that this court does not lack Subject Matter Jurisdiction as the STEPHEN JONATHAN WASHINGTON appeared specially not generally to challenge subject matter jurisdiction. "Once jurisdiction is challenged, the court cannot proceed when it clearly appears that the court lacks jurisdiction, the court has no authority to reach merits, but, rather, should dismiss the action." Melo v. US, 505 F2d 1026.

A judgment rendered by a court without personal jurisdiction over the defendant is void. It is a nullity. [A judgment shown to be void for lack of personal service on the defendant is a nullity.] Sramek v. Sramek, 17 Kan. App. 2d 573, 576-77, 840 P.2d 553 (1992), rev. denied 252 Kan. 1093 (1993).

"Court must prove on the record, all jurisdiction facts related to the jurisdiction asserted." Latana v. Hopper, 102 F. 2d 188; Chicago v. New York, 37 F Supp. 150.

"The law provides that once State and Federal Jurisdiction has been challenged, it must be proven." Main v. Thiboutot, 100 S. Ct. 2502 (1980).

"Jurisdiction can be challenged at any time." and "Jurisdiction, once challenged, cannot be assumed and must be decided." Basso v. Utah Power & Light Co., 495 F 2d 906, 910.

"Defense of lack of jurisdiction over the subject matter may be raised at any time, even on appeal." Hill Top Developers v. Holiday Pines Service Corp., 478 So. 2d. 368 (Fla 2nd DCA 1985)

12.      I believe to claim STEPHEN JONATHAN WASHINGTON was not present, at 1 P. M. on February 23, 2016 leads me to believe that you may be guilty of fraud.

13.      I require that the case be dismissed because the Plaintiff was present.

14.      STEPHEN JONATHAN WASHINGTON has a right to question the accuser such care is owed to defendant.

15.      Plaintiff negligence in failure to appear is breach of that duty; Plaintiff's negligent conduct resulted in Defendant's loss of rights to question the accuser.

14. Defendant suffered substantial and was denied due process of law and moves the court to dismiss the matter without prejudice.

WHEREFORE ROSEMARY LEBRON, Defendant demands judgment for money damages, with interest from March 12, 2009, together with the cost of this action against NEW YORK HOUSING AUTHORITY, Plaintiff, together with such other and further relief as the Court may deem reasonable and just under the circumstances.

RESPECTFULLY SUBMITTED this 1st March 2016.

STEPHEN JONATHAN WASHINGTON, Defendant

PLAINTIFF ADDRESS:

THIS IS NOT A PUBLIC COMMUNICATION

Notice to Agent is Notice to Principal Notice to Principal is Notice to Agent

Silence is Acquiescence, Agreement, and Dishonor This is a self-executing contract.

Collin county

Texas state

United States of America 1787 AD

NOTICE OF INTERNATIONAL COMMERCIAL CLAIM WITHIN THE ADMIRALTY ab initio ADMINISTRATIVE REMEDY

[28 U.S.C. §1333, §1337, §2461 and §2463]

Certified Mail

Date: 12/10/16


FIRST NOTICE OF DEFAULT


LIBELLANT:

John, ope Trustee, Executive Trustee for the Private Contract Trust known as OPE JOHN

C/O     Notary Witness

Notary Address:

Notary City, State, Zip

LIBELLEE:

HOPE JOHNSON

2355 LEBANON ROAD # 12207

FRISCO, TX 12232

This demand for dismissal is applicable to all successors and assigns.

Libellant is entitled to performance and stipulated damages agreed to by Libellees failure to respond or rebut the DEMAND FOR DISIISSAL FOR LACK OF JURISDICTION AND DENIAL FOR DUE PROCESS OF LAW ab initio ADMINISTRATIVE REMEDY File CERTIFIED

MAIL #       dated    OF CLAIM, hereinafter "ICC".

Additionally, Libellees have failed to respond to the NOTICES OF DEMAND FOR LACK OF SUBJECT MATTER JURISDICTION AND DENI-

AL DUE PROCESS OF LAW THAT WERE DELIVERED BY NOTARY PRESENTMENT dated       OF FIRST NOTICE OF FAULT.

As per Libellees agreement to Silence is Acquiescence amounting to dismissal as you are in dishonor allotted time granted in the said Notice and Demand for Lack of Jurisdiction, as the terms and conditions did clearly manifest, this document is a demand for dismal of the agreed.

Silence is Acquiescence.

DEMAND FOR DISMISSAL

Libellant grants Libellee Three (7) days, exclusive of the date of receipt, to answer by certified mail of the claims contained in this document. Failure to settle is a commercial dishonor [UCC3-505]. This is a UCC CONFIRMATORY WRITING and STATUTE STAPLE and is a perfected Contract upon the completion of this commercial process.


It is mandatory that if Libellee elects to respond to the foregoing, any such response must be done by oath SWEAR UNDER PENAL-TY OF PERJURY THAT THE

INFORMATION CONTAINED IN YOUR DOCUMENTS IS TRUE AND

CORRECT as stated in Libellant's ICC mailing location exactly as shown below:

Johnson, Hope Trustee, Executive Trustee for the Private Contract Trust known as HOPE JOHNSON

C/o     Notary Witness

Notary Address:

Notary City, State, Zip

CONTRACTUAL NOTICE OF DESMISSAL

Libellant is moving for dismissal [U.C.C. 3-501 and U.C.C. Article 9] causing this NOTICE OF DEMAND AND SETTLEMENT service upon the Libellee by certified mail. This is a commercial process within the Admiralty.

Libellee is granted Three (7) days [Truth in Lending Act at Regulation Z at 12 CFR and portions of 15 USC], exclusive of the day of service to respond as stated above and as evidenced in Libellant's Demand for Dismissal.

COMMERCIAL AFFIDAVIT OATH AND VERIFICATION

The C.O.R.P.O.R.A.T.I.O.N.

(Crooked Officials Robbing People of Rights Against Truth in Our Nation) BOOK TITLE

Collin county     )

) ss     Commercial Oath and Verification

Texas state     )

I, Johnson, Hope Trustee, Executive Trustee for HOPE JOHNSON, under my unlimited liability and Commercial Oath, proceeding in good faith, being of sound mind, having first-hand knowledge, state that the facts contained herein are true, correct, complete and not misleading, under penalty of International Commercial Law.

EXPRESS SPECIFIC RESERVATION OF RIGHTS:

I explicitly reserve all my Natural rights as an American under contract Law of the Divine Creator without prejudice and, without recourse to me. I do not consent to compelled performance under any contract that I did not enter knowingly, voluntarily and in-tentionally. I do not accept the liability of the benefits or privileges of any unrevealed contract or commercial agreement.

By:

By: John, ope Trustee, Executive Trustee for the Private Contract Trust known as OPE JOHNSON

JURAT

Texas state     )

) ss

Collin county     )

The above-named Libellant, Johnson, Hope Trustee, Executive Trustee for OPE JOHN appeared before me, a Notary, subscribed, sworn to the truth of this contractual NOTICE OF DEMAND FOR PAYMENT AND SETTLEMENT for closing of the escrow.

under oath this   day of   , 2016.

Notary  SEAL

My Commission expires


Tazadaq Shah

c/o 3319 My Domicile

New York, New York [nondomestic 12345] Attornatus Privatus


United States District Court Southern District of New York

239

The C.O.R.P.O.R.A.T.I.O.N.

(Crooked Officials Robbing People of Rights Against Truth in Our Nation) BOOK TITLE

Filed:    Clerk or Deputy Clerk:

ORDER TO CLERK OF COURT TO PERFORM SPECIFIC DUTIES

Comes now the above-entitled court and orders as follows, DISCUSSION AND CONCLUSION OF LAW

1.      The Clerk of the Court or Clerk at this office is a ministerial position not having authority of a tribunal. As such it is required to carry out it is duties without acting as a tribunal, but by merely performing the duties authorized by the court. One of those is a duty owed to the plaintiff to file documents presented for the record. Failing to file a document for the record is a criminal offense.

2.      A document is considered filed once it is received.

3.      The clerk of the court, like a recorder, is required to accept documents filed.

4.      The Federal Rules of Civil Procedure was the agreed format for the court proceedings.

5.      A paper is filed upon delivering it (A) to the clerk. FPRC 5(d)(2)

6.      The job of the clerk of the court "is to file pleadings and other documents, maintain the court's files and inform litigants of the entry of court orders." Sanders v. Department of Corrections, 815 F. Supp. 1148, H49(N.D. Ill. 1993). (Williams v. Pucinski, 01C5588 (N.D.Ill. 01/13/2004).)

7.      The duty of the clerk is to make his record correctly represent the proceedings in the case. Wetmore v. Karrick, 27 S. Ct. 434, 205 U.S. 141 (U.S. 03/11/1907 Failing to file documents presented and reflect the documents on the docket is a failure to per¬form the ministerial duties of the Clerk of Court.

8.      It is hereby the order of this court of record that the Clerk of the Court for the United States District Court Southern District of New York fulfill its obligations under the authority of law and file any documents presented for said purpose.

WITNESS: The SEAL of the COURT this _____ day of , 2018.

THE COURT

Tazadaq Shah

Attornatus Privatus

Tazadaq's Legal Brief that he used when Charged with Driving Without a License

The following is Tazadaq's Trial Brief used in a Traffic trial case while he was traveling. When the black robe saw what was being

QUIET TITLE

STATE OF NORTH CAROLINA        } SUPERIOR COURT DISTRICT 10

COUNTY OF WAKE   }

}

The C.O.R.P.O.R.A.T.I.O.N.

(Crooked Officials Robbing People of Rights Against Truth in Our Nation) BOOK TITLE

}

}

Lamar Staton and Wife   }

Wanita Staton

5429 Neuse View Drive

Raleigh, North Carolina near [27610]

Non-Domestic

Plaintiffs

      vs.    )

)      Case NO.:

POORE SUBSTITUTE, LTD   )

)

WAKE COUNTY SHERIFF   )

      Defendants     ) Action to Quiet Title

)      to Private Allodial Property

)

)

)

)      The Constitution for the

)      United States of

)      America,

)      Article Three and

)

)      Trial by the Jury Demanded

)

TO ALL PARTIES OF INTEREST:

I, Wanita Staton and Lamar Staton Bennett, rely upon Haines v. Kerner, 404 US 519 (1972), pursuant to the limitations imposed upon me as Plaintiff and this Tribunal by the Constitution of the State of North Carolina and the Fifth, and Seventh and Fourteenth Amendments to the Constitution of the United States, and the Northwest Ordinance of 1787. We purchased the home, which are the subject of this lawsuit, from OWNIT MORTAGAGE SOLUTIONS INC., who required no down payment and executed an original promissory note and deed of trust, which was executed by the Plaintiffs and Roper & Coleman with the original lender. Roper and Coleman have since privately agreed in principle to disclaim any right, title and interest in the property and are currently no longer in business. HSBC BANK USA NATIONAL ASSOCIATION subsequently purchased the note and deed of trust from ROPER & COLE¬MAN. We, Wanita Staton and husband Lamar Staton have authority and unalienable right to demand that the Defendants; 1.) show how and when they came to have a security interest in my private property described in AFFIDAVIT OF INTEREST OF FULL

NAME EXHIBIT "E", 2.) show how when and by what means they have filed a claim.

against the original Warranty Deed petitioned for and granted for the said home described in Exhibit A, 3.) provide evidence that there is valuable consideration for the alleged bank loan, 4.) provide evidence that the Defendant POORE SUBSTITUTE, LTD has the right to lend credit and 5.) provide evidence that the right to subrogation exists, and provide evidence that the mortgage debt complies with all requirements of the Federal and State Constitution or; 6.) forever abandon any claim of interest in our property and stop the fraudulent and scandalous action to foreclose on their fraudulent chattel paper, for which no valuable consideration was ever provided in the original mortgage.

We have named WAKE COUNTY SHERIFF as a Defendant to ensure that said Sheriff refrains from any and all unlawful activities at the direction of POORE SUBSTITUTE, LTD that will be inconsistent with our ownership and lawful control of the private property, which is the subject of this action to quiet title. We fully understand that the courts in North Carolina routinely the Sheriff to be called upon to carry out an unlawful act in violation of our property rights. In furtherance of that goal, we have asked the court, as part of the relief sought herein, for an order of cease and desist, commanding the Defendants to cease and desist from any actions to foreclose on the note and deed of trust in light of the lack of the right of subrogation and the failure of consideration, which is discussed below. We are not asking for financial compensation from the WAKE COUNTY SHERIFF in this action to quiet title.

ALL PARTIES PLEASE TAKE NOTICE:

We, Lamar Staton, and wife Wanita Staton, Your Affiant (s), purchased the building located at 5429 Neuse View Drive Raleigh, North Carolina near [27610] Non-Domestic from OWNIT MORTAGAGE SOLUTIONS INC., expecting that we would be doing business with Roper & Coleman as the lender and holder of the note, by paying the monthly payments due on the note. I, Wanita Staton, am one of the people of North Carolina for which the North Carolina Constitution was created in this court of record, and I Lamar Staton am one of the people of North Carolina for which the North Carolina Constitution was created in this court of record, com-

plain of the fraudulent acts and deceptive banking practices of the Defendant, POORE SUBSTITUTE, LTD who has pur-

chased a note created and executed by ROPER & COLEMAN. The note was purchased without any valuable consideration and without the Defendant POORE SUBSTITUTE, LTD pledging any pre-existing money or any of their own assets in the transaction and without the Defendant, POORE SUBSTITUTE, LTD incurring any financial cost in the transactions associated with the alleged loans of public currency otherwise known as Federal Reserve Notes. It is well understood by bank accountants and CPAs that a promissory note, when deposited, is treated by the banks as the same as the deposit of cash or a paycheck by the customer. In this context the

Plaintiffs are the banks customer. The alleged loan was funded by the creation of a demand deposit account by both ROPER & COLEMAN and later by POORE SUBSTITUTE, LTD Which was derived by depositing the promissory note into said demand deposit account and the converting the funds created by that promissory note, WHICH WAS THE BORROWERS MONEY, into a source of funding for the public currency loaned, MAKING THE LOAN TRANSACTION A MUTUAL LOAN BETWEEN THE LENDER AND THE BOR¬ROWER. Neither ROPER & COLEMAN nor the Defendant, POORE SUBSTITUTE, LTD used or pledged any of their own pre-existing money, pre-existing assets, or depositor's money in the transaction. The Defendant, POORE SUBSTITUTE, LTD has not and will not incur any financial loss or damages by our failure to pay the note. Furthermore, the Defendant, does not have the right of subrogation as a stranger to the transaction, and as someone who has not paid the entire mortgage debt in full, see 73 AM JUR Second,

Section 90.

North Carolina Superior courts are courts of record, and it is, therefore, is important to understand the characteristics of a court of record as follows: Please see Black's Law Dictionary, Fourth Edition pages 425 and 426 for further discussion of the court of record as follows; "Courts of record are those whose acts and judicial proceedings are enrolled or recorded for a perpetual memory and

testimony and which have the power to fine and imprison for contempt     A "court of record" is a judicial tribunal having attrib-

utes and exercising functions independently of the Magistrate designated generally to hold it and proceeding according to the course of the common law, its acts and proceedings being enrolled for a perpetual memorial. Jones v. Jones; 188 Mo. App.220 175 S.W. 227, 229; Ex Parte Gladhill, 8 Metc., Mass. 171, per Shaw, C. J. See also Ledwith v Rosalski; 244 N.Y. 406,155 N.E.688,

689." (emphasis mine).

## JURISDICTION

Our court of record is convened in this matter pursuant to Article Three of our Constitution for the United States of America, as a Judicial court of Law in our Judicial Branch of government, while in session under the rules of the Common Law as guaranteed by the Seventh Amendment and the Northwest Ordinance of 1787, in Article Two. See Callan v. Wilson, 127 US 540 (1888) for authority that Article Three of the United States Constitution provides for and mandates common law jurisdiction and venue.

Our one supreme court, which is now styled as Superior court was created by constitutional convention on the seventeenth day of the ninth month in the year of our Lord one -thousand -seven -hundred and eighty -seven and is not to be confused with the United States Supreme Court which was created by congress in the year of our Lord one thousand -seven -hundred and eighty -nine as an inferior court to our one supreme court. Any reference back to the original Judiciary Acts of Congress or other historical documents will confirm that this is what was described by the phrase "one supreme court" in Article Three of the original Constitution for the United States of America.

Under the Seventh Amendment to the Constitution for the United States of America, I am entitled to a common law trial by the jury. On dry land, any action must be adjudicated under common law pursuant to the Seventh Amendment; 443 Cans of Frozen Egg Product v. United States of America; 226 US 172 (1912). Additionally, a court of record is a court which exercises jurisdiction under the course of the common law, please see Black's Law Dictionary, Fourth Edition, pages 425 and 426.

VENUE

Wake County Superior Court, North Carolina republic, under the rules of the Common Law, is the proper venue for this matter to be heard by consent of all parties on the following grounds: The location of the court will be the most convenient forum for all parties, and since any issue in controversy allegedly and originally arose in that same geographic area.

STATEMENT OF THE FACTS OF THE CASE

First, as property owners in Wake County, we, Lamar Staton, and wife Wanita Staton recorded the deed, to said property described in warranty Deed in the United States of America venue, we have a common undivided interest in the property. We have a Warranty Deed on public record showing ownership where is yours, POORE SUBSTITUTE, LTD? We are the "Good Title holder (s). see Warranty Deed for evidence of the deed recorded in allodial title under the venue of the United States of America It is no longer in the venue of the UNITED STATES. This house is now our private property to which we have Good title, which means absolute ownership. we own the house in allodium and in "Dominium Directum Et Utile", please see Fairfax v. Hunter; 7 Cranch 603, 3 L. Ed. 453. We have complete and absolute dominion in our property, which is the union of the title and the exclusive use of it. We became aware, after careful study and analysis, that the original note and deed of trust that we executed claims a security interest in

the subject property based upon the transfer of Federal Reserve notes, which is commercial paper, as described in Clearfield Trust Company v US; 318 US 363; which states, "the United States as a drawee of commercial paper [federal reserve notes] stands in no different light than any other drawee" (bracketed portion ours).

The Defendant, POORE SUBSTITUTE, LTD is preparing to foreclose, based upon their attempt to collect the Mortgage. After reviewing the legal issues surrounding the request for payment, we discovered that the US Supreme Court has stated that the right of subrogation does not exist for a stranger to the transaction, Aetna L. Ins. Co. v. Middleport, 124 US 534. We also realized, after careful study and analysis, that the Federal Reserve System never provides anything of substance or intrinsic value when they create the credit, which is only a bookkeeping entry for the loan which is created by completing a ledger entry in the records of the bankers.

who wrote the original note and deed of trust, Please See Exhibit A.? The Defendant, POORE SUBSTITUTE, LTD     in this

matter will not incur a financial cost or damages by our failure, to pay the alleged balance due on the note in this matter. When the Defendant creates money, it does not cost them anything to create said money.

We base our statement of fact upon pages 9,10, 11, 22, 23, and 24 of the House Banking and Currency Committee Report called "Money Facts" published in 1964, which states on page 23 the following: "The business of banks is to lend money. The profit comes from the difference between the cost of creating money and the price they charge borrowers for that money. Now the cost of creating money is negligible. Congress has delegated the power to create money to the banking system without a charge. The banks do not pay a license fee or a payment charge for their reserves. Thus, the raw materials the banks use cost them nothing." (Emphasis added). My statement is derived from the technical descriptions of banking practices found in Money Facts, published in 1964 by the house banking committee, which is hereby incorporated by reference in this action to quiet title as Exhibit B. The organic law of this nation requires that "no state shall... make anything but gold and silver coin a tender in payment of debts", Constitution for the united states of America, Article One, Section Ten. The current Federal Reserve Banking Scheme is based upon the deliberate and planned to raise of interest rates by the Federal Reserve Bank of New York in October of 1929, and the subsequent deliberate crash of the stock market in 1929, called black Monday. The Bankers, stockholders in the Federal Reserve Bank, then with their proxies and agents in the government, the criminal element in government, hereinafter CEG, forced the UNITED STATES into a permanent state of declared national emergency on March 9, 1933, in the Emergency Banking Bill, 48 Stat.1, Public Law 89-719; declared by President Roosevelt, being bankrupt and insolvent in Several Executive Orders No. 6073, 6102, No. 6101, No. 6260 and was later seconded by Congress on June 5, 1933 with the passage of HJR 192, making all Americans the 'enemy' in paragraph 5(b) of the Trading with Enemies Act. Please see Senate Report 93- 549, dated 1973, for confirmation of the above. Said Bankers then placed the UNITED STATES into receivership based upon the Bankruptcy filed by an Act of Congress, HJR 192, dated June 5, 1933.

The real party in interest for the bankruptcy was never stated, but is clearly the British Royal Family, based upon the Treaty of Peace of 1783, and Jays Treaty 1791. These two documents created a fraudulent reversal of the State of Independence won by a long and bloody battle with the British during the Revolutionary War, by stating that King George is the Prince of the United States of America in the Treaty of Peace of 1783, and the subsequent paying of reparations in Jay's treaty. Neither treaty appears to have been ratified by Congress and specifically contravened direct orders by Congress to the treaty negotiators, John Jay, John Adams, and Benjamin Franklin. As a result, these treaties were not executed under the authority of the body politic and are without force and effect in law.

Through the above-described actions by the bankers and American government officials who committed acts of treason against the American people, the bankers, through their manipulation of Congress and President Roosevelt in 1933, and earlier, in the eighteenth Century, the treaty negotiators, the Bankers obtained control over our currency system, forced us into bankruptcy and created a new government under the bankruptcy, with new emergency powers for the reconstituted government.

The new currency, after the bankruptcy in 1933, became a debt instrument, which the American people must pay with no backing by gold and silver, as required under Article One, Section Ten of our Federal Constitution. All bank loans in the continental United States are fraudulent in their very nature because the Federal Reserve Notes they are based on are only based upon bookkeeping entries by the bankers and represent no value, and no valuable consideration. The original mortgage is therefore chattel paper with no valuable consideration and therefore the whole mortgage contract is based upon fraud and a lack of valuable consideration.

since Federal Reserve Notes have no intrinsic value whatsoever and are just bookkeeping entries under the 1933 bankruptcy. If said currency, Federal Reserve Notes, were backed by something of intrinsic value, then the currency could be valuable consideration, because the currency, could be exchanged for something of recognized value, and the lender of the Federal Reserve Notes, would then be pledging their own assets in the transaction. We, Wanita Staton and husband Lamar Staton, the Plaintiffs, are not a surety for this fraudulent national debt. We are not a subject of the British Royal Family, we are not US Citizens under the jurisdiction of Washington, D.C., and we are not co-bankrupt debtors for this fraudulent debt, and we are not part of the fraudulent Federal Reserve Banking Scheme.

The C.O.R.P.O.R.A.T.I.O.N.

(Crooked Officials Robbing People of Rights Against Truth in Our Nation) BOOK TITLE

The banks involved in this matter, are committing fraud and fraudulent conversion by attempting to transform the mortgage backed by no valuable consideration, into a security device which can be used to obtain a lien and subsequent ownership of our property, all without lawful money, which is mandated by Article One, Section Ten as stated above and without due process of law; a trial by the jury of our peers, as required by the Fifth and Seventh Amendments, respectively.

The Plaintiff's predecessor-in-interest did not loan anything of substance or intrinsic value, but they loaned their own credit in the transaction. Federal Reserve notes are bank credit and as such are not backed by gold or silver coin as required under Article One, Section ten of the US Constitution. This is an absolute requirement pursuant to the ruling by the US Supreme Court in Woodruff v. Mississippi, see Woodruff v. Mississippi; 162 US 291;16 S. Ct. 820; 40 L. Ed. 973. We quote Woodruff v. Mississippi, supra, as fol¬lows; "the power to borrow money, simply, meant the power to borrow whatever was money according to the Constitution of the United States and the laws passed in pursuance thereof, and the power to issue negotiable bonds included the power to make that payable in such money. This the law presumed, and to proceed on an implication to the contrary was to deny the holders of these bonds, after their purchase, a right arising from the Constitution and laws of the United States." (Emphasis added.) Fur¬thermore, the common law does not recognize a contract to be valid where there is no valuable consideration, such as this case, where nothing of substance or value was loaned in the transaction. The "money" loaned was bank credit, created by a series of bookkeeping entries created by OWNIT MORTAGAGE SOLUTIONS INC., which was derived from the sale of the promissory note to OWNIT MORTAGAGE SOLUTIONS INC., and subsequently, sale of the note to the Defendant.

This fraudulent mortgage can, under this fraudulent banking scheme, thus be converted into a fraudulent lien based upon no valu¬able consideration, obtained by establishing a banking system of bookkeeping entries for commercial federal reserve 'credit' with no backing by gold or silver, as required by Article One, Section Ten of our Federal Constitution, or anything of substance or intrin¬sic value and then placing a fraudulent lien or security device on our land and using this fraudulent devise and claiming to be the holder in due course on the deed to our land.

The bankruptcy of the UNITED STATES under HJR 192 removed gold backing from the currency as of June 5, 1933, under said Act of Congress, and set up the fraudulent and pernicious Federal Reserve bankruptcy system. The defendants, as a result, operate under a presumptive claim of ownership, which is ultimately based upon no valuable consideration and upon the Bankruptcy of the UNITED STATES declared by Congress on June 5, 1933, under House Joint Resolution 192, dated June 5, 1933 and the State of Declared National Emergency declared by Congress on March 9, 1933.

Both of these events forever altered the structure and fabric of American government as it was established by the founding fathers during and after the period of the revolutionary war from 1775 until about 1792 and gave, through sedition, a financial stronghold to the international bankers who hold a stockholders position in the Federal Reserve Bank/System, and who, are belligerent foreign principals in a dramatically altered American Government/ Federal Reserve Banking scheme that is operating without the authority of the American people.

Full disclosure was never given to the American people of the names of the creditors or the nature of the obligation the American people have been forced to take on under the Federal Reserve Banking Scheme and the bankruptcy of the United States and state governments as accommodation parties. See also Senate report 93-549. Nowhere in the blueprint for the federal and state governments, our American Constitution, is there a provision

246

for foreign or domestic financiers and industrialists to take over the reins of government through a perpetual state of bankruptcy, with no named creditors, no financial reorganization plan and no accountability by elected officials for having paid the Federal Reserve trillions of dollars and billions of dollars' worth of gold, for their service of "loaning money into circulation" and thereby bankrupting the federal and state governments.

Please see Exhibit B, Money Facts, a report by the House Banking Committee, published in 1964, page 9 for a discussion of how.

banks get money and how their Reserves are created. The British Royal Family appears to be the real party in interest based upon the Treaty of Peace of 1783 and Jays Treaty, which appears to give The British Royal Family a fraudulent dominion over the United States of America, as the 'Prince of the United States of America' in the First paragraph of the Treaty of Peace. This was contrary to the explicit instructions given to the Treaty delegation of John Adams, Benjamin Franklin, and John Jay by the Congress of the Unit¬ed States prior to their trip to Paris to negotiate the Treaty.

The above provision of the Treaty of Peace is therefore not a lawful provision. In addition, the original mortgage is void, unenforce¬able and without force and effect, because of a lack of valuable consideration, and breach of contract.

Second; The assign, POORE SUBSTITUTE, LTD alleged purchased the note and deed of trust for the house buildings which is the sub¬ject of this dispute from the original lender, OWNIT MORTAGAGE SOLUTIONS INC and attempted to collect payment on the note.

without the right of subrogation. The assign, POORE SUBSTITUTE, LTD, made a demand for payment and then moved.

for foreclosure on the note even though they do not have the right of subrogation as a party who is not a cosigner to the note and the action by the original lender selling the land and home to a stranger to the transaction is not agreed to by us and is therefore an unlawful act, and a breach of trust, see Aetna L. Ins, Co. v. Middleport, 124 US 534.

I sent the lender a written request to validate the debt, see Exhibit C. They did not respond to my request. The lender is currently in default on my request that they provide a validation of the debt and prove that they have the right of subrogation. This failure to answer is an admission of the truth and validity of the contents of the constructive notice under the doctrine of latches, res adjudicates, nil deceit, silence by acquiescence and tacit procuration.

The Uniform Commercial Code also reflects these principals of common law that once a debtor makes a good faith offer of performance and it is not accepted, the obligation is extinguished, pursuant to UCC 3-603. The defendants cannot produce a verified claim for which relief can be granted.

We received a Notice to Sale from the Defendant on December 17,2012 with the intent to sale on January 3,20012. The defendant is required to allow a period of 20 days which the defendant has failed to do according to 45.21.16

They steadfastly refused to respond to our constructive notice, See Exhibit C.

Third; The mortgage note, and deed of trust cannot form the basis of any kind of lien or security against our house because we are the assignee to the original warranty Deed, without the defendants in this matter ever having filed a claim against the original Warranty Deed., neither the defendants nor the original mortgage holder has any legitimate or lawful claim to the house. We, the Plaintiff in this matter, have Good title, which is the highest title anyone can have on their home. No one has superior title. As the Plaintiff, we, Lamar Staton, and wife Wanita Staton seek to quiet title against all claims by defendants to any security interest, lien, right, title or interest, in our house. The Defendants adverse fraudulent claims are without any rights whatsoever, without any foundation in law, and cannot in any way extinguish our lawful common law exclusive claim to our own house.

Fourth; We believe that the organic laws of the United States of America, including all founding documents and charters give us sovereignty and thereby a right to private citizenship good titles to homes and access to common law courts, which are derived from the people of the body politic, which created the government and all the rights and freedoms which are associated with the organic laws created by the body politic. I cite the following case below:

The US Supreme Court has affirmed the notion that each Citizen is sovereign and that state governments are bound by the Federal

Constitution: "From the crown of Great Britain the sovereignty of their country passed to the people of it, and it was then not an uncommon opinion that the un-appropriated lands, which belonged to that crown, passed not to the people of the colony or states

within those limits they were situated, but to the whole people        'We the people of the United States do ordain and establish this.

constitution.' Here we see the people acting as sovereigns of the whole country; and in the language of sovereignty, establishing a constitution by which it was their will, that the State governments, should be bound, and to which the State constitutions should be made to conform.

It will be enough to observe briefly, that the sovereignties in Europe, and particularly in England exist on feudal principals. That system considers the prince as the sovereign, and the people as his subjects; it regards his person as the object of allegiance and excludes the idea of his being on an equal footing with a subject either in a court of justice or elsewhere.

That system contemplates him as being the fountain of honor and authority; and from his grace and grant, derives all franchises, immunities, and privileges; it is easy to perceive, that such a sovereign could not be amenable to a court of justice, or subjected to judicial control and actual constraint.

The same feudal ideas run through all their jurisprudence, and constantly remind us of the distinction between the prince and the subject. No such ideas obtain here; at the revolution, the sovereignty devolved on the people; and they are truly the sovereigns of the country, and they are sovereigns without subjects...and have none to govern but themselves; the citizens of America are equal as fellow-citizens, and as joint tenants in the sovereignty.

From the differences existing between feudal sovereignties and governments founded on compacts, it necessarily follows, that their respective prerogatives must differ. Sovereignty is the right to govern; the nation or state sovereign is the person or persons in whom that resides. In Europe, the sovereignty is generally ascribed to the prince; here it rests with the people; there the sover¬eign administers the government, here never in a single instance; our governors are the agents of the people, and at most stand in the same relation to their sovereign, in which the regents of Europe stand to their sovereign.

Their princes have personal powers, dignities and preeminence, our rulers have none but official; nor do they partake in the sovereignty otherwise, or in any other capacity, then as private citizens." Chisolm v. Georgia; 2 Dall (U.S.) 419 (1793) (emphasis mine).

FIRST CAUSE OF ACTION (Quiet Title)

First. The defendants do not have a security interest in our house because of the lack of the right of subrogation. They claim that their purchase of the note from the original lender forms the foundation of their authority to take our land by a foreclosure action.

There is no right of subrogation for the Defendant, POORE SUBSTITUTE, LTD   Additionally, there is no valuable consid-

eration, since only Federal Reserve Notes were received, which are not backed by any hard asset of the bank or anything which has any redemption value. None of the Plaintiffs remember ever signing over a security interest, based upon valuable consideration to the defendants or anyone else. The defendant, POORE SUBSTITUTE, LTD, purchased the promissory note from ROPER & COLEMAN, who purchased the note from the original lender, OWNIT MORTAGAGE SOLUTIONS INC, for an undisclosed amount, even though they were not a cosigner on the original note, meaning they did not have the right of subrogation. As a result of their not having the right of subrogation, the Defendant, POORE SUBSTITUTE, LTD, is a stranger to the transaction and has no right, title or interest to our land and buildings ANY FORECLOSURE ACTION BY THEM is unenforceable and void ab into, from the beginning. The Defend¬ant, POORE SUBSTITUTE, LTD, had a duty, as an alleged creditor to prove that they have a right of subrogation if they are a co¬signer, and prove that they are a co-signer, if in fact they are, and additionally, prove that they have paid the entire debt in full, prior to taking steps to foreclose on our house, which is the subject of this civil action. The Defendant, POORE SUBSTITUTE, LTD did not do this, and by their failure to prove that they are a co-signer on the original note and that their failure to prove that they have paid the entire mortgage debt in full, they have failed to perform a duty, which they are required to perform under North Carolina.

law.

"Subrogation in equity is confined to the relation of principal and surety and guarantors, to cases where a person to protect his own junior lien is compelled to remove one which is superior, and to cases of insurance.... Anyone who is under no legal obligation or liability to pay the debt is a stranger, and, if he pays the debt, a mere volunteer.". (emphasis mine) Aetna Life v. Middleport, 124 US 534, quoting Soppier v. Garrets, 20 Bradwell App Ill. 625. The defendant, POORE SUBSTITUTE, LTD, were clearly never cosigners or sureties in the original Promissory note. The Wake County Sheriff has an auxiliary role to play in this matter, assisting POORE SUBSTITUTE, LTD in their unlawful activities.

The Defendants violated our right to due process of law, as guaranteed under the Fifth and Fourteenth Amendments to the US Constitution by presenting themselves as a party who has a right to enforce the original contract, although they clearly are not now, nor have they ever been a co-signer to the original note. Because they have no right of subrogation, they have no right to enforce the note, and thereby no right to foreclose or to claim any right, title, or interest in the house. We have a right to expect that anyone who is attempting to foreclose on the house has the right to do so as someone who has standing. The Defendant clearly has never had standing to foreclose, based upon the above case law and facts. Please note that the Defendant, POORE SUBSTI¬TUTE,

LTD, has never claimed that they have the right of subrogation. They have never brought forward evidence that refutes, rebuts, challenges, or denies our statement of fact that the Defendant, POORE SUBSTITUTE, LTD, does not have the right of subrogation and is not a co-signer. North Carolina Courts are bound by the US Constitution and laws passed in pursuance thereof. This requirement is found in the North Carolina Constitution of 1849 under Article Six, Section Seven, which states, in relevant part:

"Sec. 7. "I,        , do solemnly swear (or affirm) that I will support and maintain the Constitution and laws of the United.

States, and the Constitution and laws of North Carolina not inconsistent therewith, and that I will faithfully discharge the duties of

my office as      , so help me God.

When there is fraud involved, then any action that flows from that fraud is null and void and without force or effect in law, Ex Dollo Malo Non-Orator Action, out of fraud no action arises. Additionally, if this is true the Defendants are liable for fraud, fraudulent conversion, and attempted theft of private home. This claim of ownership of our building without a judicial trial by the jury, and without due process of law, access to an appeals process, a final judgment by a court, represents a taking of house without due process of the law in violation of the Fifth Amendment to our Federal constitution.

The Fifth Amendment to our Federal Constitution of 1787, guarantees that no person shall be deprived of life, liberty, or property without due process of law. We, Lamar Staton, and wife Wanita Staton, The Plaintiffs, do not recall ever having been given a summons or subpoena or other lawful notice requiring our presence in court in a Quiet Title Action. We do not recall a trial by the jury, final judgment, access to the appeals process or having seen a court order regarding a determination of Title in an action to Quiet Title. The Seventh Amendment to our federal constitution guarantees common law. The defendants actions are not the result of a common law ruling and due process in a court of law, "The 7th Amendment to the Constitution preserves the right of trial by jury in suits at common law involving more than $20, and provides that no fact tried by a jury, shall be reviewed otherwise than accord¬ing to the rules of the common law.", see 443 Cans of Frozen Egg Product v. United States of America; 226 US 172.

The defendants have failed to prove or show a court order authorizing private property to be liened, levied or seized based upon a determination of title in an Action to Quiet Title as required under the rules of the common law, and the Fifth and Fourteenth Amendments. The Defendants are attempting to use the organs and institutions of government to obtain title to the property and hold a foreclosure sale without due process of law, and without a trial by the jury under the rules of the common law. The common law right of due process is found in the Fifth, Seventh and Fourteenth Amendments to our federal constitution. The actions taken by the defend¬ants, attempt to deprive us of our liberty and property without due process of law. Article Three of the original constitution for the United States of America calls for either law or equity courts, depending on the circumstances, see Callan v. Wilson, 127 U.S. 540, (1888) "And as the guaranty of a trial by jury, in the third article, implied a trial in that mode, and according to the settled rules of common law". Actions by them to claim to have a security interest in our private building and personal property and claim authority-ty to hold a foreclosure sale is an action beyond the scope of their authority. This is described by the United States Supreme Court as tyranny in; United States v. Lee; 106 US 196, 1S. Ct. 240 (1882) where the United States claimed ownership of property via a tax.

sale some years earlier, the court stated as follows:

"No man in this country is so high that he is above the law. No officer of the law may set that law at defiance with impunity. All the officers of the government, from the highest to the lowest are creatures of the law and are bound to obey it. It is the only supreme power of our system of government, and every man who by accepting office participates in its functions is only the more strongly bound to submit to that supremacy, and to observe the limitations which it imposes upon the exercise of the authority which it.

gives     Shall it be said ... that the courts cannot give remedy when the citizen has been deprived of his liberty by force, his estate.

seized and converted to the use of the government without any lawful authority, without any process of law, and without any compensation, because the president has ordered it and his officers are in possession? If such be the law of this country, it sanctions a tyranny which has no existence in the monarchies of Europe, nor in any other government which has a just claim to well-regulated liberty and the protection of personal rights." In the above-cited case the government can be considered as similar and applying in like manner as the defendants in the above captioned case. If government agencies cannot take private property without due process of law, how can a bank or mortgage company do so?

The Supreme Court also reaffirmed the right to enjoy private property and not be deprived of it without due process of law in Lynch v. Household Finance Corp.; 405 US 538 (1972).

"Such difficulties indicate that the dichotomy between personal liberties and property rights is a false one. The right to enjoy property without unlawful deprivation, no less than the right to speak or the right to travel, is in truth a "personal" right whether the "property" in question be a welfare check, a home, or a savings account. In fact, a fundamental interdependence exists between the personal right to liberty and the personal

right in property. Neither could have meaning without the other. That rights in property are basic civil rights has long been recognized. J. Locke Of Civil Government 82- 85(1924); J. Adams A Defense of the Constitutions of Government of the United States of America, in F. Coker Democracy, Liberty and Property 121-132 (1942); 1 W. Blackstone, Commentaries 138-140."

The taking of private property without due process is clearly a violation of civil liberties as well as personal rights. One of the settled principles of our Constitution is that these Amendments are to protect only against invasion of civil liberties by the government whose conduct they alone limit. Burdeau v. McDowell; 256 US 465, 41 S. Ct. 574, 65 L Ed. 104813 ALR 1159 (1921); Weeks v. Unit¬ed States; 232 US 383, 34 S. Ct. 341, 58 L. Ed. 652, (1914); Hall v. United States; 41, F 2d 54(9th Cir. 1930); Brown v. United States; 12 F 2d. 926 (9th Cir. 1926). Therefore, the organs of government cannot be used to participate and assist in the unlawful plunder of our house.

Second. In the United States of America, after of the Revolutionary War of 1775, feudal titles came to an end and were replaced by allodial titles. This structural change in the nature of titles, which came with self-government, is aptly described by the Pennsylva¬nia Supreme Court in Wallace v Harmstad 44 Pa. 492; 1863 (1863) which states the following.

"I see no way of solving this question except by determining whether our Pennsylvania titles are allodial or feudal. It seems strange that so fundamental a question as this should be in doubt at this day.

"He defines a feud as a tract of land held by a voluntary and gratuitous donation, on condition of fidelity and certain services, and allodial lands as those whereof the owner had the dominium directum et verum the complete and absolute property, free from all.

services from any lord

"... the Revolution would have operated very inefficiently towards complete emancipation.

if the feudal relation had been suffered to remain. It was therefore necessary to extinguish all foreign interest in the soil, as well as foreign jurisdiction in the manner of government.

"we are then to regard the Revolution and these Acts of the Assembly as emancipating every acre of the soil (of Pennsylvania)

from the grand characteristic of the feudal system."

From this we conclude that titles in all of the several states of the United States of America are purely allodial. Our allodial title means that we are not vassals, serfs, or indentured servants. The defendant, POORE SUBSTITUTE, LTD does not have a lawful claim to our building. The defendant, POORE SUBSTITUTE, LTD, does not have a higher title than we do, or any right, title, or interest in our house except perhaps by fraud, which is void ab initio, since fraud vitiates everything.

Third. Our seal, which is our signatures on the Certificate of title (Warranty Deed) show ownership of our house. We Wanita Staton and Husband Lamar Staton are the owners of the house which is on public record. Claims by government agencies are no different than claims by private corporations and banks, such as the defendants are. Neither the defendants nor the original mortgage holder filed any sort of competing claim, or any other sort of claim in the patent proceeding for this house See also Field v. Seabury; 19 How 323; 15 L. Ed. 650; "A court of law in a state where strict common law prevail will not look behind or beyond the grant, to the rights upon which it is founded, nor examine the progressive stages of the title antecedent to the grant conclusive against the government and all claiming under junior patents and titles." United States v. Maxwell Land Grant Co.; 121 US 325; 7 S. Ct. 1015. Stone v. US; 2 Wall 525; 17 L. Ed 765.

Therefore, pursuant to these US Supreme Court rulings neither the defendants nor the original mortgage holder have any claim to or right, title or interest in our private land and home. We, Wanita Staton and Husband Lamar Staton, the Plaintiffs in this matter have allodial title, which is the highest title anyone can have on their home. Allodial title is defined as "one that is free". [Stewart v. Chicago Title Ins. Co., 151 Ill. App. 3d 888 (Ill. App. Ct. 1987)] No one has superior title. As the Plaintiffs, we, Gail-Joy-Bennett: Wofford, Dana E. Wofford, and Mark-Evan: Bennett, seek to quiet title against all claims by the defendants to any security interest, lien, right, title or interest, or power to take control of our property. The Defendant, POORE SUBSTITUTE, LTD adverse fraudulent claims is without any rights whatsoever, without any foundation in law, and cannot in any way extinguish our lawful common law exclusive claim to our own private allodial real property. We, Wanita Staton and husband Lamar Staton, the Plaintiffs in this matter, seek to quiet title as of the date of the constructive notice mailed to the Defendant.

Fourth. The Defendants Have no Right of Subrogation as a Stranger to the Transaction, a mere volunteer and as a Party who has not Tendered the Full Amount of the Mortgage Debt. The right of Subrogation does not exist for the Defendants or their assigns, agents, or principals. The assignment of the note and deed of trust for our property is unlawful since the assignee was a stranger to the transaction and has not provided evidence that they paid off the entire mortgage in full. , POORE SUBSTITUTE, LTD has failed to provide any evidence in this matter of payment of the entire Mortgage debt in full, therefore under the doctrine of latches, the presumption that the Defendant, M & T BANK, did not pay the entire mortgage debt in full is unrebutted and is therefore a fact undisputed and agreed to by the Defendants, see, 73 Am Jur Second, Section 90 which states that a right of subrogation does not exist for a mere volunteer, or someone who has not paid the entire mortgage debt in full. Please review the following for affirmation that the right of subrogation does not exist for the Defendant in this matter; Henningsen v. United States Fidelity & G. Co.; 208 US 404; 52 L. Ed 547, 28 S. Ct. 389; Prairie State National Bank v. United States; 164 US 227; 41 L. Ed. 412; 17 S. Ct. 142; Aetna L. Ins. Co. v. Middleport; 124 US 534; 31 L. Ed. 537; 8 S. Ct. 625; McBride v. McBride; 148 Or 478 36 P 2d 175.

AS A RESULT, THE DEFENDANT, POORE SUBSTITUTE, LTD, HAS NO RIGHT, TITLE, OR INTEREST IN THE PROPERTY, WHICH IS THE SUBJECT OF THIS ACTION TO QUIET TITLE, AS ONE WHO DOES NOT HAVE THE RIGHT OF SUBROGATION OF THE ORIGINAL NOTE THAT THEY ALLEGEDLY PURCHASED AND THAT WAS ALLEGEDLY ASSIGNED TO THEM. THEY HAVE NO STANDING TO FORECLOSE ON OUR PROPERTY.

Fifth. The Defendants cannot foreclose without a Judicial Determination of The Status of The Defendants as The Owner in a Court of Common Law and by Way of a Quiet Title Action.

The Defendants, by their actions are attempting to foreclose and force us out of the subject property without due process of law.

Pursuant to the rules of the common law, the Defendants do not have the right to foreclose by way of a demand for insurance payments. Pursuant to the Fifth Article of Amendment to our Federal Constitution, the Defendants cannot seek to obtain non-judicial remedies to obtain title, thereby claiming to have a 'perfected title', and thereby circumventing the due process requirements as guaranteed under the Fifth Amendment, by way of the Fourteenth Amendment. The quiet title action must be adjudicated prior to any foreclosure action taken or being tried in court. Any unlawful action taken by the Defendant must be preceded by a final judgment in an action to quiet title, and therefore their planned foreclosure is violative of our due process rights. The US Supreme Court also reaffirmed the right to enjoy private property and not be deprived of it without due process of law in Lynch v. Household Finance Corp.; 405 US 538 (1972). The Defendant is proceeding as if rights were waived. We have never waived any rights in this matter, knowingly, intelligently, or voluntarily, including our right to judicial due process, please see Brady v US; 397 US 742 at 748.

The outcome of this quiet title case will determine the ownership of the property and the validity of the claims of the parties. The foreclosure action planned by the Defendant, , POORE SUBSTITUTE, LTD lacks personal and subject matter jurisdiction because; 1.) of the misrepresentation of material facts by said Defendant that they have the right to foreclose 2.) the use of the all capitalized names as the straw man ( corporate fiction), 3.) the fact that the attempted seizure of the private property in question is not lawful because it violates the doctrine of due process established by the US Supreme Court in Lynch v Household Finance, supra, by skipping and circumventing the requirement to file an Action to Quiet Title to determine with certainty who has title to the property and 5.) it violates our due process rights as Plaintiff in the Quiet Title Action. When a court proceeds in an action such as the unlawful detainer case for anything other than dismissal, under these circumstances, all its judgments are void.

"The jurisdiction of the court depends on the correctness of the allegation." US v Percheman (1833) 32 US 518 L.Ed. 604 at 617; "Where a court has jurisdiction it has a right to decide every question which occurs in the cause, and whether its decision be cor¬rect or otherwise, its judgment until reversed, is regarded as binding in every other court. But if it acts without authority, its judgments and orders are regarded as nullities. They are not voidable, but simply void. ". Wilcox v Jackson; 13 Peters 264 (1839); quoting Elliot et al v Piersol; 1 Peters 340.

Sixth. The Deed of Trust and Note are not valid because of Inherent Fraud in the Note and Deed of Trust.

The Defendants based their claim upon a mortgage contract (Note and Deed of Trust), which is in its very nature fraudulent. There is no valuable consideration in the existing mortgage contract because there was nothing of intrinsic value loaned in the agreement. The mortgage company loaned Federal Reserve notes, which are commercial paper pursuant to a decision by the United States Supreme Court, see Clearfield Trust Company v US: 318 US 363. The mortgage contract violates Article One, Section Ten of the US Constitution and the Constitution for the United States of America. The mortgage contract violates The Coinage Act of 1792. In the United States of America, no state can make anything but gold and silver coin a tender in payment of debt, see Federal Const. Art. 1 Sec.10. Gold and silver coin has intrinsic value and is exclusively lawful money in the United States of America. The Mortgage contract (note and deed of trust) did not provide for the loaning of gold and Silver coin and did not provide for the repayment of the debt in gold and silver coin, as required under our Federal Constitution, Art. 1, Sec. 10, and is therefore not a lawful contract, because something other than gold and silver coin was made a tender in payment of debt. The mortgage contract, note and deed of trust is unconstitutional, see Woodruff v. Mississippi; 162 US 291;16 S. Ct. 820; 40 L. Ed. 973; Julliard v Greenman; 110 US 421, at 447, 4 S Ct. 122, 28 L. Ed. 204, See also Knox v Lee; 79 US (12 Wall 457, 20 L. Ed 287.

The collection of this alleged debt is unconstitutional, see Julliard v Greenman; 110 US 421, at 447, 4 S Ct. 122, 28 L. Ed. 204, See also Knox v Lee; 79 US (12 Wall 457), 20 L. Ed 287; Woodruff v. Mississippi, 162 US 291, which states; " For the power to borrow money, simply meant the power to borrow whatever was money according to the Constitution of the United States and the laws passed in pursuance thereof, and the power to issue negotiable bonds therefore included the power to make them payable in such money. This the law presumed, and to proceed on an implication to the contrary was to deny to the holders of these bonds, after their purchase, a right arising under the Constitution and laws of the United States." In two of the above cases, the US Supreme Court stated that the use of paper money was acceptable under the above-cited sections of the US Constitution, because the currency at the time of these rulings was backed by silver and gold coins. Woodruff v. Mississippi, and Article One, Section Ten

of the US Constitution must be held as controlling in this matter as the supreme law of the land, since the court is required to be faithful to the law and cannot engage in judicial nullification.

Seventh. The Defendants Cannot Validate the Debt, Therefore the obligation is extinguished, and any claim, by them, to the land is void. The Defendants agent and debt collectors failed to validate and verify the debt in accordance with the Fair Debt Collection Practices Act Title 15 USC, § 1692 and numerous sections of the Uniform Commercial Code, all of which reflect the rules of the common law. In my constructive notice I offered to pay the Defendant, POORE SUBSTITUTE, LTD if they would validate the debt and demonstrate that they have the right of subrogation. They have failed to respond to our constructive notice and are, therefore in default on our offer. As a result of the foregoing the obligation is extinguished, see Walker v. Houston; 215 Cal 742; 12 P2d 953 at 953, 87 A.L.R. 937.

Eighth. The Defendants in this matter have not responded to my request to validate the debt as required in the Offer of Performance, therefore the obligation is extinguished, See Exhibit C. Please note the Defendants claim that they have the right to foreclose, however, the right of subrogation does not exist for the Defendant, POORE SUBSTITUTE, LTD, as a stranger to the transaction, pursuant to the case law below; see 73 Am Jur Second, Section 90 which states that a right of subrogation does not exist for a mere volunteer, or someone who has not paid the entire mortgage debt in full. Please review the following for affirmation that the right of subrogation does not exist; Henningsen v. United States Fidelity & G. Co; Supra; Prairie State National Bank v. United States; Supra; Aetna L. Ins. Co. v. v. Middleport; Supra; McBride v. McBride; Supra. AS A RESULT OF THE FOREGOING US SUPREME COURT RULINGS, THE DEFENDANTS DO NOT HAVE THE AUTHORITY TO FORECLOSE BECAUSE THEY DO NOT HAVE THE RIGHT OF SUBROGATION. THEREFORE, THEY CANNOT VALIDATE THE DEBT BECAUSE THEY ARE NOT THE ORIGINAL LENDER AND CANNOT ENFORCE THE NOTE THAT THEY CLAIM TO HAVE PURCHASED FROM THE ORIGINAL LENDER.

In addition, the Defendants never proved that the full amount of the mortgage was paid further amplifying the fact that a right of subrogation does not exist. In most cases the mortgage companies and banks sell the notes to each other for pennies on the dollar, meaning that they do not pay the entire mortgage debt in full, thereby providing another reason why they do not have the right of subrogation.

Ninth. We have a Common law Lien against the property which must be satisfied before any equity liens are satisfied, See Exhibit D. Common law liens in law supersede mortgages and equity liens, Drummond Carriage Co.v. Mills; 74 NW 966 (1898); Hewitt v. William; 47 La. Ann. 742; 17 So. 269; Carr v. Dail; 19 SE 235; MacMahon v. Lundin; 58 NW, 827; and may be satisfied only when a Court of Common Law pursuant to order of the elected Sheriff under of Article Seven of the Bill of Rights.

Tenth. The Uniform Commercial Code also reflects these principals of common law that once a debtor makes a good faith offer of performance and it is not accepted, the obligation is extinguished, pursuant to UCC 3-603. The Offer of Performance is the necessary instrument to cause the discharge of the alleged debt in this matter. Please note under the tender laws, if the payment is made and refused, the debt is discharged, please see UCC 3 - 603 and UCC 2-511. Also, under The Truth in Lending Act, Title 15, Section 1601, Under Regulation Z the Defendant has to object to the tender of payment within three days or be barred from objecting later. See Nygaard v. Continental Resources, Inc; 598 N.W. 2d 851, 39 UCC 2d 851. As the Plaintiffs we have no other re¬course or remedy. We offered to pay the entire debt in full if the Defendant, POORE SUBSTITUTE, LTD, would validate the debt, SEE EXHIBIT C, and prove that they have a right of subrogation. The Defendant, POORE SUBSTITUTE, LTD did not accept our offer. The Defendant thereby violated our right to due process of law, by failing to either accept our conditional offer to pay the debt by validating the debt and proving that they have the right of subrogation or disclaiming any right, title, or interest in the property.

"A tender is an offer of performance, made with the intent to extinguish the obligation (Civil Code Section 1485) When properly made, has the effect of putting the other party in default if he refuses to accept it," Wiesenberg v. Hirshorn, 97 Cal App. 532, 275, P 997; Lovetro V. Steers 234 Cal App. 2d 461, 44 Cal. Rptr. 604; Holland v. Paddock, 142 Cal App. 2d 534, 298 P 2d 587. "...The imposition of such conditions is waived by the offeree if he does not specifically point out the alleged defects in the tender. " Civil Code Sec. 1501; Code of Civil Procedure Sec. 2076; Hohener v. Gauss (1963) 221 Cal. App. 2d 797, 34 Cal. Rptr. 656. "The rationale of the requirement of specific objection is that the offeror should be permitted to remedy any defects in his tender; the oferee is therefore not allowed to remain silent at the time of the tender and later surprise the offeror with hidden objections, " Thomassen v. Carr, (1967) 250 Cal. App. 2d 341, 350, 58 Cal Rptr. 297; Riverside Fence Co. v. Novak, (1969) 78 Cal. Rptr. 536; See Walker v. Houston; 215 Cal 742; 12 P2d 953 at 953, 87 A.L.R. 937. The Defendant never accepted my offer to pay the debt by failing to com¬ply with my condition precedent. They did this by failing to prove that they have the right of subrogation and failing to validate the debt.

The Uniform Commercial Code also reflects these principals of common law that once a debtor makes a good faith offer of perfor¬mance and it is not accepted, the obligation is extinguished, pursuant to UCC 3-603. The conditional offer to pay is the necessary instrument to cause the discharge of the Defendant's Demand for Payment in this matter. Please note under the tender laws, if the payment is made and refused, the debt is discharged, please see UCC 3 - 603 and UCC 2-511. See Nygaard v. Continental Re¬sources, Inc; 598 N.W. 2d 851, 39 UCC 2d 851. As the Plaintiffs we have no other recourse or remedy other than this action to quiet title.

The lender never produced a verified claim demonstrating that something of value or substance was loaned in the transaction. Therefore, the Defendants have no right to pursue this matter in court under Title 15 USC, Sections 1692 (g) and(e).

The Defendants never produced a verified claim demonstrating that something of value or substance was loaned in the transaction. Therefore, the Defendant has no right to demand payment. Also, our good faith offer of performance was not accepted and therefore the obligation is extinguished.

Eleventh. Under the Seventh Amendment to the Constitution for the United States of America, I am entitled to a common law trial by the jury, 443 Cans of Frozen Egg Product v. United States of America 226 US 172, 50 at 52 Morris v United States 8 Wall. 507, 19 L. ed. 481 The Sarah 8 Wheat. 391, 5 L. Ed. 644 50 at 51 United States v. La Vengence (reported in 3 Dall. 297, 1 L. Ed. 610) United States v The Sally (in 2 Cranch 406, 2 L. Ed 320 and United States v The Betsy (in 4 Cranch 443, 2 Led. 673). "An unconstitutional act is not law; it confers no rights; it imposes no duties; affords no protection; it creates no office; it is in legal contemplation, as inoperative as though it had never been passed." -- Norton vs. Shelby County; 118, US 425 p. 442. See also, Miranda v. Arizona; 384 U.S. 436 (1966) "Where rights secured by the Constitution are involved, there can be no rule making or legislation which would abrogate them" emphasis mine.

On dry land, any action must be adjudicated under common law pursuant to the Seventh Amendment. According to the US Supreme Court, in 443 Cans of Frozen Egg Product v. United States of America; Supra, the US Supreme Court stated as follows; "The 7th Amendment to the Constitution preserves the right of trial by jury in suits at common law involving more than $20, and pro¬vides that no fact tried by a jury, shall be reviewed otherwise than according to the rules of the common law."

Twelfth. The Fair Debt Collection Practices Act must be adhered to in North Carlonia, as in all other jurisdictions in the United States and the United States of America. If a debt cannot be validated by the creditor, it is unenforceable and the creditor must cease and desist all collection activities pursuant to Title 15, § 1692(g). A notice by the debtor that the debt is being disputed is all that is needed to compel the creditor to stop collecting the debt until debt validation has been completed. See Clarks Jeweler's v. Humble, 823 P 2d 818, 16 Kan App 2d 366 (1991). Furthermore, all collection agencies and debt collectors include a clause in their collection notices, which is a notice to the debtor that the debt collector is attempting to collect a debt. This provides tacit acknowl-

edgment that the debt collectors must comply with Title 15, § 1692 et seq. The debt collectors cannot identify anything of sub-stance or value loaned in the transaction and therefore cannot validate the debt. Be advised that "verification" is defined (in Black's Law Dictionary, Sixth Edition) as follows: "Confirmation of correctness, truth, or authenticity by affidavit, oath, or deposition. Affidavit of truth of matter stated and object of verification is to assure good faith in averments or statements of party."

Thirteenth. The Defendant, POORE SUBSTITUTE, LTD, has no right to lend credit as this is a violation of their corporate charter and violates Federal law, and is prohibited under the doctrine of ultra vires.

The United States Supreme Court and the lower courts have long recognized that the banks cannot loan credit.

"In the federal courts, it is well established that a national bank has not.

power to lend its credit to another by becoming surety, endorser, or guarantor for him." Farmers and Miners Bank v. Bluefield Nat 'l Bank, 11 F 2d 83, 271 U.S. 669.

"A national bank has no power to lend its credit to any person or corporation."

. . . Bowen v. Needles Nat. Bank, 94 F 925 36 CCA 553, certiorari denied in 20 S. Ct 1024, 176 US 682, 44 LED 637.

"The doctrine of ultra vires is a most powerful weapon to keep private corporation within their legitimate spheres and to punish them for violations of their corporate charters, and it probably is not invoked too often." Zinc Carbonate Co. v. First National Bank, 103 Wis 125, 79 NW 229. American Express Co. v. Citizens State Bank, 194 NW 430.

"A bank may not lend its credit to another even though such a transaction turns out to have been of benefit to the bank, and in support of this a list of cases.

might be cited, which-would look like a catalog of ships." [Emphasis added] Norton Grocery Co. v. Peoples Nat. Bank, 144 SE 505. 151 Va 195.

"It has been settled beyond controversy that a national bank, under federal.

Law being limited in its powers and capacity, cannot lend its credit by guaranteeing.

the debts of another. All such contracts entered into by its officers are ultra.

vires . . ." Howard & Foster Co. v. Citizens Nat'l Bank of Union, 133 SC

202, 130 SE 759(1926).

"Neither, as included in its powers not incidental to them, is it a part of a bank's business to lend its credit. If a bank could lend its credit as well as its money, it might, if it received compensation and was careful to put its name only to solid paper, make a great deal more than any lawful interest on its money would amount to. If not careful, the power would be the mother of panics, . . . Indeed, lending credit is the exact opposite of lending money, which is the real business of a bank, for while the latter creates a liability in favor of the bank, the former gives rise to a liability of the bank to another. I Morse. Banks and

Banking 5th Ed. Sec 65; Magee, Banks and Banking, 3rd Ed. Sec 248." American Express Co. v. Citizens State Bank, 194 NW 429.

"It is not within those statutory powers for a national bank, even though solvent, to lend its credit to another in any of the various ways in which that might be done." Federal Intermediate Credit Bank v. L 'Herrison, 33 F 2d 841, 842 (1929).

"There is no doubt but what the law is that a national bank cannot lend its credit or become an accommodation endorser." National Bank of Commerce v. Atkinson, 55 E 471.

"A bank can lend its money, but not its credit." First Nat'l Bank of Tallapoosa v. Monroe. 135 Ga 614, 69 SE 1124, 32 LRA (NS) 550.

".. . the bank is allowed to hold money upon personal security; but it must be money that its loans, not its credit." Seligman v. Charlottesville Nat. Bank, 3 Hughes 647, Fed Case No.12, 642, 1039.

"A loan may be defined as the delivery by one party to, and the receipt by another party of, a sum of money upon an agreement, express or implied, to repay the sum with or without interest." Parsons v. Fox; 179 Ga 605, 176 SE 644. Also see Kirkland v. Bailey, 155 SE 2d 701 and United States v. Neifert White Co., 247 Fed Supp 878, 879.

Fourteenth. A party alleging to be creditor must prove standing.

The Defendants have failed or refused to produce the actual note, which the Defendants allege that we owe. Where the foreclosing party cannot prove the existence of the note, then there is no note. To recover on a promissory note, the Defendant must prove: (1) the existence of the note in question; (2) that the party sued signed the note; (3) that the Defendant is the owner or holder of the note; and (4) that a certain balance is due and owing on the note. See in Re: SMS Financial LLC. v. Abco Homes, Inc. No.98-50117 February 18, 1999 (5th Circuit Court of Appeals.) Volume 29 of the New Jersey Practice Series, Chapter 10 Section 123, page 566, emphatically states, "...; and no part payments should be made on the bond or note unless the person to whom payment is made is able to produce the bond or note and the part payments are endorsed thereon. The mortgagor would normally have a Common law right to demand production or surrender of the bond or note and mortgage, as the case may be. See Restatement, Contracts S 170(3), (4) (1932); C.J.S. Mortgages S 469 in Carnegie Bank v Shalleck; 256 N.J. Super 23 (App. Div 1992), the Appellate Division held,

"When the underlying mortgage is evidenced by an instrument meeting the criteria for negotiability set forth in N.J.S. 12A:3-104, the holder of the instrument shall be afforded all the rights and protections provided a holder in due course pursuant to N.J.S. 12A:3-302" Since no one is able to produce the "instrument" there is no competent evi¬dence before the Court that any party is the holder of the alleged note or the true holder in due course. New Jersey common law dictates that the plaintiff proves the existence of the alleged note in question, prove that the party sued signed the alleged note, prove that the plaintiff is the owner and holder of the alleged note, and prove that certain balance is due and owing on any alleged.

note. Federal Circuit Courts have ruled that the only way to prove the perfection of any security is by actual possession of the se¬curity. See Matter of Staff Mortg. & Inv. Corp., 550 F.2d 1228 (9th Cir 1977), "Under the Uniform Commercial Code, the only no¬tice sufficient to inform all interested parties that a security interest in instruments has been perfected is actual possession by the secured party, his agent or bailee." Bankruptcy Courts have followed the Uniform Commercial Code. In Re Investors & Lenders, Ltd. 165 B.R. 389 (Bkrtcy.D.N.J.1994), "Under the New Jersey Uniform Commercial Code (NJUCC), promissory note is "instrument," security interest in which must be perfected by possession.

Fifteenth. To prove damages in foreclosure of a debt, a party must enter the account and general ledger statement into the record through a competent fact witness.

To prove up a claim of damages, the foreclosing party must enter evidence incorporating records such as a general ledger and accounting of an alleged unpaid promissory note, the person responsible for preparing and maintaining the account general ledger must provide a complete accounting which must be sworn to and dated by the person who maintained the ledger. See Pacific Concrete F.C.U. V. Kauanoe, 62 Haw.334, 614 P.2d 936 (1980), GE Capital Hawaii, Inc. v. Yonenaka 25 P.3d 807,96 Hawaii 32, (Hawaii App 2001), Fooks v. Norwich Housing Authority; 28 Conn.L. Rptr. 371, (Conn. Super.2000), and Town of Brookfield v. Can-dlewood Shores Estates, Inc.; 513 A.2d 1218, 201 (1986). See also Solon v. Godbole.

163 Ill. App. 3d 845, 114 Il.

Sixteenth. The Defendant, POORE SUBSTITUTE, LTD, has not incurred a financial loss in the lending of Federal Reserve Notes. Ex¬hibit B proves the factual lack of any financial loss or any assets of the alleged creditor pledged in the transaction. As anyone re¬viewing this exhibit can see, the banks in the United States of America create money at no cost to themselves. Please see page 23 Question number 125. The statement by the House Banking Committee is as follows; "The business of banks is to lend money. The profit comes from the difference between the cost of creating money and the price they charge borrowers for that money. Now the cost of creating money is negligible. Congress has delegated the power to create money to the banking system without a charge. The banks do not pay a license fee or a payment charge for their reserves. Thus, the raw materials the banks use cost them nothing." Emphasis added. Thus, the Defendant, POORE SUBSTITUTE, LTD, cannot allege that they incurred a financial loss, and they have no standing to or foundation to allege that they will incurr a financial loss, based upon the above statement issued by the House Banking Committee.

SECOND CAUSE OF ACTION

(Slander of Title, fraudulent conversion)

First. Wanita Staton and husband Lamar Staton, hereby allege and re-allege all the foregoing Paragraphs as part of this Cause of Action with the same force and effect as if fully set forth herein. Based upon the foregoing the Defendants are slandering title to the subject property and is attempting an act of fraudulent conversion. The Defendants has a duty to refrain from attempting to foreclose when they lack the right of subrogation. We ask the court to provide declaratory relief to order the defendants to cease and desist and abate any attempt to conduct a foreclosure sale, abate, curtail, cease, and desist any collection activities and foreclo¬sure activities by the defendants for lack of due process lack of a claim filed against the original land patent, and breach of contract. The Defendant, POORE SUBSTITUTE, LTD, has not produced any evidence whatsoever that they are a co-signer on the original promissory note. The Defendant, POORE SUBSTITUTE, LTD, has, therefore, no right of subrogation and no right to foreclose on our property. The Defendant, POORE SUBSTITUTE, LTD, has never produced any evidence that they have paid the entire mortgage debt in full, thereby failing to prove a second element that is required of someone who is claiming to have a right of subrogation, as discussed above. The Defendant, POORE SUBSTITUTE, LTD, therefore, has no right of subrogation as a stranger to the original transaction and as someone who has not paid the entire mortgage debt in full. See Aetna Life v. Middleport, 124 US 534. In an action to annul a promissory note and deed of trust which were then in the hands of an assignee, evidence supported findings that foreclosure during litigation would produce great or irreparable injury to the plaintiffs and therefore issuance of a preliminary injunction restraining assignees from disposing of a note and deed or from foreclosing was not an abuse of discretion, see, Daniels v.

Williams; 270 P. 2d 556, 125 C.A. 2d 310. In this case we are not asking for a restraining order, however we are asking for an order to cease and desist.

Second. The Defendants have never produced the following; A.) evidence of a lien, a security interest or some kind of right, title or interest in the property or any sort of claim that is superior to our own, based upon a right of subrogation and upon valuable consideration and a judgment; This is also required by the rules of the common law, pursuant to the Seventh Amendment, see 443 Cans of Frozen Egg Product v United States of America; to identify the valuable consideration or lawful money that gives them power to enforce the original mortgage contract.

Therefore, Under the doctrine of latches the Defendants are barred from now claiming to have a right of subrogation and thereby any right, title or interest in the property or a lien or a security interest over us, Wanita Staton and husband Lamar Stanton, the Plaintiffs, or our private property described in Exhibit A. Under the principal of estoppel by silence, the Defendant, POORE SUBSTI¬TUTE, LTD remains silent and still does not respond to the constructive notice or issues of law raised in the constructive notice.

THIRD CAUSE OF ACTION

(fraud, fraudulent inducement, insurance fraud)

We, Wanita Staton and husband Lamar Statont, hereby allege and re-allege all the foregoing Paragraphs as part of this Cause of Action with the same force and effect as if fully set forth herein. The Defendant, POORE SUBSTITUTE, LTD has no right to demand that any insurance be purchased by the Plaintiffs, because they are a stranger to the transaction and have no right of subrogation.

Request for Relief

Wherefore, we, Wanita Staton and Husband Lamar Staton, the Plaintiffs, pray for a judgment against the Defendants as follows:

One. For abatement of any and all past, current and future claims of any right, title or interest in our home, abatement of de¬mands for mortgage payments, current past and future, discharge of any current or past demands for payment and we ask that the Defendants be ordered to remove our house described in Exhibit A from any list of assets on their books and remove any records of this fraudulent debt with credit reporting agencies. We further ask that the unlawful PLANS taken by the defendants to place the property for sale to the public in an unlawful foreclosure proceeding, in violation of the due process provisions of the Fifth and Fourteenth Amendments to the US Constitution, be abated and that they cease and desist their actions and activities in pursuance thereof.

Two. For a judgment that because the above-described property is held in good title by us, Wanita Staton and husband Lamar Staton, The Plaintiffs, and that no superior title exists by anyone, including the defendants, and defendants have no security interest, right, title or interest or lien in said home, the defendants must be found to be without any lawful claim against our home, and be compelled to disclaim any right title or interest in the subject home.

Three. For an order of Cease and Desist, ordering the Defendants and their agents, including any unregistered foreign agents, to cease and desist any further actions to foreclose on this alleged debt, because of the failure of consideration and because of the lack of the right of subrogation, and therefore, the lack of any standing to sue for foreclosure or for unlawful detainer by the De-fendants. In addition, we ask for a court order of Cease and Desist ordering the Sheriff to refrain from enforcing any and all actions.

for unlawful detainer or foreclosure, taken by this Defendant, POORE SUBSTITUTE, LTD, or their agents and assigns, because they do not have the right of subrogation as a stranger to the transaction.

Punitive and Compensatory Damages

We, Wanita Staton and Lamar Staton allege and re-allege all the foregoing Paragraphs as part of this Cause of Action with the same force and effect as if fully set forth herein. We, Wanita Staton and husband Lamar Staton, the Plaintiffs in this matter further seek costs and fees from Defendant, POORE SUBSTITUTE, LTD , if the Defendants do not immediately stop their foreclosure on our home in the amount of two hundred dollars in lawful money, silver specie, silver one ounce coins, minted in the united states of America and punitive and compensatory compensation for the costs of this suit intentional infliction of emotional distress against the Plaintiff , POORE SUBSTITUTE, LTD in the amount of Five thousand dollars of lawful money, silver specie, silver one ounce coins minted in the United States of America, sum certain. We ask for compensation and damages from, POORE SUBSTITUTE, LTD. We ask for no compensation or damages from the Wake County Sheriff.

Signed in the fourth century of the independence of the United States of America. All rights specifically reserved. Respectfully submitted,

Verification

We have read the Action to Quiet Title to our home And for Declaratory Relief and know the contents thereof to be true; and the same is true of our own knowledge, except to the matters which are therein stated on our information and belief, and as to those matters, we believe them to be true. The foregoing is true, correct, complete and not misleading.

Sealed by the voluntary act of My own hand on this          day of the

month, in the Year of our Lord, two thousand and Twelve, in the fourth century of the Independence of America.

Wanita Staton

Lamar Staton


LIST OF EXHIBITS

A.      WARRANTY DEED

B.      HOUSE BANKING AND CURRENCY COMMITTEE REPORT

C.     REQUEST FOR VALIDATION OF DEBT LETTER/ DEED OF RELEASE

D.     COMMON LAW LIEN

E.     AFFIDAVIT OF INTEREST OF FULL NAME


File ends here END OF DOCUMENT END OF DOCUMENT

The SSN traps

When we filed for the SS#, we were considered one of the following (1) A U.S. Citizen; (2) A Naturalized Citizen (3) A 14th Amendment Citizen; or (4) A Sovereign citizen. Since the 4th was not offered, we should have chosen (4) Other.

We discovered the absolute solution to IRS taxes in the United States of America. This absolute solution is the direct result of un-distending what "The Social Security Administration" (SSA) is and what it does.

WHAT IT IS:

The (SSA) is a sub-part of the corporation known as "The United States Government". Congress formed The United States Government as a Corporation in an Act called "The District of Columbia Organic Act of 1871". This means we are not talking about the national government of the United States of America, we are talking about the private corporation named "The United States Government" (Corp U.S.)

WHAT IT DOES:

When, for whatever reason, a Moor determines that they want a Social Security account, they make an application for that trust in SSA for such an account. The SSA # creates a "trust and makes an account number for your trust in SSA's General Trust Fund. The account number for the trust is known as the "Social Security Number (SS#). The SSA make the applicant the trustee for the trust. They name the trust with a title that sounds like the trustee's name, but it is spelled in all capital letters. In other words, at your

request, the trust SSA creates for you is given account number in the general Trust Fund and becomes a taxpayer in the District of Columbia. It abides in the District of Columbia from the date it was created and exists forever. Even though you may reside else-where, when you act as trustee to that trust, you act in Washington, D. C

People are born, their parents give them names, which names are proper nouns (proper nouns are spelled with the initial letter of each word capitalized). The trust the SSA created is given a name, which sounds like the applicant's name, except that it is spelled with all CAPITAL LETTERS That name is a title—title to a trust. When anyone uses that Title, they are using the name of the trust. You can be sure they are using the name of the trust when, along with the title, they use the account number of the trust.

Think about it. When a person goes to get a job with a company which person is applying for the job, the trust, or the man? If it is the trust, then when the trust is paid for its services, the pay will be made in the trust name and/or SS#? If it is the man, then when the man is paid for his services, the pay will be made in the name of the man and the SS# will not be used. Look at the check-is it in the trust's name and/or SS#, or is it only in the man's name?

When a man opens a bank account, does he open it in the name of the trust, or does he open the account in his own name? When he buys a house gets a loan, does he use the trust name and/or SS# or his own natural name only? The answer is that if he used the trust name and SS#, it is the trust that opens bank account or buys the house. Notice where the action takes place. Though the trustee may live or reside in some other location, the trust.

exists in Washington, D. C. Therefore, the action takes place in Washington D.C. which is the trust "situs". In other words, Washington, D. C. is the place where the trust's legal or taxing actions takes place. When the trust acts it acts in Washington, D.C. only, regardless of where the trustee is when the action takes place.

Now ask yourself two questions: First, "Are you a federal employee"? and second, "When you perform an action for someone, do you expect to be paid for it"? Remember your answers. They are the keys to unraveling the tax questions presented by most tax protesters and the solutions given by the IRS. When taxed, we must remember that the person being taxed is the Person employed in the tax jurisdiction. We asked the question before, "Who was employed'? If the person employed was the trust, then the proper IRS form to file is the Form 1041. If the person that was employed was a human, then the IRS says the proper form to file is Form 1040.

If you took at the OMB number in the top right-hand corner of the IRS forms, you would find a number.

required by the Paper Reduction Act. That number is required to be cross referenced to the code section that necessitates the use of the form and that has been OMB authorized for such use. The cross-reference index shows the 1040 form is allowed to be used in accordance with a code section within Title 26 & 31, which section only applies to federal employees. That means that only federal employees can use Form 1040. Therefore, if you use Form 1040, you are claiming to be a federal employee. If you are not a federal employee and use Form 1040, you are lying to the IRS, which is a crime according to U.S. Criminal code. What happens when people act as trustee of a trust, they are protected by the Corporation's sole nature of the position-trustee. However, when a trustee begins to receive benefits from the trust outside of the trustee's fiduciary fees, the trustee creates a General Partnership with the trust. General Partnership are equally, collectively, and severally liable for the obligations of all of the other General Partners within the

Partnership.

TAXABLE:

Now, let us put it all together, SSA created a trust with a SS# and if that trust were employed it would constitute a federal employee, not because Corporation U.S. is the employer, but because of who the trust's creator is. If you are a General Partner with a federal employee, then you are equally, collectively and severably liable for their obligations. When you buy groceries with funds from the SS# trust, it appears that you are a General Partnership with the trust. Therefore, when the trust owes a mandatory tax so do its General Partners. The IRS has no authority to deal with humans other than Federal Employees (Form 1040) and Nonresident Aliens or U.S. Citizens that owe a tax in Puerto Rico (Form 2555). If you have created a General Partnership with the trust, then you owe all taxes the trust is liable for just as much as the trust does and you are just as much a federal employee as is the trust. Therefore, a proper form to file would be the Form 1040.

## TAX FREE:

What if the trust were to file its own taxes? Even if you had a General Partnership, any tax obligation would have already been met and there would be no tax obligation remaining for the General Partner. The proper form for a partnership to file is a Form 1041. About all there is to calculating a Form 1041 is you take the funds that were in the trust's account at the beginning of the year and subtract them from the funds in the account at the end of the year and the result is the net gain or loss. Then you subtract the net gain or loss from the year's increase, which gives you the amount spent by the trust.

## ARE YOU A FEDERAL EMPLOYEE?

NOW, the obvious question is "Are you a federal employee"? Answer, No! If you are not a Federal Employee, then the Form IO40 is the wrong form to be filed "When you perform an action for someone, do you expect to be paid for it"? The answer is obviously "YES'. Then ask yourself, "What was your wage"? I expect your wage will have been an all-expense paid wage. Now go back to the amount spent by the trust and notice that all the funds spent by the trust were spent on the trustee. Remember back to the time when you got the jobs you performed for the trust. Did you not plan on using the funds you generated from the trust to meet all your expenses? Then notice that the funds spent by the trust were all your wages. That means the amount spent by the trust goes on Form 1041 at the line designated for Fiduciary Fees. If you calculate the form you will likely notice that there are no taxes owed by the trust.

That means that even if there were a General Partnership between the trust and the trustee, there is no tax obligation for the General Partner. The only real problem left is that most of the people at the IRS think you owe that tax. That is because when SSA creates the trusts, they do it constructively (without an (1) indenture (without a deed) according to statute. We solved that problem by creating a proper indenture and by then sending that indenture to the SSA.

This methodology is being taught now and, in every case, it has been used, the IRS has paid every claim by returning the past three year's taxes to everyone that claimed then.

This information is given out for educational purposes only. Each person must understand and use it at their own risk.

(1) INDENTURE-A deed to which two or more persons are parties, and in which these enter reciprocal and corresponding grants or obligations towards each other; whereas a deed poll is properly one in which only the party making it executes it, or binds himself/herself it as a deed, though the grantors or grantees therein may be several in number. 3 Washb. Real Prop 311. See Indent, v. (To cut in a serrated or waiving line) To bind by indentures; to apprentice as to indent a young man to a shoemaker. Black's Law 4h Edition.

Internal Revenue Service (IRS) Take It or Leave It

If the Income Tax were allowable in the united states of America, it would have been instituted July 4,

1776. If the Income Tax were allowable in Texas, it would have been instituted March 5, 1836.

Two things make you subject to the income tax:

The Social Security Number

And Use of the Zip Code

The C.O.R.P.O.R.A.T.I.O.N.

(Crooked Officials Robbing People of Rights Against Truth in Our Nation) BOOK TITLE

Just as there are two united states: the UNITED STATES democracy corporation and the united states of America the republic of we the people; there are two post offices: The United States Post Office and the United States Postal Service. The United States Post Office is non-domestic (see DMM 122.32 as amended) and is for "we the people" outside of the federal territories, whereas the

United States Postal Service is domestic, is for government use and is for federal territories. Whenever you use zip codes, you are stating that you live in a federal territory or that you are living in a state as a federal employee or citizen subject to all the codes, rules, and regulations of the federal corporation. General delivery seems to be the best way to get your mail, as some suggest that the use of an address or post box also grants federal jurisdiction. You are not a USPS customer, so you do not have to fill out a USPS Form to Request General Delivery nor is general delivery only available for 30 days as the USPS will tell you, because again, you are not a customer, you are a transient - just a passing through.

It is alright for you to use the social security number and to receive benefits, if you do so as the agent for the fiction via the redemption process. The Internal Revenue Service (IRS) is NOT an agency of the government. The IRS came into the United States through the Bretton-Woods Agreement. It operates on the premise that someone has said they owe money to the IRS and the IRS can collect it.

The American people have been turned upside down by the premise to self-assess and to voluntarily comply via payments made under the penalty of perjury. This is the only self-assessment and voluntary compliance of any taxation placed upon the American people. When you self-assess your own taxes and voluntarily comply under the penalty of perjury, you have become an IRS agent against yourself and subject to Section 6065 of the Internal Revenue Code.

Section 6065 of the Internal Revenue Code states: (1) Verification of returns. Except as otherwise provided by the Secretary, any return, declaration, statement, or other document required to be made under any provision of the Internal Revenue laws or regu¬lations shall contain or be verified by a written declaration that it is made under the penalties of perjury. There are many valid ar¬guments about: the definition of income, Title 26 never having been properly ratified and passed into positive law and that Ameri¬cans cannot be directly taxed on their private property.

compensation. These are all true, but they do not matter because if you have a bank account, you have agreed to follow all the rules and regulations of the bank. One of those rules is Title 26! Your signature card is your contract with the IRS as it says that you agree to abide by all the rules and regulations of the

It is all about returns. It is called an Income Tax Return and is subject to the law of contracts. The person making the offer of contract is the one who is returning the contract and the receiver of the contract has the right to accept or reject that contract within a 72-hour period, Truth in Lending Act. There are three ways to deal with the Income Tax. Please stay with the Internal Revenue Service Codes to keep from being harassed and charged as a tax protester.

1.      You can proceed as you always have by either filling out the 1040 per the instructions of the IRS, having it done by a CPA (who is a registered agent of the IRS), or H&R Block or any person

knowledgeable in the filling out of the forms. Then pay everything that you have agreed to pay and pay it on time.

2.      Have the District Director of the IRS fill out the Form 1040 and return it to you.

The C.O.R.P.O.R.A.T.I.O.N.

(Crooked Officials Robbing People of Rights Against Truth in Our Nation) BOOK TITLE

(A)     Take the 1040 form and fill out the name and the address in all capital letters and place the social security number on the form and mail It to the District Director of the IRS in your area and notify him to fill it out and return it to you.

(B)     Upon receiving the return, if it is not signed under the penalty of perjury (per Section 6065 of the IRC), reject it, and return their offer of contract for failure to swear under the penalty of

perjury.

(C)     Because the IRS will never sign under the penalty of perjury, simply return to the IRS any letter, declaration or document received from that point on for failure to make their declaration, document, or letter under the penalty of perjury.

(D)     Instruct the District Director to return to you all monies withheld during the year.

3. Or you can file a trust Form 1041 and as trustee or fiduciary of the trust you may file for the trust. (A) The all-capital letter name by which they address you has been set up as a trust under the

Social Security Administration and has been given the social security number as the number for the trust. You as the American National are then appointed as trustee or fiduciary of the trust. You, being the trustee of a trust, must adhere to the contract of the trust and fulfill the

trust as it is written. (B) No trust pays taxes. The money made by the trust is dispersed to the beneficiaries of the trust on a Schedule K-1. Then the beneficiary pays the taxes on the dispersed earnings. In filing

your form 1041, the income is your W2 or 1099 or wherever you derive income from for that year and is to be placed in the "other income" line of the 1041. The fiduciary then is paid all the income that the trust has made that year. This gives a net taxable income of zero and instructs the IRS to return to the fiduciary any taxes that were taken and the fiduciary will take care of the commercial affairs of the trust. See sample form.

ALWAYS REMEMBER, WHEN YOU RECEIVE ANY DOCUMENT, DECLARATION, LETTER OR FORM OF ANY KIND ISSUED FROM THE IRS OFFICE, IMMEDIATELY RETURN IT FOR THEIR FAILURE TO SIGN THE DOCUMENT UNDER PENALTY OF PERJURY!

Without Prejudice all rights reserved UCC1_308 In connection with my signature indicates that I have reserved my common law rights not to be compelled to perform under any contracts that I did not enter knowingly, voluntary, and intentionally.

And furthermore, I do not accept the liability.

associated with the compelled benefit of any unrevealed contract or commercial agreement.

When asked "Are you *John Doe?

", You could ask, "Could you rephrase the question, that I am able to answer without incriminating myself as being something that.

is not living? I am not a name; however, I do have a name, which I will not enter without disclosure and or consideration of any hidden or unseen contract being made or existing. If unable to rephrase the question, then I would like to move to subject matter of jurisdiction, and who has wanted for it."

Rejection without dishonor

Do not forget about "Rejection Without Dishonor". You can stay in honor and reject a presentment. Example is if there is error in price or the contract is defective.

I have told a judge a long time ago "That I respectfully reject you without dishonor because I'm not the defendant."

1.      provide me with the legal contract or agreement I signed that obligates me to return moneys borrowed

2.      provide me with proof of collateral the opposing party has pledged in consideration for

3.      prove that such contracting person has violated any legal agreement or contract and proof if damages to the party making such claim.

UCC 3-603(b) - TENDER OF PAYMENT - discharge of obligation U.C.C. - ARTICLE 3 - NEGOTIABLE INSTRUMENTS .PART 6. DISCHARGE AND PAYMENT

3-603. TENDER OF PAYMENT.

b) If tender of payment of an obligation to pay an instrument is made to a person entitled to enforce the instrument and the tender is refused, there is discharge, to the extent of the amount of the tender, of the obligation of an endorser or accommodation party having a right of recourse with respect to the obligation to which the tender relates.

ACCEPTANCE OF OATH OF OFFICE

John Quincy Jones c/o (street address) city, state, by [00000] Tele: 000-000-0000

(FILL IN NAME OF COURT HERE)

THE STATE OF (NAME OF STATE), Plaintiff-in-Error,

vs.


JOHN QUINCY JONES, <sic> <misnomer>

Aggrieved Defendant     )

)       Case No.        (enter your case number)

ACCEPTANCE OF CONSTITUTIONS

AND OATH OF OFFICE

Date: __ Day of ____ (month), 2006 (date of trial)

__: __ A.M. or P.M. (time of trial), Traffic Court

The C.O.R.P.O.R.A.T.I.O.N.

(Crooked Officials Robbing People of Rights Against Truth in Our Nation) BOOK TITLE

Notice for        , (name) _____ (title, i.e., Judge, Commissioner, Magistrate,

(county) District Attorney, etc.)

Point of Law: All contracts commence with an offer and only become binding upon acceptance. See: "Contracts" by Farnsworth, third edition, sect. 3.3, pages 112, 113. Infra.

The organic Constitutions of the United States of American, and the State of        (name of state, Upper & Low-

er Case Type) and the Oath of Office of the above-named PUBLIC SERVANT, amounts to nothing more than an offer of an intention to act or refrain from acting in a specified way between the respective governments and the private American people and for other purposes.


Be it known by these presents that I, John Quincy Jones, do hereby accept the organic Constitutions of the United States

of America and of the State of     (name of state, Upper- & Lower-Case Type) and the Oath of Office of the above named.

PUBLIC SERVANT as your open and binding offer of promise to form a firm and binding contract between the respective govern-ments, their political instrumentalities and the above-named PUBLIC SERVANT and myself in my private capacity.

I expect that, as a PUBLIC SERVANT, you will perform all your promises and stay within the limitations of your constitu¬tions, create no unfounded presumptions, seek only the true facts, and tell the truth at all times and respect and protect my right of personal liberty and private property and all rights antecedent thereto.

The foregoing Notice of Acceptance of Constitutions and of Oath of Office is made explicitly without recourse and now constitutes a binding contract and any deviation there from will be treated as a breach of contract and a violation of substantive due process.

VERIFICATION

I, John Quincy Jones, declare under penalty of perjury in accordance with the laws of the United states of America that the foregoing is true correct and complete to the best of my knowledge and belief.

(Declarer's Signature)

(Witness Signature)        (Witness Signature)

Address of Witness:        Address of Witness:




Dated:

The C.O.R.P.O.R.A.T.I.O.N.

(Crooked Officials Robbing People of Rights Against Truth in Our Nation) BOOK TITLE

THIS INSTRUMENT IS NON-NEGOTIABLE

"Contracts" by Farnsworth, third edition, sect 33, pages 112,113

Offer and Acceptance. The outward appearance of the agreement process, by which the parties satisfy the requirement of bargain imposed by the doctrine of consideration, varies widely according to the circumstances. It may, for example, involve face-to-face negotiations, an exchange of letters or facsimiles, or merely the perfunctory signing of a printed form supplied by the other party. Whatever the outward appearance, it is common to analyze the process in terms.

of two distinct steps: First, a manifestation of assent that is called an offer, made by one party (the offeror) to another (the offer-ee).

and second, a manifestation of assent in response that is called an acceptance, made by the offeree to the offeror. Although courts apply this analysis on a case-by-case basis, depending on the circumstances, it gives a reassuring appearance of consistency.

What is an "offer"? It can be defined as a manifestation to another of

assent to enter a contract if the other manifests assent in return by some action, often a promise but sometimes a performance. By making an offer, the offeror thus confers upon the offeree the power to create a contract. An offer is nearly always a promise and, in a sense, the action (promise or performance) on which the offeror conditions the promise is the "price" of it becoming enforceable. Offer, then, is the name given to a promise that is conditional on some action by the promise if the legal effect of the promise's taking that action is to make the promise enforceable. Empowerment of the offeree to make the offeror's promise enforceable is thus the essence of an offer. When does a promise empower the promisee to take action that will make the promise enforceable? In other words, when does a manifestation of assent amount to an offer? This is one of the main sub-jects of this chapter.

What is an "acceptance"? It can be defined as the action {promise or performance} by the offeree that creates a contract (ie, makes the offeror's promise enforceable). Acceptance, then, is the name given to the offeree's action if the legal effect of that ac¬tion is to make the offeror's promise enforceable. When does action by the promise make the promise enforceable? In other words, when does the promise's action amount to an acceptance? This is another of the main subjects of this chapter. Because of the requirement of mutuality of obligation, both parties are free to withdraw from negotiations until the moment when both are bound. This is the moment when the offeree accepts the offer. It therefore follows, as we shall see later in more detail, that the offeror is free to revoke the offer at any time before acceptance.

**In conclusion:** If you find the information in this book or any of our videos of value and would like to show your appreciations by donating for our time and energy, and education to the people, please paypal and donate to heavymentalborngod@yahoo.com donate whatever value that you feel that this information and my time and energy is worth donating $500, $100, $20, $10, $5, or even $1, like the video and sub-.

scribe.

Shalawam, first giving all praises to the god of our forefathers Abraham, Isaac, and Jacob, Yahawah. My family I only ask that you do not be like 95% of the people that I talk to that I suggest they get both of My books Commercial Warfare We the people vs Despotism, The Infliction of Commerce, also a good book on contract law Brains Blum's book, that they get a Black's Law 4th dic¬tionary, get a Webster Col-ligate Dictionary, listen to a good motivational speaker such as Les Brown, Eric Thomas, James Allen to help one change one's thinking and most Importantly study the Bible! What most people do not know is that one thing that used to be required for all Law students was to study the bible it was a part of their curriculum. If you fail to do these things you will not know how to properly respond to offers; this entire game is about offer and acceptance which is contact law. It is imperative to overstand contact law. It is always about the contact and their interest is always fiat currency read CFR 72.11 its all commercial.

Subscribe to Deprogramed Enlightener and Undaunted National on YouTube. Be sure to tell others about the success that you have had with the Right Knowledge that you learned from Tazadaq Yahawah (Gods') man. shalom

The C.O.R.P.O.R.A.T.I.O.N.

(Crooked Officials Robbing People of Rights Against Truth in Our Nation) BOOK TITLE

The C.O.R.P.O.R.A.T.I.O.N.

(Crooked Officials Robbing People of Rights Against Truth in Our Nation) BOOK TITLE

The C.O.R.P.O.R.A.T.I.O.N.

(Crooked Officials Robbing People of Rights Against Truth in Our Nation) BOOK TITLE

North Carolina )        In the General Court of Justice

              )        CMS Court Type Court Division

        Forsyth County )        CM SCIS Case Number

LOC User1

State of North Carolina)

)

v.        )        DEMAND FOR PROBABLE CAUSE

          )        HEARING AND MOTION FOR

CMS DefendantNameFull)        RECORDING OF HEARING

Defendant)

Now comes the defendant and pursuant to N.C.G.S. 15A-606 and requests the Court to calendar a hearing in this matter immedi¬ately in compliance with the statutory requirements. Defendant, who has been found by the Court to be indigent, further moves that said hearing be recorded and transcribed at State expense. In support of this motion defendant shows unto the Court as fol¬lows:

Defendant was charged with the felony charge(s) now pending against defendant on or about CMSOffenseDate.

Defendant's case has not received a probable cause hearing within the time allowed by statute and defendant has not waived said hearing.

Without waiver of probable cause, which defendant has not waived, by statute a hearing must be held within 15 days of defend-ant's first appearance. Said appearance was on or about CMSServiceDate and no such hearing has been had as of today.

Pursuant to statute any defendant may provide for the recording of all proceedings in his case. N.C.G.S. 15A-1241. Recordation is required to preserve the defendant's 6th Amendment right to confront and cross-examine the witnesses against him, including impeachment with prior statements.

Defendant has been found to be indigent by the Court and accordingly, pursuant to Ake v. Oklahoma, 470 U.S. 68 (1985), defend¬ant is entitled to the furnishing of services in defense of his case at the expense of the State.

Defendant requests that his probable cause hearing be recorded and that such services be provided at the expense of the State.

This the 18 November 2018.

CMS Defense Attorney Assistant Public Defender Suite 400, 8 West 3rd Street Winston-Salem, NC 27101 (336) 761-2510

Certificate of Service

The C.O.R.P.O.R.A.T.I.O.N.

(Crooked Officials Robbing People of Rights Against Truth in Our Nation) BOOK TITLE

This is to certify that the undersigned has this day.

served this paper upon all other parties to this matter by hand.

delivering a copy thereof to the office of those persons listed

below:

CMS Prosecuting Attorney, ADA

Forsyth County DA's Office

Seventh Floor, Hall of Justice Building

Winston-Salem, NC 27101

This the 18 November 2018.

CMS DefenseAttorney

| North Carolina ) | In the General Court of Justice |
| ) | CMSCourtType Court Division |
| Forsyth County ) | CMSCISCaseNumber |

LOCUser1

State of North Carolina)

)

v.        )        ORDER FOR PROBABLE CAUSE

         )        HEARING AND FOR

CMS Defendant Name Full)        RECORDING OF HEARING

Defendant)

Pursuant to the motion of the defendant in this matter and heard before the undersigned this day, the Court enters the following order.

A probable cause hearing in this matter shall be and hereby is scheduled for in District Court 1C.

The above date has been agreed upon by the State and Defendant in this matter and is the involved officers' next court date.

Pursuant to the defendant's request and the defendant's indigent status, the Probable Cause hearing in this matter shall be record¬ed by an official Court Reporter and the expense of this service shall be borne by the State.

Defendant's counsel shall make a request of the Trial Court Administrator for assignment of an official Court Reporter to the Dis¬trict Court morning session in courtroom 1C to record the hearing in this matter. If for any reason the Trial Court Administrator is unable to provide for a Court Reporter assigned to the Courthouse to report the hearing, then defense counsel shall arrange for the services of a private licensed Court Reporter to report the hearing.

This order shall constitute authority for the State to pay for the services of a court reporter to report this hearing, said services to

be compensated for at the established rate for official court reporters in the employ of the State.

This the _____ day of   , 200___.

Nunc Pro Tunc this the ____ day of        , 200____

District Court Judge, Presiding


Cause No.

STATE OF TEXAS          §         IN THE          COURT

§

V.        §          COURT DESIGNATION

§

***        §          COUNTY, TEXAS

MOTION TO SUPPRESS EVIDENCE OF THE ARREST BASED ON LACK OF          PROBABLE CAUSE BASED ON VIDEOTAPE AS

PRESENTED IN WHITELEY V.        WARDEN, WYOMING STATE PENITENTIARY, 401 U.S. 560, 91 S. Ct. 1031, 28 L. Ed. 2d 306 (1971)

TO THE HONORABLE JUDGE OF SAID COURT:

NOW COMES ***, the Defendant in the above styled and numbered cause and files his/her motion to suppress evidence based on the lack of evidence of probable cause as shown in the videotape and in support thereof would show the Court as fol¬lows:

I.

Probable cause means that there is a reasonable ground for belief of guilt. Brinegar v. United States, 338 U.S. 160, 69 S. Ct. 1302, 93 L. Ed. 1879 (1949).

II.

The videotape is the best evidence of the state of the Defendant at the time of the arrest, having been made shortly after the ar¬rest. The videotape, itself, shows a sober person.

III.

Both the physical and mental faculties of the Defendant do not show that there was sufficient evidence to support and independent judgement of probable cause, which is what is required, of course, for an arrest without a warrant. Whiteley v. Warden, Wyoming State Penitentiary, 401 U.S. 560 (1971). Therefore, the arrest and continued custody should not have taken place, and, absent a warrant, which would not have passed judicial muster, the Defendant should have been released from custody following the vide¬otape. Gerstein v. Pugh, 420 U.S. 103, 95 S. Ct. 854, (1975).

IV.

The legal requirements for an arrest without a warrant are just as stringent as the requirements for an arrest with a warrant. In other words, the evidence that would have been presented before a neutral magistrate must have convinced a neutral magistrate that there was reasonable ground for belief of guilt. Brinegar, 338 U.S. 160 (1949). It is submitted that a reasonable magistrate,

looking at this videotape, would not have issued a warrant. Whiteley, 401 U.S. 560 (1971).

V.

The State argued in Whiteley that the Court should employ a less stringent standard for reviewing a police officer's assessment of probable cause as a prelude to a warrantless arrest than a Court would employ in reviewing a magistrate's assessment as a prelude to issuing an arrest warrant or a search warrant. Whiteley, 401 U.S. at 566. The Court in Whiteley, rejected that position, noting that prior Supreme Court cases had also rejected that decision and that the reason for its rejection is "both fundamental and obvious: less stringent standards for reviewing the officer's discretion in effecting a warrantless arrest and search would discourage resort to the procedures for obtaining a warrant." Id.

VI.

The law in Texas regarding warrantless arrests is "more stringent than the demands of the U.S. Constitution," since warrantless arrests must be specifically authorized by statute. Witt v. State, 745 S.W.2d 472, 476 (Tex. App.—Houston [1st Dist.] 1988, rev. ref would); Stevenson v. State, 780 S.W.2d 294 (Tex. App.—Tyler, 1989) (Statutes governing warrantless arrests are to be strictly construed and the burden is on the State to show that warrantless arrests come within the statutory exception).

VII.

For purposes of making a warrantless arrest under Tex. Code Crim. Proc. art. 14.03(a)(1), arrest of the suspect based on events as consistent with innocent activity as with criminal activity is unlawful. Hoag v. State, 728 S.W.2d 375 (Tex. Crim. App. 1987).

VIII.

It is the objective analysis and not the subjective intent of the police that is controlling about the determination of whether there is probable cause for an arrest under Texas law. Johnson v. State, 722 S.W.2d 417 (Tex. Crim. App. 1986) (overruled on other grounds). Moreover, the Court is not bound by the officer's subjective conclusion about whether probable cause to arrest exists when they independently scrutinize the objective facts. Johnson v. State, 751 S.W.2d 926 (Tex. App.—Houston [1st Dist.] 1988, pet. ref would).

IX.

Although facts known to the officer at the time the Defendant was placed in the County Jail might have raised suspicions concerning him, if they do not constitute probable cause, then the arrest is illegal. Sweeten v. State, 693 S.W.2d 454 (Tex. Crim. App. 1985).

WHEREFORE PREMISES CONSIDERED, the Defendant respectfully prays that the Court.

find there was not probable cause to arrest the Defendant for driving while intoxicated and order that all evidence seized as a re¬sult of the unlawful arrest of the Defendant be suppressed and not be admitted into evidence upon the trial of this case.

Respectfully Submitted,

Attorney Name State Bar Number Address

City, State, Zip Phone

Fax

Attorney for Defendant ***

CERTIFICATE OF SERVICE

This is to certify that a true and correct copy of the foregoing Motion to Suppress Evidence of the Arrest Based on Lack of Probable Cause Based on Videotape as Presented to a Neutral Magistrate in Whiteley v. Warden, Wyoming State Penitentiary, 401 U.S. 560

(1971) was served upon the attorney for the State on          , 200___.

Attorney for Defendant

Cause No.

STATE OF TEXAS          §          IN THE          COURT

§

V.          §          COURT DESIGNATION

§

***          §          COUNTY, TEXAS

ORDER

CAM E ON this day to be heard Defendant's Motion to Suppress Evidence of the Arrest Based on

A judgment that is "void" may be attacked by motion under rule 60(b), regardless of whether the motion is made within one year or is made later [1], by an independent suit in equity if for some reason the motion under 60(b)

would not provide adequate relief [2]; or by denying the validity of the judgment when it is relied on in a subsequent action.

Many decisions characterize a judgment that has been procured by fraud as "void," though more often, such a judgment is characterized as "voidable." The distinction has never been noticeably clear, and the purpose of making it not consistently articulated.

One purpose of the distinction is to give effect to the concept that the person seeking to nullify the judgment should ordinarily do so by going into the court that rendered the judgment rather than attempting to do so in an independent suit. Hence, it has been said that a "void" judgment can be attacked in an independent suit but a "voidable" one must be attacked by a 60(b) type of motion. But if the proposition is accepted that the applicant for relief should always be required to use a 60(b) motion unless it would not provide adequate relief [3], then the distinction is unnecessary.

At any rate, a judgment rendered by a court that lacks jurisdiction is universally characterized as "void."[4] Traditional doctrine had been that such a judgment is a legal nullity. In modern decisions, however, the problem is recognized as being more complicated [5]. That is, there may be situations in which a court, lacking jurisdiction has rendered a judgment that should nevertheless be given effect. In this regard, it is important to distinguish between jurisdiction over the person and jurisdiction over the subject matter.

Jurisdiction over the person may be lacking because the process employed did not give adequate notice to the person against whom judgment was rendered [6], or because that court lacked the required contacts with the case [7], or because, although jurisdiction was secured over a party purporting to represent the person, the representation was fundamentally inadequate [8].

Unless the party somehow learned of the action and made an appearance to contest the exercise of jurisdiction over his person [9], the judgment is void on Due Process grounds in all these circumstances. Many decisions also hold a judgment void where the party obtained actual notice from a court that had sufficient contacts with the case, but the process was not in technical compliance with the rules governing mechanics of service [10]. Inasmuch as the party in that situation had actual notice and could have raised his technical objection by special appearance, however, it is not at all clear why the judgment should be treated as void, particularly if the statute of limitations has run on the claim by the time the judgment is attacked.

The problem of lack of subject matter jurisdiction is more complicated. The old vintage rule was that a judgment of a court lacking subject matter jurisdiction was a legal nullity [11]. This rule was subject to various saving qualifications, e.g., that jurisdiction was presumed if the rendering court was one of general jurisdiction, that evidence outside the record was inadmissible to prove lack of jurisdiction, etc. But it had the effect of making judgments potentially vulnerable if any substantial question of subject matter jurisdiction was presented.

The modern view, not yet fully accepted, takes a different approach, at least where the lack of jurisdiction was not entirely obvious. In this approach the critical questions are, first, whether the party against whom the judgment was rendered had opportunity to do so. The questions present themselves in three contexts: where the question of jurisdiction was raised in the original action; where the party charged with the judgment appeared in the action, thereby having an opportunity to challenge jurisdiction, but did not raise the jurisdictional question; and where the judgment was rendered by default.

If the question of jurisdiction was raised and adjudicated in the original action, the modern view is that the judgment is not subject to subsequent attack, on the premise that a court has an auxiliary jurisdiction to determine its jurisdiction [12]. Although some authorities suggest that this rule is inapplicable to courts of limited jurisdiction, there seems no reason why it should not be. An erroneous determination of the jurisdictional question can be remedied by review through appeal or extraordinary writ, and failure to pursue such a remedy should foreclose subsequent disputation of the issue.

If the party charged with the judgment appeared in the action, there is almost equally strong reason for holding that the question of subject matter jurisdiction may not be raised by subsequent attack on the judgment [13]. By hypothesis, the party had opportunity to raise the jurisdictional defense. There is little reason for saying it should survive the judgment when defenses on the merits would not. Moreover, the party who obtained the judgment may be assumed to suppose it is valid and justifiably guide his subsequent conduct accordingly. Nevertheless, many authorities still adhere to the view that the jurisdictional question can be subsequently raised, by motion under Rule 60(b) or its analogues, by separate suit in equity, or by attacking the judgment when it is relied upon by an opponent. However, most of the cases in which such an attack has been allowed have involved no intervening reliance interests and either a judgment of a tribunal of limited jurisdiction or grounds of attack having Constitutional implications [14]. Even in these situations the tendency seems to be to sustain the judgment except when its enforcement would affect the government itself or the administration of a scheme of remedies having significance beyond the immediate parties.

When the judgment has been entered by default, the judgment is usually regarded as open to attack if rendered without subject matter jurisdiction. When the default was entered without Constitutionally adequate notice, the judgment is in any event infirm on Due Process grounds [14]. If notice was adequate, however, it can be said that the party had opportunity to raise the question of subject matter jurisdiction and should be foreclosed from subsequent opportunity to do so. On the other hand, default judgments are in any case disfavored [16], the more so if the rendering court apparently lacked the authority it purported to exercise. The better rule would seem to be to hold such a judgment void, except when it has given rise to substantial interests of reliance of which the person against whom it was rendered was aware [17]. Binding the person to the judgment in the latter situation can be justified not so much on a principle of res judicata as upon one of equitable estoppel [18], for a judgment is not the only basis upon which one's rights may be treated as finally concluded.

1. See Fed. R. Civ. P 60(B)(4).

2. See Sec. 13.15 supra.

3. See Sec. 13.15 at note 2 supra.

4. See 11 Wright & Miller, Federal Practice and Procedure sec. 2862.

5. See Boskey and Brauncher, Jurisdiction and Collateral Attack, 40 Colum. L. Rev. 1006 (1940).

6. E.g., Walker v. City of Hutchinson, 352 U.S. 112, 77 S. Ct. 200, 1 L.Ed. 2d 178 (1956). See also United States v. Brand Jewelers, Inc., 318 F. Supp. 1293 (S.D.N.Y 1970) (injunction by the United States against procuring judgments based on "sewer service"); see Tuerkheimer, Service of Process in New Youk City: A Proposed End to Unregulated Criminality, 72 Colum. L. Rev. 847 (1972).

7. E.g., Hanson v. Dencla, 357 U.S. 235, 78 S. Ct. 1228, 2 L. Ed. 2d 1283 (1958).

8. See Restatement of Judgments Second sec. 86(2) (Tent. Draft No. 2, 1975).

9. If he made an appearance and contested jurisdiction, the determination of that issue is res judicata. See Baldwin v. Iowa State Traveling Men's Assn., 283 U.S. 522, 51 S. Ct. 517, 75 L. Ed. 1244 (1931); Durfee v. Duke, 375 U.S. 106, 84 S. Ct. 242, 11 L. Ed. 2d 186 (1963).

10. See, e.g., Central Operating Co. v. Utility Workers of America, 491 F.2d 245 (4th Cir. 1974).

11. See Dobbs, The Decline of Jurisdiction by Consent, 40 N.C.L. Rev. 49 (1961).

12. Durfee v. Duke, 375 U.S. 106, 84 S. Ct. 242, 11 L. Ed. 2d 186 (1963).

13. See generally Dobbs, Beyond Bootstrap: Foreclosing thte Issue of Subject-Matter Jurisdiction Before Final Judgment, 51 Minn. L. Rev. 491 (1967). See Restatement of Judgments sec. 10.

14. Ibid. See, e.g., United States v. United States Fidelity & Guaranty Co., 309 U.S. 506, 60 S. Ct. 653, 84 L. Ed. 894 (1940); Jordan v. Gilligan, 500 F.2d 701 (6th Cir. 1974).

15. See notes 6-8 supra.

16. See sec. 13.14 text following note 5 supra.

17. See Restatement of Judgments sec. 117.

18. See sec. 11.31 supra.

## RULE 60. RELIEF FROM JUDGMENT OR ORDER

(a) Clerical Mistakes. Clerical mistakes in judgments, orders or other parts of the record and errors therein arising from oversight or omission may be corrected by the court at any time of its own initiative or on the motion of any party and after such notice, if any, as the court orders. During the pendency of an appeal, such mistakes may be so corrected before the appeal is docketed in the appellate court, and thereafter while the appeal is pending may be so corrected with leave of the appellate court.

(b) Mistakes; Inadvertence; Excusable Neglect; Newly Discovered Evidence; Fraud, etc. On motion and upon such terms as are just, the court may relieve a party or a party's legal representative from a final judgment, order, or proceeding for the following reasons: (1) mistake, inadvertence, surprise, or excusable neglect; (2) newly discovered evidence which by due diligence could not have been discovered in time to move for a new trial under Rule 59(b); (3) fraud (whether heretofore denominated intrinsic or extrinsic), misrepresentation, or other misconduct of an adverse party; (4) the judgment is void; (5) the judgment has been satisfied, released, or discharged, or a prior judgment upon which it is based has been reversed or otherwise vacated, or it is no longer equitable that the judgment should have prospective application; or (6) any other reason justifying relief from the operation of the judgment. The motion shall be made within a reasonable time, and for reasons (1), (2), and (3) not more than one year after the judgment, order, or proceeding was entered or taken. A motion under this subdivision (b) does not affect the finality of a judgment or suspend its operation. This rule does not limit the power of a court to entertain an independent action to relieve a party from a judgment, order, or proceeding, or to grant relief to a defendant not actually personally notified as provided in Title 28, U.S.C., Sec. 1655, or to set aside a judgment for fraud upon the court. Writs of coram nobis, coram vobis, audita querela, and bills of review and bills in a bill or review, are abolished, and the procedure for obtaining any relief from a judgment shall be by motion as prescribed in these rules or by an independent action.

FRCP 60

A motion to set aside a judgment as void for lack of jurisdiction is not subject to the time limitations of Rule 60(b). See Garcia v. Garcia, 712 P.2d 288 (Utah 1986).

There is only an immaterial procedural difference between the relief sought pursuant to Rule 60(b) and the relief sought in an independent action. Hadden v. Rumsey Prods., 196 F.2d 92 (2d Cir. 1952); 7 Moore's Federal Practice, § 60.38(3) (2d ed. 1971))

A judgment is void, and therefore subject to relief under Rule 60(b)(4), only if the court that rendered judgment lacked jurisdiction or in circumstances in which the court's action amounts to a plain usurpation of power constituting a violation of due process. United States v. Boch Oldsmobile, Inc., 909 F.2d 657, 661 (1st Cir. 1990)

Where Rule 60(b)(4) is properly invoked on the basis that the underlying judgment is void, "'relief is not a discretionary matter; it is mandatory.'" Orner v. Shalala, 30 F.3d 1307, 1310 (10th Cir. 1994) (quoting V.T.A., Inc. v. Airco, Inc., 597 F.2d 220, 224 n.8 (10th Cir. 1979)).

For a judgment to be void, there must be some jurisdictional defect in the court's authority to enter the judgment, either because the court lacks personal jurisdiction or because it lacks jurisdiction over the subject matter of the suit. Puphal v. Puphal, 105 Idaho 302, 306, 669 P.2d 191, 195 (1983); Dragotoiu, 133 Idaho at 647, 991 P.2d at 379.

A void judgment is one that has been procured by extrinsic or collateral fraud or entered by a court that did not have jurisdiction over the subject matter or the parties. Rook v. Rook, 233 Va. 92, 95, 353 S.E.2d 756, 758 (1987)

Law Review Articles

Allocating the Burden of Proof in Rule 60(b)(4) Motions to Vacate a Default Judgment for Lack of Jurisdiction

Misc. Cases on Void Judgments

Diamond v. Diamond

More

United States v. One Rural Lot NO. 10,356, ETC.

OSHA decision on ADANLOCK OFFICE ENVIRONMENTS, DIV. OF SUPERIOR JAMESTOWN CORP

Latimer v. Latimer, a void divorce

PHYLLIS C. HUDSON v. SC DEPT. OF HIGHWAYS - judgment finding a void judgment itself found void - Rule 54(c) does not result in a void judgment unless the judgment by default was different in kind from or exceeded in amount than that prayed for in the demand for judgment.

Meyer v. Meyer

Hamill v. Bay Bridge

People of Illinois v. Harvey. I read section 2-1401, like Rule 60 of the Federal Rules of Civil Procedure (Fed. R. Civ. P. 60), as replacing traditional collateral proceedings as the proper vehicle for attacking void judgments. See Malone v. Cosentino, 99 Ill. 2d 29, 33 (1983) (final judgments can only be attacked on direct appeal, or in one of the traditional collateral proceedings now defined by statute). ... Considering these concerns, I believe the better course of action is simply to recognize that a motion for relief from a void judgment may be brought under section 2-1401 of the Code of Civil Procedure. This clarifies the basis of jurisdiction and provides the procedural mechanism for exercising the principle of law with which every member of this court agrees, i.e., that a motion attacking a void judgment may be brought at any time.

KANSAS ex rel. KOONTZ v. CLUBB However, when a judgment is attacked under K.S.A. 60-260(b)(4) as being void, there is no question of discretion on the part of the trial court.

MEDINA v. AMERICAN FAMILY MUTUAL - A judgment against an alleged tortfeasor that is void due to lack of personal service cannot be successfully used to collect under the injured party's underinsured motorist coverage when the insurance company has not otherwise submitted to jurisdiction in the case. "avoid act cannot be ratified." In re Garcia, 105 B.R. 335 (N.D.Ill. 1989).

A party may attack a void judgment at any time in a motion separate and apart from a section 2-1401 petition. R.W. Sawant, 111 Ill. 2d at 310; City of Chicago v. Fair Employment Practices Comm'n, 65 Ill. 2d 108, 112 (1976); Barnard v. Michael, 392 Ill. 130, 135 (1945); see State Bank v. Thill, 113 Ill. 2d 294, 308-09 (1986); Cavanaugh v. Lansing Municipal Airport, 288 Ill. App. 3d 239, 246 (1997); In re Marriage of Parks, 122 Ill. App. 3d 905, 909 (1984); First Federal Savings & Loan Ass'n v. Brown, 74 Ill. App. 3d 901, 905 (1979).

A court may not render a judgment, which transcends the limits of its authority, and a judgment is void if it is beyond the powers granted to the court by the law of its organization, even where the court has jurisdiction over the parties and the subject matter.

Thus, if a court is authorized by statute to entertain jurisdiction in a particular case only and undertakes to exercise the jurisdiction conferred in a case to which the statute has no application, the judgment rendered is void. The lack of statutory authority to make order or a judgment is akin to lack of subject matter jurisdiction and is subject to collateral attack. 46 Am. Jur. 2d, Judgments § 25, pp. 388-89.

A void judgment is to be distinguished from an erroneous one, in that the latter is subject only to direct attack. A void judgment is one which, from its inception, was a complete nullity and without legal effect. Lubben v. Selective Service System, 453 F.2d 645, 649 (1st Cir. 1972)

A judgment rendered by a court without personal jurisdiction over the defendant is void. It is a nullity. [A judgment shown to be void for lack of personal service on the defendant is a nullity.] Sramek v. Sramek, 17 Kan. App. 2d 573, 576-77, 840 P.2d 553 (1992), rev. denied 252 Kan. 1093 (1993).

"Where there are no depositions, admissions, or affidavits the court has no facts to rely on for a summary determination." Trinsey v. Pagliaro, D.C. Pa. 1964, 229 F. Supp. 647.

(Crooked Officials Robbing People of Rights Against Truth in Our Nation) BOOK TITLE

"A court cannot confer jurisdiction where none existed and cannot make a void proceeding valid. It is clear and well-established law that a void order can be challenged in any court", OLD WAYNE MUT. L. ASSOC. v. McDONOUGH, 204 U. S. 8, 27 S. Ct. 236 (1907).

"The law is well-settled that a void order or judgement is void even before reversal", VALLEY v. NORTHERN FIRE & MARINE INS. CO., 254 U.S. 348, 41 S. Ct. 116 (1920)

"Courts are constituted by authority and they cannot go beyond that power delegated to them. If they act beyond that authority, and certainly in contravention of it, their judgements and orders are regarded as nullities; they are not voidable, but simply void, and this even prior to reversal." WILLIAMSON v. BERRY, 8 HOW. 945, 540 12 L. Ed. 1170, 1189 (1850).

"Once jurisdiction is challenged, the court cannot proceed when it clearly appears that the court lacks jurisdiction, the court has no authority to reach merits, but rather should dismiss the action." Melo v. U.S. 505 F 2d 1026

"There is no discretion to ignore lack of jurisdiction." Joyce v. U.S. 474 2D 215.

"The burden shifts to the court to prove jurisdiction." Rosemond v. Lambert, 469 F 2d 416

"Court must prove on the record, all jurisdiction facts related to the jurisdiction asserted." Latana v. Hopper, 102 F. 2d 188; Chicago v. New York 37 F Supp. 150

"The law provides that once State and Federal Jurisdiction has been challenged, it must be proven." 100 S. Ct. 2502 (1980)

"Jurisdiction can be challenged at any time." Basso v. Utah Power & Light Co. 495 F 2d 906, 910.

"Defense of lack of jurisdiction over the subject matter may be raised at any time, even on appeal." Hill Top Developers v. Holiday Pines Service Corp. 478 So. 2d. 368 (Fla 2nd DCA 1985)

"Once challenged, jurisdiction cannot be assumed, it must be proved to exist." Stuck v. Medical Examiners 94 Ca 2d 751. 211 P2d 389.

The C.O.R.P.O.R.A.T.I.O.N.

(Crooked Officials Robbing People of Rights Against Truth in Our Nation) BOOK TITLE

"Jurisdiction, once challenged, cannot be assumed and must be decided." Maine v Thiboutot 100 S. Ct. 250.

"The law requires proof of jurisdiction to appear on the record of the administrative agency and all administrative proceedings." Hagans v Lavine 415 U. S. 533.

Though not specifically alleged, defendant's challenge to subject matter jurisdiction implicitly raised claim that default judgment against him was void and relief should be granted under Rule 60(b)(4). Honneus v. Donovan, 93 F.R.D. 433, 436-37 (1982), aff'd, 691 F.2d 1 (1st Cir. 1982).

Kocher v. Dow Chem. Co., 132 F.3d 1225, 1230-31 (8th Cir. 1997) (if there is an "arguable basis" for subject matter jurisdiction, a judgment is not void).

Lubben v. Selective Service System, 453 F.2d 645, 649 (1st Cir. 1972) ("A void judgment is to be distinguished from an erroneous one, in that the latter is subject only to direct attack. A void judgment is one, which, from its inception, was a complete nullity and without legal effect.").

Stoll v. Gottlieb, 305 U.S. 165, 171- 72, 59 S.Ct. 134 (1938) ("Every court in rendering a judgment tacitly, if not expressly, determines its jurisdiction over the parties and the subject matter.").

GEICO v. Jackson, 1995 U.S. Dist. LEXIS 16814, *1 (1995) ("[A] default judgment constitutes an implicit ruling on subject matter jurisdiction and an erroneous determination does not make the judgment void under Rule 60(b)(4)").

"Either a judgment is valid, or it is void, and the court must act accordingly once the issue is resolved." In re Marriage of Hampshire, 261 Kan. 854, 862, 934 P.2d 58 (1997).

"A judgment is void if the court acted in a manner inconsistent with due process. A void judgment is a nullity and may be vacated at any time.

Ex-parte

In reference to case number 13-4099—EX-REL UNITED STATES ANTONIO RASHAAD DOVINE VS UNITED STATES OF AMERICA, Mr. Dovine is operating in sui juris status and is in propria persona. This ex-parte request is made to this court as-king this court to vacate the VOID Judgment passed by the United States District Court for the Eastern District of North Carolina, made by a kangaroo jury after a kangaroo trial and a VOID sentence passed by Louise Flanagan against Dovine, Antonio R. on February 4th, 2013. Mr. Dovine has been involuntarily committed to USP LEE in Virginia, under the Racketeering Chapter of title 18 United States Code.

The judgment is not Voidable but Void when the judgment is made lacking subject matter and personal jurisdiction of the matter. The law is clear that even if jurisdiction is presumed to be had, it is lost when substantial rights of the accused are violated.

1.      The unclean hands of the United States Attorney and court and members of the court, including but not limited to the bar members, the clerks, the court reporters and the judges and magistrates, and the jurors and witnesses.

2.      There is no petition in the record of the case.

3.      The courts committed fraud in the procurement of jurisdiction by filing and possibly adjudicating the case in the Western District and then transferring it to the Eastern District and simulating a kangaroo trial.

4.      The judge did not produce an Oath of Office from Chambers when requested and to date there appears to be no oath on held in her chambers as required. Her own clerk admitted that the oath is not available at the clerks' office or at the judge's chambers'.

5.      The petitioner Mr. Dovine is not an employee or citizen of the United States or The State of North Carolina, as the term citizen and employee would cause one to be subject to the authority and rules and codes of the United States. Statutory jurisdiction only exists if there is a valid contract with all the principles making the contract a valid legal and lawfully binding contract. The statutory jurisdiction as well as the subject matter jurisdiction remains unproven on the record. Even though the accused never plead guilty or not guilty but appropriately challenged jurisdiction and demand that jurisdiction be proven for and on the record before he would be able to properly address the bill and the charges.

6.      The true meaning of jurisdiction is Oath Spoken, and unless you can produce for and on the record a valid binding and legitimate oath of office on file with the Secretary of State of North Carolina, United States of America etc where Mr. Dovine took an oath of office, then it is proven fact in law and on the record that the Court does not have in personam jurisdiction over the living breathing sentient body, spirit, or mind of the Petitioner.

7.      Void judgments are those rendered by a court which lacked jurisdiction, either of the subject matter or the parties. Wahl v. Round Valley Bank 38 Ariz, 411, 300 P. 955(1931), Tube City Mining & Millng Co. v. Otterson, 16 Ariz. 305, 146p 203(1914); and Millken v. Meyer, 311 U.S. 457, 61 S. CT. 339,85 L. Ed. 2d 278 (1940).

with subject matter jurisdiction is that it can never be presumed, never be waived, and cannot be constructed even by mutual consent of the parties. Subject matter jurisdiction is two part: the statutory or common law authority for the court to hearthe case and the appearance and testimony of a competent fact witness, in other words, sufficiency of pleadings.

8.      Subject matter failings are usually the following:

(1)      No petition in the record of the case, Brown v. VanKeuren, 340 Ill. 118,122 (1930).

9.      (2)      Defective petition filed, Same case as above.

10.      (3)      Fraud committed in the procurement of jurisdiction, Fredman Brothers Furniture v. Dept. of Revenue, 109 Ill. 2d 202, 486 N.E. 2d 893(1985)

11.      (4)      Fraud upon the court, In re Village of Willowbrook, 37 Ill, App. 3d 393(1962)

12.      (5)      Judge does not follow statutory procedure, Armstrong v. Obucino, 300 Ill 140, 143 (1921)

13.      (6)      Unlawful activity of a judge, Code of Judicial Conduct.

14.      Violation of due process, Johnson v. Zerbst, 304 U.S. 458, 58 S.Ct. 1019(193; Pure Oil Co. v. City of Northlake, 10 Ill.2d 241, 245, 140 N.E. 2d 289 (1956); Hallberg v Goldblatt Bros., 363 Ill 25 (1936), (If the court exceeded its statutory authority. Rosenstiel v. Rosenstiel, 278 F. Supp. 794 (S.D.N.Y. 1967)

15.      any acts in violation of 11 U.S.C. 362(a), IN re Garcia, 109 B.R. 335 (N.D> Illinois, 1989).

Where no justiciable issue is presented to the court through proper pleadings, Ligon v. Williams, 264 Ill. App 3d 701, 637 N.E. 2d 633 (1st Dist. 1994)

Where a complaint states no cognizable cause of action against that party, Charles v. Gore, 248 Ill App. 3d 441, 618 N.E. 2d 554 (1st. Dist. 1993)

where any litigant was represented before a court by a person/law firm that is prohibited by law to practice law in that jurisdiction

16.      The United States of America is not a country and is the stile (style) of the government created by the constitution of 1789. The United States of America is named as the Plaintiff in a Civil matter being adjudicated as a criminal case cannot be a victim in any case as it does not exist in real life to be injured or harmed. United States of America was called to the stand and did not admit, when asked who in the court has a claim against the Defendant the record will show that no one had a claim, thus no cause, no claim, no case.

17.      Lack of Service, no summons or properly served pleadings were ever submitted to the petitioner.

18.      There were no pre-trial hearings which violated another constitutionally protected due process rights of the accused.

19.      The true nature and cause were not made known to the accused and the accused was denied right to counsel.

20.      The search and seizure constitutionally protected rights of the accused were not protected, upheld, and were blatantly violated and disregarded by the arresting officers at the Raleigh Police Department, the US Marshall Service, the IRS, and the holding facilities, jails, USP LEE members. There is/was no probable cause to arrest the

petitioner on the night of May 3, 2011, the seizure of the Petitioners body and person by the US Marshall Service based on an arrest warrant issued by a clerk of court and not by magistrate or judge and not after a Probable Cause hearing or summons served on the accused and refused by the party summonsed to appear having been executed and on a Memorandum from the United States Attorney at the DOJ in Raleigh NC.

21.     The so-called Attorney who was put on the case, his reason was a conflict of interest, any conflict of interest, was always a conflict and he should have removed himself before making any type of filing or even speaking with the petitioner regarding the case or defenses, strategies etc. Any bar member appointed to this case, especially one who has a title of Nobility and has given up United States of America citizenship and allegiance is to the Crown and by the true 13th amendment and are barred from courts in America.

22.     When the court is engaged in profiting and gaining financially from a case there can be no real justice and no real adjudication based on the law and the appearance of impartiality, fairness, unalienable rights and Bill of Rights, human rights, birthrights, and rights which are not enumerated. Thus, when the court acts outside of its scope and in a capacity, which does not display the very appearance of fair dealings the proceedings are Null and Void.

23.     The Jury was convened unlawfully and from invalid venue. The jury was unqualified as US citizens to be seated on a jury in North Carolina.

24.     Not only is the code in title 18 section 1951 void for vagueness, but the terms also that define, whoever and commerce are ambiguous and therefore void due to the ambiguity the code begins with the term "whoever" and in the definition section under the same it defines "whoever" as a specific group of entities and the term includes is used which is a limitation term. Therefore, things not specifically named are excluded unless they are of the same type.  Hobbs Act robbery comes under the Racketering chapter 95 in the USC Title 18 otherwise known as RICO. The alleged acts do not constitute or resemble any type of organized crime or criminal enterprise.

25.     Title 18 of the U.S.C. is prima facie law and the petitioner formally challenged the validity and requires the complete de jure law as originally passed by both the house and senate and signed into law by the President of the United States of America de jure.

26.     The prison sentence passed by Louise Flanagan is VOID and the petitioner dutifully and honorably Demand this court to Vacate Immediately and without further delay or distress or process.

27.     The impartiality of the judge and the prosecutor and the Attorneys who all are paid out of appropriated funds and because of their membership with the bar they all stand to gain from a conviction and prison sentence.

28.     The fact that the prosecutor did not have a bond in this case and did not provide the letter and receipt from the OID and money order issue from the Secretary of Puerto Rico as the rule, so states reflect the attempt to make the defendant responsible for the bond and the defendant did not agree to stand in a surety or give bond for the benefit of the prosecutor.

29.     The fact that the records have been altered and misleading this court as this case was not heard in or at Raleigh and this is a requirement. Raleigh is the proper venue, and no stipulation was made or agreed to either in fact or implied.

30.     There is no evidence, and the petitioner believes none exist showing where a judge or magistrate ordered the grand jury investigation based upon an affidavit by a victim. There is no complaint, there is no sworn affidavit, there is no summons or valid warrant issued for the arrest and confinement of Mr. Dovine.

31.     The IRS is an unnamed indispensable party, the Secretary of Treasury is also an unnamed indispensable party, the ATF is also an unnamed indispensable party, the Customs Board and Patrol is an unnamed indispensable party and there is a strong possibility of more unnamed unknown indispensable parties.

32.     The district court is not constitutional court. Therefore, the court lacks jurisdiction and authority unless consented to by all parties. There is NO CONSENT GIVEN BY THE PETITIONER/ACCUSED. The accused is not a juvenile, nor delinquent, does not acknowledge fictions nor consent to be governed by fictional, corporate, acting under color of law and authority pretended to be granted by the governed.

33.     The accused has the right to be a "person" recognized by the law with privileges and benefits of "the person". Accordingly he has not delegated or granted powers to the federal government or The State, and is entitled to equal protection, due process, to be indicted by a lawfully drawn Grand Jury, present his case on his own behalf or to be represented by counsel, entitled to bail in all cases when death is not the penalty, entitled to face his accuser, entitled to a defense, entitled to have witnesses on his behalf be subpoenaed, entitled to have a true and clear and concise statement of the accusation, the indictment did not give definitions to terms, the indictment did not read the charge out as it is in the code, verbatim or otherwise. The regulation known as the CFR is essential to the code having any foundation is omitted from the indictment, thus misleading the jury and the defendant as to what is being charged and to whom the code is applicable to be enforced against. The indictment appears to be an information signed and submitted by the prosecuting attorney only, and not by an impartial, properly qualified, and lawfully drawn grand jury. There was no return in open court or to a magistrate or judge of an indictment and no judge or magistrate authorized or signed the arrest warrant giving authority to the US Marshal Service to arrest the petitioner.

34.     All the four (4) court forced attorneys have done things to hinder the petitioner from having a fair, speedy trial, they have impaired any and all defense, have refused to raise issues that have merit and that are grounds for dismissal, vacation of judgment.

35.     The exclusionary rule was not enforced adequately, and the exclusionary rule is one of utmost importance to an accused and is remedy that must be afforded when procedural violation occurs. The initial arrest was unwarranted and there was no probable cause for the initial arrest. The petitioner gave a coerced confession and other information to the police which then gave cause to have warrants issued. The confession was thrown out, however the information which led to evidence which incriminated the petitioner further was part of the poisonous tree as well and should have been thrown out as well. Any competent learned man of law who recognized the confession was coerced therefore would have asked for all the evidence obtained thereafter to be excluded as well.

36.     The petitioner is entitled to be brought into a constitutional tribunal under the laws of His Sovereign and to be tried before a jury of His Peers.

37.     No man or woman has made a claim against the petitioner and The United States of America has not made a claim of injury or damage in which the petitioner may answer to.

38.     The framework of laws and rules that govern the administration of justice in cases involving an individual who has been accused of a crime, beginning with the initial investigation of the crime, and concluding either with the unconditional release of the accused by virtue of acquittal (a judgment of not guilty) or by the imposition of a term of punishment pursuant to a conviction for the crime.

39.     At trial, a criminal defendant has several constitutional rights, including the right to counsel, the right to a public trial, the right to a trial by jury, the right to a fair and impartial trial, the right to confront witnesses in court, the right to compulsory process to obtain witnesses, and the privilege against self-incrimination. Violation of any of these rights may result in the reversal or vacation of a conviction on appeal.

40.     There are exceptions and nuances to most of the procedural trial rights. Under the Sixth Amendment, if a defendant is indigent, or unable to afford an attorney, the court will appoint an attorney. This right applies only for felony charges and cases in which actual imprisonment may be imposed. Accordingly, an indigent who [is not represented by counsel at trial] may not be sentenced to incarceration, regardless of whether conviction of the offense warrants incarceration (Scott v. Illinois, 440 U.S. 367, 99 S. Ct. 1158, 59 L. Ed. 2d 383 [1979]

41.

42.     A criminal defendant has the right to an attorney from the first critical stage of the criminal process through the end. An attorney must be present at the request of the defendant during such events as interrogation, lineup identifications after charges have been filed, preliminary hearings before the court, trial, and sentencing.

## Conclusion

The are many out there that doubt that Tazadaq is the truth and that this worked for those that endured until the end. Those naysayers need to be kicked out of your life. If you want to change your life read this book another 6 times. If you fail to do what is suggested, you will not have success. You have done it your way long enough. I cannot tell you what to do I can only tell you that Ihave an 812-credit score and rising and can live anywhere I chose with such a credit score. Because it is not about how much fist money you have because there is no real money since 1933 therefore it is all about credit. Become a creditor contact me at taza-daqshah@yahoo.com or simply visit www.truedisciplesofchrist.org/shop Please join our assembly if you want to change your life and be a warrior in the army of the Lord.

If you genuinely want to be a free man/woman, a free National by taking the proper steps and placing the proper documents on record and the proper agents and agencies on notice then contact us via www.truedisciplesofchrist.org/shop. You should do what is asked before you go in dishonor of another single contract. I get tons of emails all the time about people wanting to become a SPC but many shy away once I suggest that they provide a gift of $$$$ for time, research, energy, and devotion, this is a small donation for the information that you receive. I just do not comprehend the concept of waiting something for free, that if applied correctly will change your life If you want to stop being a ward of the state and revoke power of attorney of the De facto then you should become a SPC (Secured Party Creditor) now.

Remember you are either a debtor or a creditor. Creditors win debtors always pay a fine or go to jail. Creditors are free and are no longer under the power and authority of a defacto color of law system if you stay in honor. To start your process simply donate on cash.me/$tazadaqshah or paypal.me/tazadaq. The process usually takes up to two weeks to complete. Your package will be mailed to you upon completion USPS tracking number. If you decide to mail a blank money order instead. Please emails your first last and middle name and your domicile (address) to creditorsdebtorscontracts@yahoo.com once you have made donation. A P.O Box or second address would be ideal for the debtor but not mandatory. Please also leave a number where you can be reached. Once the payment is made you will get a confirmation email from PayPal as will I.

You do not need a PayPal account to donate via PayPal, you can use a Debit, Gift card, or Credit card. Because of the nature of this information, it is nonrefundable because once you have the information you can use it at will. The donation is for our time, energy, education and up to dated researched information. "For the scripture saith, thou shalt not muzzle the ox that treadeth out the corn. And the labourer is worthy of his reward". (wages) 1st Timothy 5:18. You have just completed reading the onl bok of its kind. Others will try to emulate it but the Most High gave this mission to Tazadaq. Now go out and see the world for how it really is and win!

You now should have the mind state of a creditor. Please go to Amazon and write a review on this book. Make it a great day! Please pray for me (Tazadaq) the enemy wants to stop this truth. Keep your head up and face all hardship wholeheartedly and endure all rightness that brings about pleasure. Strength is born out of struggle for it develops moral character within. When we abort the path to struggle, we hinder the development of our character. We must never take the road of lesser resistance it is usually the wrong path. From birth both the baby and mother must endure the struggle of traveling through the birth canal and the pain and struggle of having the womb strength beyond imagination. Thus, we see from our beginning into the word we had to undergo struggle yet what a precious reward for struggle, the gift of life. Make it a great day if it is not going so well remember we can change the reality of our existence and it all begins with just a thought. Here is some of my work to paint another reflection of reality.

They will do whatever they can to being me down or make me appear as if I did some wrong to stop this message. In the event of my demise for this truth I teach please martyr me beloved. The world will remember my name Tazadaq.

Shalawam ahchyam praise be Yahawah Ba ha Sham Yahawashi for keeping True Disciples of Christ (TDOC) in the spirit of 2 Samuel 23:8–38, הַגִּבֹּרִ֔ים ha-Gibbōrîm, Legal information and Education Is Not Legal AdviceThis website, videos, or documents is a service made available by TDOC, its partners, affiliates, or subsidiaries ("Provider"). This Website, videos, documents provide general information related to the law and lawyers designed to help users safely cope with their own legal needs. This website does not provide legal advice and Provider is not a law firm, neither do the provider desire to be a lawyer. None of our customer service representatives are lawyers and they also do not provide legal advice. Although we go to great lengths to make sure our information is accurate and useful, we recommend you consult a lawyer if you want legal advice. No attorney-client or confidential relationship exists or will be formed between you and Provider or any of our representatives.

That talk that Nazi don't want simps to hear. Tuesday Nights 9:30 PM est. YouR Host Taz talking that talk

Made in the USA
Columbia, SC
25 March 2024